COUNTRY L
M A

Guide to Rural

WALES

By James Gracie

© Travel Publishing Ltd

Published by:
Travel Publishing Ltd
7a Apollo House, Calleva Park
Aldermaston, Berkshire RG7 8TN
ISBN 1-904-43463-0
© Travel Publishing Ltd
Country Living is a registered trademark of The National
Magazine Company Limited.

First Published: 2002
Second Edition: 2005
Third Edition: 2007

COUNTRY LIVING GUIDES:

East Anglia	Scotland
Heart of England	The South of England
Ireland	The South East of England
The North East of England	The West Country
The North West of England	Wales

PLEASE NOTE:

All advertisements in this publication have been accepted in good faith by Travel Publishing and they have not necessarily been endorsed by *Country Living* Magazine.

All information is included by the publishers in good faith and is believed to be correct at the time of going to press. No responsibility can be accepted for errors.

Editor:	James Gracie
Printing by:	Scotprint, Haddington
Location Maps:	© Maps in Minutes ™ (2007) © Crown Copyright, Ordnance Survey 2007
Walks:	Walks have been reproduced with kind permission of the internet walking site © www.walkingworld.com
Walk Maps:	Reproduced from Ordnance Survey mapping on behalf of the Controller of Her Majesty's Stationery Office, © Crown Copyright. Licence Number MC 100035812
Cover Design:	Lines & Words, Aldermaston
Cover Photo:	Bluebells in Spring, Nantlle Ridge, Cwm Pennant, Snowdonia © www.photolibrarywales.com
Text Photos:	Text photos have been kindly supplied by © Bob Brooks, Weston-super-Mare and © www.picturesofbritain.co.uk

Foreword

From a bracing walk across the hills and tarns of The Lake District to a relaxing weekend spent discovering the unspoilt hamlets of East Anglia, nothing quite matches getting off the beaten track and exploring Britain's areas of outstanding beauty.

Each month, *Country Living Magazine* celebrates the richness and diversity of our countryside with features on rural Britain and the traditions that have their roots there. So it is with great pleasure that I introduce you to the *Country Living Magazine Guide to Rural England* series. Packed with information about unusual and unique aspects of our countryside, the guides will point both fair-weather and intrepid travellers in the right direction.

Each chapter provides a fascinating tour of Wales, with insights into local heritage and history and easy-to-read facts on a wealth of places to visit, stay, eat, drink and shop.

I hope that this guide will help make your visit a rewarding and stimulating experience and that you will return inspired, refreshed and ready to head off on your next countryside adventure.

Susy Smith

Editor, Country Living magazine

PS To subscribe to *Country Living Magazine* each month, call 01858 438844

Introduction

This is the 3rd edition of the *Country Living Guide to Rural Wales* and we are sure that it will be as popular as its predecessors. Regular readers will note that the page layouts have been attractively redesigned and that we have provided more information on the places, people and activities covered by the guide. Also, in the introduction to each village or town we have summarized and categorized the main attractions to be found there which makes it easier for readers to plan their visit. James Gracie, a very experienced travel writer has, of course, completely updated the contents of the guide and ensured that it is packed with vivid descriptions, historical stories, amusing anecdotes and interesting facts on hundreds of places in Wales.

The coloured advertising panels within each chapter provide further information on places to see, stay, eat, drink, shop and even exercise! We have also selected a number of walks from www.walkingworld.com (full details of this website may be found to the rear of the guide) which we highly recommend if you wish to appreciate fully the dramatic landscapes, rich cultural heritage and rural charm of this wonderful Celtic country.

The guide however is not simply an "armchair tour". Its prime aim is to encourage the reader to visit the places described and discover much more about the wonderful towns, villages and countryside of Wales. In this respect we would like to thank all the Tourist Information Centres who helped us to provide you with up-to-date information. Whether you decide to explore this country by wheeled transport or on foot we are sure you will find it a very uplifting experience.

We are always interested in receiving comments on places covered (or not covered) in our guides so please do not hesitate to use the reader reaction forms provided at the rear of this guide to give us your considered comments. This will help us refine and improve the content of the next edition. We also welcome any general comments which will help improve the overall presentation of the guides themselves.

For more information on the full range of travel guides published by Travel Publishing please refer to the order form at the rear of this guide or log on to our website (see below).

Travel Publishing

Did you know that you can also search our website for details of thousands of places to see, stay, eat or drink throughout Britain and Ireland? Our site has become increasingly popular and now receives monthly hundreds of thousands of visits. Try it!

website: www.travelpublishing.co.uk

Contents

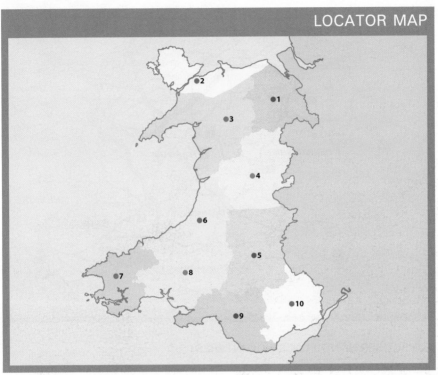

LOCATOR MAP

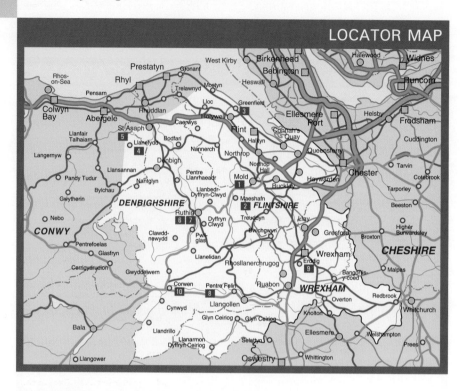

LOCATOR MAP

ADVERTISERS AND PLACES OF INTEREST

🏛 historic building   🏛 museum   🏛 historic site   ⌂ scenic attraction   🌱 flora and fauna

1| North Wales Borderlands

This area of Wales, the North Wales Borderlands, can easily be overlooked by visitors as they speed westwards, but it is a mistake not to stop and explore the towns, villages and countryside, as they are rich in history, heritage and scenic beauty. One of the best ways of seeing the countryside is by bicycle. The Flint to Chester section of the North Wales Coastal Route is in place and, for a completely traffic-free route, the circuit of Llyn Brig reservoir is recommended. This region of Wales also offers some of the best mountain biking in Britain, and among the most challenging rides are those in the Clwydian Range and through Clocaenog Forest near Denbigh.

Each of the different areas has its own special character and scenery: the Clwydian Hills, a (a 22-mile long chain of heather-clad hills and a designated Area of Outstanding Natural Beauty); the Dee estuary; the broad, gentle sweep of the Vale of Clwyd with historic towns like Ruthin, St Asaph, Denbigh and Rhuddlan; Wrexham, the largest town in North Wales, and its surrounds; The Maelor (once a detached portion of Flintshire), where the Cheshire Plains transform into the Welsh Hills; Chirk and the beautiful Ceiriog Valley. The Romans certainly forayed into the area from their major town of Chester and there is also evidence of Celtic settlements.

However, it was during the 13th century that Edward I, after his successful campaign against the Welsh, set about building his ambitious Iron Ring of huge fortresses along the Dee estuary and the North Wales coast. Each was built a day's march from its neighbours, and the first was begun at Flint in 1277. This was the cutting-edge military technology of its day and, though the great fortresses are now in ruins, the remains of the massive project - the largest seen in Europe - are still very much in evidence.

Plus this area of Wales teems with wildlife. In fact, the land around the Dee estuary is home to a great number of waders and wildfowl which feed on the mudflats left by the retreating tides.

Between the estuary and the Clwydian Range lie small, compact villages as well as the market towns of Mold and Holywell, a place of pilgrimage that became known as the Lourdes of Wales. The range, a grassy line of hills above the Vale of Clwyd, offers fabulous views and exhilarating walks; it is one of the eight designated Areas of Outstanding Natural Beauty in Wales.

Further south lie Llangollen and the Dee Valley. Llangollen is a delightful old town in a picturesque riverside setting which is not only a charming place to visit but is also the home of the annual International Music Eisteddfod (not the same as the National Eisteddfod). An eisteddfod was, originally, a meeting of bards where prizes were awarded for poetry reading and singing and, while local events still draw people from all over the country, the event at Llangollen has a true international flavour with such eminent figures as Luciano Pavarotti having graced its stage. The town is also famous for the Llangollen Railway, a re-opened section of the Barmouth - Ruabon line which closed in 1960.

Though this northern gateway to the country is not a particularly large area, it boasts all but one of the 'Seven Wonders of Wales', wonders which while not quite as spectacular as the more familiar Seven Wonders of the World are nonetheless all interesting in their own right and well worth a visit. They are listed in the famous 19th century rhyme:

> Pistyll Rhaeadr and Wrexham Steeple,
> Snowdon's Mountain without its people,
> Overton Yew Trees, St Winefride's Well,
> Llangollen Bridge and Gresford Bells.

The Borderlands offer an impressive variety of attractions, from castles and country houses to churches and museums, country parks and farm parks, lakes and canals, and leisure pursuits from walking, cycling and riding to birdwatching and golf (more than 20 courses). There is also superb fishing for salmon and trout on the Rivers Dee and Clwyd, sea fishing in the Dee estuary and trout or coarse fishing at numerous lake fisheries. Festivals and other special events are staged throughout the year, and visitors are welcome to attend many rehearsals as well as performances by renowned Welsh choirs - a unique and moving experience that will long be remembered.

Mold

🏛 St Mary's Parish Church	🏛 Mold Museum
🏛 Bailey Hill	🍂 Loggerheads Country Park
🌳 Daniel Owen	🌳 Richard Wilson
🖋 Clwyd Theatr Cymru	🖋 Mold Carnival

Flintshire was one of the few counties in Britain to have detached portions. The largest was known as *Maelor Saesneg*, or 'Flintshire Detached'. At one time it was part of Cheshire, but in 1536 was transferred to Wales by Richard II. In 1974 it became part of Wrexham Maelor District, which later became the County Burgh of Wrexham. To complicate matters, the burghs of Prestatyn, Rhyl and St Asaph were once in Flintshire as well, and there was another detached portion around Marford and Rossett.

Mold was Flintshire's county town, and is proud to claim the novelist, tailor and Methodist preacher **Daniel Owen** (1836 - 1895) as one of its own. He is often hailed as Wales' greatest novelist, and writing only in Welsh, it was his honest accounts of ordinary life that were to make him one of the greatest 19th century novelists and also to gain him the title the 'Welsh Dickens'. His most famous books were *Rhys Lewis* and *Enoc Huws*. Owen's statue stands outside the town library, which is also the home of **Mold Museum**, where a room is dedicated to Owen's memory.

Though born in Montgomeryshire, Mold claims landscape painter **Richard Wilson** (1713 - 1782), as its own. After pursuing a career in London, he returned to his native

---

TOWER

Nercwys, nr Mold, Flintshire CH7 4EW
Tel: 01352 700220
e-mail: enquiries@towerwales.co.uk
website: www.towerwales.co.uk

Tower is a Welsh fortified border house, the only example to survive intact, and Grade I listed for outstanding historical interest. Starting life some 500 years ago, it has changed through successive generations from being a lair for raiders and the scene of constant border hostilities into the peaceful home of the current owners Charles and Mairi Wynne-Eyton. The house, which lies a mile south of Mold and just 10 miles from the English border, is approached through parkland and stands in ornamental gardens with a small lake and lots of wildlife.

Tower is a unique base for a break, with three very comfortable guest rooms, each named after a past family member. They combine abundant character with up-to-date amenities, with mostly antique furniture, family portraits, en suite or private bathroom, large double or king-size beds, beverage tray, television, clock-radio and thoughtful extras such as fruit, flowers and books.

A generous Welsh breakfast is served at the library end of the drawing room. The whole house is filled with echoes of the past, and group visits can be arranged by appointment on certain days of the year.

🏛 historic building   🏛 museum   🏛 historic site   🍂 scenic attraction   🌿 flora and fauna

Wales and settled in Mold to concentrate on the dramatic scenes of mountainous Welsh countryside which became his trademark. He died in Colomendy, and his grave and memorial can be found near the north entrance to **St Mary's Parish Church**. It was one of his descendants, Brian Wilson, who founded the American group the Beach Boys. Dating from the 15th century and built by

Loggerheads Country Park

Margaret Beaufort, Countess of Richmond, to celebrate her son Henry VII's victory at Bosworth in 1485, the church has some interesting stained glass windows as well as some fine architectural ornamentation. A light and airy building, this church was constructed on the site of an earlier church whose original oak roof, carved with Tudor roses, has been retained in part.

The church stands at the foot of **Bailey Hill**, the site of a Norman motte and bailey fortification which was built at this strategic point overlooking the River Alyn by Robert de Montalt, who may have given the town its English name. First captured by the Welsh in 1157 and then again by Llywelyn the Great in 1199, ownership of the castle passed through many hands and today, not surprisingly, little remains of the fortress, as its site is now marked by a bowling green. Bailey Hill may have given the town its Welsh name of *Yr Wyddgrug*, which means 'The Mound'.

On the outskirts of Mold lies **Clwyd Theatr Cymru**, which offers a wide range of entertainment including theatre, music and frequent exhibitions of art, sculpture and photography. It has a bar, coffee shop,

bookshop, free covered parking and disabled access. Every June it hosts the **Mold Carnival**. The composer Felix Mendelssohn was said to have been inspired by the town's surroundings when writing his opus *Rivulet*, and the nearby limestone crags provide panoramic views over the surrounding countryside.

One such scenic area lies four miles west of Mold on the A494 - **Loggerheads Country Park**, which is situated on the edge of the Clwydian Range. Classified as an Area of Outstanding Natural Beauty, this large park is an ideal environment for all the family, especially younger members, as there are various trails which are each about one-and-a-half miles long. The trails all start near the late-18th century mill building that used water from the River Alyn to drive a water wheel and two sets of stones to grind corn from the local farms. A regular bus service takes you to Loggerheads from both Mold and Chester.

Around 200 years ago, Loggerheads was a centre for lead mining, due to the plentiful supply of ore-bearing limestone, and many relics of those days can still be seen within the quiet woodland. There is a fine selection of

THE MINERS ARMS

Village Road, Maeshafn, Denbighshire CH7 5LR
Tel: 01352 810464

Managed by Gilly and John Walker, **The Miners Arms** is a picturesque old inn dating from the early 1700s which was originally a row of miners' cottages. It is located in the village of Maeshafn which lies three miles from Mold, one mile from the A494 and accessed from either Llanferres or Gwernymynydd. Set in an attractive upland wooded area in the Clwydian range, an area of outstanding natural beauty close to Loggerheads Country Park, it was formerly a mining and quarrying community.

During the summer months, the front of the inn is adorned with colourful hanging baskets, while the interior of the inn is delightfully cosy, with a log fire for those chilly autumn and winter days. There are two comfortable bars, and a restaurant that seats sixteen. There are extensive lunch and dinner menus, with only fresh local produce being used in the kitchen wherever possible. The menus are changed frequently, and people come from near and far to sample the food. Lunches are served from Wednesday to Saturday, on Sunday traditional Sunday lunch is sreved. Dinner is served from Tuesday to Saturday evenings. You are advised to book in advance for weekend sittings. Groups and small private events can be catered for.

The bars sell a great range of drinks, from real ales, beers, wines to spirits and soft drinks. There are occasional folk nights, and on the first Sunday of August the inn hosts a music festival. There is plenty of outdoor seating at the frontof the pub.

The Miners Arms is closed on Monday and Tuesday lunchtimes.

---

local arts, crafts and souvenirs on display in the Craft Shop at the **Loggerheads Countryside Centre**, where there is also a tea room.

Around Mold

RHOSESMOR
3 miles N of Mold on the B5123

🏛 Parish Church of St Paul   🏚 Moel y Gaer

🏚 Wat's Dyke

Moel y Gaer, near this small village, was considered to be a fine example of an Iron Age hill fort until archaeological digs unearthed evidence that suggested this site had been inhabited from as far back as 3500 BC.

To the west of the Rhosesmor lie the remains of a short section of **Wat's Dyke**, a much shorter dyke than Offa's which is thought to have been built by the Mercian King Aethelbald in the 8th century. Just under 40 miles long, the dyke ran southwards from the Dee estuary to Oswestry.

The Parish Church of St Paul dates from 1876, when the parish of Caerfallwch, in which Rhosemor is situated, was formed. The village was once a centre of lead mining, and beneath it are natural and man-made tunnels. There is even said to be an underground lake, the largest in Europe.

HALKYN
4½ miles N of Mold on the B5123

🏛 Parish Church of St Mary   🌄 Halkyn Mountains

The village lies close to the long ridge of the **Halkyn Mountains** which rise to some 964

🏛 historic building   🏛 museum   🏚 historic site   🌄 scenic attraction   🌿 flora and fauna feet at their highest point and are scarred by the remnants of ancient lead mines and quarries, some of which date back to Roman times. In the 17th century, Derbyshire lead miners were brought here to work in the newly opened lead mines. The medieval parish church was demolished in 1878, and the present **Parish Church of St Mary** was built some distance away in the same year.

Flint Castle

FLINT
5 miles N of Mold on the A5119

 Flint Castle 🦆 Ian Rush

Flint can boast two historical firsts: it was the first associated borough in Wales to receive a charter (in 1284) and it was also the site of the first of Edward I's Iron Ring fortresses. Dotted along the North Wales coast, a day's march apart, Edward I's ring of massive fortresses represented Europe's most ambitious and concentrated medieval building project, started after the Treaty of Aberconwy in 1277 and completed in 1284 by James of St George.

Flint Castle, now in ruins, stands on a low rock overlooking the coastal marshes of the Dee estuary and the Wirral peninsula. Originally surrounded by a water-filled moat, the remains of the Great Tower, or Donjon, are an impressive sight. Set apart from the main part of the castle, this tower, which is unique among British castles, was intended as a last retreat and, to this end, was fully self-sufficient, even having its own well.

Flint Castle featured in the downfall of Richard II, when he was lured here in 1399 from the relative safety of Conwy Castle and was captured by Henry Bolingbroke, Duke of Lancaster and the future Henry IV. The imprisonment of Richard is remembered in Shakespeare's *Richard II*, where, in response to Bolingbroke's, "My gracious Lord, I come but for mine own," the defeated Richard replies, "Your own is yours, and I am yours, and all." At this point even the King's faithful greyhound is said to have deserted him.

During the Civil War, the town and castle remained in Royalist hands, under the leadership of Sir Roger Mostyn, until 1647, when both were taken by General Mytton, who was also responsible for dismantling the castle, thus creating the ruins we see today.

Ian Rush, the Welsh international footballer, though born in St Asaph, went to school in Flint.

HOLYWELL
7 miles N of Mold on the A5026

🏛 St Winefride's Chapel 🏛 St Winefride's Well

🏛 Parish Church of St James 🦆 Gutun Owain

🏛 Basingwerk Abbey 🦆 Gerard Manley Hopkins

🏛 Greenfield Valley Heritage and Country Park

The town is well worth visiting solely on account of its fine town centre, which boasts over 60 listed buildings dating from Georgian and Victorian times. Thursday and Saturday are market days, when stalls crowd the main street. In the town lies one of the Seven Wonders of Wales, **St Winefride's Well**, which was once a place of pilgrimage and, at one time, was referred to as the Lourdes of Wales. According to tradition, Winefride, the niece of St Beuno, was beheaded by Prince Caradoc after refusing his advances. It is claimed that a spring gushed from the place where her head fell and that she returned to life after her uncle had replaced her head. Winefride (Gwenfrewi in Welsh) went on to become an abbess at Gwytherin Convent near Llanrwst and, in 1138, her remains were given to Shrewsbury Cathedral. Caradoc was struck dead by lightning on the spot. Thought to have healing qualities, the well has been visited by pilgrims since the 7th century and still is,

particularly on St Winefride's Day, the nearest Saturday to 22nd June. The well, and the Vale of Clwyd, is beloved of the poet **Gerard Manley Hopkins**. He trained as a priest at St Beuno's College, Tremeirchion, and St Winefride's Well inspired him to write a verse tragedy, which contains many beautiful, evocative lines:

> *The dry dene, now no longer dry nor*
> *dumb, but moist and musical.*
> *With the uproll and downcarol of day*
> *and night delivering water.*

On Wales in general he was equally lyrical:

> *Lovely the woods, water, meadows,*
> *combes, vales,*
> *All the air things wear that build this*
> *world of Wales.*

St Winefride's Chapel was built by Margaret Beaufort (the mother of Henry VII)

Greenfield Valley Heritage Park

Greenfield, Holywell, Flintshire CH8 7GH
Tel: 01352 714172 Fax: 01352 714791
website: www.greenfieldvalley.com

Referred to as the Borderlands best kept secret, the Greenfield Valley Heritage Park is one and a half miles of woodlands, reservoirs, ancient monuments and industrial history. The park is freely accessible year round attracting over 100,000 visitors per year. Within the Park is a Farm and Museum Complex with an attractive collection of original and reconstructed local buildings. A 16th century farmhouse, early 19th century cottage, black-smith's forge, Victorian schoolroom and farm buildings provide an atmospheric backdrop to agricultural displays and exhibits. The museum holds events most weekends throughout the season. The whole site is a fascinating insight into times past.

There are farm animals to see and feed, an adventure playground and an indoor activity area. Facilities include a Visitor Centre, Environment Centre, free coach and car parking, toilets, cafe and gift shop. The museum and associated facilities are open from the beginning of April to the end of October.

🏛 historic building   🏛 museum   🏛 historic site   🍃 scenic attraction   🌿 flora and fauna in around 1500 to enclose three sides of the well. The Victorian statue of St Winifride has a thin line round the neck showing where her head was cut off. Also here stands the **Parish Church of St James**, which was built in 1770 and it probably stands on the site of the original chapel which was constructed by St Beuno in the 7th century.

Basingwerk Abbey, to the east of Holywell, was built by Cistercian monks in 1132. The abbey functioned as a self-sufficient community, as the Cistercians lay great emphasis upon agricultural labour. Although this was an English house, Basingwerk absorbed Welsh culture and the Welsh bard, **Gutun Owain**, was associated with the abbey from where he wrote *The Chronicle of Princes*, which is also known as the *Black Book of Basingwerk*.

The abbey survived until the Dissolution of the Monasteries in the 16th century. In a tranquil setting that contrasts with the busy roads not far away, this magnificent ruin contains an arch which, despite weather beaten columns and faded 'message of love', is a fine example of Norman ecclesiastical architecture. In one of the buildings the remains of timber beams can be seen that once supported a roof.

Linking Holywell with the ruins of the abbey is the **Greenfield Valley Heritage and Country Park** (see panel opposite), a 70-acre area of pleasant woodland and lakeside walks with a wealth of monuments and agricultural and industrial history. There are animals to feed, an adventure playground and picnic areas. In the 18th and 19th centuries this was a busy industrial area which concentrated on the newly established production processes for textiles, copper and brass.

NORTHOP
4 miles N of Mold on the A5119

🏛 Parish Church of St Peter and St Eurgain

🏛 Grammar School 🕯 William Parry

A church existed in Northop as early as the 6th century. The present **Parish Church of St Peter and St Eurgain** was extensively rebuilt in the mid 19th century, and much of the medieval fabric was lost. St Eurgain was the niece of St Asaph, the second bishop of St Asaph diocese. The church's tower is 98 feet high, and one of the landmarks of the area. The town's old **Grammar School**, dating from the 16th century, still stands in the churchyard.

The town was the birthplace (date unknown) of **William Parry**, a leading Catholic who was supposedly involved in a plot to assassinate Elizabeth I. He was the son of Harry ap David, and his real name was William ap Harry. He was eventually hung in 1585, and nowadays historians believe that he was innocent.

EWLOE
4 miles E of Mold on the B5125

🏛 Ewloe Castle

Ewloe (pronounced 'Yoo-low') was once famous for the manufacture of bricks and earthenware tiles. Hidden in a steeply wooded glen area are the remains of **Ewloe Castle**, a fortification which was built by the Welsh. It was founded by Llywelyn ap Gruffyd, known in English as 'Llywelyn the Last' in 1257 after he had retaken this part of Wales from the English. Some 150 years later, a tower, two wards protected by a curtain wall and an outer ditch were added but the castle failed to live up to expectations, and by the late 13th century it ceased to have any military significance.

Hawarden Castle

village close to the English border has two castles, one a ruin dating from the 13th century and another that was once the home of the Victorian Prime Minister, William Gladstone. **Harwarden Castle**, Gladstone's home for some 60 years after his marriage to the daughter of Sir Stephen Glynne in 1839, was started in 1750 and enlarged and castellated by Sir Stephen in 1809. The remains of the older castle, chiefly the circular keep and the hall, still stand in **Castle Park**.

The town achieved temporary fame when the footballer Michael Owen bought a full street of houses here, called Austen Close, to house his family.

CONNAH'S QUAY
5 miles NE of Mold on the B5129

🍃 Wepre Country Park

This is the largest town in Flintshire, and is wholly industrial in nature, having three power stations and a steelworks. The town is said to get its name from the former landlord of an inn that stands near the docks. To the south of the town is the 160-acre **Wepre Country Park**, where there are ancient woodlands, walks, a fishing pool and a visitor centre.

HAWARDEN
5 miles E of Mold on the A550

🏛 Harwarden Castle   🏛 Parish Church of St Deiniol

🏛 Gladstone Memorial Chapel

🏛 St Deinol's Residential Library   🏛 Castle Park

Mentioned in the *Domesday Book*, this small

The **Parish Church of St Deiniol**, as well as having stained glass windows by Burne-Jones, also houses the **Gladstone Memorial Chapel**, where marble effigies of the distinguished statesman and his wife, who are buried in Westminster Abbey, can be seen. The church was largely rebuilt after a deliberate fire in 1857, though records go back showing that one existed in the 12th century. The parish was once a 'peculiar', which means that the rector was not answerable to any bishop. He therefore wielded considerable power, and had his own ecclesiastical court. He could also issue marriage licenses and prove wills.

The village's connections with Gladstone continue to this day as the former Prime Minister donated his collection of books to the famous **St Deinol's Residential Library**, which lies adjacent to the church.

🏛 historic building   📷 museum   🏛 historic site   🍃 scenic attraction   🌿 flora and fauna

CAERGWRLE

6 miles SE of Mold on the A541

🏰 Caergwrle Castle   ⛰ Waun-y-Llyn Country Park

⛰ Hope Mountain

Once occupied by the Romans as an outpost station for nearby Chester, **Caergwrle Castle**, which stands on a high ridge, probably started life as a Bronze Age hill fort. It was Dafydd, brother of Llewelyn the Last, who constructed the fortification in 1277 more or less in its present form and it was from here, in 1282, that Dafydd launched his last Welsh attack on the English King Edward I. He had formerly been Edward's ally, and after being captured some time later, he was hung, drawn and quartered for treason at Shrewsbury.

To the west of the village is **Waun-y-Llyn Country Park**, at 74 acres one of the smallest in Wales. Close by is **Hope Mountain**, where there are spectacular views towards the Cheshire Plain.

CILCAIN

3½ miles W of Mold off the A541

🏰 Jubilee Tower   ⛰ Clwydian Range

⛰ Moel Famau

This charming hamlet in the heart of the Clwydian Range has a medieval church with a double nave, a hammerbeam roof and stained glass. The smooth browned slopes of the **Clwydian Range** ascend from the broad and fertile planes of the Vale of Clwyd, with **Moel Famau** (The Mother of Mountains) being, at 1,820 feet, the range's highest peak. It is well worth the climb to the summit as not only are there the remains of a **Jubilee Tower**, started in 1810 to commemorate George III's Golden Jubilee (since blown down in a storm in 1852) but the panoramic views are breathtaking.

Westwards lies the Vale of Clwyd with the river stretching down to the Irish Sea, while to the east the land rolls gently down to the Dee estuary.

CAERWYS

8½ miles NW of Mold on the B5122

🏰 Parish Church of St Michael

Originally a Roman station, Caerwys grew to become a village of such significance that it received a charter from Henry III, making it the smallest town in Britain with a royal charter. Once an important market town, Caerwys is credited with being the place where, in around 1100, Gruffydd ap Cynan called the first Eisteddfod. This cultural feast was revived in the 16th century by Henry VIII, who said that it was to be for 'craftsmen of music and poetry'. Elizaberth I, his daughter, declared in 1568 that it was to be the official home of yearly the Eisteddfod.

The present **Parish Church of St Michael** was first recorded in 1291. The tower is from that date, though the chancel and nave are possibly 14th century. However, it is known that an earlier church stood on the site, and that Prince David and Henry III met here in 1244.

AFONWEN

8 miles NW of Mold on the A541

🎨 Aronwen Craft and Antiques Centre

Another small village in the Clwydian Range, Afonwen is home to one of the largest craft and antique centres in north Wales. **Afonwen Craft and Antique Centre** not only has a whole host of crafts, accessories and gifts for sale, including furniture, crystal, china and silver, but also holds regular exhibitions and demonstrations.

WHITFORD
10 miles NW of Mold on the A5026

🏛 Parish Church of St Mary and St Beuno

🏛 Maen Achwyfaen   🕊 Thomas Pennant

Close to the village can be found a curious monument, **Maen Achwyfaen** (The Stone of Lamentation). This Celtic cross, sculpted in the shape of a wheel, is said to have been erected in about 1000 and is the tallest such cross in Britain. The person or event it commemorates is unknown. The **Parish Church of St Mary and St Beuno** dates from a rebuild in 1845/46, though there are still some medieval fragments. The renowned 18th century writer **Thomas Pennant** is buried in the graveyard. He was born in 1726 in Downing Hall (no longer standing) and is best known for his book *A Tour in Wales*. He also wrote about tours through Scotland and England. He has been described as one of the greatest travel writers of his time, and published books on the fauna and flora of Wales, as well as its antiquities. Though he travelled constantly through the country, he could speak no Welsh, and had to rely on others to translate the language into English for him.

Denbigh

🏛 Denbigh Castle   🕊 Catherine of Berain

🕊 Humphrey Llwyd   🏛 Parish Church of St Marcella

🕊 Thomas Edwards   🏛 Parish Church of St Dyfnog

🕊 Henry Morton Stanley   🏛 Back Row   🏛 Town Walls

Recorded as a small border town in the 11th century, Denbigh, whose Welsh name Dinbych means a small fortified place, grew to become a residence for Welsh princes and a leading centre of Welsh power. Today, it still retains a charm that is enhanced by buildings dating from the 16th century onwards, and most of the centre is now a conservation area. The old town is concentrated around **Denbigh Castle**, built on the site of a Roman settlement and commands good views over the Vale of Clwyd.

It was one of the biggest and most imposing fortifications in Wales and its ruins are still an impressive sight as they crown the top of a steep hill above the town. It was originally a stronghold of the Welsh prince Dafydd ap Gruffydd, brother of Llewelyn the Last, but when Henry de Lacy, Earl of Lincoln, was given the Lordship of Denbigh by Edward I during his campaigns against the Welsh, he began construction of the new castle in 1282, the year the town fell

Denbigh Castle

to Edward. De Lacy removed all traces of the older Welsh fortification and, at the same time, created a new English borough protected by town walls.

Over 3,000 labourers worked on the castle and the walls. The walled town was completed by 1311 but it was subject to sporadic attacks during its occupation including, in 1402, by Owain Glyndwr, who laid siege to the town and again, during the Wars of the Roses, when the old town was burnt to the ground. In 1645, during the Civil War, Charles I stayed at the castle, which was held for him by Colonel William Salisbury (nicknamed Old Blue Stockings because of his flashy taste in hosiery). It later endured a six-month siege before falling, in October 1646, to Parliament forces, after which the castle and the walls gradually fell into disrepair. But a large stretch of the **Town Walls** still exists and can be walked today, providing a splendid historic view of the town, particularly the section that includes Countess Tower and the Goblin Tower.

Denbigh developed gradually round its market place and town square, and by the time of the first Elizabethan era it was one of the largest and richest towns in North Wales, and also a centre of culture. Elizabeth's favourite Robert Dudley, Earl of Leicester, was Lord of Denbigh until his death in 1588. Of particular interest is **Back Row**, where part of Denbigh's original medieval street pattern still exists and where several 15th century buildings, including the Golden Lion Inn, still give a flavour of those times.

The **Parish Church of St Marcella** (also known as the Eglwys Wen, or the 'white church') is one of the most magnificent churches in Denbighshire. It was largely rebuilt in the 15th century, incorporating a double knave - a well known feature in this part of Wales - and originally had a whitewashed exterior. Its interior is as inspiring as its exterior, with hammer-beamed roofs, stone sculptures and imposing monuments. One of the monuments is to **Humphrey Llwyd**, the physician, musician, antiquarian and Member of Parliament. He was born in Denbigh 1527, and made the made the first accurate maps of Wales which were published in an atlas of 1573 printed in Antwerp. He is sometimes known as the Father of Modern Geography. **Thomas Edwards** was another noted native of the town, and now lies in the churchyard. Born in 1739, he went on to become an actor and playwright under the name of Twm o'r Nant, and he was given the nickname the Welsh Shakespeare

One of the few towns in Wales approved of by Dr Samuel Johnson during his travels through the Principality, Denbigh was also the birthplace of **Henry Morton Stanley**. He was born John Rowlands in 1841, the illegitimate son of John Rowlands and Elizabeth Parry, and grew up partly in the care of relatives and partly in the workhouse in St Asaph. In his late teens he sailed from Liverpool to New Orleans as a cabin boy. There he was befriended by a merchant, Henry Hope Stanley, whose first and last names he took - the Morton came later. He spent the next few years as a soldier, sailor and journalist, and his several commissions for the *New York Herald* culminated in a quest to find the explorer David Livingstone, who had set out for Africa to search for the source of the Nile.

At the head of an American-financed expedition, and keeping his intentions hidden from the British, he set out from Zanzibar and struggled to Ujiji, where in 1871 he found the explorer and addressed him with the immortal words, "Dr Livingstone, I presume". The two became firm friends, and Livingstone continued his quest after being restocked with provisions. He died a year later. Stanley wrote about his expedition and returned to Africa to take up the exploration where Livingstone left off. He was involved in numerous adventures and enterprises, mainly with Belgian backing, and was instrumental in paving the way for the creation of the Congo Free State. On his return to Britain, he married, spent some years as a Member of Parliament and was knighted by Queen Victoria. He died in London in 1904 and was buried in the churchyard of St Michael in Pirbright; his rough granite headstone bears the inscription "Africa".

Another child of Denbigh was the Elizabethan beauty **Catherine of Berain**, a distant relation of Elizabeth I who married four times and produced so many descendants that she was known as 'Mam Cymru', or 'Mother of Wales' (see also Llanrwst).

Three miles south of Denbigh, on the A525 Ruthin road at Llanrhaeadr-yng-Nghinmeirch, stands the 15th century **Parish Church of St Dyfnog**, whose chief treasure is a marvellous Tree of Jesse window. The Tree of Jesse, most often seen depicted in church windows, details the family tree of Christ down from Jesse, the father of King David. It was made in 1553, and was saved from destruction during the Civil War by being buried in a dug-out chest, which can also be seen in the church. St

LLAETH Y LLAN VILLAGE DAIRY GUEST HOUSE

Llannefydd, Near Denbigh, Conwy LL16 5DR
Tel: 01745 540256
e-mail: llaeth@villagedairy.co.uk
website: www.villagedairy.com

Nestling in the tranquil hills between Denbigh and the coast, **Llaeth Y Llan** is an historic 17th century farmstead transformed by owners Gareth and Falmai Roberts into a renowned modern dairy and visitor centre. It produces prize-winning yoghurts that are rich and creamy, using only the finest and freshest of ingredients. It has won a True Taste of Wakes award, as well as many others, and so good are the yoghurts that it supplies Waitrose, Harrods and Selfridges.

There are three ranges - the traditional variety in 14 delicious flavours, the indulgent liqueur dessert combinations, and the breakfast range, which is the most recent. There are guided tours round the dairy to see how the yoghurts are produced, though these must be booked in advance. You can also see the floral garden with its beautiful waterfall, something that is sure to delight young and old.

New for 2007 is overnight B&B accommodation in the comfortable, well-appointed farmhouse. There are three en suite bedrooms furnished and decorated in a country style, and the tariff includes a full breakfast, featuring, of course, the breakfast range of yoghurts produced on the premises.

So for the creamiest yoghurts and the most comfortable B&B accommodation, make your way to the Lleath Y Llan Village Dairy Guest House.

🏚 historic building　🏛 museum　🏚 historic site　🦢 scenic attraction　� flora and fauna

Dyfnog lived during the 7th century, and founded the church because of a holy well that still exists in the woods behind the building.

Around Denbigh

BODFARI
3 miles NE of Denbigh on the B5429

🏛 The Parish Church of St Stephen

🏛 St Deifar's Holy Well

Situated in the heart of the Vale of Clwyd, at the foot of the Clwydian Range, Bodfari marks the abrupt change in landscape from arable fields to heath and moorland. The **Parish Church of St Stephen** dates mainly from a rebuilding of 1865, though it has a fine east widow with good stained glass. Thought to have been the site of a Roman station, the village is famous for **St Deifar's Holy Well**, which can be found at the inn next to the church. Mothers used to dip their babies in the waters three times to prevent them crying in the night.

TREMEIRCHION
6 miles NE of Denbigh on the B5429

🏛 Parish Church of Corpus Christi

🏛 Bachegraig Gatehouse   🕭 Hester Lynch Piozzi

This small village is home to several buildings of interest. The 14th century **Parish Church of Corpus Christi** is the only church in Britain with that dedication, which means 'body of Christ'. It is a simple building with combined nave and chancel, but houses an interesting 14th century canopied tomb containing the effigy of a vested priest while, in the chancel, a tablet commemorates **Hester Lynch Piozzi** (1741-1821), a writer who is better known as Dr Johnson's friend Mrs

Thrale. She was the wife of Henry Thrale, a Southwark brewer who died in 1781. While married to him, she had fallen in love with an Italian music master called Gabriel Piozzi who had been hired to give music lessons to her daughter. In 1784, she married Gabriel, a union which was not approved of by her family or friends, including Johnson and Boswell.

She inherited a house in Tremeirchion she had known in her childhood which was dilapidated and in need of great repair. The couple rebuilt the house, living there happily until Piozzi's death. Hester is best remembered nowadays for two books, *Anecdotes of the Late Samuel Johnson. LLD.*, *During the Last Twenty Years of His Life*, and *Letters To and From the Late Samuel Johnson LL.D., to Which Are Added Some Poems Never Before Printed.*

In 1567, Sir Richard Clough, a wealthy merchant, built a house, Bachegraig, near the village. Though the house is now demolished **Bachegraig Gatehouse** still stands and its unusual architectural style so shocked the local inhabitants that they thought the devil must have been the architect and had also supplied the bricks. The local story has it that the devil baked the bricks in the fires of hell; to this day, a nearby stream is known as Nant y Cythraul or the Devil's Brook.

ST ASAPH
6 miles N of Denbigh on the A525

🏛 St Asaph's Cathedral   🏛 Translator's Memorial

🏛 Elwy Bridge   🕭 William Morgan

This small town on a ridge between the River Clwyd and Elwy has city status because of its cathedral. Standing on a hill and constructed on the site of a Norman building, **St Asaph's Cathedral** is not only the Britain's smallest

🎞 stories and anecdotes   🕭 famous people   🎨 art and craft   ✏ entertainment and sport   🚶 walks

St Asaph's Cathedral

medieval cathedral but it has also had to endure a particularly stormy past. It was founded in AD 560 by St Kentigern (also known as St Mungo). Born in Scotland, St Kentigern left in AD 553 after Christianity collapsed in the Kingdom of Strathclyde, and made his way to Wales, founding churches as he went. He eventually settled in Llanelwy (St Asaph's Welsh name, meaning 'church, or parish, of Elwy') and founded a monastery there. When he returned home in AD 573 he left the monastery in the hands of his favourite pupil, St Asaph.

The cathedral was sacked by Henry III's forces in 1245 and then destroyed during Edward I's conquest of Wales some 37 years later. Edward wished to rebuild at nearby Rhuddlan but Bishop Anian II insisted that the new cathedral remain at St Asaph. The

building as we see it today was begun by Anian and completed by his two successors.

In 1402 the woodwork was burnt during Owain Glyndwr's rebellion (it was subsequently restored by Bishop Redman) and by the 17th century matters were so desperate that many of the possessions were sold and the Bishop's Palace became a tavern! However, St Asaph's Cathedral has survived and today it holds several treasures including a first edition of the William Morgan Welsh Bible (dating from 1588) that was used at the Investiture of Charles as the Prince of Wales in 1969.

Bishop of St Asaph from 1601 to 1604, **William Morgan** began his mammoth task of translating the Bible into Welsh while he was a rector (see also Penmachno). His work was not as well regarded then as it is now, and during his ministry over the parish of Llanrhaeadr ym Mochnant his congregation grew so upset with his neglect of his pastoral duties for his translation work that he had to be escorted by armed guards to the church. Not only was the finished work of importance to the Welsh churches, each one of which received a copy, but it also set a standard for the Welsh language, which, without being codified, could have been lost forever. A special monument, the **Translator's Memorial**, commemorates and names those who, under Morgan's guidance, assisted him in translating the Bible. Major restoration work on the cathedral was entrusted to Sir George Gilbert Scott, who also worked on the restoration of the cathedrals at Bangor and St David's as well as building many churches and houses throughout the United Kingdom. (The Scott dynasty takes a bit of sorting out: Sir George Gilbert Scott (1811-1878), the most prolific builder and restorer, had two architect sons, George Gilbert Scott Jr (1839-1897) and

THE TWEEDMILL FACTORY OUTLET

Llannerch Park, St Asaph, Denbighshire LL17 0UY
Tel: 01745 730072
e-mail: enquiries@tweedmill.co.uk
website: www.tweedmill.co.uk

With over 30,000 square feet of quality products all at affordable prices, a visit to Tweedmill Factory Outlets is a must! Womenswear-menswear-childrenswear-shoes-gifts and home accessories are all there at affordable prices.

The outlet sits two miles south of the small cathedral City of St. Asaph in Denbighshire, on the A525, and is a favourite stopping off point for locals and tourists alike who know and appreciate quality items at affordable prices. There is ample free parking for everyone, so shopping here is an enjoyable experience, with none of the fuss or bother normally associated with the high street. Take your time looking around the outlet, as we normally have at least 50,000 perfect items of clothing and accessories, as well as 5,000 pairs of shoes and 100,000 homeware

items. Most of the items are discounted with some up to half the recommended retail price, so there is no reason for you not to take your time to look around and get yourself a bargain.

The place is warm and inviting during the winter months, and cool and relaxing in the summer. It also has a beautiful country setting, which makes a visit a real pleasure. There are many departments each with a huge range of bargains. There is ladies wear, menswear, children's wear, homeware, perfume, handbags and luggage, a cookshop, furnishings and gifts-in fact something for everyone. Why not make a full day of it? You can enjoy a meal in Drapers café-bar, which is so good it holds a coveted award from Les Routiers, and offers quality food using where possible fresh local produce. Why not try the Warehouse café, which is self service, though serviced from the same kitchen. Toasties-sandwiches-baked potatoes-cakes-they are all here, along with teas, coffee and cold drinks.

The Tweedmill Factory Outlet positively welcomes coach parties, and makes the perfect stopping off point to do some serious shopping or enjoy a relaxing meal or drink. Opening times are Monday to Saturday 9.30am-6.00pm with late night until 8pm on Thursdays and 11am-5pm on Sundays. The only day they close is Christmas Day! Wheelchairs are available, so there is easy access throughout as well as air conditioned fitting rooms.

So pay the factory outlet a visit, and be prepared to encounter bargains galore! You will want to come back!

John Oldrid Scott (1842-1913). John Oldrid's son Sir Giles Gilbert Scott (1880-1960) was responsible for Liverpool Cathedral.)

In the centre of St Asaph is **Elwy Bridge**, which is believed to date from the 17th century although it was the fine renovation work by Joseph Turner in 1777 that allows it to carry today's heavy traffic. The River Elwy is linked with a particularly fishy tale about Bishop Asaph, after whom the town is named. One day, Queen Nest, the wife of Maelgwn Gwynedd, King of North Wales, lost a precious ring - the ancient and sacred ring of the Queens of the North - while bathing in the river. Upset and fearing her husband's anger, the Queen went to St Asaph to ask for his help in retrieving the ring. Comforting the lady, St Asaph invited the royal couple to dine with him the following evening where he told Maelgwn about the loss of the ring. The king's terrible rage could only just be contained by St Asaph and he suggested they begin their meal. As the king cut into the locally-caught salmon that started the feast, the sacred ring fell out on to his plate!

However, Glasgow - where Kentigern founded that city's cathedral - claims the events took place there, though the circumstances are slightly different.

RHUDDLAN
8 miles N of Denbigh on the A525

🏛 Rhuddlan Castle	🏛 Parliament House
🏛 Gillot's Tower	🏛 Dominican Friary
🏛 Parish Church of St Mary	🏛 Twt Hill
🎭 Statute of Rhuddlan	

The site of an early Norman stronghold can be seen **Twt Hill**. The stronghold dates from the 11th century, and was built by Robert of Rhuddlan, known as the 'Terror of North Wales'. At one time it may have incorporated a stone tower, though nothing can now be seen of it. The place was abandoned in about 1277, when Edward I built **Rhuddlan Castle** nearby. One of the Iron Ring of fortresses built by Edward I, as one of the most massive and impenetrable of his defences, it was the king's headquarters during his campaign and it was from here that Edward issued the **Statute of Rhuddlan** (in March 1284) that united the Principality of Wales with the Kingdom of England. He also gave the town a Royal Charter when his sovereignty was confirmed.

The statute, which lasted until the Act of Union in 1536, was enacted on the site now occupied by **Parliament House** (the old court house) and there is a commemoration tablet on the wall which is said to be from the original building. Although the castle, like many, was partially destroyed during the Civil War, the town is still sometimes referred to as the Cradle of Wales.

Rhuddlan Castle

🏛 historic building   📷 museum   🏛 historic site   🗺 scenic attraction   🌿 flora and fauna

While the castle in its heyday was a magnificent example of medieval defensive building, the most impressive engineering feat in the area was the canalisation of the River Clwyd to give the castle access, by ship, to the sea some three miles away. The remains of the dockgate, **Gillot's Tower**, can still be seen. This was built by James of St George, who was also responsible for the interesting concentric plan of the castle which allowed archers, stationed on both the inner and outer walls, to fire their arrows simultaneously.

At one time a **Dominican Friary** stood close to Twt Hill, though the remains are now on private property. The **Parish Church of St Mary** was founded in the 13th century, with an extra nave being added 200 years later. However, the original church may have been built about 1080. At one time it was considered as the place to build a new cathedral for what is today the Diocese of St. Asaph. There is the tombstone of an archbishop in the church - but an unusual one. He was William de Freney, Archbishop of Edessa in Syria. It was originally part of the Dominican friary, but was brought to the church in 1536. It was de Freney's uncle who had been sent to England by the Pope to found the Dominican order in the country.

DYSERTH
10 miles N of Denbigh on the A5151

🏛 Parish Church of St Bridget 🏛 Bodrhyddan Hall

🏛 Merseyside Children's Holiday Camp

🏛 St Mary's Well 🏞 Dyserth Waterfall

Lying in the foothills of the Clwydian Range, below Craig Fawr's slopes, this village, in the scenic Vale of Clwyd, boasts a 60-foot waterfall known as the **Dyserth Waterfall**, as well as the charming **Parish Church of St Bridget**, which dates from the 13th century.

Just to the west of the village lies **Bodrhyddan Hall**, the impressive 17th century manor house of the Conwy family who have had their home here since the early 15th century. The hall houses the Charter of Rhuddlan, and visitors can also see, around the fireplaces in the white drawing room, panels that came from the chapel of a Spanish Armada ship that foundered off the coast of Anglesey. For the more ghoulish, one of the rooms contains an Egyptian mummy. Other notable items include Hepplewhite chairs, suits of armour and ancient weapons, and a family portrait by Sir Joshua Reynolds. **Bodrhyddan Gardens** are also of interest, the main feature being a box-edged Victorian parterre designed by William Andrews Nesfield, father of the famous William Eden Nesfield, who remodelled the house in 1875. William E had a very varied life, being a soldier and a watercolour painter before taking up garden design when he was over 40. He worked on well over 200 estates, among the most notable being the Royal Botanic Gardens at Kew. A much older part of the garden at Bodrhyddan is centred around a well house (bearing the inscription 'Inigo Jones 1612') containing a spring, **St Mary's Well**, that may once have had pagan significance.

In 1909 a man called Arthur Lee founded the **Merseyside Children's Holiday Camp** here, and for 75 years it provided holidays for poor children from Liverpool and Birkenhead. It's site is now occupied by a hotel and country club.

BODELWYDDAN
8 miles N of Denbigh off the A55

🏛 Marble Church 🏛 Bodelwyddan Castle

St Margaret's Parish Church is known as the **Marble Church**, and was built between 1856

🎭 stories and anecdotes 🐦 famous people 🎨 art and craft 🚶 entertainment and sport 🚶 walks and 1860 by Lady Willoughby de Broke as a memorial to her husband. The landmark white spire is of local limestone, while inside is an arcade made of 14 different types of marble. In the churchyard are buried several Canadian soldiers from a nearby camp who were shot for mutiny in 1918

Opposite the eye-catching church stands **Bodelwyddan Castle**, a Victorian country house and estate which occupies the site of a 15th century house. The castle is the Welsh home of the National Portrait Gallery, and as well as the wonderful collection of Victorian portraits on display, visitors can see beautiful furniture on loan from the Victorian and Albert Museum and sculptures from the Royal Academy. Anyone tiring of the glorious pieces exhibited here can relax and play one of several hands-on Victorian games and inventions in the gallery, while outside are picnic tables, an adventure playground, maze, terrace café and secret woodland walk. A hands-on science centre is the latest attraction.

18th and 19th century landscaped parkland surrounds the castle and here, too, is an Arts and Crafts walled garden originally planted by TH Mawson, with some redesign work being undertaken by H Moggridge in 1980.

RUTHIN
7 miles SE of Denbigh on the A525

🏛 Parish Church of St Peter	🏛 Old Grammar School
🏛 Old Courthouse	🏛 Ruthin Gaol
🏛 Nant Clwyd House	🏛 Ruthin Castle
🏛 St Peter's Square	🏛 Maen Huail

This old market town lies in the Vale of Clwyd, more or less surrounded by a ring of hills, with a layout that appears to have changed little from medieval days. In fact, a description of Ruthin made in Elizabethan times, where it is described as "the grandest market town in all the Vale, full of inhabitants and well replenished with buildings", is as true today as it was then. **St Peter's Square** is a good place from which to view the town; it was here in 1679 that a Catholic priest was hung, drawn and quartered. Situated behind a magnificent set of 18th century wrought iron gates stands the town's splendid **Parish Church of St Peter**. Founded in the late 13th century as a collegiate church, its notable features include an early 16th century oak roof that consists of 408 carved panels. Behind the church there are some beautiful buildings in the collegiate close - 14th century cloisters, the **Old Grammar School** of 1284 and 16th century almshouses.

St Peter's Square itself is edged with many lovely buildings, including the particularly eye-catching 15th century Myddleton Arms with its unusual Dutch style of architecture and its seven dormer windows that have been dubbed the 'Eyes of Ruthin'. At one time there were around 60 inns and

Nant Clwyd House, Ruthin

pubs in Ruthin - one for every 10 men in the town - and nine of these were to be found around the square. On the south side of St Peter's Square stands the impressive wattle and daub **Old Courthouse**, which dates from 1401 and was a temporary resting place for prisoners, who were kept in the cells below the magnificent beamed court room.

On Clwyd Street, a major new attraction opened in May 2002. This is **Ruthin Gaol**, through whose gates thousands of prisoners - men, women and children, the guilty and the innocent - passed between 1654 and 1916. Visitors (all volunteers these days!) can see how prisoners lived their daily lives: what they ate, how they worked, the punishments they suffered. The cells, including the punishment, 'dark' and condemned cell, can be explored,

and there are hands-on activities for children. In Castle Street can be found one the oldest town houses in North Wales. **Nant Clwyd House** is a fine example of Elizabethan architecture although the present 16th century building shows traces of an earlier house. During the reign of Elizabeth I it was the home of Dr Gabriel Goodman, an influential man who was the Dean of Westminster for 40 years. He established Ruthin School in 1595 and the town's almshouses. Ruthin is also renowned for **Maen Huail**, a stone that stands in the market place and which, according to legend, marks the place where Huail was beheaded by King Arthur because of rivalry in love.

Ruthin Castle, begun in 1277 by Edward I, was the home of Lord de Grey of Ruthin who, having proclaimed Owain Glyndwr a

ELFAIR

18 Stryd Clwyd, Rhuthun, Sirddinbych LL15 1HW
Tel/Fax: 01824 702575

Behind the smart and inviting blue-painted exterior of a building dating back to Tudor times, **Elfair** is stocked with gifts and crafts made in Wales and reflecting Welsh life, culture and heritage. It has been run since the early 1990s by Mrs Sioned Evans, former teacher and mother of four, and her husband, and in the ground floor (with a separte children's room) and cellar customers will find an outstanding selection of crafts, souvenirs, gifts and homeware that

includes traditional love spoons, cards for all occasions, framed prints and photographs, kitchenware, glassware, bone china, pottery, jewellery, T-shirts, toys, soft toys and Welsh-themed CDs and DVDs.

There are also aprons in the Welsh national colours, textiles, throws, blankets, ornaments in slate and books, in

both Welsh and English about Wales and Welsh topics. One room is filled with things for children. The shop is open from 9.30 to 5 Monday to Saturday.

traitor to Henry IV, was given a large area of land originally held by the Welshman. After Glyndwr crowned himself Prince of Wales, de Grey was the first to suffer when Ruthin was attacked in 1400. Though the town was all but destroyed, the castle held out and survived the onslaught. During the Civil War, the castle again came under siege, this time surviving for 11 weeks in 1646 before eventually falling to General Mytton, who had the building destroyed. Partially restored and then owned by the Cornwallis-West family, Ruthin Castle played host, before and during World War I, to many famous and influential Edwardians including the Prince of Wales (later Edward VII), the actress Mrs Patrick Campbell and Lady Randolph Churchill, the mother of Winston Churchill. Today, the castle, with its charming grounds and roaming peacocks, is a

hotel that specialises in medieval banquets.

LLANARMON-YN IÂL

11 miles SE of Denbigh on the B5431

🏠 Parish Church of St Garmon

The capital of the Lâl region and occupying an attractive position on the banks of the River Alun, at the southern end of the Clwydian Range, this small village is noted for the **Parish Church of St Garmon**. It has been considerably altered over the years, and now only one of the two naves is wholly medieval. The fine Llwd memorial dates from 1639, and there are two medieval effigies (one of a knight and one of a bishop) rescued from Valle Crucis Abbey (see also Llangollen). Up until Tudor times pilgrims would flock to the shrine of St Garmon here.

🏠 historic building   🏠 museum   🏛 historic site   🌀 scenic attraction   🌿 flora and fauna

LLANFIHANGEL GLYN MYFYR
11 miles SW of Denbigh on the B5103

🏯 Parish Church of St Michael 🐟 Llyn Brenig

🐟 Llyn Alwen 🌲 Clocaenog Forest

This sleepy village lies in the fertile vale through which the River Alwen runs. Just to the north lies the **Clocaenog Forest**, Wales' second largest commercial plantation, which covers much of the southern moorland between the vales of Clwyd and Conwy. Managed by the Forestry Commission, it has well-marked forest trails of varying lengths that lead walkers through the mixed plantations of larch, spruce, pine, beech, oak and ash.

On the edge of the forest lies **Llyn Brenig**, a massive man-made reservoir that was completed in 1976 to accompany the smaller **Llyn Alwen**, which dates from the early 1900s. Close to the dam, and reached along the B4501, is a Visitor Centre which explains the local history and ecology of this tranquil Welsh valley as well as acting as a starting point for lakeside walks. By the lake, depending on the time of year, butterflies such as Orange Tip and Tortoiseshell can be seen and, along with the water sports on the lake, fishing is also available.

The **Parish Church of St Michael** is basically medieval, though it was partially rebuilt in 1852 and restored in 1902

CERRIGYDRUDION
12½ miles SW of Denbigh on the B4501

🏯 Parish Church of St Mary Magdalene

📖 Y Fuwch Frech

This village's name, often misspelt as 'Druidion', means 'Place of the Brave' and has no connection with Druids. There are many tales of fairy cattle to be found in Wales,

creatures that are thought to have descended from the aurochs, the wild cattle that roamed Britain in prehistoric times. Cerrigydrudion has it own cow, **Y Fuwch Frech** (the freckled cow), who lived on nearby Hiraethog mountain. For years she supplied the area with milk and would always fill any receptacle brought to her. One day, a witch began to milk her into a sieve and continued until the cow went insane and drowned herself in Llyn Dau Ychen. The **Parish Church of St Mary Magdalene** is said to have been founded as early as AD 440. The present building is medieval, and was mentioned in the Norwich Taxation documents of 1254. It was enlarged in 1503 and restored in 1874.

GWAENYNOG BACH
1½ miles W of Denbigh on the A543

🏯 Gwaenynog Hall

During the late 19th and early 20th centuries Beatrix Potter was a frequent visitor to the beautifully situated estate of **Gwaenynog Hall** (not open to the public), which was owned by her uncle Fred Burton. It is thought that her sketches, dating from a visit in 1909, of the kitchen garden (which has now been restored) were the basis for *The Tale of the Flopsy Bunnies* and also the working environment of the fictional Mr McGregor the gardener, who wanted to bake Peter Rabbit in a pie.

Llangollen

🏯 Parish Church of St Collen 🏯 Plas Newydd

🏯 Llangollen Bridge 🏯 Pontcysylte Aqueduct

🏯 Valle Crucis Abbey 🏛 Llangollen Wharf

🐟 World's End 🖋 International Musical Eisteddfod

🏛 Lower Dee Exhibition Centre 🏛 Dr Who Exhibition

🏛 International Model Railway World 🏛 Eliseg's Pillar

📖 stories and anecdotes 🐟 famous people 🖋 art and craft 🖋 entertainment and sport 🌲 walks

🏠 Llangollen Motor Museum	🏠 Dapol Toy Factory
🏠 Llangollen Canal Exhibition Centre	
🏚 Castell Dinas Bran	🍃 Horseshoe Pass
🐦 Ladies of Llangollen	🏚 Ffynnon Collen
🍃 Royal International Pavilion	🍃 National Eisteddfod
🍃 Canoe Centre and International Canoe Course	

The town, which is in the Dee Valley, takes its name from its founder, a monk called St Collan, who set up his cell and monastery here in the 7th century. A legend says that he was instructed to ride a horse for one full day along a valley and then stop. At the place where he stopped, he was to mark out the boundaries of a monastery. This he did, and it soon became an important place. Another story tells of St Collan, after fighting with a giantess in a nearby mountain pass, washed off the blood in a well, known locally as **Ffynnon Collen** (St Collen's Well).

The **Parish Church of St Collen** is largely Perpendicular, though there is an Early English doorway. It is, like many churches in this part of Wales, double-naved, and its chief glories are the two late medieval roofs.

The town nowadays draws visitors from all over the world who come here for the annual **International Musical Eisteddfod** which has been held since 1947. For six days every July, musicians, choirs, folk singers and dancers from all over the world, many performing in their national costumes, converge on the town to take part in this wonderful cultural event that is centred around the **Royal International Pavilion**. Between 2,000 and 5,000 competitors take part, and, in a small town with only 3,000 inhabitants, crowds of around 120,000 people are not unknown. Dylan Thomas was a regular visitor, and Luciano Pavarotti, Tiri Te Kanawa and Placido Domingo have taken part. This event should not be confused with the **National Eisteddfod**, the annual Welsh language cultural

River Dee, Llangollen

🏠 historic building	🏠 museum	🏚 historic site	🍃 scenic attraction	🐦 flora and fauna

festival whose venue alternates between the north and south of the country.

The first recorded eisteddfod was held at Cardigan Castle in 1176, and the modern eisteddfod began as a competition between bards at the Owain Glyndwr hotel in Corwen in 1789; it became a truly national event at Llangollen in 1858, when thousands of people came to Llangollen from all over the country. Music, prose, drama and art are included in the festival, which culminates in the chairing and investiture of the winning poet.

Throughout the rest of the year there are many other attractions in Llangollen to keep visitors satisfied. In particular, close to the river, is the **Lower Dee Exhibition Centre**, which incorporates three attractions in one place. The **Doctor Who Exhibition** is the world's largest collection of memorabilia dedicated to the cult television programme, while the **International Model Railway World** is the world's largest permanent exhibition of model railways. Finally, visitors young and old will find the **Dapol Toy Factory**, where many of the models for the other two exhibitions on the site are made, a

Llangollen Motor Museum

Pentre Felin, Llangollen LL20 8EE
Tel: 01798 860324
e-mail: llangollenmotormuseum@hotmail.com
website: www.llangollenmotormuseum.co.uk

The **Llangollen Motor Museum** is located near the town, nestling between the Llangollen Canal and the river. The building, dating back to the 1820s, was originally a slate dressing works and had many other uses before becoming a museum in 1985. The museum demonstrates in an informative , yet informal, way the charm and character of our motoring past, and the collection comprises more than 60 vehicles, from cars and motor bikes to invalid carriages and pedal cars. There is a recreation of a 1950s village garage complete with petrol pumps and the owners' living quarters. Included in the museum's collection are a Model T Ford, a splendid 1925 Vauxhall 38/93, a 1925 Citroën Boulangere from the vineyards of France and many of the cars that grandad used to drive. Among the motor bikes are great British names, including Norton, Triumph, Ariel, Sunbeam and BSA. The Museum is owned and run by the Owen family, headed by Gwylim, who was involved in the design and construction of cars at Vauxhall, his wife Ann and one of his sons, Geoffrey, who is a car restorer. For those who like to repair and restore their own vehicles, the Museum keeps a large stock of spares for classic cars, mainly from the 1960s.

The Museum also has a small exhibition showing the history and development of the British canal network and life on the canals through models, paintings, pottery and other memorabilia. School parties are welcome, and for car clubs a private field is available for picnics or overnight camping. The Llangollen Motor Museum, which has a refreshment and souvenir shop, is open Tuesday to Sunday March to October; winter opening by arrangement.

fascinating place to wander around. The **Llangollen Motor Museum** (see panel on page 25) features over 60 cars, motor bikes and even pedal cars from the earliest days of motoring to the present day.

Much later, in the 19th century, Llangollen was famous as the home for 50 years of the **Ladies of Llangollen**, Lady Eleanor Butler and Miss Sarah Ponsonby. These two eccentric Irish women ran away from their families in Ireland and set up home together in 1780 in a cottage above the town. As well as devoting their lives to "friendship, celibacy and the knitting of blue stockings", the ladies also undertook a great deal of improvements and alterations that turned a small, unpretentious cottage into the splendid house - **Plas Newydd** - that is seen today. The marvellous 'gothicisation' of the house was completed in 1814 and some of the elaborate oak panels and the glorious stained glass windows were donated to the couple by their famous visitors, who included Sir Walter Scott, William Wordsworth, the Duke of Gloucester and the Duke of Wellington. The ladies were both buried in the churchyard of St Collen, sharing a grave with their friend and housekeeper Mary Caryll.

Although, after their deaths, some of the ladies' displays were dispersed, the work on the house was continued by another owner, General Yorke, and Plas Newydd is still well worth visiting. A small museum contains relics of the Battle of Waterloo. The gardens are interesting and, while the formal layout to the front of the house was created after the ladies had died and the terraces have been altered since they lived here, they still reflect the peace and quiet the couple

were seeking as well as containing more interesting curios from those early Regency days. Plas Newydd is open every day from Easter to October.

Back in the town centre and spanning the River Dee is the eye-catching **Llangollen Bridge** dating from 1347 and originally constructed by John Trevor, who went on to become the Bishop of St Asaph. One of the Seven Wonders of Wales, this four-arched bridge has been rebuilt and widened in places over the years and is still used by today's traffic. The **Canoe Centre and International Canoe Course** is on the banks of the Dee, to the west of the bridge. The river is used for slalom competitions, and competitions are held in the winter months. Visitors can also take part in canoeing. On the north side of the

Llangollen Station

river is **Llangollen Station**, home of the Llangollen Railway Society. Since taking over the disused line in 1975, the Society has restored the railway track and journeys along the banks of the River Dee can be taken on this delightful steam railway. The station houses a museum with a collection of engines, coaches and rail memorabilia. From **Llangollen Wharf** pleasure cruises along the Llangollen Canal have taken place since 1884. Some trips are horse-drawn, while others cross the **Pontcysylte Aqueduct** in the narrow boat *Thomas Telford*.

Also on the Llangollen Canal, a branch of the Shropshire Union Canal, is the **Llangollen Canal Exhibition Centre**, and just a short walk further on is **Castell Dinas Bran**. Although the remains of this Iron Age hill fort are not extensive, the climb is well worth the effort as the view over the town and the Vale of Llangollen is quite breathtaking. **World's End,** on the north side of the town, has been known by that name for centuries, and offers woodland walks plus a link with the last, as it is supposed to have associations with King Arthur. One of its peaks is called Craig Arthur, and Guinevere was supposed to have been held captive here when she was kidnapped.

The main route north out of Llangollen passes the impressive ruins of **Valle Crucis Abbey** (see walk on page 28). Situated in green fields and overshadowed by the surrounding steep-sided mountains, this was an ideal place for a remote ecclesiastical house, the perfect spot for the Cistercians,

Offa's Dyke Path

medieval monks who always sought out lonely, secluded places. This abbey was founded in 1201 by Madog ap Gruffyd, the Prince of Powys, and was a very suitable location for the monks of this austere order. Despite a fire, the tower collapsing and the Dissolution in 1535, the ruins are in good condition and visitors can gain a real feel for how the monks lived and worked here. Notable surviving original features include the west front with its richly carved doorway and rose window, the east end of the abbey and the chapter house with its superb fan-vaulted roof. Also to be seen are some mutilated tombs which are thought to include that of Iolo Goch ('Iolo the Red'), who lived between1320-1398 and was a bard of Owain Glyndwr. Valle Crucis means

Horseshoe Falls, Valle Crucis Abbey and Llangollen Canal

Distance: *2.6 miles (4.2 kilometres)*

Typical time: *90 mins*

Height gain: *130 metres*

Map: *Explorer 256*

Walk: *www.walkingworld.com ID:1646*

Contributor: *Pat Roberts*

Parking is at the start of the walk, in the Llantilsilio Car Park and Picnic Area. This is on a B road off the A542 from Llangollen to the Horseshoe Pass

DESCRIPTION:

The walk is short and takes in Valle Crucis Abbey before going round or over Velvet Hill. The choice is yours, over-the-top if you are fit and round-the-base if you are not. The walk starts with a visit to Horseshoe Falls, where the water is diverted from the River Dee to the start of the Llangollen Canal. It then follows the canal towpath, passing Berwyn Station on the Llangollen railway. There is a real chance of seeing steam trains here and also horse-drawn barges on the canal.

FEATURES:

Hills or Fells, River, Toilets, National Trust/NTS, Wildlife, Birds, Flowers, Great Views, Butterflies, Woodland, Ancient Monument

WALK DIRECTIONS:

1 | Walk down to the bottom corner of the picnic site and some steps down to the road, where go right and down. On the opposite side of the road, take this flight of stone steps down towards the canal. Cross the canal via an irom footbridge, to descend steps at the rear entrance of the hotel, where turn right along the canal to Horseshoe Falls.

2 | Horseshoe Falls, where water is diverted from the River Dee to form the Llangollen Canal. This is a beautiful spot. Retrace your steps along the canal.

3 | On reaching the rear of the hotel, walk past the iron steps descended earlier and continue along the canal. When you reach the Iron Bridge Hotel & Restuarant, follow the towpath on the right bank of the canal.

4 | Just after passing the motor museum, pass seats carved out of the trunks of trees and reach a bridge over the canal. Cross this bridge to reach the road, where go right and up.

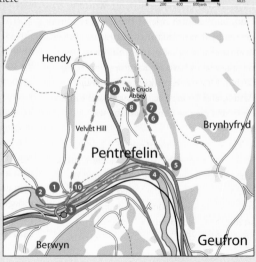

5 | Soon see a track on the other side of the road and a sign on the wall "Valle Crucis Abbey". Follow this stony track across fields, with good views all around.

6 | We found this gate misleading. There is a sign on the stile pointing left along the track, but when we were there the sheep feeding-troughs were denying access to the path. The stony track just goes on, so we went through the gate.

7 | Where the track swings right, there is a stile ahead; IGNORE IT. Just after the track swings right, there is a path down on the left, which leads down to a stream with a footbridge over it. Once over the stream, pass between the caravans to reach the entrance to Valle Crucis Abbey.

8 | Valle Crucis Abbey was founded in the 13th Century for the Cistercian Monks. It is in the care of CADW and there is a small entrance fee. From the abbey entrance, walk up the

tarmac road serving the caravan site. When you pass the site office, bear to the right and up to the road. Cross over.

9 | This footpath takes you up and over Velvet Hill. There are wonderful views from the top, with a sense of remoteness. For anyone who is less energetic, there is an easier route which goes AROUND Velvet Hill. Just past the footpath sign, take this quiet road to the left. It curves round the hill, but drops down quite quickly near the bottom. It is always manageable. Just as this narrow road meets the main road at the bottom, there is a National Trust sign on the left "Velvet Hill." The footpath over the top of the hill comes down onto the road.

10 | On reaching this road, turn right. The main entrance to the picnic site is straight ahead, but there is also an entrance down the minor road to the left, signed "Corwen".

'Valley of the Cross' and refers to **Eliseg's Pillar**, which stands about half a mile from the abbey and was erected in the early 9th century. The inscription on this Christian memorial cross is now badly weather beaten but fortunately a record was made in 1696 of the words. It was erected in memory of Eliseg, who annexed Powys from the Saxons, by his great-grandson Concenn. The pillar was broken by Cromwell's men and not re-erected until the 18th century.

A little further northwards along this road lies the spectacular **Horseshoe Pass** which affords remarkable views of the surrounding countryside. From the top of the pass can be seen the Vale of Clwyd and the ridge of Eglwyseg Rocks where Offa's Dyke path (see Prestatyn) runs.

Around Llangollen

JOHNSTOWN
6 miles NE of Llangollen on the B5605

🌱 Stryt Las Park

On the B5605 between Johnstown and Rhosllanerchrugog lies **Stryt Las Park**, a predominantly wetland area with a large lake and three small ponds. This Site of Special Scientific Interest is home to one of Europe's largest colonies of the Great Crested Newt. The park is open daily, the visitor centre daily in summer, weekends only in winter. In Rhosllanerchrugog, the Stiwt is a forum for Welsh language choirs, stage performances and crafts.

📖 stories and anecdotes   🦜 famous people   🎨 art and craft   ✒ entertainment and sport   🚶 walks

BERSHAM
7½ miles NE of Llangollen off the A483

🏛 Clywedog Valley and Trail   🕊 Davis Brothers

🏚 Bersham Ironworks

Bersham lies in part of the **Clywedog Valley and Trail** that skirts around the south and west of Wrexham and includes several places of industrial interest. It passes through Plas Power and Nant Mill, woods that stretch along the River Clywedog between Bersham and Coedpoeth. A well-preserved section of **Offa's Dyke** cuts through Plas Power (see Prestatyn). The village was established around 1670 and was the home of the **Davis Brothers**. The fine workmanship of these two famous iron masters can be seen in the beautiful gates at Chirk Park (see Chirk) and at St Giles' Church in Wrexham.

The master and owner of **Bersham Ironworks** from 1762, John 'Iron Mad' Wilkinson, was himself famous for the cannons he bored for use in the American War of Independence and for the cylinders he produced for James Watt's steam engines. The ironworks are open in the summer, the Heritage Centre all year round.

WREXHAM
9½ miles NE of Llangollen on the A483

🏛 Parish Church of St Giles   🕊 Judge Jeffreys

🏚 Clywedog Valley and Trail   🕊 Elihu Yale

🏛 King's Mill   🏛 Wrexham Museum   🏚 Erddig

🖈 Wrexham Science Festival

This once small market town, which is considered to be the unofficial capital of North Wales, is now a busy place with plenty to offer the visitor. Growing and prospering around the commercial importance of its brick and tile manufacturing, brewing, steel and coal, Wrexham still holds a variety of markets today. An interesting experience for city dwellers is the cattle market held on Saturdays where farmers from the surrounding area come to socialise and oversee transactions and where visitors can wander around soaking up the rural atmosphere.

For those wishing to find out more about the town and its social, industrial and local history then **Wrexham Museum**, housed in the County Buildings that were originally constructed as the militia barracks in 1857, is a good place to start. The discovery of a skeleton nearby - it became known as Brymbo Man - traces the town's history back as far as the Bronze Age while the Romans are also known to have settled in the Wrexham area. Both Roundhead and Cavalier troops were garrisoned in the town during the Civil

Wrexham Parish Church

🏛 historic building   🏛 museum   🏚 historic site   🏛 scenic attraction   🌿 flora and fauna

War and, in 1882, Britain's first lager brewery was built here. The suburb of Acton was the birthplace of **Judge Jeffreys**, the notoriously harsh lawman who was nicknamed 'Bloody' for his lack of compassion and his belief in swift justice.

Perhaps Wrexham's best known building, and one that's a particular favourite of American tourists, is the **Parish Church of St Giles** that dominates the town's skyline. It is famous for being the burial place of **Elihu Yale**, the benefactor of Yale University, who was laid to rest here on his death in 1721. His father had emigrated from Wrexham to North America in 1637, and Elihu was born soon afterwards in Boston. In 1691 Elihu sent a cargo of books and Indian goods from Fort Madras where he was Governor. The sale of the books enabled him to initiate the University of Yale in 1692. The memorial quadrangle at Yale has a Wrexham Tower (see also Bryneglwys). Yale's tomb in St Giles was restored in 1968 by members of Yale University to mark the 250th anniversary of the benefaction and it can be found in the churchyard to the west of the tower. His tomb is inscribed:

Born in America, in Europe bred,
In Africa travelled and in Asia wed,
Where long he lived and thrived; in London dead.
Much good, some ill he did; so hope's all even,
And that his soul through mercy's gone to heaven.

Erddig

Nr Wrexham LL13 0YT
Tel: 01978 355314

Two miles south of Wrexham, in a glorious 2,000-care estate and country park, **Erddig** is one of the most fascinating houses in Britain, not least because of the unusually close relationship that existed between the owners and their servants. This is movingly illustrated by the extraordinarily detailed exhibition of family memorabilia collected by the servants and on show to visitors. The late 17th century mansion was begun by Joshua Edisbury, the High Sheriff of Denbighshire, who subsequently fled, unable to meet his debts. The house passed into the hands of the Meller family and to their descendants until finally coming under the ownership of the National Trust. The stunning state rooms display most of their original 18th and 19th century furniture and furnishings, including some exquisite Chinese wallpaper.

The outbuildings have been restored, including kitchen, laundry, bakehouse, stables, sawmill, smithy and joiner's shop, and visitors can wander around the country park and the dairy farm. The large walled garden has been restored to its 18th century formal design and incorporates Victorian additions, notably a parterre and yew walk, as well as a canal garden and fish pool; it also contains the National Ivy Collection, and a narcissus collection. Erddig is open to the public between late March and early November except Thursday and Friday. It has a plant sales area, a shop and a licensed restaurant. Video presentations are available, and conducted tours by prior arrangement.

You that survive and read his tale take care
For this most certain exit to prepare.
When blest in peace, the actions of the just
Small sweet and blossom in the silent dust.'

The church itself is also well worth taking the time to look over; its 136 foot pinnacle tower is one of the Seven Wonders of Wales. Begun in 1506 and much restored, this Gothic tower still carries some of the original medieval carvings, in particular those of St Giles, which are recognisable by his attributes of an arrow and a deer. Elsewhere in the church are a colourful ceiling of flying musical angels, two very early eagle lecterns, a Burne Jones window and the Royal Welsh Fusiliers chapel.

Just to the south of Wrexham and found in a glorious 2,000-acre estate and country park, is **Erddig** (see panel on page 31), one of the most fascinating houses in Britain, with stunning state rooms, exhibitions of family memorabilia collected by the servants, restored outbuildings and exquisite grounds that include the National Ivy Collection.

Along with Erddig, which lies within the **Clywedog Valley and Trail**, is **King's Mill**, a restored mill that dates from 1769 although an older mill has been on the site since 1315.

Every year in early spring the town hosts the **Wrexham Science Festival**.

GRESFORD
13 miles NE of Llangollen on the B5445

🏛 Parish Church of All Saints   🏛 Gresford Bells

🎞 Gresford Colliery Disaster

This former coal mining town was the site of the **Gresford Colliery Disaster** in 1934 that killed 266 men. The colliery closed in 1973 but the wheel remains in memory of those who lost their lives in this terrible disaster.

The town's **Parish Church of All Saints** is one of the finest in Wales, with notable medieval screens, stained glass, font and misericords, and a memorial to the mining disaster; it is also home to the famous **Gresford Bells**, one of the Seven Wonders of Wales, which are still rung every Tuesday evening and on Sundays.

HOLT
15 miles NE of Llangollen on the B5102

🏛 Holt Bridge   🏛 Holt Castle   ⚲ H.G. Wells

🏛 Parish Church of St Chad

The River Dee, which marks the boundary between Wales and England, runs through this village and its importance as a crossing point can be seen in the attractive 15th century **Holt Bridge**. The village of Holt was also the site of a Roman pottery and tile factory that provided material for the fort at nearby Chester. For a short while, the town had a very famous inhabitant - **H.G. Wells**, who was a teacher at the local school. There are scant remains of **Holt Castle**, or Castrum Leonis as it was called, built by John de Warren in the 13th century. The **Parish Church of St Chad** originally dates from the late 14th century, though it was almost completely rebuilt between 1871 and 1873.

BANGOR-IS-Y-COED
11 miles E of Llangollen on the B5069

🏛 Parish Church of St Dunawd   ⚲ Racecourse

Bangor-is-y-coed ('The Place of the Choir Below the Wood'), also known as Bangor-on-Dee, is in the area known as the Maelor, where the Cheshire Plains meet the Welsh Hills. The **Parish Church of St Dunawd** dates from the early 14th century and later, and is named after a Welsh saint who founded a monastery here in about AD 560. Due to its support of the Celtic peoples in their struggle against the Anglo Saxons, it was destroyed in 607 by Ethelfrid of Northumbria in what turned out to be the last victory by the Saxons over Celtic Christianity. Apparently, 1,200 monks were laid to the sword as Ethelfrid considered praying against him was tantamount to

Pontcysyllte Aqueduct

fighting against him. Those fortunate enough to have survived are thought to have travelled to Bardsey Island. Local legend also suggests that Owain Glyndwr married Margaret Hanmer in the hamlet of Hanmer, just four miles away. The village is well known to race-goers as it is home to a picturesque **racecourse**, situated on the banks of the River Dee, that stages several national hunt meetings annually. The village itself has a charming 17th century bridge said to have been built by Inigo Jones.

OVERTON
10 miles E of Llangollen on the A539

🏛 Parish Church of St Mary 🌿 Overton Yew Trees

This substantial border village is home to another of the Seven Wonders of Wales - the **Overton Yew Trees**, 21 trees that stand in the churchyard of the **Parish Church of St Mary**. Dating from medieval times, these tall, dark and handsome trees have a preservation order placed upon them. Within the church itself there are some interesting artefacts from the 13th century.

CEFN-MAWR
4½ miles E of Llangollen on the B5605

🏛 Pontcysyllte Aqueduct 🐟 Ty Mawr Country Park

Towering some 126 feet above the River Dee and carrying the Llangollen branch of the Shropshire Union Canal, **Pontcysyllte Aqueduct** is a magnificent construction some 1,007 feet in length. Built in 1805 by Thomas Telford, this cast iron trough supported by 18 stone pillars was much scorned by people at the time although today it is greatly admired and is still used regularly by pleasure boats. **Ty Mawr Country Park** is well worth a visit.

CHIRK
5½ miles SE of Llangollen on the B5070

🏛 Parish Church of St Mary 🏛 Chirk Castle

This attractive border town's origins lie in the 11th century castle of which, unfortunately, little remains except a small motte close to the town's **Parish Church of St Mary**. The church dates originally from Norman times, but it has been added to and restored over the years. It was originally dedicated to St, Tysilio, the son

---

🎭 stories and anecdotes   🎨 famous people   🎨 art and craft   🎶 entertainment and sport   🚶 walks of a Powys prince, but became St Mary's in the 16th century. Today, Chirk is perhaps better known for the National Trust owned **Chirk Castle** which lies a mile outside the town, and goes back almost 700 years. The magnificent iron gates were made and erected in 1701 by the Davis Brothers, and are one of the glories of the grounds (see also Bersham).

The Myddleton family of Chirk Castle have a red hand on their coat of arms that, legend has it, appears there as a reminder of the family's past misdeeds and could not be removed until a prisoner had survived 10 years in the castle dungeons. In the centre of Chirk is a war memorial designed by Eric Gill.

Just south of the town are two splendid constructions that span the Ceiriog valley: the first, an aqueduct built in 1801 by Thomas Telford, carries the Llangollen branch of the Shropshire Union Canal, while the other is a viaduct built in 1848 to carry the then new Chester to Shrewsbury railway line over the River Ceiriog.

GLYN CEIRIOG
2½ miles S of Llangollen off the B4500

🏛 Parish Church of St Ffraid   ⚜ Ceiriog Forest

🏛 Chwarel Wynne Mine Museum

This former slate mining village is more properly called Llansantffraid Glyn Ceiriog, and is home to the **Chwarel Wynne Mine Museum** which, as well as telling the story of the slate industry that used to support the village, gives visitors a guided tour of the caverns where the slate was mined. There is also a nature trail around the surrounding countryside. A narrow gauge tramway, the Glyn Valley Railway, once linked the Shropshire Union Canal at Gledrid with the quarries and mines at Glyn Ceiriog. Opened in

1873 and originally horse-drawn, it was later converted to steam and diverted through Chirk Castle estate to meet the Great Western Railway at Chirk station. It carried slate, silica, chinastone and dolerite downstream and returned with coal, flour and other commodities. It also carried passengers, and though it closed in 1935, the bed of the tramway can still be seen here and there, and the Glyn Valley Tramway Group was founded in 1974 to conserve evidence of the GVR. The Group has little museums in the Glyn Valley Hotel at Glyn Ceiriog and the former waiting room at Pontafog station, and a GVR Museum and Visitor Centre is to be established in the old locomotive shed and yard at Glyn Ceiriog.

The village lies in the secluded Vale of Ceiriog, and just to the west is the beautiful **Ceiriog Forest** which offers surprisingly pastoral views and vistas along with forest walks and trails. The **Parish Church of St Ffraid** (another name for Bridget) was completely rebuilt in about 1790.

LLANARMON DYFFRYN CEIRIOG
6½ miles SW of Llangollen on the B4500

🏛 Parish Church of St Garmon   🏛 Tomen Garmon

⚜ Ceiriog   ⚔ Ceiriog Trail

This peaceful village in the heart of the Vale of Ceiriog was the birthplace of the famous Welsh bard, **Ceiriog**, whose real name was John Hughes (1832-1887). A collector of folk tales as well as a poet, he is sometimes called the 'Robert Burns of Wales'. The 14-mile Upper **Ceiriog Trail** for walkers, mountain bikers and horse riders passes his home, Pen-y-Bryn. In the churchyard of the **Parish Church of St Garmon**, built in 1846, are yew trees, one of which may be over 1,000 years old. Also in the churchyard is a small tumulus which may date from the Bronze Age. Local legend says it is **Tomen Garmon**, from which St Garmon preached and in which he was later buried.

LLANTYSILIO
1 mile W of Llangollen off the A5

🏛 Parish Church of St Tysilio   🏛 Horseshoe Weir

🐾 Helena Faucit

Situated on the banks of the River Dee, and close to Thomas Telford's **Horseshoe Weir** which was built in 1806 to supply water to the Llangollen Canal, lies the **Parish Church of St Tysilio**. A Norman building, it was here, in 1866, that Robert Browning worshipped, and a brass plaque placed by Lady Martin commemorates his visit. Lady Martin, also known as the actress **Helena Faucit**, lived in the house next to the church. She, too, is remembered at the church by a chapel that was built following her death in 1898. In 1885 she published a book called *On Some of Shakespeare's Female Characters*, which was popular in its day.

GLYNDYFRDWY
4 miles W of Llangollen on the A5

🏛 Parish Church of St Thomas   🐾 Eos Griffiths

🏛 Owain Glyndwr's Mound

Once within the estate of Owain Glyndwr, this village lies on the historic and important A5 and between the Berwyn and Llantysilio mountains. A mound by the road, known as **Owain Glyndwr's Mound**, was once part of an impressive earthwork fortress that was later incorporated into part of the Welsh hero's manor house and estate. It was here, in 1400, that he declared himself to be Prince of Wales. Though it looks much older, the **Parish Church of St Thomas** dates only from 1858.

Much more recently, Glyndyfrdwy has become known as the home of the Dutch Butterfly Man, **Eos Griffiths**, who is known world wide for creating the bright and colourful ornamental butterflies that can be seen adorning homes from Scandinavia to Australia.

CORWEN
9 miles W of Llangollen on the A5

🏛 Parish Church of St Mael and St Suilen

🏛 Rug Chapel   🏛 Parish Church of All Saints, Llangar

🏛 Caer Derwyn   🐾 Owain Glyndwr

This market town, in a pleasant setting between the Berwyn Mountains and the River Dee, has, for many years, been known as the 'Crossroads of North Wales'. The town's origins can be traced back to the 6th century when the Breton-Welsh saints, Mael and Sulien, founded a religious community here. The **Parish Church of St Mael and St Sulien** still bears their name. This church was founded in the 12th century, though what can be seen nowadays dates mainly from the 13th to 15th centuries. It has an incised dagger in a lintel of the doorway that is known as **Glyndwr's Sword**. The mark was reputedly made by Glyndwr when he threw a dagger from the hill above the church in a fit of rage against the townsfolk. However, the dagger mark actually dates from the 7th to 9th centuries and there is another such mark on a 12th century cross outside the southwest corner of the church.

The town was also once the headquarters of Owain Glyndwr, who gathered his forces here before entering into his various campaigns. Owain Glyndwr (c1354-c1416), the self-styled Prince of Wales, led the last major attempt to shake off the yoke of the

CORWEN MANOR

8 London Road, Corwen, Denbighshire LL21 0DR
Tel: 01490 413196

Corwen Manor started in 1839 as the old Union Workhouse. It was bought by Alan and Sandra Sayer in 1989 and is now a thriving craft centre with a workshop making candles. The craft shop has a full range of Welsh gifts, hand made products from North Wales and a wool shop.

The candle workshop is best known for its wide range of novelty candles, all made in Wales. So whether you collect frogs, dogs, cats, pigs, dragons, owls or teddy bears, you're sure to find them here. There is also a full range of candle-making and craft supplies on sale, plus a range of love spoons, both standard or personalised - the perfect gift or souvenir.

There is also a full range of personalised goods for that special occasion, from candles to gifts. For the fisherman it stocks a fine selection of tackle and bait for all types of fishing, such as game, sea and course.

Corwen Manor also has a delightful café selling drinks and snacks.

So if you're anywhere near Corwen make sure you set aside plenty of time to take a look at this fine craft centre.

English. His status as a national hero was reinforced with the rise of Welsh Nationalism from the 18th century onwards. Descended from the Princes of Powys, he studied law in London and served with Henry Bolingbroke, an opponent of Richard II who was later to become Henry IV. When he returned to Wales, he encouraged resentment against the oppressive English rule. In September 1400, a year after Bolingbroke had usurped the throne, Glyndwr entered into a feud with a neighbour, Reynold, Lord Grey of Ruthin, which sparked an uprising in North Wales and a national struggle for independence. Glyndwr formed an alliance with King Henry's most influential and powerful opponents and by 1404 controlled most of Wales and embarked on a series of campaigns. But by the next year

he had twice been defeated by Henry IV's son Prince Henry (later Henry V), his English allies had been eliminated and even help from the French was fruitless.

By 1409 Glyndwr's main strongholds were in English hands and his campaigns came to an unsuccessful conclusion.

It was in the Owain Glyndwr Hotel in 1789 in Corwen that a local man, Thomas Jones, organised a bardic festival that laid the foundations for the modern eisteddfod. Across the River Dee from the town lies **Caer Derwyn**, a stone rampart around a hill that dates from Roman times.

To the west of Corwen and set in pretty, landscaped grounds is the simple, stone built **Rug Chapel**. A rare example of a private

🏛 historic building   🏛 museum   🏛 historic site   ♤ scenic attraction   🌾 flora and fauna chapel that has changed little over the years, Rug was founded in the 17th century by Old Blue Stockings, Colonel William Salisbury, in collaboration with Bishop William Morgan (the first translator of the Bible into Welsh) and its plain exterior gives no clues to its exquisitely decorated interior. It is testimony to Salisbury's 'high church' outlook, and is best described as a 'painted chapel'. Few parts have been left unadorned and, as well as the beautifully carved rood screen (a Victorian addition), the ceiling beams are painted with rose motifs. However, not all the decoration here is exuberant; there is also a sombre wall painting of a skeleton as a reminder of mortality. The architect Sir Edwin Lutyens acknowledged that his work was influenced by this beautiful chapel and evidence can be seen of this in his most elaborate commission, the Viceroy's House, New Delhi, which was completed in 1930.

Another interesting religious building can be found just to the south of Rug, in the direction of Llandrillo. The **Parish Church of All Saints** at Llangar, overlooking the confluence of the Rivers Dee and Alwen, is medieval, and though it was superseded in the 19th century by a new church at Cynwyd, this small place still retains many of its original features. In particular, there are some extensive 15th century wall paintings and a minstrels' gallery. Both Rug Chapel and Llangar church are now cared for by CADW - Welsh Historic Monuments.

LLANDRILLO
12 miles SW of Llangollen on the B4401

🏠 Parish Church of St trillo   ⛰ Craig Berwyn

🏃 Berwyn Mountains

The road to Llandrillo, from the north,

follows the Vale of Edeirion and the River Dee as it weaves its way below the northwest slopes of the **Berwyn Mountains**, another mountain range that is popular with walkers and visitors. This small village is a good starting point for walks in the Berwyns and footpaths from the village lead towards **Craig Berwyn**, whose summit is over 2,100 feet above sea level. The name means 'church of St Trillo', and the successor of the church he founded here, the **Parish Church of St Trillo**, was built in the mid 19th century on a site that had been occupied by a place of worship for centuries. The east window is worth seeing.

BRYNEGLWYS
5 miles NW of Llangollen off the A5104

🏠 Parish Church of St Tysilio   🏠 Plas-Yn-Yale

Standing on the slopes of Llantysilio Mountain, the large 13th century **Parish Church of St Tysilio**, in the heart of the village is, surprisingly, connected with the family who helped to found Yale University in the United States. Close to the village lies **Plas-Yn-Yale**, the former home of the Yale family and the birthplace of Elihu Yale's father. Elihu himself was born in 1647 in Boston, Massachusetts, and went on to become a governor of India before coming to England. Known for his philanthropy, Elihu was approached by an American College who, after receiving generous help, named their new college in Newhaven after him. In 1745, 24 years after his death, the whole establishment was named Yale University. Elihu Yale is buried in the Church of St Giles in Wrexham (see also Wrexham).

LOCATOR MAP

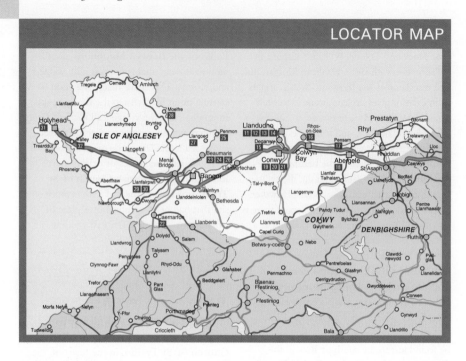

ADVERTISERS AND PLACES OF INTEREST

Accommodation, Food and Drink

Arts and Crafts

Fashions

Giftware

Home and Garden

Places of Interest

Specialist Food Shops

🏠 historic building   🏛 museum   🏛 historic site   🝆 scenic attraction   🌿 flora and fauna

2 North Wales Coast & Anglesey

The coast of North Wales draws visitors in their thousands to its holiday resorts, but this very traditional region, where Welsh is still spoken on a daily basis, has many other treasures, both man-made and natural. The coastline from Prestatyn to Bangor was, before the coming of the railways, littered with small fishing villages. During the 19th century, as the hours of mill workers from the industrial towns of Lancashire and the Midlands were reduced, the concept of an annual holiday, albeit in some cases just the odd day at the seaside, became widespread. Served by the newly built railway network, the fishing villages expanded to accommodate visitors. Boarding houses and hotels were built for the society visitors coming to take the sea air, and amusements and entertainment were soon a regular feature. Llandudno still retains much of its Victorian and Edwardian charm, while other resorts, such as Rhyl, have tried to counter the unsettled British summer weather by the creation of indoor complexes.

Prestatyn, to the east, lies at one end of Offa's Dyke (see Prestatyn). Built more as a line of demarcation rather than a fortification, the dyke runs from the coast southwards to Chepstow. Still substantially marking the border with England, many sections of the ancient earthwork are visible and can be seen from the waymarked footpath that runs the length of the dyke. It was also along the coast that Edward I built his Iron Ring of castles and while many are in ruins, two in particular are exceptional. Conwy Castle, now a World Heritage Site, was built in such a position that the

surrounding land provides suitable protection from attack. Caernarfon Castle, as much a royal residence as a fortress, was the place where Edward, in 1301, crowned his own son (later Edward II) as Prince of Wales. There were princes before this. In 1218 Llywelyn the Great and his descendents were given the title by his brother-in-law, Henry III of England. However, Edward II was the first heir to the English throne to have the title bestowed on him. Centuries later, in 1969, it was in the grounds of the splendid castle ruins that Queen Elizabeth invested the same title on her eldest son, Prince Charles.

Caernarfon and Bangor lie at opposite ends of the Menai Strait, the channel of water that separates mainland Wales from the Isle of Anglesey. It was not until the 19th century that a bridge was constructed across the strait, and Thomas Telford's magnificent Menai Suspension Bridge of the 1820s was joined, some 30 years later, by Stephenson's Britannia Bridge. Two great monuments to 19th century engineering, the bridges still carry traffic, both road and rail.

The Isle of Anglesey, with its rolling hills, fertile farmland and miles of wild and craggy coastline, has attracted settlers from the Stone Age onwards and is littered with evidence of Neolithic, Bronze Age and Iron Age people. Anglesey has its impressive castle, Beaumaris, built by Edward I to repel invasion from its neighbours. Today's invaders are largely tourists and holidaymakers, attracted by the elegant seaside resorts, the fishing, the sailing and the walking.

LYMPLEY LODGE

Colwyn Road, Craigside,
Llandudno, Conwy LL30 3AL
Tel: 01492 549304
e-mail: patricia@lympleylodge.co.uk
website: www.lympleylodge.co.uk

Set beneath the Little Orme on the edge of Llandudno, **Lympley Lodge** is a beautiful Victorian villa built in the 1870s that has been sympathetically converted into a superb guest house that boasts the very best in Welsh hospitality. It is the perfect base for exploring not only the delights of one of Wales' premier holiday resorts, but the whole of North Wales, an area that brims with history, scenic splendour and delightful places to visit.

There is a choice of three individually designed guest rooms, each one spacious, elegant and extremely comfortable. The Woodland is a double room, and has a Victorian brass bed and en suite bathroom; the Marina is a twin room with two single Victorian brass beds and an en suite shower room; and the Orme is a double room with en suite shower room, antiques and great views towards the sea. They all come with tea/coffee making facilities, hair dryer, clock/radio alarm, books, toiletries and fresh flowers.

The guest sitting room/library, with its antique furniture and comfortable seating, is on the first floor, and commands great views out over the sea. Here you can watch TV, read a paper or book, or relax as you admire the view. It makes a great place to plan your next day's outing.

The breakfast room is equally as appealing, and it is here that the Lympley Lodge's renowned Welsh breakfasts are served every morning. Only the finest of local produce - much of it free range - is used wherever possible to produce dishes that are tasty, hearty and always filling. Of course, lighter options are also available, and there are always plenty of fresh fruits, yoghurt, cereals, tea and coffee.

In addition to the guest rooms, a ground floor, self-contained holiday apartment is available to rent on a weekly or longer basis. It sleeps two, and comes fully furnished and equipped for a holiday to remember. It can be rented from March to October every year, and a brochure is available by phoning the number above.

There is just so much to see and do, not only in Llandudno, but in the whole of North Wales, and Lympley Lodge is the place to stay. People return to it again and again, and you're sure to do the same if you make it your base while on holiday!

Llandudno

🏛 Church of St Tudno   🏛 Deganwy Castle

🗻 Great Orme   🏛 The Rabbit Hole

🏛 Llandudno Museum   🗻 Promenade

🏛 Whire Rabbit Statue   🏛 Great Orme Tramway

🏛 Great Orme Copper Mine   🌱 Bodafon Farm Park

Originally just a collection of fishermen's cottages, Llandudno - the 'Queen of Welsh resorts' - was developed in the 1850s under the watchful eye of the Liverpool surveyor, Owen Williams. A delightful place that is a wonderful example of Victorian architecture, Llandudno was planned around a pleasant layout of wide streets and, of course, the Promenade, the essential feature of a resort from that age. The **Promenade** is now lined with renovated, redecorated and elegant hotels and the wide boulevard gives it an air of the French Riviera. Off the Promenade towards the Little Orme by the fields, **Bodafon Farm Park** is a working farm and also home to the North Wales Bird Trust. Farm attractions include sheep shearing, ploughing, harvesting and collecting eggs. The Trust houses 1,000 birds, including eagle owls and falcons. A permanent Victorian puppet show can be watched on the promenade close to the **Pier**, which in 1914 the Suffragettes attempted to burn down. Later, Ringo Starr, of Beatles fame, worked on the pleasure streamers that docked at Llandudno pier.

Along the seafront can also be found the **White Rabbit Statue**, from Lewis Carroll's much loved story *Alice In Wonderland*. The

CLIFTON VILLA

28 Chapel Street, Llandudno, Conwy LL30 2SY
Tel: 01492 877697
e-mail: zena.cliftonvilla@yahoo.co.uk
website: www.cliftonvilla-guesthouse.com

For the last two years, Zena and Nigel Pugh have run **Clifton Villa** in the centre of Llandudno, and is a comfortable, friendly, welcoming and affordable guest house. It is only a couple of minutes away from all the town's main attractions, and yet plenty of off-street parking is easily available.

Zena and Nigel offer 11 extremely comfortable and well-appointed rooms to discerning guests. Each one has been furnished and decorated to a high standard, reflecting the care that is taken to ensure that you have a memorable and enjoyable stay. Seven of the rooms are fully en suite, and all have a colour TV, tea and coffee making facilities, hair dryer and thermostatically controlled radiators.

The bed and breakfast tariff includes a full cooked breakfast, served in the spacious breakfast room. Lighter options are also available if required. The produce is sourced locally wherever possible, and great care is taken to ensure that your every need is taken care of, including special dietary needs, which can be catered for by prior notice.

Zena and Nigel are keen to welcome you to their friendly establishment - one that you will remember for a long time, for all the right reasons!

🎬 stories and anecdotes   🦜 famous people   🎨 art and craft   🖋 entertainment and sport   🚶 walks

Llandudno Pier

characters of the day as William Gladstone and Matthew Arnold as well as Lewis Carroll. Though little is known today of Carroll's stay with the family, visitors can be certain that it was on the broad, sandy beaches at Llandudno that the Walrus and the Carpenter 'wept like anything to see such quantities of sand' and it was the White Knight who considered "boiling it in wine" to prevent the Menai Bridge from rusting. The Visitor Centre at **The Rabbit Hole** presents an interesting audio-visual exhibition that is dedicated to Alice and her time in Wonderland.

tribute is to the real Alice - Alice Liddell - who came here on holiday with her family; it was also at Llandudno that her parents spent their honeymoon. Among the visitors to Dean Liddell's holiday home were such notable

NO 9 GUEST HOUSE

Chapel Street, Llandudno LL30 2SY
Tel: 01492 877251
Email: amandalynmiller@tiscali.co.uk
Website: www.no9llandudno.co.uk

No. 9 Guest House is ideally located in the Victorian resort of Llandudno, providing a central base for exploring the Snowdonia National Park and North Wales coast. A wealth of outdoor activities are within easy reach along with historic country houses, castles and other places of interest. No. 9 has comfortable and elegant bedrooms individually furnished to compliment the many original features of this much-loved Victorian town house. All bedrooms are en suite, with TV/DVD/CD, central heating thermostats, hairdryers, hospitality trays and all the comforts one would expect in a quality guest house.

No. 9 offers great value for money combined with high standards of service in a warm, informal atmosphere. Breakfast is served in a sunny, spacious dining room with fresh produce from local suppliers. A classic British breakfast is served with many dishes to choose from and homemade bread is a speciality.

Before booking give No. 9 a call to discuss your requirements with Amanda, the owner who always goes that little bit further to make her visitors' stay extra special. No. 9 Guest House offers the very best in service and efficiency at prices you can certainly afford.

🏛 historic building   🏛 museum   🏛 historic site   🌣 scenic attraction   🌿 flora and fauna

Although Llandudno is very much a product of the Victorian age, it earlier played host to Bronze Age miners and the Romans and, in the 6th century, St Tudno chose Great Orme as the site of the cell from where he preached. The saint was one of the seven sons of King Seithenyn, whose kingdom, it is said, sank beneath the waves of Cardigan Bay. The cell's successor is the **Church of St Tudno**, which was Llandudno's parish church when it was a fishing village, and which dates mainly from the 15th century. In 1852 it lost its 'parish church' status. One of its treasures is a roof boss depicting Christ's 'stigmata' - the wounds to his hands and feet where he was nailed to the cross and the wound in his side. At **Llandudno Museum** visitors are taken through the town's history, from ancient times to the present day, by a collection of interesting exhibits: a child's footprint imprinted on a tile from the Roman fort of Canovium (Caerhun), objets d'art collected from all over the world by Francis Chardon.

As well as being the home of Llandudno's roots, the massive limestone headland of **Great Orme** still dominates the resort today and also separates the town's two beaches. Two miles long, one mile wide and 679 feet high, its name, Orme, is thought to have originated from an old Norse word for sea monster. In what is now a country park, there are prehistoric sites in the form of stone circles and burial sites and the remains of Bronze Age mines. The summit can be reached by the **Great Orme Tramway**, a magnificent monument to Victorian

WONDERLLANDUDNO LTD

1 Mostyn Street, Llandudno, Conwy LL30 2NL
Tel/Fax: 01492 875962

'Probably the finest gift shop in Wales' reads the sign outside this splendid corner shop in the heart of Llandudno. That claim takes a lot of living up to, but step inside **Wonderllandudno Ltd** and you'll probably agree that this is no idle boast.

Gifts, crafts and souvenirs are displayed on tables, on shelves, in cabinets – even hanging from the ceiling! Cards for all occasions, pencils, pens and stationery, novelty mugs, sunglasses, canes and umbrellas, jewellery, watches and clocks, mobiles, soft toys, model kits, sweets and soft drinks, newspapers, things for the beach, ornaments and trinkets......the list is almost endless. The shop also has a large display of collectable cars, buses and trucks bringing collectors here from far and wide.

This splendid establishment stands close to the seafront in the 'Queen of Welsh resorts', famed for its broad sandy beaches, Victorian architecture and the looming headland of Great Orme with its tramway and copper mine. There's always plenty to occupy the visitor to Llandudno, and there's no finer place than Wonderllandudno to find something different to take home as a souvenir of a visit.

NORTH WALES HOLIDAY COTTAGES AND FARMHOUSES

Contact: Bob and Barbara Griffiths
39 Station Road, Deganwy, Conwy LL31 9DF
Tel: 08707 559888
e-mail: info@nwhc.co.uk   website: www.northwalesholidaycottages.co.uk

One popular way of enjoying your holiday is to go self-catering, and becoming, for a short while, a part of the community in which you are staying. Not only are you closer to the natural beauty of an area, you are immersed in the cultural and social life of the locality. For those interested in enjoying North Wales like this, the premier company for providing high quality accommodation is North Wales Holiday Cottages and Farmhouses, whose experience, expertise and comprehensive local knowledge is demonstrated in their brochure, or on their website. However, nothing can replicate the vast fund of knowledge of both the properties, and the area, that the staff has. All of the staff live locally, and have intimate knowledge of most of the properties. You are virtually guaranteed that, when you make an enquiry, someone on duty in the office will know both the property you are interested in, and its locality.

To see just what a superb and professional service Bob and Barbara Griffiths, and the rest of the friendly, helpful staff can provide, why not write or ring and request a brochure, or visit their website at www.northwalesholidaycottages.co.uk. There is bound to be something in the 54 pages of properties to both tempt you, and fulfill your requirements, with levels of appointment and luxury to satisfy everyone, from someone looking for a simple, comfortable base, to those with the most fastidious of tastes. There are cottages in the hills with walking from the doorstep, relaxing waterside properties, others with wonderful views and many in Areas of Outstanding Natural Beauty. The birdlife is wonderful and of course there seems to be a castle around almost every corner. Virtual tours of many of the properties can be seen on the website, along with news of what's going on in the area.

engineering constructed in 1902 that is Britain's only cable hauled, public road tramway. The **Great Orme Copper Mine** is the only Bronze Age copper mine in the world open to the public. Visitors can explore the 3,500-year-old passages, see the great opencast mine workings, peer into the 470ft shaft and discover how our ancestors turned rock into metal. The Visitor Centre is open to non-mine visitors, and also at the site are a tea room serving Welsh cream teas and a shop selling a wide variety of books, minerals, fossils and other souvenirs. Great Orme is home to a herd of wild goats descended from a pair presented to Queen Victoria by the Shah of Persia.

Great Orme Copper Mine

Just south of Llandudno, on Conway Bay, lies Deganwy, a once thriving fishing village that shares the same stretch of coastline though it has now been taken over by its larger neighbour. Often mentioned in Welsh history, Deganwy was a strategically important stronghold and **Deganwy Castle** was the seat of Maelgwn Gwynedd as early as the 6th century. The first medieval castle was probably built here by Lupus, Earl of Chester, shortly after the Norman Conquest. The scant remains seen today are, however, of a castle built by one of the Earl's successors in 1211. Henry II was besieged here by the Welsh and Deganwy was finally destroyed by Llewelyn ap Gruffyd (Llewelyn the Last) in 1263.

Around Llandudno

LLANSANFFRAID GLAN CONWY
3 miles SE of Llandudno off the A470

🏠 Felin Isaf   🏠 Parish Church of St Ffraid

In Garth Road **Felin Isaf** has two working watermills and a museum describing the history of the site and the various uses and types of mills. The **Parish Church of St Ffraid** is medieval in origin, though it was largely rebuilt in 1839.

BODNANT
6 miles S of Llandudno off the A470

🌳 Bodnant Gardens

Situated above the River Conwy and covering some 80 acres are the famous Edwardian **Bodnant Gardens**, laid out by the 2nd Lord Aberconwy in 1875 and presented to the National Trust in 1949.

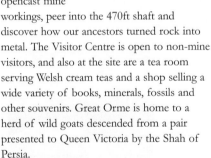

🎬 stories and anecdotes   🐦 famous people   🎨 art and craft   🎵 entertainment and sport   🥾 walks

RHOS-ON-SEA

3½ miles E of Llandudno on the B5115

🏠 Bryn Eurin   🐾 Revd W. Venable Williams

🎭 Harlequin Puppet Theatre

This very sedate North Wales coastal resort has a breakwater to shelter the pleasure boats and, along the promenade, is the small **Chapel of St Trillo**. Though the chapel's age is unknown it is said to have been built above an ancient holy well and also on the spot from where, reputedly, Owain Gwynedd set sail, in 1170, and eventually landed on the North American continent - some 322 years before Columbus made his historic voyage to the New World! It is said to be the smallest church in Britain, as it can only seat six people. Southwest of the town

is **Bryn Eurin**, all that is left of a prehistoric fort.

On the promenade is a monument to the **Revd W. Venable Williams**, He helped in the development of Rhos, but was in many ways a controversial figure He resisted the demands of local farmers to have their tithes reduced, and had his mission church in Colwyn Bay set on fire because of this. He also tried frantically to stop Colwyn Bay from splitting from his own parish of Llandrillo yn Rhos, taking his fight all the way to Parliament and even Queen Victoria.

The **Harlequin Puppet Theatre** can be found on the town's promenade. When built in 1958, it was Britain's first permanent theatre specially for puppet shows, and continues to present shows to this day.

TABITHA JANE

8B Rhos Parade, Penrhyn Avenue, Rhos on Sea,
North Wales LL28 4RD
Tel: 01492 543058
e-mail: smoggs@tiscali.co.uk

Tabitha Jane has been in Rhos on Sea for over 12 years, and during that time has gained an enviable reputation as being the place to go for quality leather goods, as well as jewellery, scarves, belts, luggage, gloves and gift items to suit all ages.

It is owned and managed by the husband and wife team of Pauline and Peter Williams, who have both been involved in leather - both production and sales - for many years, and have an in-depth knowledge that makes shopping here a delight. They have a traditional outlook on retailing - value for money, great service, helpful, friendly advice and always time for a short chat.

The shop itself is a fascinating place, crammed with leather goods of all kinds, and yet feeling spacious and light. Browsing is positively encouraged, and there is absolutely no obligation to buy. Bridge - Tula - Jane Shilton - Fiorelli - Gianni Conti - Marta Ponti - Radley - they're all here, and a few more famous names as well.

Phone calls and emailed orders are positively welcome, and if you call in there is always time for a friendly chat. This is the perfect place to buy that special gift for a loved one, or indeed to treat yourself. Rhos on Sea is renowned for the quality of its shopping, and in Tabitha Jane you will find one of the best leather shops in North Wales. Pay it a visit and see for yourself.

🏛 historic building   🏛 museum   🏛 historic site   🔍 scenic attraction   🌿 flora and fauna

Colwyn Bay

conservation centre for rare and endangered species that is best known for the Chimp Encounter, its collection of British wildlife and its feeding of the sealions. The zoo's gardens, laid out by TH Mawson at the end of the 19th century, incorporate both formal terraces and informal woodlands with paths offering superb views of Snowdonia as well as the Conwy estuary and the North Wales coast. The Tarzan Trail Adventure Playground is a surefire winner with young visitors.

LLISFAEN
7 miles SE of Llandudno off the A55

🏛 Parish Church of St Cynfran

The **Parish Church of St Cynfran** was supposedly founded in AD 777 the by the saint of the same name. The present church has been heavily restored, though parts date from the 14th century, with masonry from an even earlier building incorporated. Cynfran himself is a shadowy figure, said to be the son of King Brychan of Brecknock, himself a saint. There is a holy well to the north of the church.

ABERGELE
10½ miles E of Llandudno on the A548

🏛 Gwrych Castle 🏛 Parish Church of St Michael
🪨 Cefn-Yr-Ogo 🎬 Abergele Train Disaster

Along with **Pensarn**, its neighbour on the coast, Abergele is a joint resort which, though more modest than such places as Rhyl, Prestatyn and Colwyn Bay, is justly popular

COLWYN BAY
5 miles SE of Llandudno on the A55

🐑 Welsh Mountain Zoo 🐿 Terry Jones
🐿 Timothy Dalron 🐿 Bertrand Russell

A more genteel place than the resorts found to the east, Colwyn Bay was built largely during the 19th century to fill the gap along the coast between Rhos-on-Sea and the village of Old Colwyn. As a result, there are many fine Victorian buildings to be seen, and the beach is served by a promenade along which most of the town's attractions can be found. Colwyn Bay includes among its famous sons ex-Monty Python **Terry Jones** and a former James Bond, **Timothy Dalton**. The philosopher **Bertrand Russell** (1872-1970) was cremated with no ceremony at Colwyn Bay crematorium and his ashes scattered in the sea.

Although Colwyn Bay lies on the coast it is also home to the **Welsh Mountain Zoo**, a

🎬 stories and anecdotes 🐿 famous people 🎨 art and craft 🖋 entertainment and sport 🚶 walks with those looking for a quieter seaside holiday. Outside the town, on Tower Hill, is the mock-Norman **Gwrych Castle**, built in 1814 and formerly the seat of the Earl of Dundonald. It is now a holiday centre and among its many attractions are medieval jousts and banquets. The **Parish Church of St Michael** is medieval in origin, though it was heavily restored in the mid 19th century. Outside the church is a **Penitential Stone**. This was where people had to do penance for their sins by standing and asking the congregation for mercy as they left the church. Also in graveyard is the mass grave of those people killed in the **Abergele Train Disaster,** which took place on August 20th 1868, when the Irish mail train from London was hit by wagons that had rolled down an incline towards it. They were being shunted onto a side line at the time, and their brakes had not been applied. It would have been a simple collision had not two of the wagons contained 50 barrels of paraffin. On impact, the wagons exploded, causing the front carriages of the mail train to catch fire. Thirty three people were killed, making it, up until that time, the worth rail disaster in British history.

Another incident took place on June 30th 1969, when two members of the Mudiad Amddiffyn Cymru (Welsh Defence Movement), Alwyn Jones and George Taylor, were killed when a bomb they were planting on the line went off prematurely. The royal train was due to pass on its way to Caernarfon for the investiture of Prince Charles as Prince

SYMBOLS EMBROIDERY

82 Marine Road, Pensarn, Abergele LL22 7PR
Tel: 01745 833365
e-mail: enquiries@embroideryatsymbols.co.uk

Dorothy Bacon opened **Symbols Embroidery** in 1991, and since then her business has become one of the best known of its kind in the country. She embroiders garments of every kind for your business, your hobbies, your sports organisation or indeed for anything you choose. It is a small company that puts the personal touch first, and offers exceedingly high standards of service coupled with great value for money.

No job is too large or too small for Dorothy, and she has undertaken work for military regiments, town criers, businesses, golf clubs, bands and a whole host of organisations who will testify to her skills. A carefully embroidered badge or logo will enhance your business and get your name known. Or if you wish, you can get a polo shirt embroidered in any design for your own personal use or as a thoughtful gift for a loved one.

Big or small, Dorothy can embroider something that will suit you perfectly. She has even personalised wedding dresses for that extra special day. So call in and see her, and discuss your own needs. There is no obligation, and you will get friendly, personal service.

🏠 historic building 🏛 museum 🏛 historic site 🌿 scenic attraction 🌱 flora and fauna

GELE BUTCHERS

23 Market Street, Abergele, Conwy LL22 7AG
Tel: 01745 823993 Fax: 01745 822940
e-mail: grahamandhazel@btinternet.com website: www.gelebutchers.net

After being in the butchery trade for 20 years, Graham Beach and Hazel Jones took over **Gele Butchers**, where Graham learnt his trade as an apprentice in 1986. They pride themselves on doing things the traditional way here, using only local Welsh beef and lamb, all fully traceable to its source farm.

The shop enjoys an equally fine reputation for its hand-made sausages and burgers, home-cured bacon, cooked meats and black pudding – and the super pies, all baked daily on the premises. Customers in the spotless modern interior can also buy free-range eggs, Welsh cheese and yoghurt and Darlington preserves and chutneys. The website allows online shopping.

of Wales, and they wanted to stop it as a protest (see also Caenarfon)

Situated on higher ground behind the castle are the natural caverns of **Cefn-Yr-Ogo** whose summit commands magnificent views of the surrounding coastline.

RHYL

14 miles E of Llandudno on the A548

🦪 Sun Centre 🐟 SeaQuarium 🐦 Nerys Huighes

Little more than a couple of fishermen's cottages until its development as a seaside resort from 1833, Rhyl used to be the destination for many workers and their families from the industrial towns and cities of Wales, the Midlands and the northwest of England. Though the heyday of this once elegant resort has long since passed, Rhyl still has a lot to offer the holiday maker.

As well as the full range of amusement arcades and seaside attractions, Rhyl is home to two large and exciting complexes: the **Sun Centre**, one of the first all-weather leisure attractions in the country, with indoor surfing and daredevil water slides and flumes; and **SeaQuarium**, where visitors can enjoy a seabed stroll surrounded by sharks, rays and other ocean creatures.

Nerys Hughes, the actress from the TV series *The Liver Birds* and *District Nurse*, was born in Rhyl, and **Carol Voderman**, though born in Bedford, attended school in the town when her family moved to North Wales.

To the southwest of the town lies the

mouth of the River Clwyd, which is crossed by Foryd Bridge, and to the south lies Rhuddlan Marsh where, in AD 795, Caradoc was defeated by Offa of Mercia.

PRESTATYN

16½ miles E of Llandudno on the A548

🏠 Prestatyn Castle   🏛 Offa's Dyke   🐦 John Prescott

🏃 Offa's Dyke National Trail

With three great beaches - Ffrith Beach, Central Beach and Barkby Beach - Prestatyn has proved a popular holiday destination over the years and, as expected, all types of entertainment are available, making the town an ideal centre for family holidays Although the town undoubtedly expanded with the opening of the Chester to Holyhead railway line in 1848, people were flocking here 50 years before, lured by descriptions of the air being like wine and honey and with the abundant sunshine being deemed excellent in the relief of arthritic conditions and nervous disorders.

However, Prestatyn's origins go back to prehistoric times, as excavated artefacts have shown. While the Roman's 20th legion was stationed at Chester, it is thought that an auxiliary unit was based at a fort on what is now Princes Avenue. The discovery in 1984 of a Roman bath house in Melyd Avenue would certainly seem to support this assumption.

The settlement is mentioned in the Domesday Book as Prestetone, from the Anglo-Saxon Preosta Tun (meaning a settlement in which two or more priests reside). It was Lord Robert Banastre who was responsible for building the Norman **Prestatyn Castle**. It was of a typical motte and bailey design, but all that remains of the fortification today is one stone pillar on the

top of a raised mound that can be found close to Bodnant Bridge.

Prestatyn lies at one end of the massive 8th century earthwork **Offa's Dyke**. Although the true origins of the dyke have been lost in the mists of time, it is thought that the construction of this border defence between England and Wales was instigated by King Offa, one of the most powerful of the early Anglo-Saxon kings. From 757 until his death in 796 he ruled Mercia, which covers roughly the area of the West Midlands. He seized power in the period of civil strife that followed the murder of his cousin King Aethelbald and, ruthlessly suppressing many of the smaller kingdoms and princedoms, created a single settled state that covered most of England south of Yorkshire. His lasting memorial is the dyke, which he had built between Mercia and the Welsh lands. With an earthwork bank of anything up to 50 feet in height and a 12ft ditch on the Welsh side, much of this massive feat of engineering is still visible today. The northern end of **Offa's Dyke National Trail** leads up the High Street, climbs the dramatic Prestatyn hillside and wanders through the Clwydian Range. This long-distance footpath of some 180 miles crosses the English-Welsh border ten times and takes in some extraordinarily beautiful countryside. From the Clwydian Hills through the lush plains of England and the much fought over lands of the Welsh borders, the footpath not only covers some superb terrain but also allows those walking its route to see a great variety of flora and fauna as well as take in the traditional farming methods that have survived in the more remote areas of this region.

John Prescott the labour politician was born in Prestatyn in 1938.

🏠 historic building   🏛 museum   🏛 historic site   🐦 scenic attraction   🌿 flora and fauna

LLANASA

20 miles E of Llandudno off the A548

🏛 Parish Church of St Asaph and St Cyndeyrn

🏛 Gyrn Castle

The **Parish Church of St Asaph and St Cyndeyrn** largely dates from the 15th century, though there has been a church on the site since at least the 6th century. It incorporates some stained glass windows from Basingwerk Abbey (see Holywell), which was dissolved by Henry III in 1536. Close by the village stands **Gyrn Castle** which originates from the 1700s and was castellated in the 1820s. It now contains a large picture gallery, and its grounds offer some pleasant woodland walks.

TRELAWNYD

19 miles E of Llandudno on the A5151

🏛 Parish Church of St Michael 🏛 Gop Hill

🎵 Trelawnyd Male Voice Choir

Formerly called Newmarket, this village is well known for its Bronze Age cairn, **Gop Hill**, the biggest prehistoric monument in Wales, which marks the place where, traditionally, Offa's Dyke began, although the town of Prestatyn also claims this honour. The **Trelawnyd Male Voice Choir**, with over 100 members, is reckoned to be one of the best choirs in North Wales. The **Parish Church of St Michael**, which measures only 55 feet by 19 feet, was rebuilt in 1724, though a church has stood on the site for centuries.

MELIDEN

17 miles E of Llandudno on the A547

🏛 Parish Church of St Melyd 🌿 Craig Fawr

Meliden is a former mining village, and in the 19th century several hundred miners worked in the local mines. Just to the south of

Meliden lies **Craig Fawr**, a limestone hill that supports a wide variety of flowers and butterflies, including the Brown Argus, a rare sight in North Wales, whose larvae feed on the Common Rockrose. Nature trails have been laid around the site that not only take in the myriad of wildlife and plants but also an old quarry where the exposed limestone reveals a wealth of fossils left deposited here over 300 million years ago. The short walk to the summit is well worth the effort as there are panoramic views from the top over the Vale of Clwyd, the coastline and beyond to Snowdonia.

The **Parish Church of St Melyd** is mentioned in the Domesday Book, though the present church largely dates from the 13th century and later. It is the only church in Wales dedicated to that particular saint. The half-timbered south porch, which seems out of place tacked onto a stone building, was added in 1884. It also has a 'Devil's Door' (now bricked up) which allowed the devil to leave the church when summoned to do so by the priest. When the churchyard wall was rebuilt some time ago, a surprising number of skeletons were unearthed. It is thought that these may have been people who were thought at the time to be in league with the devil, and who were not allowed to be buried in consecrated ground. The relatives got round this ecclesiastical edict by burying them half in and half out of the churchyard.

POINT OF AYR

21½ miles E of Llandudno off the A548

Marking the western tip of the Dee estuary and with views across the river mouth to Hilbre Island and the Wirral, this designated RSPB viewing point is an excellent place to observe the numerous birds that come to feed

🎬 stories and anecdotes 🦅 famous people 🎨 art and craft 🎭 entertainment and sport 🚶 walks on the sands and mudflats left by the retreating tide.

LLANFAIR TALHAIARN
11½ miles SE of Llandudno off the A544

🝔 Mynydd Bodran   🐟 John Jones

This village, the start of a walk to the Elwy Valley, is the burial place of **John Jones** (1810-1869), another poet who was acclaimed as the Welsh Robert Burns (see also Llanarmon Dyffryn Ceiriog). The waymarked walk is basically a circuit of **Mynydd Bodran**, which rises to nearly 950 feet above the Elwy and Aled Valleys and provides some spectacular views.

LLANGERNYW
10½ miles SE of Llandudno on the A548

🏛 Parish Church of St Digian

🏛 Sir Henry Jones Museum   🌿 Llangernyw Yew

This quiet Denbighshire village was the birthplace, in 1852, of Sir Henry Jones, who became known as 'the cobbler philosopher'. Born the son of a local shoemaker, Henry Jones left school at the age of 12 to become apprenticed to his father but, after the long working day, Henry continued his studies well into the evenings. His hard work paid off and he won a scholarship to train as a teacher and then went on to study philosophy before eventually becoming Professor of Moral Philosophy at Glasgow University. A well-known and highly regarded academic and a widely acclaimed lecturer on social affairs and liberalism, Henry received his knighthood in 1912, and was made a Companion of Honour in 1922. He died in the same year. Though Sir Henry is buried in Glasgow, this village has not forgotten its local hero. In 1934, Jones' childhood home, Y Cwm, was purchased by a fund set up to honour his memory and his

work. Today, the **Sir Henry Jones Museum** takes visitors on a tour through the family house - the tiny kitchen and bedroom where the family lived and shoemaker's workshop where Henry and his father worked.

The whitewashed **Parish Church of St Digian** dates from the 13th century, though it was much restored in the 1800s. In the churchyard is the **Llangernyw Yew**. The oldest known tree in Wales, and one of the oldest living things in the world, the yew is estimated to be over 3,000 years old. An old legend says that every Easter and July 31st the angel of death - known as the Angelystor in Welsh - appears beneath the tree's boughs and solemnly announces the names of the people of the parish who will die within the next six months. A story is told of one Shôn ap Robert, who mocked the legend while drinking in a local pub. His friends challenged him to visit the yew tree on the next July 31st, and he took up the challenge. The first name he heard as he approached the tree was his own, and though he declared jokingly that he was not yet ready to die, within six months he was being buried in the churchyard.

Conwy

🏛 Conwy Castle   🏛 Town Walls   🏛 Toll House

🏛 Suspension Bridge   🏛 Conway Mussel Museum

🏛 Plas Mawr   🏛 Teapot Museum and Shop

🏛 Aberconwy House   🐚 Conway Yachting Festival

🏛 Britain's Smallest House   🏛 Conway Rail Bridge

🏛 Parish Church of St Mary and all Saints

Situated opposite Deganwy, on the south bank of the Conwy estuary, Conwy has in recent times returned to something of its former self with the completion of the tunnel that carries the A5 under the estuary. No longer

---

🏛 historic building   🏛 museum   🏛 historic site   🝔 scenic attraction   🌿 flora and fauna

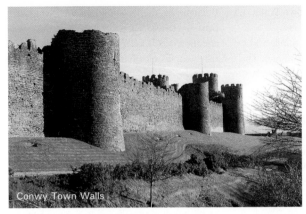

Conwy Town Walls

of what was one of the most picturesque of the many Welsh fortresses remain eye-catching to this day. **Conwy Castle** is situated on a rock which overlooks the River Conwy and its estuary, from which it commands wonderful views of the whole area.

Begun in 1283, the castle's construction was largely finished by the autumn of 1287 and, compared with some of Edward's castles, Conwy is of a relatively simple design which relies on its position rather than anything else to provide a defence against attack. The town was walled at

harassed by heavy traffic, the town is a delight to wander in, its small streets steeped in history and the whole place dominated by another of Edward I's great castles. The ruins

BEYOND THE NINTH WAVE

4 High Street, Conwy, North Wales LL32 8DB
Tel/Fax: 01492 582212
website: www.beyondtheninthwave.co.uk

One of the many fine old properties on the main street of Conwy, **Beyond the Ninth Wave**, its name derived from Celtic legend, is a former art gallery where Vicki and Tony Price offer visitors an eclectic selection of gifts, cards and home accessories. The shop is a relaxed interpretation of modern and historical design.

The owners source their stock from all around the UK and Europe, and products from Sia, Balagan Jewellery and Burleigh Pottery sit comfortably alongside traditional Japanese Dolls, elegantly dressed teddy bears and table linen. Truly there is something for everyone.

The same ethos and eye for design has created the

courtyard Coffee Shop, an ideal spot to relax with a freshly ground cappuccino coffee, a pastry and a newspaper. And the Danish pastries really do come from Denmark.

🎞 stories and anecdotes   🐦 famous people   🎨 art and craft   🏛 entertainment and sport   🚶 walks

the same time and today the **Town Walls** still encircle the vast majority of Conwy, stretching for three quarters of a mile and including 22 towers and three gateways. The castle was also built to be a suitable royal residence and in fact was used twice by Edward I: once on his way to Caernarfon where his son, the first English Prince of Wales was born, and again in 1294, when trying to put down the rebellion of Madoc ap Llewelyn. Now a World Heritage Site, the castle not only offers visitors spectacular views from its battlements but the huge curtain walls and the eight massive round towers are still a stirring sight. In 1399, Richard II stayed at the Castle before being lured out and ambushed by the Earl of Northumberland's men on behalf of Henry

Bolingbroke, the Duke of Lancaster, who later became Henry IV. Conwy was given the attention of Owain Glyndwr during his rebellion, his men burning it to the ground.

As with other castles further east, Conwy was embroiled in the Civil War. A Conwy man, John Williams, became Archbishop of York and, as a Royalist, sought refuge in his home town. Repairing the crumbling fortifications at his own expense, Archbishop Williams finally changed sides after shabby treatment by Royalist leaders and helped the Parliamentary forces lay siege to the town and castle, which eventually fell to them in late 1646.

The town developed within the shadows of its now defunct fortress, and slate and coal extracted from the surrounding area were

RHYWBETH-I-BAWB

5a High Street, Conwy LL32 8DB
Tel: 01492 573334   Fax: 01492 592926

Marilyn and Elwyn Watson have filled their shop with a fine selection of goods that reflect all aspects of Welsh culture and heritage – the Welsh people, the Welsh language, the Welsh sporting prowess, the Welsh countryside. Even the front of their charming little single-fronted shop is painted in the red, green and white colours of the national flag.

Customers at **Rhywbeth-i-Bawb** are welcome to browse at leisure in the shop, and among the frequently changing stock are rugby shirts, rugby balls, footballs, caps, Welsh and Celtic T-shirts and jewellery, fabrics, lapel badges and many other souvenirs and gifts to take home as reminders of a stay in the lovely town of Conwy with its castle, bridges, cobbled streets and distinguished houses large and small.

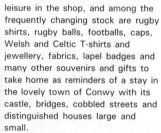

The name Rhwbeth-i-Bawb means something for everyone, and the shop does indeed offer something to suit all ages and pockets.

🏯 historic building   🏛 museum   🏚 historic site   🌄 scenic attraction   🌾 flora and fauna

shipped up and down the coast from Conwy. Later, the town fathers approached Thomas Telford, who planned a causeway and bridge, as Conwy's trade and links grew with the outside world. Built in 1826, the elegant **Suspension Bridge** replaced the ferry that previously had been the only means of crossing the river so close to its estuary. The **Toll House** (NT) has been restored and furnished as it would have been a century ago. This suspension road bridge, its design sympathetic to its surroundings, was soon followed by the construction of railways. By the side of Telford's bridge stands the Robert Stephenson designed tubular **Conwy Rail Bridge** of 1846. Both builders breached the town walls in styles that complemented the town's architecture and the two structures are still admired today.

Bridges, however, are not the only architectural gems Conwy has to offer. **Plas Mawr** (Cadw), an Elizabethan town-house on the High Street, is one of the best preserved buildings from that period in Britain. Built for the influential merchant Robert Wynn between 1576 and 1585, the house has an interesting stone façade and over 50 windows. Plas Mawr (the name means Great Hall) is particularly noted for its fine and elaborate plasterwork, seen to striking effect in the glorious decorated ceilings and friezes and in the glorious overmantel in the hall. The authentic period atmosphere is further enhanced by furnishings based on an inventory of the contents in 1665. The house came into the possession of the Mostyn family during the 18th century and in 1991 was given by Lord Mostyn to the nation. Close by is **Aberconwy House** (NT), a delightful medieval merchant's home that dates from the 14th century. The rooms have been decorated and furnished to reflect various periods in the house's history.

Occupying part of the site of a 12th century Cistercian Abbey, founded by Llwelyn the Great in 1199 and then moved to Maenan by Edward I, is the **Parish Church of St Mary and all Saints**. Some interesting features still remain from that time though there have been many additions over the centuries. The 15th century rood screen is particularly fine. This was the burial place of the Princes of Gwynedd, and Llwelyn himself.

Conwy's **Teapot Museum and Shop**, on Castle Street, is an interesting and unusual attraction where visitors can see a unique collection of antique, novelty and humorous teapots that date from the mid-1700s to the

---

YESTERYEARS TOY SHOP

6 High Street, Conwy,
North Wales LL32 8DB
Tel: 01492 592224
e-mail: yesteryears2001@aol.co

Yesteryears Toy Shop must be the most fascinating shop in Conwy. It sells a marvellous range of fine toys that are sure to bring back memories of childhood, and all at competitive prices. Everything from puppets to dolls houses and rocking horses to castles are here, along with 'retro' toys, tin pedal cars and theatres. There are toys for the young and the not-so-young - call in and be entranced by everything you see!

📖 stories and anecdotes   🐦 famous people   🎨 art and craft   🖋 entertainment and sport   🚶 walks

Britain's Smallest House

Conwy Bay, a mermaid begged the local fishermen who found her to carry her back to the sea. The fishermen refused and, before she died, the mermaid cursed the people of the town, swearing that they would always be poor. In the 5th century, Conwy suffered a fish famine that caused many to avow that the curse was fulfilled.

St Brigid is connected to another fish famine story. Walking by the riverside carrying some rushes, she threw the rushes upon the water. A few days later the rushes had turned into fish and ever since they have been known as sparlings or, in Welsh, brwyniaid - both meaning rush-like. On the quayside the fishermen still land their catches, and from here pleasure boat trips can be taken. Nearby can be found what is claimed to be **Britain's Smallest House**, measuring 10 feet by 6. It seems that its last tenant was a fisherman who was 6' 3" tall - he was presumably also a contortionist! Conwy was once a famous pearl fishing centre and had a thriving mussel industry, whose history is told in the **Conwy Mussel Centre**, open daily from mid-May to September. The **Conway River Festival** takes place every year in August, and is the premier yachting occasion for the whole of the Irish Sea.

present day. Many of the pieces on show have taken their place in the annals of teapot history, including the celebrated Worcester 'aesthetic' teapot of 1880, the Wedgwood cauliflower pot of 1775 and the Clarice Cliffe tepee-shaped pot of 1930. It is housed in one of the towers on the town walls, and was founded by a collector in the 1960s. It is the leading museum of its kind in Britain. The museum shop is also a must for tea enthusiasts, as it not only sells a wide variety of teas but also a mass of tea paraphernalia.

It is not surprising that the town and the surrounding area have strong links with the sea and Conwy also has a traditional mermaid story. Washed ashore by a violent storm in

Around Conwy

ROWEN
4 miles S of Conwy off the B5106

🏛 Parish Church of St Celynin   🏛 Maen-y-Bardd

🏛 Caer Bach   🌱 Parc Mawr   🌱 Parc Glyn

⚜ Tal-y-fan

From this very pretty, quiet village a track, which was once a Roman road, skirts by the foot of **Tal-y-fan**, which reaches 2,000 feet at its peak. Roughly six miles in length, the path passes by **Maen-y-Bardd**, a Neolithic burial chamber, and eventually drops down towards the coast at Aber. Another, circular, walk of about five miles, one of several in the Conwy Valley devised by Active Snowdonia, passes many impressive cromlechs and standing stones. The route also takes in **Caer Bach**, where there are traces of a Neolithic settlement, the wonderfully unspoilt 14th century **Parish Church of St Celynin** and the Woodlands Trust's **Parc Mawr** woods.

Just to the east of Rowen lies **Parc Glyn**, a traditional Welsh farm that specialises in the breeding and conservation of rare farm animals. Along with the sheep, cattle and pigs, there are peacocks, guinea fowl, ducks and geese. Surrounding the animal and bird paddocks, are scenic picnic areas and pleasant mixed woodland.

TREFRIW
8 miles S of Conwy on the B5106

🏠 Trefriw Woollen Mill 🏭 Fairy Falls 🐟 Taliesin

This village, nestling into the forested edge of Snowdonia in the beautiful Conwy valley, sits on an old Roman road. It was once one of the homes of Llywelyn the Great, and the **Parish Church of St Mary** stands on the site of a former church built by him to please his wife, who refused to climb to the church at Llanrhychyrn, above the village. Standing eight miles from the sea, it was once the biggest inland port in Wales. The village today has two main attractions, **Trefriw Woollen Mill** and the local chalybeate springs. The woollen mill has been in operation since the 1830s and it is still owned by descendants of Thomas Williams, who purchased it in 1859. It is run by hydro-electric power generated from the

two lakes - Crafnant and Geirionydd - which lie to the west of the village. While the source of power is modern, the tapestries and tweeds produced here from raw wool are very traditional.

A footpath above the woollen mill leads to **Fairy Falls**, where in the early 19th century a forge was founded to make hammers and chisels for use in the slate quarries. It closed at the beginning of the 20th century. Sometime between AD 100 and AD 250, while prospecting for minerals in this area, the Romans opened up a cave where they found a spring rich in iron (chalybeate). Covered in later years by a landslide, it was not until the 18th century that the spring was uncovered by Lord Willoughby de Eresby, owner of nearby Gwydir Castle, who went on to built a stone bathhouse. Taking the waters became so popular that by 1874 the original bathhouse was replaced with a pumphouse and bath, and the bottled water was exported worldwide. Following a decline during much of the 20th century, interest in the natural spring waters has been rekindled. Visitors can take the waters, view the museum artefacts in the tea room and browse in the spa beauty shop.

Lake Geirionydd, to the south of the village, was the supposed birthplace, in the 6th century, of the great bard **Taliesin**, to whom in 1850 Lord Willoughby erected a monument. Taliesin was possibly the earliest poet to write in the Welsh language. He was referred to as the 'chief bard of Britain', and is said to have served at the court of at least three British kings. In 1863, a local poet, Gwilym Cowlyd, being dissatisfied with the National Eisteddfod, started an arwest, a poetical and musical event that was held in the shadow of the monument every year until 1922. The monument fell down in a storm in

1976 but was restored in 1994. It lies on one of Active Snowdonia's Conwy Valley walks, which also passes Fairy Falls and old mine workings; it skirts Lake Crafnant and provides memorable views at many points along its route.

LLANRWST

10 miles S of Conwy on the A470

🏛 Parish Church of St Grwst 🏛 Gwydir Uchaf Chapel

🏛 Gwydir Chapel 🏛 Llanrwst Almshouses

🏛 Old Bridge 🏛 Gwydir Castle 🏛 Tu Hwnt i'r Bont

🏛 Battle of Llanrwst

The market centre for the central Conwy Valley owes both its name and the dedication of its church to St Grwst (Restitutus), a 6th

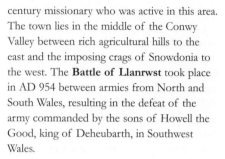

century missionary who was active in this area. The town lies in the middle of the Conwy Valley between rich agricultural hills to the east and the imposing crags of Snowdonia to the west. The **Battle of Llanrwst** took place in AD 954 between armies from North and South Wales, resulting in the defeat of the army commanded by the sons of Howell the Good, king of Deheubarth, in Southwest Wales.

Famous for its livestock fairs and the manufacture of grandfather clocks and Welsh harps, it was also known for its woollen yarn and its sail-making industry. The **Parish Church of St Grwst** with its fine rood screen dates from 1470, though the tower and north aisle are 19th century. The 1470 building replaced a thatched church from 1170 that was destroyed in the fighting of 1468. Next to the church lies **Gwydir Chapel**, famous for its richly carved Renaissance interior. This was the private chapel of the Wynn family and among its treasures is an imposing stone sarcophagus of the Welsh prince Llewelyn the Great. This chapel should not be confused with **Gwydir Uchaf Chapel** which lies on the opposite bank of the river Conwy and is particularly noted for its ceiling covered with paintings of angels. The **Llanrwst Almshouses** date from 1610, and were built by Sir John Wyn of Gwydir. They were closed in 1976, and now house a small museum.

Below the chapel lies **Gwydir Castle**, the Wynn family's Tudor mansion which has, in its grounds,

River Conwy, near Llanrwst

🏛 historic building   🏛 museum   🏛 historic site   🔾 scenic attraction   🍀 flora and fauna

Gwydir Chapel, Llanrwst

Tu Hwnt i'r Bont (the House over the Bridge), a 16th century courthouse which has since been divided into two cottages and is now a tea room. At one point the town was governed neither by the Welsh nor the English, giving rise to the saying 'Cymru, Lloegr a Llanrwst' - 'Wales, England and Llanrwst'. At one time, it even applied (tongue in cheek, it has to be said) for independent membership of the United Nations.

BETWS-Y-COED
12 miles S of Conwy on the A5

The 'Gateway to Snowdonia' - see next chapter.

CAPEL CURIG
9 miles S of Conwy on the A5

🏛 Church of St Julitta   ⛰ Mount Siabod

🖋 Plas-y-Brenin

some fine cedars of Lebanon planted in 1625 in celebration of the marriage of Charles I to Henrietta Maria of France. Here, too, is an arch built to commemorate the end of the War of the Roses, while inside the much restored house is a secret room, once hidden by a wooden panel, which is home to the ghost of a monk said to have been trapped in the tunnel that leads the arch. A walk west from the town takes in these historic buildings, the remains of an old crushing mill and the site of the old Hafna Galena Mine. Gwydir Castle was the home of Catherine of Berain, Elizabeth I's cousin (see also Denbigh). Although called a castle, it is, in fact, a fine Tudor house.

Back in town, the **Old Bridge** is thought to have been designed by Inigo Jones; it was built in 1636 by Sir Richard Wynn. Next to it stands

Situated at the junction of the mountain roads to Beddgelert, Llyn Ogwen and Betws-y-Coed, Capel Curig has the reputation of being the wettest place in Wales. However, it is popular with climbers as well as hill walkers and anglers, who use the village as a base. A walk south of the village passes by lonely Llyn y Foel and climbs the steep ridge of Daiar Ddu to the top of **Mount Siabod**. The reward for this expenditure of energy is the most spectacular panoramic view of many of Snowdonia's great peaks. **Plas-y-Brenin**, the National Mountain Centre, provides excellent facilities for climbing, canoeing, dry slope skiing and orienteering.

The former **Parish Church of St Julitta** was founded by St Curig, a 6th century bishop. The smallest church in Snowdonia, it is being gradually restored by the 'Friends of St Julitta'. It was deconsecrated in the 1970s. St Julitta was a wealthy Turkish widow who was the mother of Cyriacus, who was killed by the Roman governor of Seleucia when he was three years old. Julitta was martyred, and her son was also declared a martyr.

Bangor

🏛 Bangor Cathedral	🖋 Theatre Gwynedd
🏛 Gwynedd Museum and Art Gallery	🦅 Aled Jones
🏛 Menai Suspension Bridge	🏛 Britannia Bridge
🏛 Victoria Pier	🏛 University College of North Wales
🏛 Penrhyn Castle	🏛 The Swellies	🦅 Bryn Terfel

A cathedral and university city, Bangor incorporates a wide variety of architectural styles that remind the visitor that this is not only an interesting and stimulating place but also one with a long history. A monastic community was founded here as early as AD 525 by St Deiniol, and the town's name is derived from the wattle fence which surrounded the saint's primitive enclosure -

the term 'bangori' is still used in parts of Wales to describe the plaiting of twigs in a hedge. However, there were settlers in the area long before St Deiniol, including the Romans at nearby Segontium, and the **Gwynedd Museum and Art Gallery** is just the place to discover not only the area's 2,000 years of history, but also to see the reconstructions of domestic life in days gone by. The art gallery exhibits a range of work by artists from all ages. Close by in Deiniol Street is **Theatre Gwynedd**.

The main church of the oldest bishopric in Britain, **Bangor Cathedral** dates from the 13th century and has probably been in continuous use for longer than any other cathedral in Britain. During the Middle Ages, the cathedral became a centre of worship for the independent principality of Gwynedd, and the tomb of Owain Gwynedd, buried here after his death, became a starting point for pilgrims setting out on the arduous journey to

Menai Suspension Bridge

🏛 historic building   🏛 museum   🏛 historic site   🦅 scenic attraction   🦅 flora and fauna

Bardsey Island. Restored in 1866, the cathedral also contains a life-size carving of Christ dating from 1518 while, outside, there is a Biblical garden that contains plants which are associated with the Bible.

Until the slate boom of the 19th century, Bangor remained little more than a village, albeit with an impressive church. Its position on the Menai Strait that separates Anglesey from the mainland, made this the ideal place for nearby Penrhyn Quarry to build its docks, and the town soon flourished as a commercial centre. Its importance increased further when the **University College of North Wales** was founded here in 1884. Improvements in the roads and then the coming of the railways to the North Wales coast also saw Bangor grow in both stature and importance. The **Menai Suspension Bridge** was built by Thomas Telford between 1819 and 1826 and was the first permanent crossing of the Menai Strait. Before its completion the crossing had been made by ferry, and cattle on their way to and from market would swim the channel. Another deciding factor in building the bridge was the treacherous currents to be found in the strait. The worst accident took place in 1785, when a ship carrying 55 people ran aground on a sandbar. Efforts to refloat it proved fruitless, and when it became swamped with water and keeled over only one person survived. Rocks and reefs called **The Swellies** just beneath the surface between the two bridges also cause whirlpools. This was where HMS Conway was lost in 1953.

However, there was much local opposition to the construction, not only from the ferrymen but also from ship-owners worried that the structure would impede the passage of their tall ships. As a result of this concern, the road bridge stands at a height of 100 feet.

The **Britannia Bridge**, a mile further southwest from Telford's bridge, is a combined road and rail crossing and was built between 1846 and 1850 by Robert Stephenson. In 1970 a fire meant that it has to be rebuilt. The lions guarding the bridge are by John Thomas, who was responsible for much of the sculpture at the Houses of Parliament. Also jutting out into the Menai Strait from the town is the 1,500-foot long **Victoria Pier**, which was built in 1896. As well as being attractive, the pier is a pleasant place from which to view Snowdonia, the coast and the small boats passing by, and to admire the houses, some of them quite magnificent, which stand beside the water. Both pleasure and fishing trips can be taken from the pierhead. Bangor is a major centre of the mussel industry.

The town was the birthplace of two singers - **Bryn Terfel**, the international operatic tenor, and **Aled Jones**, singer of *Walking in the Air*. Surprisingly, on the sound track of the film *The Snowman*, someone else sings the song.

To the west of the town and overlooking Beaumaris on the Isle of Anglesey lies **Penrhyn Castle** (NT), a dramatic neo-Norman construction built by Thomas Hopper between 1820 and 1845, and incorporating Doll and Railway Museums.

Around Bangor

ABERGWYNGREGYN
6 miles E of Bangor off the A55

🏛 The Cross   🔅 Rhaeadr Aber Falls

Well to the south of the village lie **Rhaeadr Aber Falls**, reached by taking a footpath through sheltered woodland, where the drop of the river is said to be among the steepest in

Rhaeadr Aber Falls

Church of St Mary and Christ dates from 1864, and was built by local benefactor Colonel John Platt.

PENMAENMAWR
10 miles E of Bangor off the A55

🏠 Parc Plas Mawr   🏛 Cefn Coch

A tiny quarrying village before the arrival of the railway in 1848, this small holiday resort, with its sand and shingle beach, has changed little since William Gladstone holidayed here in the 19th century, and it still boasts many fine Victorian buildings. Gladstone was a frequent visitor, and there's a bust of him on a granite obelisk in Paradise Road. Penmaenmawr has a small industrial heritage park, **Parc Plas Mawr.** It features not only industrial heritage, but works of art such as sculpture and objects carved from wood. The foundations of a house owned by the Derbyshire family have been uncovered by archaeologists.

In the town's steep mountain-backed hinterland can be found many prehistoric sites including one of Wales' best known Bronze Age stone circles, **Cefn Coch**. An urn was uncovered here containing the remains of a child as well as a bronze dagger said to be evidence of a ritual sacrifice that once took place here.

Wales. Above the village is **The Cross**, a huge cross marked out by trees on the hillside. Some people claim it was planted as a memorial to the crew of a German bomber that crashed on the hillside. The reality is more mundane - it was planted by scientists from Bangor University in the mid '50s as an experiment in sheep management.

LLANFAIRFECHAN
8 miles E of Bangor on the A55

🏠 The Parish Church of St Mary and Christ

🌱 Traeth Lafan

An excellent base for energetic walks amid stunning scenery, Llanfairfechan also has a long stretch of sandy beach and a nature reserve at **Traeth Lafan. The Parish**

BETHESDA
7 miles SE of Bangor on the A5

🏛 Penryn Slate Quarries   🍂 Nant Ffrancon Pass

🍂 Carneddau Estate

This old quarry town takes its name from the Nonconformist chapel that was built here and served many of the 2,300 men and their families who worked in the quarry at its peak in 1875. The gouged rock of the **Penrhyn**

Slate Quarries forms a huge hillside amphitheatre; it was the largest open cast slate mine in the world and still produces high-quality slate 250 years after it was first worked.

From the town, the main road travels through the beautiful **Nant Ffrancon Pass**, which runs straight through and up the valley of the River Ogwen and into the Snowdonia National Park. Five miles south of Bethesda on the A5, Llyn Idwal is one of several lakes on the National Trust's **Carneddau Estate**. In 1954 it was declared the first National Nature Reserve in Wales.

Caernarfon

🏰 Caernarfon Castle 　🏰 Parish Church of St Mary

🏰 Hanging Tower 　🕊 David Lloyd-George

🏛 Museum of the Royal Welsh Fusiliers

🏛 Caernarfon Air World 　🚂 Welsh Highland Railway

🏛 Segontium Roman Fort and Museum

🕊 Sir Hugh Owen 　🚶 Lôn Las Menai

Situated on the right bank of the River Seiont, near the southwest end of the Menai Strait, Caernarfon (the name means 'fort on the shore') is a town steeped in history as well as a

Segontium Roman Fort

Beddgelert Road, Caernarfon, Gwynedd LL55 2WG
Tel: 01286 675625
website: www.segontium.org.uk

The Segontium Roman fort was an auxiliary fort built by the Romans when they spread their conquest of Britain into Wales, and dates back to 77 AD. Although it was a remote outpost, it is one of the most well known Roman sites in Britain and attracts thousands of visitors each year. From records, it is clear that it held a regiment of up to 1,000 auxiliary soldiers until about 394 AD. These troops were non citizens who would be in the service of the Roman army for 25 years. It was a very strategic establishment, as it controlled access to Angelsey, and protected the Welsh coast from the sea bound Irish raiders. Apart from being of military use, Segontium was also the administrative centre for north west Wales.

Visiting the fort, it is apparent that you are encouraged to have a 'hands on' approach. The fort is active in that it allows visitors into the remains so that you can not only see the remains, but experience them too. The museum tells the story of the conquest and occupation of Wales and contains fine examples of the finds excavated from the Segontium site. Here you can get a vivid idea of life in this part of occupied Britain. The Segontium Roman Museum opened in 1924 vividly portrays the story of the conquest and occupation of Wales by the Romans and displays the finds from nearby auxillary fort of Segontium, one of the most famous in Britain. The site was one of the first Roman sites to be developed as a historical venue.

📖 stories and anecdotes 　🕊 famous people 　🎨 art and craft 　🎭 entertainment and sport 　🚶 walks bastion of the Welsh language and national pride. The history of Caernarfon goes back to Roman times. **Segontium Roman Fort and Museum** (see panel on page 63), half a mile from the town centre on the road towards Beddgelert, is the only place in Wales where it is possible to see something of the internal layout of an auxiliary station. Built to defend the Roman Empire against attack from rebellious tribes, the fort dates back to AD 77, when the Roman conquest was finally completed following the capture of Anglesey. Certainly this was one of the most important garrisons on the edge of the Roman Empire and, during its life, it was not only a military but also an administrative centre for northwest Wales. It is believed that Constantine the Great was born here. Excavations of the site have revealed coins which show that the fort was garrisoned at least until AD 394 and this long occupation can be explained by its strategic position controlling the fertile lands and mineral rights of Anglesey and providing a defence against Irish pirates. The well-preserved site is managed by CADW and the Museum, which is run by the National Museum and Galleries of Wales, displays many items, including coins, pottery and weapons which have been uncovered during excavation work.

Caernarfon Castle

However, it is another great construction and symbol of military power - the impressive **Caernarfon Castle** - that still dominates the town today. The most famous of the numerous great fortresses in Wales, the castle was begun in 1283 by Henry de Elreton, who was also building Beaumaris Castle, under the orders of Edward I. It took some 40 years to complete. Built not only as a defence but as a royal palace and a seat of government, the castle's majestic appearance was no accident as it was designed to be a dream castle and is based around two oval-shaped courts divided by a wall. The outer defences are strengthened at intervals by towers and are, in places, up to 15 feet thick! Many attempts were made by the Welsh, over the years, to destroy the castle but their failure is confirmed by the presence of this magnificent building today. It was here that, in 1284, Edward I crowned his son the first English Prince of Wales and the castle was once again used for such an investiture when, in 1969, the Queen crowned Prince Charles Prince of Wales. Many protests were planned about the investiture, but it passed off peacefully. However, two members of the Mudiad Amddiffyn Cymru (Welsh Defence Movement) were killed at Abergele the day before as they tried to plant a bomb on the line to stop the royal train (see also Abergele) Also at the castle, and housed in the Queen's Tower, is the **Museum of the Royal Welsh Fusiliers**, the country's oldest regiment.

The castle sits where the River Seiont meets

the Menai Strait, the expanse of water that separates mainland Wales from the Isle of Anglesey. Close by, the old Slate Quay, from where slate was once shipped, is now the place from where fishing trips and pleasure cruises depart up the Strait to Beaumaris. Castle Square, on the landward side of the castle, holds markets and here, too, can be found statues of two famous Welshmen: the gesticulating, urging **David Lloyd-George**, once a member of Parliament for the area, and **Sir Hugh Owen**, the founder of Further Education in Wales.

The Anglesey Hotel and the **Hanging Tower** stand by the castle walls and were a customs house until 1822. The last hanging to take place in the tower was in 1911 when an Irishman named Murphy was executed for murdering a maid. It is said that when he died the bell clapper in the **Parish Church of St Mary** fell off. The church itself was founded in 1307 and, though much of it has since been reconstructed, the arcades of the eastern and southern walls are part of the original 14th century building.

Northgate Street is called, in Welsh, Stryd Pedwar a Chewch - meaning four and six street. Apparently it originates from the time when sailors flocked to this part of town looking for lodgings: four pence for a hammock and six pence for a bed!

From the town, walkers can enjoy a scenic footpath, the **Lôn Las Menai**, which follows the coastline along the Menai Strait towards the village of Y Felineli (see below) and from which there are views across the water to the Isle of Anglesey. Caernarfon is the terminus of the **Welsh Highland Railway**, which is owned and operated by the Ffestiniog Railway, the oldest independent railway company in the world.

To the southwest of Caernarfon and overlooking Caernarfon Bay is **Caernarfon Air World**, located on the site of an RAF station that was built in 1940 and which is also the home of the first RAF mountain rescue team. As well as offering pleasure flights to visitors, there is the Aviation Museum, housed in one of the great hangars which not only displays over 400 model aircraft but has various planes and helicopters on show and also provides visitors with the opportunity to take the controls in a flight trainer.

Y FELINHELI
4 miles NE of Caernarfon off the A487

The Greenwood Centre 🔍 Glan Faenol

Situated south of this village is **The Greenwood Centre**, a forest heritage and adventure park. Opened in the early 1990s, this centre concentrates on exploring and explaining man's relationship with trees and how, by using conservation techniques, the loss of trees from the countryside can be halted whether in the equatorial rain forests or ancient temperate forests of Europe. The skills of ancient carpenters and joiners are also on show, particularly in the Great Hall, a building that was constructed entirely using medieval skills and knowledge and is held together by 500 oak pegs!

A couple of miles further east off the A487, bordering the Menai Strait, is **Glan Faenol** (NT), which includes parkland and farmland around Vaynol Hall, once one of the largest estates in North Wales. This is an important habitat for wildlife, and a pleasant walk leads to the sea and two viewing platforms. The estate has tracts of ancient woodland and several follies, including one built to rival the Marquess Column on Anglesey. The views of Snowdonia and across the strait are memorably depicted in one of Rex Whistler murals at Plas Newydd.

Isle of Anglesey

Menai Bridge

🏛 Menai Suspension Bridge   🏛 St Tysilio's Church
🌱 Pili Palas

Acting as a gateway to Anglesey, this largely Victorian town grew and developed after the construction of Thomas Telford's **Menai Suspension Bridge**, which connects the island to mainland Wales. The waterfront is a popular place for anglers and for those wishing to view the annual Regatta on the Menai Strait held every August, and the promenade, known as the Belgian Promenade because it was built by refugees from Belgium who sought shelter here during the First World War.

On Church Island, reached by a causeway from the town, there is the 14th century **St Tysilio's Church**, built on the site of a foundation by St Tysilio in AD 630. The site is thought to have been visited by Archbishop Baldwin and Giraldus when they may have landed here in 1188. It can be reached by a short causeway from the Belgian Promenade.

For a place with a difference, **Pili Palas** (Butterfly Palace) is an interesting and unusual attraction that will delight everyone. The vast collection of exotic

butterflies and birds, from all over the world, can be seen in tropical environments, where visitors can not only marvel at the colourful creatures but also see the wonderful tropical plants. There is also a Tropical Hide, an amazing Ant Avenue and a Snake House and while adults relax in Pili Palas' café children can let off steam in the adventure play area.

Around Menai Bridge

BEAUMARIS
4 miles NE of Menai Bridge of the A545

🏛 Beaumaris Castle   🏛 Courthouse
🏛 Museum of Childhood Memories
🏛 Parish Church of St Mary and St Nicholas
🏛 Beaumaris Gaol   🌱 Menai Strait Regatta

An attractive and elegant town, Beaumaris was granted a charter by Edward I in 1294 and it adopted the Norman name 'beau marais' which translates as 'beautiful marsh'. The lawned seafront, now with its elegant Georgian and Victorian terraces, was once a marsh that protected the approaches to **Beaumaris Castle**. Often cited as the most

Beaumaris Castle

technically perfect medieval castle in Britain, Beaumaris Castle was the last of Edward I's Iron Ring of fortresses built to stamp his authority on the Welsh. Begun in 1295 and designed by the king's military architect, James of St George, this was to be his largest and most ambitious project. Regarded as a pinnacle of military architecture of the time, with a concentric defence rather than the traditional keep and bailey, the outer walls contained 16 towers while the inner walls were 43 feet high and up to 16 feet thick in places. It was never actually completed, as the money ran out before the fortifications reached their full planned height. Perhaps a measure of the castle's success was that, unlike other castles built by Edward I, it never experienced military action. Now a World Heritage Site and in the hands of CADW (Welsh Historic Monuments), Beaumaris Castle is still virtually surrounded by its original moat. There was also a tidal dock here for ships coming in through a channel in the marshes - an iron ring where vessels of up to 40 tons once docked still hangs from the wall.

The **Parish Church of St Mary and St Nicholas** dates from the 14th century, and was originally the church for the castle garrison. It has noteworthy 16th century choir stalls and the stone coffin of Princess Joan, wife of Llywelyn the Great and illegitimate daughter of King John. For many years the coffin was used as a drinking trough for horses. The building has four clocks on its tower, and is said that someone who was about to be hanged in the old gaol nearby

BOLD ARMS HOTEL

Church Street, Beaumaris, Anglesey LL58 8AA
Tel: 01248 810313
e-mail: theboldarms@tiscali.co.uk

The **Bold Arms Hotel** is a lively, attractive establishment in the beautiful old town of Beaumaris, right on the Menai Straits. It is owned by Nick Beguley and managed by his daughter Hannah, and has two large fully en suite rooms for letting - soon to be four when the hotel's refurbishment is complete. Hannah places great emphasis on high standards of service, value for money and an atmosphere that is friendly and welcoming. The menu, both in the hotel itself and in its barbecues, includes many dishes prepared from local produce. She is happy to arrange golf and fishing for people staying at the hotel, which greatly adds to its attraction. There is a pool table and two 42 inch plasma screen TVs for sporting occasions.

Its sister hotel, the *White Lion Hotel* (tel. 01248 810589), is another establishment that offers only the best. It has eleven en suite rooms, and is friendly, spacious yet cosy and has a clientele that returns year after year. Why not use either hotel as a base while exploring Anglesey, or as an overnight B&B stop?

And why not eat in the *Welsh Black Steak House*, a superb restaurant that offers great food -including juicy steaks with all the trimmings - at amazing prices? It is open every evening, and a warm Welsh welcome will be extended to you.

The Bold Arms Hotel is in the centre of a town that has so much to offer the tourist. It is one of the 'five walled towns' and boasts two golf courses as well as boat trips from the pier to Puffin Island.

cursed the clock facing the gaol, saying that it would never tell the same time as the other three. It never did, until it was found out that the prevailing southwest winds were interfering with the hands. This was rectified and the clock has shown the correct time ever since.

Although Beaumarais saw little or no military action, the town briefly enjoyed notoriety as a haven for pirates, as well as being a busy trading port. With the advent of steam ships and paddle boats, the resort developed during Victorian times as visitors from Liverpool and elsewhere took the sea trip down to the town. It is now a popular place with the yachting fraternity due to its facilities and involvement in the annual **Menai Strait Regatta**.

While having connections with both sea trade and developing as a holiday resort, Beaumaris was at one time also an administrative and legal centre for the island. The **Courthouse**, dating from 1614, is open to the public during the summer and, although it was renovated in the 19th century, much of its original Jacobean interior remains. It was here, in 1773, that Mary Hughes stood in the dock and was sentenced to transportation for seven years after she had been found guilty of stealing a bed gown valued at six pence!

Close by is **Beaumaris Gaol**, which was designed as a model prison by Hansom in 1829. In this monument to Victorian law and order, the last man to hang was Richard Rowlands, who cursed the church clock

---

SHOEBOX

26 Castle Street, Beaumaris, Anglesey LL58 8AP
Tel: 01248 811188

Make your way to the **Shoebox** in Beaumaris for the very best in men's and women's footwear - everything from famous names like Rieker and Padders to Wellington boots. It offers good, old-fashioned friendly service with the personal touch, and specialises in wide fitting footwear. It stocks a large of footwear, as well as belts, shoe horns, stretchers, polish, shoe trees and gift vouchers. You can't afford to miss it.

PILOT HOUSE CAFÉ

Black Point, Penmon
Tel: 07776 006804

The Pilot House Café sits at Black Point, Penmon, housed in a building that was originally home to three lighthouse pilots and their families. Today the weary traveller can relax here and enjoy a fine selection of food and drink, all at affordable prices. Coffees, tea, hot chocolate, soft drinks and milkshakes are always available, as are filled baked potatoes, home baking, and soups. There is also a small shop selling souvenirs and gifts.

THE OWAIN GLYNDWR

Llanddona, Beaumaris, Anglesey LL58 8UF
Tel: 01248 810710
e-mail: jenoir2000@hotmail.com

In Llanddona, near Beaumaris, on the beautiful Isle of Anglesey, you will find one of the best eating houses and pubs in the area - **The Owain Glyndwr**, named after one of Wales' great heroes, who rose against the English in the 15th century. It is a family-run pub, which prides itself on its warm and welcoming environment, coupled with value for money prices and a friendly service.

The bar area is open plan yet cosy. It carries a great range of beers, wines, cider, spirits and soft drinks guaranteeing something to suit everybody's taste. The ever changing range of real cask ales has led the pub to be featured in the 2008 *Good Beer Guide*. The home cooked food, which is made to order, is outstanding, with an extensive lunch menu and a Table D'Hote evening menu which features, wherever possible, only the finest and freshest of local produce. The majority of the meals offered can be altered to suit customers with special dietary requirements i.e. coeliacs and diabetics.

The pub is warm and inviting, with an open fire that burns brightly during the colder months, fitted seating, pine tables and deep carpet. Everybody is welcome, from walkers to coach parties to those with dogs and those on horses! Whoever you are you are sure of a warm welcome here!

---

opposite as he climbed to the scaffold in 1862. Today's visitors can relive those days of harsh punishment as well as view the cells and the treadwheel and follow the route taken by the condemned men to their rendezvous with the hangman.

An equally interesting place for all the family to visit is the **Museum of Childhood Memories** in Castle Street. It is a treasure house of nostalgia with a collection of over 2,000 items in nine different rooms. Each one has its own theme, such as entertainment, pottery and glass and clockwork tin plate toys. Visitors can wander around and see the amazing variety of toys which illustrate the changing habits of the nation over the last 150 years.

LLANFAES
5 miles NE of Menai Bridge off the B5109

🏠 Parish Church of St Catherine

Now a quiet and sedate place, Llanfaes was a busy commercial village long before the establishment of Beaumaris as one of the island's major centres, and travellers from the mainland arrived here after crossing the Menai Strait from Aber and the Lavan Sands.

In 1237, Llywelyn the Great founded a monastery in the village over the tomb of Joan, his wife and the daughter of King John. The tomb can now be seen in St Mary's Church, Beaumaris, where it was moved at the time of the Dissolution. In 1295 Edward I moved the inhabitants of Llanfaes to Newborough so that he could use the stone in

---

PLAS BODFA

Llangoed, Anglesey LL58 8ND
Tel: 01248 490100
e-mail: info@plasbodfa.com
website: www.plasbodfa.com

On a hillside just two miles beyond Beaumaris stands **Plas Bodfa**, a glorious country house with breathtaking views of Snowdonia across the Menai Strait.

The building has a chequered past but is now home to a wondrous array of gifts, curiosities and crafts. The Traditional Tea Room, popular with locals and visitors alike, is famous for its unusual homemade soups and cakes. Plas Bodfa is also an exclusive outlet for the much acclaimed Elizabeth Bradley needlework kits.

The lovingly manicured grounds offer a haven of peace and relaxation on a sunny day. Repose in the Tea Garden to muse at the mountains or perhaps play a game of boules on the lawn. The paddocks are filled with cheeky ducks and chickens, miniature Shetland ponies and some very amusing guinea fowl. On sunny days the rabbits will be out on parade and the resident peacock, Bradley, is usually on hand to welcome you to the estate. All the pets are tame and friendly.

This is just a small taste of what to expect here. Evolving constantly, you are promised that Plas Bodfa is well worth a visit.

the town to built Beaumaris Castle. During World War Two, flying boats were built at a factory near the village. The **Parish Church of St Catherine** dates from 1845, and replaces an earlier church. It is an imposing, steepled building that seems much too large for the village.

LLANGOED
6 miles NE of Menai Bridge on the B5109

🏛 Castell Aberlleiniog   🏛 Haulfre Stables

In Edwardian times, this historic village was a popular resort with the lower middle classes who came here to relax in boarding houses by the sea. Llangoed's seaside charm is enhanced by its pastoral setting where a walk downstream, alongside the river, leads to **Castell Aberlleiniog**, found in the midst of some trees. This was originally a timber castle, built in around 1090 by Hugh Lupus, Earl of Chester, who, along with Hugh the Proud, Earl of Shrewsbury, exacted great cruelty on the Welsh. Lupus was later killed during an attack on the castle by Magnus, King of Norway, when he was struck in the eye by an arrow. The ruins of the bailey, which was constructed later, are still visible. Close by is the site of a battle where, in 809, the Saxons were, albeit briefly, victorious over the defending Welsh. **Haulfre Stables** is a small equestrian museum housed in a historic stable block and containing a collection of Victorian harnesses and saddlery, carts and carriages.

PENMON
7 miles NE of Menai Bridge off the B5109

🏛 Penmon Priory   🏛 Parish Church of St Seiriol

🏛 Dovecote   🏛 Puffin Island   🏛 St Seiriol's Well

On the eastern tip of Anglesey, this is a beauty spot whose lovely views across the Menai Strait go some way to explaining why it was

---

🏛 historic building   📷 museum   🏛 historic site   🐦 scenic attraction   🐾 flora and fauna

Penmon Church & Priory Ruins

and also because the young birds were considered a delicacy when pickled.

The **Parish Church of St Seiriol**, originally the priory church, was rebuilt in the 12th century and contains wonderful examples of Norman architecture and a carved cross, recently moved to the church from the fields nearby, that shows influences from both Scandinavia and Ireland. The ruins of the priory's domestic buildings include a 13th century wing with a refectory on the ground floor where traces of the seat used by the monk who read aloud during meals can still be seen.

chosen, centuries earlier, as a religious site. **Penmon Priory** was established by St Seiriol in the 6th century and in 1237 Llywelyn the Great gave the monastery and its estates to the prior of Puffin Island. St Seiriol was nicknamed Seiriol the Pale, as he used to meet and talk to St Cybi of Holyhead at a point halfway between their monasteries. Seiriol travelled westwards in the morning and eastwards in the evening, so the sun never tanned his face. St Cyri, on the other hand, travelled in the opposite direction, and was known as St Cyri the Tanned. Seirol was eventually buried on nearby **Puffin Island**, where he had also founded a monastery. Once known as Priestholm and now often called Ynys Seiriol, this island is thought once to have been connected to the mainland at one time, as St Seiriol was said to have a chapel across the bay in Penmaenmawr and ancient records tell of journeys between the two. The remains of monastic buildings that date back to the 6th century can still be seen here. The island was so named because of the large puffin colonies that nested here. However, the numbers of the nesting birds declined in the 19th century partly due to rats on the island

A nearby **Dovecote**, built in around 1600 by Sir Richard Bulkeley, contains nearly 1,000 nesting places. A path, beginning across the road, leads up to **St Seiriol's Well**, which was probably the site of the original 6th century priory. Although the upper part of the building covering the well appears to date from the 18th century, the lower portion is much older and could indeed incorporate something from the priory's original chapel.

An abandoned quarry close to the village once provided stone for Beaumaris Castle as well as the Telford and Stephenson bridges which link the island and the Welsh mainland.

PENTRAETH
4 miles NW of Menai Bridge on the A5025

🏛 Parish Church of St Mary   🏛 Plas Gwyn

🏛 Three Leaps

Before land reclamation, this sleepy village

stood on the edge of Traeth Coch (known in English as Red Wharf Bay). Its name reflects this, as it means 'head of the beach'. At low tide, the almost 15 square miles of sand supported a flourishing cockling industry. Nowadays, this is a popular place for a holiday even though it is not ideal for swimming due to the strong tidal currents. The **Parish Church of St Mary** dates originally from the 14th century, and in the graveyard is the mass grave of people who perished on the Royal Charter, a sailing ship which was blown onto the rocks near the village as it sailed from Australia to Liverpool (see also Moelfre). There are no names on the stones, as very few bodies were identified. Close to **Plas Gwyn**, an 18th century Georgian mansion, is the **Three Leaps** - three small stones in a row that commemorate a contest in AD 580 between two rivals for the hand of the grand-daughter of the warrior Geraint. The contest was won by the man who could leap the furthest, in this case, by a champion named Hywel. The stones mark his efforts, in possibly what we now know as the triple jump. The loser is said to have died of a broken heart.

BENLLECH
6½ miles N of Menai Bridge on the A5025

🏛 Castell Mawr   🪶 Goronwy Owen

With its excellent beach to attract holidaymakers, Benllech is probably the most popular resort on Anglesey, but those coming here should take care as there are strong tidal currents and the sands can be treacherous. This resort has another claim to fame, as the birthplace of the poet **Goronwy Owen**. He lived between 1723 and 1769, and spent his last years in Virginia as the rector of St Andrew's Church in Laurenceville. His fame rests on an output of just 55 poems.

Traces of a hill fort, **Castell Mawr**, can be found on the west side of Red Wharf Bay, and on the evidence of coins found here, the site could once have been occupied by the Romans.

MOELFRE
9 miles N of Menai Bridge on the A5108

🏛 Parish Church of St Gallgo   🏛 Royal Charter
🏛 Lligwy Burial Chamber   🪶 Ynys Moelfre
📷 Seawatch Centre   🏛 Din Lligwy Village

Moelfre

This is a charming coastal village with a sheltered, pebbled beach, attractive cottages and sandy beaches to both the north and the south. Fame, however, came to Moelfre in an unfortunate and bizarre way via its lifeboat which, over the years, has been involved in many rescues, two of

🏛 historic building   📷 museum   🏛 historic site   🍃 scenic attraction   🪶 flora and fauna

which are worthy of mention. Returning to Liverpool from Australia in October 1859, laden with cargo and passengers, including gold prospectors coming home after making their fortunes in the Australian Gold Rush, **The Royal Charter** sank.

A rigged iron vessel and the pride of the merchant fleet, the ship was all set to make the long passage in record time but, while sheltering from a hurricane in Moelfre Bay, she foundered with the loss of 450 passengers and crew. Only 39 people survived, and many believe that the gold still lies with the wreck out in the bay. Efforts have been made to recover the lost fortune with varying but not overwhelming degrees of success and it has been said that the larger houses around Moelfre were paid for with gold washed

ashore from the wreck. This is despite customs officers swamping the village in an attempt to ensure that any salvaged gold ended in the Exchequer rather than in the hands of the locals. Charles Dickens visited the site on New Year's Eve 1859, and apparently based a story on the disaster in *The Uncommercial Traveller* (see also Pentraeth).

One hundred years later, almost to the day, in October 1959, the coaster *Hindlea*, struggling in foul weather, had eight crew members rescued by the Moelfre Lifeboat. The rescue earned Richard Evans, the lifeboat's coxswain, his second RNLI gold medal for gallantry.

At Llanallgo, between Moelfre and Dulas, is the mainly 15th century **Parish Church of St Gallgo**, with its ancient bell, one of the oldest

Din Lligwy Village, Moelfre

Beyond the station is a small outcrop of rocks, **Ynys Moelfre**, a favourite spot for seabirds and, occasionally, porpoises. About a mile inland from the village, off the narrow road, is the impressive **Lligwy Burial Chamber**, a Bronze Age tomb with huge capstone supported by stone uprights, which lies half hidden in a pit dug out of the rock. Close by is **Din Lligwy Village**, the remains of a Romano British settlement that covers over half an acre. Certainly occupied around the 4th century AD, after the Roman garrison on Anglesey had been vacated, some of the stone walls of the buildings can still be seen and excavations of the site have unearthed pottery, coins and evidence of metal working from that period. Nearby are the ruins of the 14th century **Capel Lligwy**.

LLANDDYFNAN

5 miles NW of Menai Bridge on the B5109

🏠 Stone Science 🏛 Llanddyfnan Standing Stone

in the country. It was struck in the 13th century, and bears the inscription *Ave Maria Gracia Plena* (Hail Mary, Full of Grace), as well as the imprint of an Edward I coin struck in 1281. In the graveyard is a memorial to the victims of the *Royal Charter* tragedy. St Gallgo is famous as being the brother of Gildas, the 6th century historian of Britain, who wrote *De Excidio et Conquestu Britanniae*. He was born in the Kingdom of Strathclyde in Scotland, which at that time had strong ties with Wales, and even spoke the same language.

The **Seawatch Centre** has displays and exhibits about Anglesey's rich maritime heritage, including athe village's lifeboat.

To the west of the village lies **Stone Science**, an unusual attraction that tells the story of the earth from its beginning to the present - a journey spanning 650 million years. The museum illustrates the science with displays of fossils, crystals and artefacts, and there are numerous and varied items for sale in the Stone Science shop. Nearly opposite is the eight feet high **Llanddyfnan Standing Stone**.

LLANGEFNI

6 miles NW of Menai Bridge on the B5420

🏠 Oriel Ynys Môn

The island's main market and administrative centre, Llangefni is also the home of **Oriel**

Ynys Môn (the Anglesey Heritage Centre), an attractive art gallery and heritage centre, built in 1991, which gives an insight into the history of Anglesey. From prehistoric times to the present day, the permanent exhibition covers a series of themes including Stone Age Hunters, Druids, Medieval Society and Legends.

Llyn Cefni Reservoir to the northwest of the town is an important wildlife habitat and nature reserve overlooked by a hide; it also provides a pleasant picnic area. On the northwest edge of town by the River Cefni, The Dingle is a local nature reserve with footpaths through mature woodland. The A5114, which connects Llangefni to the A5, is the shortest A road in the British Isles.

LLANFAIR PG
1 mile W of Menai Bridge off the A5

🚉 Railway Station　　🏛 Marquess of Anglesey Column

📽 Llanfairpwllgwyngyll

Llanfairpwllgwyngyll, often called Llanfair PG, is the village with the world's longest place name. The full, tongue-twisting name is: Llanfairpwllgwyngyllgogerychwyrndrobwyllllantysiliogogogoch and the translation is even longer - St Mary's Church in a hollow of white hazel near to a rapid whirlpool and St Tysilio's Church near the red cave. The name is said to have been invented, in humorous reference to the burgeoning tourist trade, by a local man. Whether this is true or not, it has certainly done the trick, as

TAFARN TY GWYN

8 Holyhead Road, Llanfair PG,
Anglesey LL61 5UJ
Tel: 01248 715599
e-mail: Philip-stott@btconnect.com

Tafarn Ty Gwyn is a busy village pub serving good food and good beer in friendly, comfortable surroundings. It stands in the centre of Llanfair PG next to the famous railway station with its much-photographed 58-letter station sign. The pub has earned the patronage of both locals and the many visitors who come by car and coach to see the station and other local attractions. They also increasingly come to enjoy the excellent hospitality provided by Phil Stott and his wife Rose, who are leaseholders of this Scottish & Newcastle outlet. They sell a full range of S&N products including traditional cask ales and guest beers.

The menu emphasises locally sourced ingredients on a regularly changing selection of traditional home-cooked food offering restaurant quality at pub prices. The pub has a large lounge bar that hosts a quiz every Wednesday and live music every Thursday and Saturday. There's also a separate 'cellar bar' that attracts a younger set with sports TV, darts and pool, and when the sun shines the beer garden is a popular spot, particularly with families.

📽 stories and anecdotes　🦜 famous people　🎨 art and craft　🍴 entertainment and sport　🚶 walks many visitors stop by initially out of curiosity at the name.

The village, overlooking the Menai Strait, is where the Britannia Bridge crosses to the mainland. The **Marquess of Anglesey Column** looks out from here over to Snowdonia and the quite splendid views from the top of the column are available to anyone wishing to negotiate the spiral staircase of some 115 steps. The column was finished two years after the battle of Waterloo, and the statue on top of the column was added, in 1860, after the death of Henry Paget, Earl of Uxbridge and 1st Marquess of Anglesey, whom it commemorates. Paget fought alongside the Duke of Wellington at Waterloo, where he lost a leg to one of the last shots of the battle. He lived to be 85, having twice been Lord-Lieutenant of Ireland after his military career (see also Plas Newydd).

The last public toll house, designed by Thomas Telford when he was working on the London-Holyhead road in the 1820s, stands in the village; it still displays the tolls charged in 1895, the year the toll house closed. Next door is the modest building where, in 1915, the first Women's Institute in Britain was founded. The movement originated in Canada earlier in the same year.

However, the village's most famous building is its **Railway Station** - the often filmed station whose platform has the longest station sign and where the longest platform ticket in Britain could be purchased. Today, visitors can see a replica of the Victorian ticket office, examine some rare miniature steam trains and wander around the numerous craft and souvenir shops that can now be found here.

LLANGADWALADR
10½ miles W of Menai Bridge on the A4080

🏛 Parish Church of St Cadwaladr

Around the time that Aberffraw was the capital of Gwynedd, this small village was said to have been the burial place of the Welsh princes. The **Parish Church of St Cadwaladr** was founded in AD 615 as part of a royal monastery, and was probably built of wattle and daub - wattle walls covered in dried mud to provide stability and waterproofing, as the village's early name was Eglwys Ail, meaning 'wattle church'. The present building dates from the 12th century, and has a memorial stone to Cadfan, King of Gwynedd, who died in AD 625. It is embedded in the church wall, and reads *King Cadfan, the Wisest and Most Renowned of All Kings Lies Here*. Cadwaladr was Cadfan's grandson, and he died in Rome in AD 682. His body was brought here for burial.

ABERFFRAW
12½ miles W of Menai Bridge on the A4080

🏛 Parish Church of St Beuno   🏛 Church of St Cywfan

🏛 Llys Llywelyn Museum   🏛 Din Dryfol Burial Chamber

🏛 Barclodiad y Gawres Burial Chamber

Though this was the capital of Gwynedd between the 7th and 13th centuries, and therefore one of the most important places in Wales, there remains little trace of those times. In fact, no one quite knows where the court buildings were situated. However, a Norman arch, set into the **Parish Church of St Beuno** is said to be from the chapel of the royal court. The church as we see it today dates largely from the 16th century, The **Llys Llywelyn Museum**, although modest, has exhibitions recounting the area's fascinating history.

🏛 historic building   🏛 museum   🏛 historic site   ᗧ scenic attraction   ᐟ flora and fauna

On an island just offshore is the **Church of St Cywfan**. It dates originally from the 13th century, though what we see today mainly dates from the 14th and 15th centuries. At one time the building was much bigger, but when erosion started to bite at the island, and old graves started to fall into the shoreline, parts of it were demolished. By 1891 it was roofless, but money was eventually raised to refurbish it.

Inland, the **Din Dryfol Burial Chamber** provides further evidence of Iron Age life on the island while, to the north of Aberffraw, on the cliff tops above Porth Trecastell, is the **Barclodiad y Gawres Burial Chamber**. Considered to be one of the finest of its kind, this burial chamber, along with Bryn Celli Ddu, contains some notable murals. This area is also known as Cable Bay, as it is here that a transatlantic cable came ashore.

PLAS NEWYDD
2 miles SW of Menai Bridge off the A4080

🏛 Plas Newydd 🏛 Bryn Celli Ddu

Bryn Celli Ddu, a wonderful example of a Bronze Age passage grave, lies up a narrow country road close to **Plas Newydd** (NT), which is situated on the banks of the Menai Strait. The splendid mansion house was designed by James Wyatt, and is surrounded by gardens and parkland laid out in the 18th century by Humphry Repton. Not only are there fabulous views over the water to Snowdonia from the lawns but there is a woodland walk, an Australian arboretum and a formal Italian style garden terrace.

As well as Britain's largest collection of works by Rex Whistler, the house contains a military museum. It is not to be confused with Plas Newydd near Llangollen.

Passage Grave, Plas Newydd

BRYNSIENCYN
5 miles SW of Menai Bridge on the A4080

🏛 Tre-Drwy 🏛 Caer Leb 🏛 Bodowyr Burial Chamber

🏛 Castell Bryn Gwyn 🌱 Foel Farm Park

🌱 Anglesey Sea Zoo 🐿 Sir Ellis Jones Ellis-Griffith

Close to this village there was once an important centre of Druid worship, but no signs remain of the temple that stood at **Tre-Drwy**. There are, however, several other interesting remains in the area. Just to the west of the village lies **Caer Leb**, an Iron Age earthwork consisting of a pentagonal enclosure 200 feet by 160 feet encircled by banks and ditches, while, just a short distance away is **Bodowyr Burial Chamber**, a massive stone that is, seemingly, delicately perched upon three upright stones. To the south of the

Anglesey Sea Zoo

Brynsiencyn, Llanfairpwllgwyngyll, Gwynedd LL61 6TQ
Tel: 01248 430411
e-mail:info@angleseyseazoo.co.uk
website:www.angleseyseazoo.co.uk

Anglesey Sea Zoo was founded in 1983 on the site of an oyster hatchery and has developed every year to become an important visitor attraction.

The Anglesey Sea Zoo is Wales largest marine aquarium, nestling on the shores of the Menai Strait, and with over 50 species it has re-created the habitats of the fauna and flora found around Anglesey and the North Wales Coastline. From the intricacy and complexity of the invertebrates in the Bone Free Zone, your tour takes you through a Shipwreck, a walkover the Shark Pool and then on to the wonders of the Open Ocean. Our underwater camera gives you a fish's eye view of the Fish Forest looking out as well as members of your family looking in! The aim is to provide an exciting yet educational visit, incorporating the conservation efforts to preserve the local marine environment.

Tropical displays include piranhas and seahorses amongst others. Zoo staff are actively involved in seahorse conservation and support the work of Project Seahorse. Learn more about the life of a lobster at the Lobster Hatchery of Wales. Find out more about the local sealife at the supervised Discovery Pool sessions (This is a free facility available during local school holidays).

The Shop has gifts to suit all ages and pockets. For that extra special something why not visit the Pearls Shack and pick your own Japanese Pearl Oyster. Learn about how pearls form and have your pearl valued and set in a range of gold and silver jewellery. The outside facilities, including Radio Controlled Boats, Aquablast, Crazy Golf and fun Photo Boards make Anglesey Sea Zoo a great family day out.

burial chamber, and just a mile west of Brynsiencyn, are the earthwork remains of **Castell Bryn Gwyn**, a site which has been excavated and shows traces of having been used from as far back as the New Stone Age through to the time of the Roman occupation of Britain.

Back in the village and found down the small road leading to the shore lies **Foel Farm Park**, a real working farm which offers visitors the opportunity to bottle feed lambs and baby calves, cuddle rabbits, see and help with milking and enjoy the homemade ice cream. There are also covered areas for rainy days which include an adventure play den and an indoor picnic room.

Also overlooking the Menai Strait is the **Anglesey Sea Zoo** (see panel above), an award-winning attraction that takes visitors beneath the waves and into the underwater world of a wide variety of sea creatures. The imaginative and innovative displays allow visitors a unique view of these interesting beasts, which include sea horses, oysters, conger eels and rays.

In the graveyard of the Victorian parish church is a monument to the grandly named **Sir Ellis Jones Ellis-Griffith**, MP for Anglesey from 1895 until 1918. Though born in Birmingham, he was brought up in the village, and died in 1926.

DWYRAN
8 miles SW of Menai Bridge off the A4080

🐦 Bird World

Just outside the village lies **Bird World**, a wonderful family attraction set in extensive parkland, with views over to the Snowdonia mountain range, where visitors can admire the wide variety of birds on display as well as picnic in the beautiful surroundings of the lake. There is also a small animal farm and pet area for the children along with a huge indoor play barn.

NEWBOROUGH
9 miles SW of Menai Bridge on the A4080

🏛 Church of St Dwynwen   🐚 Abermenai Point

🐚 Llanddwyn Island

🐚 Anglesey Model Village and Gardens

🐦 Newborough Warren   🎨 Charles Tunnicliffe

Founded in 1303 by the former inhabitants of Llanfaes, who had been moved here by Edward I, the village stands on the edge of a National Nature Reserve that covers 1,566 acres of dunes, coast and forest. Among the many footpaths through the reserve, there are several forest trails that show how the Forestry Commission is constantly trying to stabilise the dunes. **Newborough Warren** is so called because, before myxomatosis, about 80,000 rabbits were trapped here annually. There is a route through the warren to **Abermenai Point**, but the way can be

dangerous and advice concerning tidal conditions should be sought before considering the walk.

Llanddwyn Island is also accessible on foot but again tidal conditions should be carefully studied before setting out. On the island stand the ruins of the early medieval **Church of St Dwynwen**. She is the Welsh equivalent of St Valentine, and even today St Dwynwen's Day is still celebrated in some parts of Wales. Though she is the patron saint of love, her own story was far from lovely. She was one of the 24 daughters of Brychan Brycheiniog, and said to be the prettiest. She fell in love with a man called Maelon, but when he discovered that she was already promised to someone else, he raped her and left her. She prayed to God to let Maelon truly repent, and asked for two further wishes. God obliged, the other two being that he protected the hopes and wishes of true loves and that she should never marry. Also on the island is a holy well, in which, it was once thought, a sacred fish swam that could predict the future.

Until the 1920s, marram grass, which has been grown for conservation purposes from Elizabethan times, was also a mainstay of the area, helping to sustain a cottage industry in the production of ropes, baskets, matting and thatching materials. A high embankment was built here in the 18th century by Thomas Telford to stop the sea, which had previously almost cut the island into two.

Charles Tunnicliffe, the renowned wildlife artist, had a studio on the island for over 30 years and Anglesey Council has purchased a collection of his marvellous work which can be seen at the Oriel (Gallery) Ynys Môn in Llangefni. On the A4080 signposted from Newborough, Newborough Forest is a pine forest with rides, glades and miles of walks.

🎭 stories and anecdotes   🐦 famous people   🎨 art and craft   🎪 entertainment and sport   🥾 walks

Situated between Newborough and Dwyran lies **Anglesey Model Village and Gardens**, a delightful place where visitors can wander through the attractive landscaped gardens and see many of the island's many landmarks - all built to one twelfth scale. There is a children's ride-on train, as well as the garden railway, and the gardens themselves are particularly beautiful, with many water features and a good collection of plants and trees.

Holyhead

🏛 Parish Church St Cybi 🏛 Eglwys Bedd

🏛 Four Mile Bridge 🌿 Gogarth Bay

🏚 Salt Island 🏚 Caer y Twr 🏚 Cytiau'r Gwyddelod

🏚 Trefignath 🌿 South Stack 🖉 Porth Dafarch

🌿 Ellin's Tower 🖉 Canolfan Ucheldre Centre

🖉 Trearddur Bay 🕯 Breakwater Quarry Country Park

Holyhead Mountain (Mynydd Twr) rises to

720 feet behind this town, which is usually called the largest on Anglesey though it actually sits on another island off Anglesey's coast, Holy Island. A busy rail and ferry terminal, especially for travellers to and from Ireland, Holyhead has all the facilities needed to cater for visitors passing through. It is also, despite being something of an industrial and commercial centre, a seaside resort. Its origins lie back in the times of the Romans and the early Celtic Christians. Parts of the **Parish Church St Cybi** date from the 14th to the 17th century and it is situated within the partially surviving walls of the small Roman fort, Caer Gybi (the source of Holyhead's Welsh name) and on the site of a 6th century chapel. St Cybi, who died in AD 554, was the brother of St David, patron saint of Wales, and he came here at the end of his life. His friend was St Seiriol of Penmon (see also Penmon). The shrine and relics of St Cybi was removed to Dublin by Henry IV's army when it invaded Anglesey, but

Ellin's Tower, Holyhead

🏛 historic building   🖼 museum   🏚 historic site   🌄 scenic attraction   🌿 flora and fauna

FORGET ME NOT FLORISTS

21 Stanley Street, Holyhead, Anglesey LL65 1HG
Tel: 01407 764348

The mother and daughter team of Carol Stride and Lorraine Woosnam have created, in **Forget Me Not Florists**, one of the best shops of its kind on the lovely island of Anglesey. Flowers say so much, and here you will find the perfect gift in a bunch of colourful, fresh flowers that speak of warm summer days or well-tended gardens.

The shop has been open for over two years, and since its inception it has become a very popular place, with people coming from all over to choose from its wide range. It sits close to the harbour and port, and also sells a wide range of flower accessories, plus such marvellous items as beautifully made silk flowers, plants, gift cards, chocolates, picture frames, silver candle sticks, candles, teddy bears, and so much more. Come in and look round. Take your time, as you are free to browse with absolutely no obligation to buy. The whole place is colourful and bright, as all good flower shops should be, and both Carol and Lorraine are always on hand to offer help and advice. The shop is a member of Interflora, and can provide bouquets and floral arrangements for all occasions.

Prices are always reasonable, and represent amazing value for money. So why not pay it a visit? Flowers are always welcome, and can brighten up even the darkest, wettest of days. Carol and Lorraine will offer you a warm welcome.

were lost at the Reformation. Close to the church is a smaller church, **Eglwys Bedd** ('Church of the Grave'), which reputedly contains the tomb of Seregri, an Irish warrior who was repelled by the Welsh chief, Caswallon Lawhir, in AD 550. The town's triumphal arches, built in 1821, commemorate George IV's visit here as well as the end of the A5, the major road from London.

The interesting **Canolfan Ucheldre Centre** is housed in an old convent chapel. It is an arts centre for northwest Wales opened in 1991, and presents both film, music and drama events as well as holding all manner of art and craft exhibitions and workshops. **Salt Island** (Ynys Halen), close to the town centre, is self-explanatory: a factory was built here to extract salt from the seawater. Rock salt was

added to improve the sea salt's quality and when an excise duty was charged smuggling flourished, particularly between Four Mile Bridge and the Isle of Man, where salt was duty free.

While the town itself is not without interest, it is the immediate surrounding area that draws most visitors to Holyhead. **Four Mile Bridge** connects Holy island to Anglesey, and was so called, not because it is four miles long, but because it it four miles from the ferry terminal in Holyhead. Its old name was Pont Rhyd Bont. **Breakwater Quarry Country Park**, just northwest of the town, incorporates Britain's largest breakwater. Designed by James Meadow and started in 1845, the structure, which shields an area of 667 acres, took 28 years to construct.

Holyhead Mountain

Distance: *4.7 miles (7.5 kilometres)*

Typical time: *180 mins*

Height gain: *200 metres*

Map: *Landranger 114*

Walk: *www.walkingworld.com ID:860*

Contributor: *Haydn Williams*

ACCESS INFORMATION:

From Bangor keep on the A55 right across the island to Holyhead, about 25 minutes' drive. Follow the town centre sign on the first roundabout, then follow the signs for South Stack, passing the ferry terminal on your right. Keep following the signs for South Stack to your starting point for the walk, this is at the first car park on your left (free parking). If you have got to the car park with the cafe you have gone about 300yds too far.

DESCRIPTION:

A very interesting start with a visit to the Holyhead Mountain hut group, a hill fort on the summit, 360-degree views. There are two bird reserves in the area, one of which is Ellen's Tower, where the RSPB lend out binoculars for viewing the puffins and finishes off with a walk on the cliffs. There are 263 species of wild plants in this area, a hermitage that dates from the 3rd Century, some of the most demanding cliff climbs in the UK and in Holyhead itself there is a Roman fort to visit.

FEATURES:

Hills or Fells, Mountains, Sea, Toilets, Birds, Flowers, Great Views, Food Shop, Good for Kids, Tea Shop, Woodland, Ancient Monument

WALK DIRECTIONS:

1 | The access car park; the entrance to the historic hut site is directly opposite. If you want to leave this until later, turn left onto road and turn right onto access to Foel.

2 | As you aproach the house take the dirt track to the right.

3 | Take the right-hand track that follows the line of the wall.

4 | Take the left-hand path of these two and head for the saddle. Carry on over the crossroads.

5 | Turn left at crossroads.

6 | Turn left and start going uphill again. Take the left-hand path that follows the wall going uphill.

7 | After about fifty metres turn left and head steeply uphill.

8 | After topping out, carry on down towards South Stack in the distance, but ensure that you then turn right and head for this distinctive rock.

9 | Head for the radio dishes and keep them to your right.

10 | Walk out to the headland for the view down to South Stack.

11 | After leaving the view of South Stack, carry on along the path until you come to a hole in the wall leading down to Ellin's Tower; this now belongs to the RSPB and they supply binoculars for you to look at the puffins etc.

12 | Look to the left-hand corner of the tower and follow path at this wooden handrail. Follow the path along the impressive cliffs until you come to the "dangerous cliffs" notice; turn left and head back to the car.

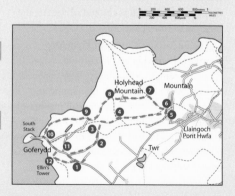

From the country park there are many walks along the coast, including a route to **South Stack**. This is a reserve of cliffs and heath teeming with birdlife, including puffins, guillemots and razorbills. The RSPB visitor centre is open daily, the café daily in summer, and the lighthouse is open daily in summer for guided tours. The lighthouse, one of the most impressive in Wales, was built in 1809 and stands on a beautiful but dangerous site reached by a steep stone stairway of over 400 steps. Above the harbour and breakwater, is a memorial to Captain Skinner, who drowned when his packet boat, *Escape*, was lost in 1832.

At the summit of Holyhead Mountain, from where, on a clear day, Snowdonia, the Isle of Man and the Mourne Mountains in Ireland can be seen, there is evidence of an ancient settlement. The remains of **Caer y Twr**, a hill fort, are visible and, close by, is **Cytiau'r Gwyddelod**, a hut settlement from the 2nd century.

Between South Stack and North Stack lies **Gogarth Bay**, where the RSPB sea bird centre includes a cavern, known as Parliament House Cave, which is used by a profusion of sea birds such as puffins, guillemots and even falcons. Visitors here can also watch the thousands of cliff nesting birds via live television pictures and enjoy the beautiful cliff top walks. **Ellin's Tower**, in the centre, is another spot favoured by ornithologists.

Aqua diving, windsurfing, water skiing and fishing are some of the many attractions of **Trearddur Bay**, a popular part of Anglesey's extensive coastline that lies just to the southwest of Holyhead. With large sandy beaches, clear water and safe bathing, it is obviously popular. The Georgian house, Towyn Lodge, on the south side of the bay, played host to Thomas Telford while he was

working on what is now the A5 road in the 19th century. A portion of the bay, **Porth Dafarch**, is owned by the National Trust. **Trefignath** is a chambered cairn with two tall pillars at each side of the entrance.

Around Holyhead

RHOSCOLYN
4½ miles S of Holyhead off the B4545

🏛 Parish Church of St Gwenfaen 🏚 Bwa Gwyn

🏚 St Gwenfaen's Well 🌊 Rhoscolyn Head

The name of this village means 'the moor of the column', the column in question thought to be a Roman one. It was once home to a thriving oyster industry that is now, sadly, in decline. China clay was also once quarried here, while the local marble was used in the construction of Worcester, Bristol and Peterborough Cathedrals.

The **Parish Church of St Gwenfaen** was originally founded in the 6th century by St Gwenfaen. **St Gwenfaen's Well** was said to have properties that cured, in particular, mental illness. **Rhoscolyn Head** is a superb headland ideal for cliff walking, and there are splendid views northwards over Trearddur Bay and, southwards, over Cymyran Bay. At **Bwa Gwyn** (White Arch) is a memorial to Tyger, a remarkable dog who, in 1817, led to safety the four-man crew from a sinking ketch. After dragging the cabin boy ashore and returning for the ship's captain, the dog collapsed and died from exhaustion.

VALLEY
3½ miles SE of Holyhead on the A5

🐦 Llyn Penrhyn

Valley sits on Anglesey, immediately opposite

CIGYDD Y FALI

The Old Court House, Station Road, Y Fali, Anglesey LL65 3EB
Tel: 01407 742391
e-mail: cigydyyfali@aol.com   website: www.valleybutchers.co.uk

Cigydd Y Fali translates as The Valley Butchers, and is a superior butchers shop within the small, picturesque village of Y Fali, about three or four miles east of Holyhead on the A5. The shop has been in existence for many years, and was taken over two years ago by Karl Jones, who has improved and built on the great reputation it has for high quality meat and other products. Cigydd y Fali has recently won 11 Gold Awards for Excellence for their meat products.

It sells only meat reared on Anglesey, and specialises in tender lamb, tasty pork and well hung beef, with people travelling from all over the island - and even from the mainland - to buy its high-quality produce. It also sells award-winning pies and sausages, which are made on the premises, as well as locally produced eggs and cheeses. Its cooked meats are all produced on the premises, ensuring maximum flavour and freshness, and the shop sells to all the major hotels and restaurants in the area.

The shop is noted for its value-for-money prices, and also features a section selling fresh fruit and vegetables. This area of Anglesey is holiday country, with many self-catering cottages, campsites and caravan parks. So the shop is also popular with holiday-makers, who appreciate the immaculately clean premises, the friendly staff and the help and advice that is always given when choosing a cut of meat. So if you're holidaying in this part of Wales, or even just passing through - then make your way to Cigydd Y Fali for the best in butcher meat and ancillary products.

Holy island. It was thought to have gained its name while Thomas Telford was cutting his road through the small hill here. Centuries earlier this was the home of Iron Age man whose weapons and horse trappings found in the area are now on display in the National Museum of Wales.

However, Valley is perhaps better known today for the nearby airfield established here during World War II as a fighter pilot base. In 1943, the American Air Force expanded the base's capability for use as an Atlantic terminal and now the RAF uses it for training flights and for Air/Sea rescue. Opposite the barracks is **Llyn Penrhyn**, a complex of reed-fringed lakes with lots of wildfowl and dragonflies. Before the bridges to Holyhead were built,

during the construction of the A5, the crossing to the town was made via Four Mile Bridge (see Holyhead).

RHOSNEIGR
7½ miles SE of Holyhead on the A4080

🏛 Parish Church of St Maelog   🌊 Cymyran Bay

🌱 Tywyn Trewan Common   🏰 Norman Court

This small resort is situated in a quiet spot, close to the sandy beaches and rocky outcrops of **Cymyran Bay**. The River Crigyll, which runs into the sea by the town, was the haunt, in the 18th century, of the 'Wreckers of Crigyll', who were famous for luring ships onto the rocks. Tried at Beaumaris in 1741, where the group of desperate men were found guilty and hanged, the wreckers became the subject of a ballad, *The Hanging of the Thieves of Crigyll*. In March 1883 the tea clipper the **Norman Court** ran aground off the coast near the village, though not as a result of wreckers. She was one of the fastest and best of the tea clippers of the day, and had become a famous name. She was carrying, not tea, but 1,000 tons of sugar for Greenock in Scotland. Twenty men were rescued from the ship, and two were lost. For over 24 hours they had been clinging to the ship's rigging. For many years after, her wreckage could still be seen.

The **Parish Church of St Maelog** dates from 1848/49, though it looks much older. There has been a church on the site since at least the 6th century, when St Maelog chose this site to establish a church and monastery. He was the brother of Gildas and St Gallgo (see Moelfre), and died in Brittany.

The 1,400 acres of gorse and dunes at **Tywyn Trewan Common** is a paradise for botanists and ornithologists.

LLANFAIRYNGHORNWY
7 miles NE of Holyhead off the A5025

🏛 The Skerries   🐾 Frances Williams

This village, on the approach to **Carmel Head**, has two claims to fame. It was here, in the 19th century, that **Frances Williams** founded the Anglesey Association for the Preservation of Life from Shipwreck. Along with her husband, who was the local rector, Frances raised funds for lifeboats on the island and, through her efforts, the first lifeboat station in the area was established. She was also noted as an artist, and some of her drawings are held by the University of Wales at Bangor.

Lying two miles offshore from the point at Carmel Head are **The Skerries**, a group of windswept islets whose Welsh name, Ynysoedd y Moelrhoniaid, means Island of

Porpoises. On the islets stands the last Lighthouse to be privately owned (ships had to pay a toll as they passed). When braziers stood there during the 18th century, they burnt approximately 100 tons of coal a night! Now automated and owned by Trinity House, its beam is rated at four million candles.

CEMAES
11 miles NE of Holyhead off the A5025

🏛 Parish Church of St Patrick. Llanbadrig

🏛 Mynachdy   🖼 Ogof y March Glas

🏛 Wylfa Nuclear Power Station   🏖 Cemaes Bay

🏛 Parish Church of St Mechell, Llanfechell

🏖 North Anglesey Heritage Coast

Boasting two glorious, safe, sandy beaches, **Cemaes Bay** is a popular place on the island that was also once a favourite with smugglers. However, today, Cemaes is a quiet and picturesque fishing village, with a small tidal harbour with much to offer holidaymakers: wonderful walks, abundant wildlife, fishing, hotels, shops, pubs and also the opportunity to learn a little of the Welsh language. It sits in the middle of the **North Anglesey Heritage Coast**, and is the most northerly village in Wales.

Ogof y March Glas - Cave of the Blue Horse - on Cemaes Bay was named after an incident that took place over 200 years ago. Following a family dispute, a young man furiously galloped away from his house near the bay on his dappled grey horse. Blinded by rage, he galloped headlong over the cliff; only his hat was ever seen again, although the carcass of his horse was found washed up in the cave.

At Llanbadrig, north of the village, is the **Parish Church of St Patrick**. 'Badrig' is actually the Welsh for Patrick, and there are

🏛 stories and anecdotes   🐾 famous people   🖌 art and craft   🎵 entertainment and sport   🥾 walks three churches in Wales dedicated to that particular saint. However, the one at Llanbadrig is the only one with a tangible connection to him. The original church dates from about AD 440, and was founded by the great man himself after he was sent by Pope Celestine I to Ireland to spread Christianity. It is said he was shipwrecked on Yns Badrig, off the coast, but managed to get to the shore, where he took refuge in St Patrick's Cave on the shore close to where the church now stands. He found a well there with fresh drinking water, and founded the church in gratitude. The present church dates from the 15th century, though there is a more modern church in the village as well. At Llanfechell, south of the village, is, the **Parish Church of St Mechell**, the nave and part of the chancel of which dates from the 13th century.

Around the headland at the western edge of the bay lies **Wylfa Nuclear Power Station**. Its visitor centre is the starting point for a guided tour of the station and also contains a mass of information about the nature trail surrounding the plant. Cemlyn Bay, home to thousands of terns between April and July, is managed as a nature reserve by the North Wales Wildlife Trust; **Mynachdy** contains old settlement sites and the remains of some long disused copper mines.

AMLWCH
14 miles NE of Holyhead on the A5025

🏛 Amlwch Railway Museum   🏚 Parys Mountain

South of this seaside town lies the pock-marked **Parys Mountain**, which has provided copper for prospectors from as early as Roman times. In 1768 a copper boom helped make Anglesey the copper centre of the world, but by 1820 the rush was over as prices fell and the mineral deposits became exhausted. The harbour, which was built during more prosperous times, is now used mainly by pleasure craft. In its heyday Amlwch had 6,000 inhabitants and 1,000 ale houses. The **Amlwch Railway Museum** has displays on trains and associated memorabilia.

Amlwch

DULAS
15 miles E of Holyhead off the A5025

🌱 Ynys Dulas

A once thriving village, Dulas was, in the early 19th century, home to both a brickworks and a shipbuilding industry. Standing at the head of the Dulas River, which runs into the bay, the village overlooks **Ynys Dulas**, a small island which lies a mile or so offshore and is the haunt of grey seals. On the island itself is a 19th century tower built as a beacon and a refuge for sailors; the lady of Llysdulas manor house once had food left there for stranded mariners.

LLANERCHYMEDD
11 miles E of Holyhead on the B5112

🏛 Parish Church of St Mary 🎣 Llyn Alaw

To the north of the village lies **Llyn Alaw**, Anglesey's largest lake, well known for its fine trout fishing as well as the abundant wildlife found around its shores. Covering some 770 acres, the lake is actually a man-made reservoir, produced by flooding marshland. It supplies most of the island's industrial and domestic needs. Some people actually believe that Llanerchymedd was the burial place of Mary, mother of Jesus. A book, *The Marian Conspiracy*, was even published claiming that the actual burial site is where the present **Parish Church**

of **St Mary** now stands. This flies in the face of Roman Catholic dogma, which teaches that Mary bodily ascended to heaven.

LLANDDEUSANT
6½ miles E of Holyhead off the A5025

🏛 Llynnon Mill 🏛 Bedd Branwen

This village is home to Anglesey's only stone tower working windmill, built in 1775-76 at a total cost of £529-11s-0d. Four storeys high, with a boat-shaped cap, it ceased milling by wind power in 1924, but was restored and opened to the public in 1984. **Llynnon Mill** not only mills stoneground flour for sale (wind and conditions willing) but also has an attractive craft shop and a popular tea room for visitors to enjoy.

Tradition has it that the green mound, **Bedd Branwen**, near the River Alaw, is the grave of Branwen, the heroine of the Welsh epic, *Mabinogion*. Opened in 1813, it later revealed a rough baked clay urn containing fragments of burnt bone and ashes. Since the discovery of more funeral urns in 1967, the site has become even more significant.

🎬 stories and anecdotes 🪶 famous people 🎨 art and craft 🎭 entertainment and sport 🚶 walks

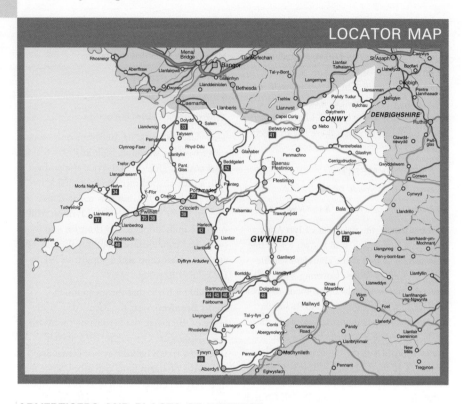

LOCATOR MAP

ADVERTISERS AND PLACES OF INTEREST

🏛 historic building   🏛 museum   🏛 historic site   🌿 scenic attraction   🌷 flora and fauna

3| Snowdonia Coast & Inland

To the south of Anglesey lies the Llyn (Lleyn) Peninsula, which forms the southern arm of the great curve of Caernarfon Bay. This is one of the most secluded and most beautiful parts of Wales, and over 100 miles of its shoreline are designated Areas of Outstanding Natural Beauty. During the Middle Ages, Bardsey Island, lying off the western tip of the peninsula, was a place of pilgrimage, and the ancient route to Aberdaron, from where the pilgrims sailed to the island, can still in parts be followed. Reminders of the area's early Christian past can be found throughout Llyn, along with more ancient monuments such as hill forts. churches and standing stones. This region, like the northern coast and the Isle of Anglesey, has been a favourite holiday destination since the coming of the railways in the mid 19th century.

The attractive Victorian resorts along the southern shore of the peninsula are sheltered and provide plenty of scope for sailing, swimming and fishing. Though born in Manchester, the place where David Lloyd George lived until he was 16 years old - Llanystumdwy - is a popular place to visit. However, the whole region is filled with splendid attractions to see and exciting things to do. Perhaps the most visited of all is the fantasy village of Portmeirion, built from the 1920s to the 1970s by Sir Clough Williams-Ellis, made famous by the TV series *The Prisoner* in 1966 and 1967.

There are three National Parks in Wales, and Snowdonia, at some 840 square miles, is the largest and certainly the most dramatic. Set up in 1951, and embracing a number of mountain and hill ranges, Snowdonia National Park (Parc Cenedlaethol Eryri in Welsh) extends southwards from Snowdon as far as Aberdovey and Machynlleth, eastwards to Bala, and northwards to Conwy. In the west the park borders the Llyn Peninsula and the Cambrian coast.

There are several routes up to the summit of Snowdon, beginning at various points around its base. Some call for more energy than others, but the least arduous ascent is by the Snowdon Mountain Railway that runs from Llanberis. The most popular walk follows the railway. In and around nearby Betws-y-Coed, the walking is gentler and includes surviving tracts of the vast forests that once covered much of Wales. From the earliest times, this region was mined for its minerals. Gold was mined here long before the Romans arrived and, as recently as the 19th century, there were mini-gold rushes in a belt that stretched from Bontddu along the line of the River Mawddach. Copper, lead and slate were also mined up until the start of the 20th century, and the scars left by those industries can still be seen today. Several of the mines have found new roles as visitor attractions, along with the little railways that once carried the minerals from the mines and quarries to the coast.

In the middle of the 19th century, the coastal villages and towns, many of them obscure, quiet fishing communities, were put on the map and changed radically in character with the arrival of the main railway network. As the fashion for sea air grew and communications were made easier, they became popular seaside resorts and, today, many of them still retain Victorian and Edwardian buildings constructed to cater for holidaymakers. The scenery throughout the region is truly inspirational, and few would disagree with the verdict of the 19th century traveller and writer George Borrow:

"Perhaps in all the world there is no region more picturesquely beautiful."

The Llyn Peninsula

DINAS DINLLE
3 miles S of Caernarfon off the A499

🏛 Fort St David   🏛 Fort Williamsburg

🏚 Dinas Dinlle Fort

Dinas Dinlle is seaside village at the mouth of the Menai Strait. With a shingle beach and cliffs overlooking Caernarfon Bay, there are many pleasant spots to picnic and enjoy the views down the Llyn Peninsula or across the bay to Anglesey. At the beach's northerly tip at Belan lies **Fort St David**, which was built in the 18th century along with **Fort Williamsburg** at Glynllivon. It was constructed by the first Lord

Newborough, who felt concern over the threat of invasion by Napoleon; his lordship also raised and equipped his own private army, The Royal Caernarfonshire Grenadiers which, by the time of his death in 1807, had cost him a quarter of his fortune. **Dinas Dinlle Fort**, overlooking she shore, is much older, as it dates from the Iron Age.

LLANDWROG
4 miles S of Caernarfon off the A499

🏛 Parish Church of St Tyrog

Llandwrog was built to serve the estate of Lord Newborough at Glynllifon Park, and memorials to the Newborough family may be seen in the **Parish Church of St Tyrog**.

Y GOEDEN EIRIN

Dolydd, Caernarfon, Gwynedd LL54 7EF
Tel: 01286 830942 Mobile: 0770 849 1234
e-mail: john_rowlands@tiscali.co.uk
website: www.ygoedeneirin.co.uk

Sitting within 20 acres of land, the four star Y Goeden Eirin is a superb bed and breakfast establishment that offers comfortable, spacious yet cosy, accommodation at affordable prices. There is a double room in the main house that boasts a TV, settee, desk, small dressing room and bathroom. An outhouse has been tastefully converted to offer two further rooms, called Cwt Môr and Cwt Mynydd (Sea and Mountain Rooms). Cwt Môr has twin beds, and has shelves full of books in English and Welsh, while Cwt Mynydd has a double bed and an old Welsh oak dresser. Each room has a TV, cafetière and herbal tea making facilities. The B&B is owned and personally managed by Eluned and John Rowlands, and they place great emphasis on making their guests very welcome, so much so that a carafe of sherry, fresh fruit or Welsh biscuits await

them in the rooms. In the summer months, it is possible to eat out of doors at the traditional slate table, admiring the surrounding scenery.

Though Y Goeden Eirin is not a restaurant in the conventional sense, both Eluned and John place great emphasis on food, and arriving here for a meal is like visiting a family home and eating with them. The establishment can hold up 12 to 15 diners in its dining room, which has a relaxed and informal atmosphere. The food is all homemade from only the finest locally sourced produce wherever possible. If you have special dietary needs, they can be discussed by phone beforehand. Y Goedin Eirin has a restaurant licence, so you can enjoy a drink with your meal.

🏛 historic building   🖼 museum   🏚 historic site   ◔ scenic attraction   🌱 flora and fauna

CLYNNOG FAWR
10 miles SW of Caernarfon on the A499

🏤 Parish Church of St Beuno   🏛 St Beuno's Well

🏛 Bachwen

This typical Llyn Peninsula village on the Heritage Coast is famous for its remarkably large and beautiful **Parish Church of St Beuno**, which stands on the site of a chapel founded by the saint around AD 616. One of the sons of the royal family of Morgannwg, St Beuno had great influence in North Wales and he built his chapel on land which was presented to him by Cadwallon, King of Gwynedd. St Beuno's burial place and his shrine can be seen in this early 16th century building, which lies on the Pilgrims' Route to Bardsey Island. For many years, his tomb was thought to have curative powers.

Nearby is **St Beuno's Well**, whose waters were also thought to cure all manner of illness and conditions, especially if the sufferer had first visited the church. Close by, and virtually on the seafront, stands the capstone and three uprights of **Bachwen**, a neolithic burial chamber.

TREFOR
3½ miles SW of Clynnog Fawr off the A499

🏛 Tre'r Ceiri   ⛰ Yr Eifl   ⛰ Gurn Ddu

⛰ Bwlch Mawr

This coastal former quarry village is dominated by **Yr Eifl** (The Rivals), which lies to the southwest and which, from its 1,850 foot summit, affords stunning views out over Caernarfon Bay to Anglesey and across the Llyn Peninsula. On the southeastern slopes of the hill is **Tre'r Ceiri** (Town of

Giants), one of the finest Iron Age forts in the country. A stone wall surrounds this once heavily populated circle of 150 huts, some of it three feet high.

The road between here and Clynnog Fawr passes by the **Gurn Ddu** and **Bwlch Mawr** hills which sweep down towards the sandy beach.

NEFYN
9 miles SW of Clynnog Fawr on the A497

🏤 Old St Mary's Church   🏛 Garn Boduan

🏛 Llyen Historical and Maritime Museum

Once a fishing village, this resort was granted a charter in 1355, along with Pwllheli, by the Black Prince. It was here in 1284 that Edward

Tre'r Ceiri, Trefor

🎞 stories and anecdotes   🐦 famous people   🎨 art and craft   🎭 entertainment and sport   🚶 walks

CAEAU CAPEL HOTEL

Nefyn, Gwynedd LL53 6EB
Tel: 01758 720240 Fax: 01758 720750
e-mail: gwestycaeaucapel@hotmail.com
web: www.caeaucapelhotel.com

Caeau Capel Hotel is a delightful Victorian country house set in an acre-and-a-half of tranquil grounds in Nefyn, on the lovely Lleyn Peninsula. Run by resident owners Ruth and Ian Stagg, the hotel has 17 tastefully furnished en suite bedrooms ranging from singles to a four-poster double and family rooms. All have TV, clock radio and tea/coffee making facilities, and some have balconies from which to enjoy the sea view. A residents' bar, two comfortable lounges and a games room with pool and darts provide ample room to relax, and there's a putting green on the front lawn.

Breakfast is served from 8.30am to 9am, and the optional evening meal at 7.30pm – home-cooked, using as much fresh local produce as possible. This is good golfing country, and the hotel has special concessions with no fewer than seven local courses, including the championship course at Royal St David's and the popular 27-hole Nefyn & District course a mile from the hotel. Many other outdoor activities are available locally, and there are interesting places to visit all around – castles, museums, gardens, National Trust houses, old mines and craft centres.

I celebrated his conquest over Wales. Housed in **Old St Mary's Church**, whose tower supports a sailing ship weathervane, is the **Lleyn Historical and Maritime Museum**, an excellent place to visit to find out more about this interesting and beautiful part of Wales. To the southwest of the village is **Garn Boduan**, an Iron Age hill fort where the foundations of over 100 buildings can still be seen. Three defensive walls surrounded the fort, though its position alone made it almost impregnable. It can be accessed from the B4354, close to its junction with the A497.

Pwllheli

🏯 Penarth Fawr

Sitting on the south coast of the Lleyn Peninsula, Pwllheli is its chief town, and is often referred to as the 'jewel' in the Welsh scenic crown. Like Nefyn, it was granted a charter in 1355. This was given by the Black Prince to Nigel de Loryng, the local lord of the manor, who had helped the Prince win the Battle of Poitiers. A popular holiday resort with all the usual amusements, this is also still a market town, though its once busy port, where wine was imported from the Continent, is now home to pleasure craft, with a 420-berth marina and an annual sailing regatta. During the National Eisteddfod in 1925, three members of the Army of Welsh Home Rulers met with three members of the Welsh Movement at the town's Temperance Hotel and joined forces to form the political party, Plaid Cymru.

BRYAN WILLIAMS

80 High Street, Pwllheli, Gwynedd LL53 5RR
Tel: 01758 612279
e-mail: shop@bwjellers.freeserve.co.uk

For over 40 years, Bryan Williams has been in the jewellery, watch making and engraving trade, and his shop in Pwllheli is known throughout the area for the wide range of items stocked and his skills in engraving and watch repair. He stocks not only watches by such makes as Lorus, Tissot, Casio, Adidas and Kenneth Cole, but also a great selection of clocks and barometers.

This is a family-owned business, and his range of fine jewellery is impressive. Here you are sure to find a souvenir or a gift for a loved one, such as Clogau Gold items, with a touch of rare Welsh gold in them! He also stocks Nao figurines as well as rings, chains, brooches in gold and silver. He carries a great stock of trophies, cups and glassware which can be engraved or etch on the premises.

Bryan, family and staff are keen to welcome you to their fascinating shop, and to the shop across the road, J & L Jewellers. You can browse to your heart's content and there is no obligation to buy. You will receive all the help and advice you need to make a purchase. The shop also offers a full watch repair service, and they will gladly change watch batteries for you. So come

---

PYSGOD LLYN SEAFOODS

Y Maes Pwllheli, Gwynedd LL53 5HA
Tel: 01758 614292
e-mail: sales@llynseafoods.co.uk website: www.llynseafoods.co.uk

If you're a lover of seafood, then head for **Pysgod Llyn Seafoods** in the centre of Pwllheli. Here you will find local fish and shellfish - all fresh and inviting - in a small, intriguing shop that has a distinct nautical theme.

It is owned and run by the husband and wife team of Kathryn and Stephen Williams, and Stephen, who is a former chef, will not only offer help and advice about your purchases, he might even throw in a recipe or two as well!

There is always a fine stock of fish on offer, from whole fish to fillets. The familiar cod, haddock and salmon are always popular, but you can also choose from the more exotic tuna and snapper, and shellfish such as crab, lobster and langoustines. The shop also sells award-winning homemade fish soup and sauces, as well as traditional fish accompaniments such as lemons, new potatoes and asparagus.

This is also the place to get all your ready meals, freshly made on the premises: fisherman's pie, seafood pancakes, marinated sea bass and so on to cook at home. The delicatessen counter features mouth-watering products including homemade patés, potted shrimps, fishcakes and tartlets.

You won't be disappointed if you come to Pysgod Llyn Seafoods.

Just to the east of the town lies **Penarth Fawr**, an interesting 15th century manor house.

Around Pwllheli

ABERERCH
2 miles E of Pwllheli off the A497

🏠 Parish Church of St Cawrdal

🕊 Robert ap Gwilym Dhu

The **Parish Church of St Cawrdal** was built in the 14th and 15th centuries on the foundations of a much older building. It was founded in the 6th century by Cawrdaf, who was the son of Prince Caradog Freichfras of Brecon. In the churchyard is the grave of **Robert ap Gwilym Dhu** (Robert Williams)

and his wife. He lived between 1776 and 1850, and was a poet and hymn writer.

CHWILOG
4¹⁄₂ miles NE of Pwllheli on the B4354

🏠 Talhenbont Hall   🏠 Parish Church of Llangybi

Close to the village lies **Talhenbont Hall**, an early 17th century manor house that was once the home of Sir William Vaughan, and was used as a garrison for Cromwellian troops. A place of history with its fair share of ghosts, the hall was used, during the Civil War, as a garrison for Parliamentary soldiers. However, what attracts most visitors to the hall are its magical grounds, through which the River Dwyfach flows in a series of waterfalls and, as well as the nature and river trails, there is an adventure playground.

PEN-LLYN LUSITANO STUD & RIDING CENTRE
Llaniestyn, Pwllheli, Gwynedd LL53 8SL
Tel: 01758 730741
website: www.lusitanocymru.co.uk

The Pendlebury family have been breeding and training horses at the **Pen-Llyn Lusitano Stud and Riding Centre** on the Llyn peninsula for over 30 years. It is famed as one of the foremost studs in the land, holding the finest bloodlines. The mares here have been bred from three of the most famous Portuguese stallions of all times.

The centre offers riding breaks for all people, from beginners to the most experienced, among some lovely countryside. There are treks along quiet country lanes, mountain treks and pub/beach rides that are all thoroughly enjoyable, plus stable days which include a hack and a lesson. The riding centre also offers pure and part bred Lusitanos for sale which may be kept at Pen-Llyn in the livery stables.

The beautifully even-tempered Lusitano (named after the Latin word for Portugal - 'Lusitania') horses are ideal for dressage, and the centre offers lessons in classical dressage individually or in groups. Janine Pendlebury was born into riding, and gives wonderful displays and 'theatre' events all over the country, including the *Sons of the Wind* performance.

So if you want to take part in horse trekking or riding, or just want to admire these wonderfully elegant and intelligent animals, come along to the stables and see them in action.

🏠 historic building   📷 museum   🏛 historic site   🍃 scenic attraction   🌿 flora and fauna

LLANGYBI

5 miles NE of Pwllheli
off the B4354

🏚 St Cybi's Well   🏚 Garn Pentyrch

St Cybi's Wells, Llangybi

Just to the north of the village is **St Cybi's Well**, which was reputed to have curative properties for such diseases and illneses as warts, blindness, scurvy and rheumatism. The well was established in the 6th century when St Cybi was in the process of setting up religious cells and a monastery in Holyhead. It is sheltered by an unusual building with beehive vaulting, which is thought to be unique in Wales. Behind it is the Iron Age fort of **Garn Pentyrch**. A story tells of a boy who played with the fairies among the stones of Garn Pentrych, and who eventually disappeared for two years, though he looked no older when he came back. The **Parish Church of Llangybi** is medieval, and services are only held here five times a year.

LLANYSTUMDWY

6½ miles E of Pwllheli on the A497

🏚 Highgate   🏚 Parish Church of St John

🏚 Memorial Gates   🏚 Lloyd George Museum

🐦 David Lloyd George

This peaceful little coastal village is best known as being the home of **David Lloyd George**, the Member of Parliament for Caernarfon for 55 years and the Prime Minister who, at the beginning of the 20th century, was responsible for social reform as well as seeing the country through the Armistice at the end of World War I. Though born in Manchester, Lloyd George's childhood home, **Highgate**, is now just as it

would have been when the great statesman lived there, and the **Lloyd George Museum** features a Victorian schoolroom and an exhibition of the life of this reforming Liberal politician. When he died in 1945, he was buried beneath the boulder where he used to sit and think while young. It sits on the outskirts of the village, across the river from the **Parish Church of St John**. Opposite his grave is a set of **Memorial Gates** presented to the village by Pwllheli in 1952. They feature an elephant and a castle - elephants are part of the town's coat of arms.

He won this tribute in Parliament from Winston Churchill: "As a man of action, resource and creative energy he stood, when at his zenith, without a rival. His name is a household word throughout our Commonwealth of Nations. He was the greatest Welshman which that unconquerable race has produced since the age of the Tudors. Much of his work abides, some of it will grow greatly in the future, and those who come after us will find the pillars of his life's toil upstanding, massive and indestructible." The Museum is open Easter to October, and at other times by appointment.

🏚 stories and anecdotes   🐦 famous people   🔎 art and craft   🖊 entertainment and sport   🚶 walks

CRICCIETH
8 miles E of Pwllheli on the A497

🏰 Criccieth Castle   🌿 Criccieth Festival

🏰 Parish Church of St Catherine

This small family resort lies near the northeast corner of Cardigan Bay and enjoys fine views down the Llyn coastline and northeastwards to Snowdonia. Unlike many of the other resorts on the peninsula, Criccieth is more reminiscent of a south coast seaside town rather than one set in North Wales.

An attractive Victorian town, it is dominated by **Criccieth Castle**, which stands on a rocky outcrop with commanding views over the sea. Built in the early 13th century by Llywelyn the Great as a stronghold of the native Welsh princes, it was captured in 1283

and extended by Edward I; but the core of the structure - the powerful twin towered gatehouse - still exists from the original fortification. Despite Edward's strengthening of the defences, in 1404 the castle was taken by Owain Glyndwr and burnt and the castle walls still bear the scorch marks. One of the best preserved of the 13th century castles to be found in the North Wales countryside, the romantic ruins of Criccieth Castle have inspired many artists down the centuries including JMW Turner, who used it as the backdrop for a famous painting of storm-wrecked sailors. The annual **Criccieth Festival** is renowned for its traditional Celtic music and song.

The **Parish Church of St Catherine** was founded, on what is thought to be the site of a

BLODAU ELERI FLORIST

34 High Street, Criccieth, Gwynedd LL52 0BT
Tel: 01766 522626
website: www.blodaueleriflorist.co.uk

The firm known as **Blodau Eleri Florist** is a family affair, and was established in 1903. So it has a long history of catering for the people of Criccieth, and supplying all their floral needs. The original high standards set over 100 years ago have been maintained and even improved since then, and it remains a highly respected shop patronised by locals and visitors alike.

They can provide flowers and gifts for any occasion, such as a birthday, Valentine's Day or an anniversary. They also provide a sympathetic, discreet yet professional service that ensures that your floral tributes reflect the love and affection that a loved one deserves at a difficult time.

The floral arrangements are inspirational, as are the gifts, which are hand-crafted to suit the occasion. These gifts can enhance any floral arrangement, and this, coupled with the range of gifts, such as balloons, teddy bears and chocolates, add that extra something. They can also supply champagnes and selected wines so that you can show your love for someone. There is a same day or next delivery service throughout Gwynedd using their own vans, and being a member of Interflora they can deliver across the UK and even worldwide. Corporate events are no problem, so call and discuss your needs.

They are located in Criccieth's High Street, and the shop always has a wide range of flowers and giftware. The design-to order service is available at all times, and the prices always reflect amazing value for money.

🏰 historic building   🏛 museum   🏛 historic site   🌀 scenic attraction   🌿 flora and fauna

Celtic monastery, by Edward I when he captured the castle and gave Criccieth its royal charter in 1284. In about 1500 it was enlarged by the addition of a northern isle and arcade, and in the 19th century it was fully restored, with the aisle (which was in imminent danger of collapsing) being rebuilt.

GOLAN
9 miles NE of Pwllheli off the A487

🏚 Brynkir Woollen Mill

Between the entrances to two wonderful valleys, Cwm Pennant and Cwm Ystradllyn, and a mile off the A487 Porthmadog-Caernarfon road, lies **Brynkir Woollen Mill**. Originally a corn mill, it was converted over 150 years ago for woollen cloth production and, though now modernised (the River Henwy is used to generate electricity although the waterwheel still turns), visitors can still see the various machines that are used in the production process: Tenterhook Willey, carders, spinning mules, doubling and hanking machines, cheese and bobbin winder, warping mill and looms.

TREMADOG
12 miles E of Pwllheli on the A487

🏚 Peniel Methodist Chapel

🏚 Parish Church of St Mary   🦉 TE Lawrence

This village, developed, like its close neighbour Porthmadog, by William Alexander Madocks, is a wonderful example of early 19th century town planning and contains many fine Regency buildings. Madocks, who was the MP for Boston in Lincolnshire, bought the land in 1798 and built Tremadog on the reclaimed land in classical style, with broad streets and a handsome market square with a backdrop of cliffs. He hoped that the town would be a key point on the intended main route from the south of England to Ireland, but his rivals in Parliament preferred the North Wales route, with Holyhead becoming the principal port. The little town of Tremadog, with its well-planned streets and fine buildings, remains as a memorial to Madocks, who died in Paris in 1828, where he is buried in the Père Lachaise cemetery (see also Porthmadog). **Peniel Methodist Chapel** is unusual, in that it is in the shape of a Greek temple, while the **Parish Church of St Mary** is a good example of a Gothic revival church. Inside is a plaque commemorating the Madocks family. The soldier and author **TE Lawrence** (of Arabia) was born in Tremadog in 1888 and the poet Shelley is known to have visited on several occasions.

PORTMEIRION
13½ miles E of Pwllheli off the A487

🏚 Plas Brondanw   🏚 Brondanw

🦉 Portmeirion Pottery

This very special village, in a wonderful setting on a wooded peninsula overlooking Traeth Bay, was conceived and created by the Welsh architect Sir Clough Williams-Ellis between 1925 and 1972. An inveterate campaigner against the spoiling of Britain's landscape, he set out to illustrate that building in a beautiful location did not mean spoiling the environment. In looks, this is the least Welsh place in Wales: the 50 or so buildings, some of which consist only of a façade, were inspired by a visit Williams-Ellis made to Sorrento and Portofino in Italy. The **Portmeirion Pottery** was established in 1960 by Clough's daughter Susan Williams-Ellis and her husband Euan. Susan had studied under Henry Moore and Graham Sutherland, and her classic designs include *Botanic Garden* (1972) and the recently relaunched *Totem* from

Portmeirion

Distance: *2.8 miles (4.5 kilometres)*

Typical time: *90 mins*

Height gain: *100 metres*

Map: *Explorer OL18*

Walk: *www.walkingworld.com ID:1952*

Contributor: *Pat Roberts*

There is a large free car park at Portmeirion. From the A487 east of Porthmadoc, at Minffordd, follow signs for Portmeirion.

DESCRIPTION:

This easy walk can be coupled with a visit to Portmeirion. It has easy walking with one climb after Waymark 06 and the views are good. If you time your walk to coincide with the Festiniog Train timetable, there are opportunities for train-spotting.

FEATURES:

River, Wildlife, Birds, Flowers, Great Views, Mostly Flat, Woodland

WALK DIRECTIONS:

1 | It is a large car park, with an entrance and an exit. Wherever you are parked in the large car park, make for the entrance and walk back up the road you drove down.

2 | Take this bridleway off to the right. It passes a few houses and a three-fingered bridleway sign, where we go straight on. There are lovely views across to the mountains. After rising slowly, the track loses some height before reaching a road.

3 | At the road, turn left to the main A487. Cross with care and continue down the narrow road straight ahead. Cross the Festiniog Railway line, eventually to reach a T-Junction.

4 | Here go left and walk this quiet minor road, eventually to reach the A487 again and walk on the pavement, maintaining direction, towards Porthmadoc.

5 | Just after the warning signs for the tolls, but before the actual toll, cross the road to a footpath sign leading up to Boston Lodge Halt. You may be lucky to see one of the steam locomotives here. Walk a few metres left to a pedestrian crossing (just sleepers over the lines).

6 | Cross the line and go over the stile. The track swings right before swinging left and following the wall on your left. It then rises quite steeply between two walls, passing through a double gate before dropping slightly to another gate.

7 | Through the gate and across the gravel track, continue in the same direction down a green track with a wall on your left.

8 | Go through this gap in a high wall and the gate behind it, to pass through a similar gap in another high wall. Ignore a path off to your right, but continue ahead through another gate and down an enclosed path. Turn left as directed to reach a ladder-stile.

9 | DO NOT CROSS THIS STILE. Turn right down a narrow path to the car park.

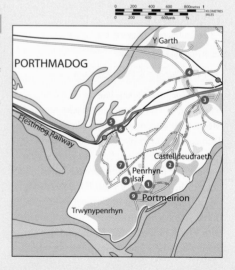

Portmeirion

amenities, which include a cinema, the **Porthmadog Pottery**, where visitors can try throwing pots, and galleries. Out of the town, towards Tremadog and across The Cob, the scenery to the left is magical and, at low tide, cattle graze alongside herons and other seabirds and waders.

Seeing Porthmadog today it is hard to believe that this was once the busiest slate port in

the 1960s. Williams-Ellis' ancestral home, **Plas Brondanw**, lies some five miles away, up the A4085 northeast of Garreg, and the marvellous gardens here make the extra journey well worthwhile. Designed to please the eye, and also provide some fabulous views over the mountain scenery, there are, among the splendid plants, charming statues and elegant topiary terraces. Although less well known than the village and gardens at Portmeirion, the gardens at **Brondanw** are considered by some to be Clough Williams-Ellis' most important creation, and certainly the most beautiful. Sir Clough continued working up until his death at the age of 94 in 1978.

PORTHMADOG
12½ miles E of Pwllheli on the A487

🏛 Maritime Museum   🏺 Porthmadog Pottery

🏛 Madog Car and Motorcycle Museum

🚂 Ffestiniog Railway   🚂 Welsh Highland Railway

This is a busy town that can become very busy as holidaymakers take advantage of its many

North Wales and, in fact, the town would never have existed had it not been for William Madocks, also responsible for neighbouring Tremadog. Member of Parliament for Boston, Lincolnshire, and a great entrepreneur, Madocks drained the mud flats that made up this estuary to create land for grazing cattle in the early 19th century. The Cob embankment, built to keep the tides at bay, enclosed some 7,000 acres of land and re-routed the River Glaslyn to produce a deep water channel that was ideal for the docks. Naming Porthmadog after himself (nearby Tremadog was named after his brother), he saw the beginning of the blossoming of the town in the 1820s. The history of the town and its waterfront is described in the **Maritime Museum** where, too, the importance of the trade in slate and Porthmadog's shipbuilding industry is told.

Porthmadog is also home to both the **Ffestiniog Railway** (see panel on page 100), the world's oldest narrow track passenger carrying railway, and the recently extended **Welsh Highland Railway**. Maintaining the theme of transport, the **Madog Car and Motorcycle Museum** displays a gleaming collection of vintage British vehicles.

LLANBEDROG

3½ miles SW of Pwllheli on the A499

🏛 Plas Glyn y Weddw   🏛 Parish Church of St Pedrog

🏛 Myndd Tir y Cwmwd   🌿 Tin Man

Named after the 6th century St Pedrog, Llanbedrog lies on the other side of **Mynydd Tir y Cwmwd** from Abersoch. The views from the summit are stunning, and another attraction is the **Tin Man**, a modern sculpture made of beachcombed material. In Llanbedrog itself is **Plas Glyn y Weddw**, a neo-Gothic mansion which houses a collection of Welsh furniture and holds various Welsh art exhibitions. The **Parish Church of St Pedrog** was founded in the 6th century by St Pedrog. The present church is mainly Victorian, though there are medieval fragments dating back to the 13th century.

Ffestiniog Railway

Harbour Station, Porthmadog, Gwynedd LL49 9NF
Tel: 01766 516000
e-mail: enquiries@festrail.co.uk
website: www.ffestiniograilway.co.uk

The world-famous **Ffestiniog Railway** was originally built to transport slate from the mines to Porthmadog, where it was transferred to ships for export and use throughout the world. Like many other little railways, its original role has been superseded, but this one has found fame as one of the country's leading attractions. The world's oldest narrow-gauge passenger-carrying railway, it runs behind steam locomotives on the 13½-mile journey from Porthmadog to Blaenau Ffestiniog; the route climbs 700 feet into Snowdonia National Park through pastures and forests, by lakes and waterfalls, round horseshoe bends and at one point turning back on itself in a complete spiral.

Calling en route at Minffordd, Penrhyn and Tan-y-Bwlch, the trip takes just over an hour. Trains can be hired for private functions, anniversaries or fine dining evenings, and the year brings many special events, including trips on vintage trains using rolling stock dating from as far back as 1860. The Ffestiniog found itself at the cutting edge of railway technology in the 1870s: pivoted wheels, or bogie, which gave a superior ride and allowed coaches to take curves more smoothly, had appeared in North America in 1873 and it was on the Ffestiniog that it first came to the UK.

There are shops selling gifts and souvenirs at the termini and Tan-y-Bwlch. Porthmadog has a café serving anything from sandwiches and snacks to three-course meals, and the café at Tan-y-Bwlch is open while the trains run. Most trains have corridor coaches where refreshments are sold.

The railway may be little, but it provides a big experience with a variety of driving programmes, starting with the more easily handled Penrhyn Lady class locomotives *Linda*, *Blanche* or *Taliesin*, leading up to the ultimate challenge of one of the famous Double Fairlies hauling 10 carriages. Drivers will enjoy one-to-one personal tuition and work an eight hour shift, with 14 miles driving and 14 miles firing. Another course involves operating one of the oldest steam engines in the sidings at Minffordd, shunting a rake of slate wagons.

🏛 historic building   🏛 museum   🏛 historic site   🌀 scenic attraction   🌿 flora and fauna

ABERSOCH
6 miles SW of Pwllheli on the A499

🏛 Castellmarch   🌱 Tudwal's Islands

🎭 March Amheirchion

A popular family resort with safe beaches, Abersoch lies on each side of the estuary of the River Soch. Its sheltered harbour attracts a wide variety of pleasure craft and just off the coast lie **St Tudwal's Islands** - so called because the saint founded a religious cell there in the 6th century. Both islands are now privately owned and are the home of bird sanctuaries.

The site of the 17th century mansion, **Castellmarch**, was said to be the home of **March Amheirchion**, one of King Arthur's Knights. Reputed to have the ears of a horse, March (the name is Welsh for horse) kept them hidden and killed anyone who saw them - burying the bodies in a nearby reed bed. However, one day a man cut one of the reeds to make a pipe. However, when it was played, it made no sound other than the words 'March has horse's ears'. When March heard about this, he set off to kill the man for mocking him, but relented when he himself tried to play the pipe and got exactly the same words. Thereafter he made no attempt to hide his ears.

RHIW
11 miles SW of Pwllheli off the B4413

🏛 Plas yn Rhiw   🕊 RS Thomas

This hamlet lies in a miniature pass and overlooks **Porth Neigwl** (Hell's Mouth), a

---

FLIPSIDE JEWELLERY

1/2 Abenuchaf, Lon Garmon, Abersoch, Gwynedd LL53 7UG
Tel: 01758 712772 Fax: 01758 712841
e-mail: simon@flipsidejewellery.co.uk
website: www.flipsidejewellery.co.uk

There are two very different faces to the ever popular Flipside jewellery. On the one hand they are the purveyors of simple and elegant handmade contemporary jewellery, created on the premises by silversmith Simon Harris who also makes use of more unusual semi precious crystals in his designs. Commissions are undertaken in silver, gold and platinum and Flipside is fast becoming a favourite for couples looking for extra special wedding rings, as they can discuss the design process with Simon in an informal and personal way.

The other renowned face of Flipside is as a destination for "fabulous, frivolous frippery from far flung corners of the world". The avid retail therapist receives a colourful welcome to this magpie's nest overflowing with bright sparkling goodies and the most disciplined customer will find it hard to walk away empty handed. They try to fulfil your quest for the perfect gift for that hard-to-buy-for person who has everything. (A designer fly swatter as an unexpected gift could be the ticket!).

Set in beautiful farm buildings, Flipside is set back from the village centre, overlooking the harbour and is just a short stroll but there is a car park if the weather is less favourable.

🎭 stories and anecdotes   🕊 famous people   🎨 art and craft   🎪 entertainment and sport   🚶 walks four mile sweep of beach so called because of its reputation for strong currents. It is now a favourite place for wind surfing.

Sheltered from strong gales by Mynydd Rhiw, **Plas yn Rhiw** is a small, part-medieval, part-Tudor, part-Georgian manor house which was given to the National Trust in 1952 by the unconventional Keating sisters from Nottingham. The three spinsters, Eileen, Lorna and Honora, purchased the property in 1938 and lovingly restored it after it had lain neglected for some 20 years. This they did with the help of their friend Sir Clough Williams-Ellis, the architect of Portmeirion.

The house is surrounded by glorious grounds, which were also restored by the sisters, providing fabulous views over Porth Neigwl. Visitors can wander through ornamental gardens and, in the spring, the bluebell and snowdrop woodlands. At one time the poet and clergyman **RS Thomas** (1913-2000) lived in one of the estate cottages, where he wrote some of his finest poetry (see also Eglwys Fach).

LLANFAELRYS
12 miles SW of Pwllheli off the B4413

🏚 Parish Church of St Maelrhys

The delightful **Parish Church of St Maelrhys** is a simple oblong measuring about 42 feet long by 12 feet wide. The nave and font dates from the 15th century. Maelrhys was born in Britanny, and was the cousin of Cadfan, abbot of Bardsey.

ABERDARON
13½ miles SW of Pwllheli on the B4413

🏚 Parish Church of St Hywyn   🏛 Castel Odo

A small and delightful village which is often busy in the height of summer. It was here, in 1405, that the Tripartite Indenture - the agreement to divide Britain with Wales becoming independent under the rule of Glyndwr - was signed. However, these plans were subsequently ruined by Henry IV and Henry V. Close to the sea and originally dating from the 6th century, the **Parish Church of St Hywyn** is thought to have sheltered the 12th century Prince of Wales, Gryffydd ap Rhys, from marauding Saxons. During the Civil War, it once again proved a place of sanctuary as Cromwell's soldiers also sought refuge here. It was founded in the 6th century by St Hywyn. Its oldesr parts date from the 12th century, though most of the building dates from an enlargement of 1417. It was closely

Abersoch

associated with the abbey on Bardsey island, and had the right of sanctuary.

Aberdaron

One of Aberdaron's most famous natives was Richard Robert Jones, the son of a local carpenter. A strange vagabond, known as Dic Aberdaron, this self-educated linguist is said to have spoken 35 languages and is renowned for having compiled dictionaries in Welsh, Greek and Hebrew. The great poet RS Thomas also hailed from Aberdaron. He wrote many inspired lines about his beloved country, summed up in this extract:

Every mountain and stream, every farm and little lane announces to the world that landscape is something different in Wales.

A mile or so from the village lies **Castel Odo**, an Iron Age fort providing evidence that there have been five different occupations of the peninsula dating back to the 4th century BC.

UWCHMYNYDD
15 miles SW of Pwllheli off the B4413

🏠 Church of St Mary 🏛 Porth Oer ⛰ Mynydd Mawr

⛰ Braich-y-Pwll

Situated on the wild and beautiful tip of the Llyn Peninsula, it was from here that the first pilgrims set out across the two-mile wide Barsey Sound to Bardsey Island in the Middle Ages. On the summit of **Mynydd Mawr**, the National Trust has converted an old coastguard hut into a small information point. The National Trust is responsible for much of the land towards the tip of the Lleyn Peninsula, including the ecologically outstanding coastal heath of **Braich-y-Pwll**, where the ruins of the **Church of St Mary**, once used by the pilgrims, can still be seen. This heath is the spring and summer home of a variety of plant life and birds, including fulmars, kittiwakes, cormorants, guillemots and the rare chough. A similar variety has its home on the tiny islands of Dinas Fawr and Dinas Bach.

Five miles east of Aberdaron, on the south side of the Peninsula, Porth Ysgo and Penarfyndd cover 245 acres of beaches and cliffs, while two miles northwest of the village Mynydd Anelog is an 116-acre area of ancient commonland with the remains of prehistoric hut circles. Here, as in the other NT stretches of coastland on the Peninsula, is found our friend the chough, a relative of the crow with a distinctive red bill. Apart from here, this rare bird is usually found only in Pembrokeshire and on a part of the western coast of Scotland. The curiously named **Porth Oer**

(Whistling Sands), located off the B4417 by Methlem, is worth a visit as at certain stages of the tide the sands seem literally to whistle when walked upon. The noise is caused by the rubbing together of minute quartz granules.

BARDSEY ISLAND
17 miles SW of Pwllheli off the B4413

🏛 Abbey of St Mary   🏛 Lord Newborough's Crypt

🏛 Lighthouse   🏚 Hermit's Cave

This wild, whale-shaped island in the Irish Sea has long been a place of pilgrimage, and has inspired many legends. One says that this is King Arthur's Avalon, another that his magician Merlin sleeps in a glass castle on the island. St Cadfan built an abbey here in the 6th century, though this would not have been an abbey as we know it today. It would have been an area of ground marked off with a low wall within which would have been chapels, churches, monks cells and other buildings. On this site, in the 12th century, was built the Augustinian **Abbey of St Mary**. It was dissolved in 1537, and now only a few walls now remain. St Dyfrig died here in AD 522, and though his remains were later transferred to Llandaff Cathedral in Cardiff, it was from about this time that Bardsey became a place of pilgrimage. At one time it was considered that three pilgrimages to this holy island was equivalent to one to Rome.

Next to the abbey ruins is **Lord Newborough's Crypt**, where the once owner of the island is buried. There is also the **Hermit's Cave**, though it is doubtful if a hermit ever lived here, as it is too small. The **Lighthouse** on the south of the island was erected in 1821, and is the only square lighthouse maintained by Trinity House.

The island is now an important bird and field observatory. Bardsey is best known for its vast numbers of breeding shearwaters. A boat makes the 20-minute trip to the island from the hidden fishing cove of Porth Meudwy by Aberdaron.

The island's name is Norse in origin and the Welsh name, Ynys Enlii, means Island of Currents - a reference to the treacherous waters that separate Bardsey from the mainland.

Llanberis

🏛 Dolbadarn Castle   🏛 Welsh Slate Museum

🗺 Snowdon   🚂 Snowdon Mountain Railway

🚂 Llanberis Lake Railway   🚂 Electric Mountain

🚂 Dinorwig Power Station   🗺 Llyn Llydaw

🗺 Padarn Country Park   🗺 Glyder Fawr

🗺 Pass of Llanberis   🐟 Marged Ifan

🎣 Kingfisher Trail   🏊 Snowdon Race

🏊 Snowdon Marathon

🌿 Cwm Derwen Woodland and Wildlife Centre

This former slate-producing community has many attractions to keep the visitor occupied although it is, perhaps, best known for the nearby mountain, **Snowdon**. Rising to some 3,560 feet, this is the highest peak in Wales and the most climbed mountain in Britain. On a clear day, the view from the summit is breathtaking, with Ireland sometimes visible. However, before setting out for the summit it is worth remembering that the weather changes dramatically here, and walkers and climbers should always be prepared. Many reach the summit the easy way, with the help of the **Snowdon Mountain Railway**, a rack and pinion system built in 1896 that has carried millions to the top of the mountain over the years. It is not surprising that this mountainous and inhospitable area is also

---

🏛 historic building   📷 museum   🚂 historic site   🗺 scenic attraction   🌿 flora and fauna

Snowdon Mountain Railway

By the side of the lake is **Cwm Derwen Woodland and Wildlife Centre**, with a woodland discovery trail and a timewalk exhibition with an audio-visual display. Here, too, is the **Welsh Slate Museum**, which tells the story of the slate industry through a variety of exhibitions, a restored slate-carrying incline, a terrace of quarrymen's cottages, audio-visual shows and demonstrations. The De Winton waterwheel is the second largest in Britain and once provided all the power for slate mines.

steeped in legend and mystery. The eagles of Snowdon have long been regarded as oracles of peace and war, triumph and disaster, and Snowdon's peak is said to be a cairn erected over the grave of a giant who was killed by King Arthur. **Llyn Llydaw**, a lake just below Snowdon, is yet another contender for the *Lady of the Lake* story. Arthur himself is supposed to have been fatally wounded at the Battle of Camlann, which some people have identified with 'cwm-y-llan', or the 'valley of the lake'.

For those wanting another train ride or are content with a more sedate journey, the **Llanberis Lake Railway** near Llanberis takes a short trip round Llyn Padarn, during which there are several different views of the mountain. The railway lies in **Padarn Country Park**, which gives access to 800 acres of Snowdonia's countryside and also includes Llyn (Lake) Padarn. The **Kingfisher Trail** is designed specifically for wheelchairs.

Bus tours take visitors deep into the mountain tunnels and the machinery rooms of the **Electric Mountain,** that control the vast quantities of water used by **Dinorwig Power Station**. In Europe's largest man-made cavern the world's most powerful hydro-electric generators are in action.

In such a rugged setting, where life has always been harsh, it comes as no surprise to find that it is said that the strongest woman ever to have lived came from Llanberis. Born in 1696, **Marged Ifan** died at the ripe old age of 105. At 70, it was said, she could outwrestle any man in Wales and could also catch as many foxes in one year as the local huntsmen in 10. After receiving many offers of marriage, Marged is said to have chosen the smallest and most effeminate of her suitors. Tradition has it that she only beat her husband twice: after the first beating he married her and after the second he became an ardent churchgoer!

The **Snowdon Race** takes place every July, and leaves from Llanberis, and finishes there as well. The mountain is five miles away, and is 3,560 feet high. The **Snowdon Marathon**, held every October, also starts and finishes at Llanberis.

The **Pass of Llanberis** (along the A4086) is one of the most desolate stretches of road in Wales and is dominated by Snowdon to the south and the curiously shaped **Glyder Fawr**, 3,279 feet to the north. Sheep graze beside the narrow road, which in some places is almost blocked by boulders and rocks.

Guarding the entrance to the pass and overlooking Llyn Padarn are the substantial remains of **Dolbadarn Castle** which was built by Llywelyn the Great. After the battle of Bryn Derwin, where Llywelyn defeated his two brothers, the victor held Owain ap Gryffydd prisoner here for some 22 years. The last stronghold of the independent princes of Gwynedd, it was from here, in 1283, that Dafydd ap Gryffydd fled from the

English forces of Edward I. The exterior scenes for the film *Carry On Up The Khyber* were shot in and around Llanberis.

BETWS-Y-COED
14½ miles E of Llanberis on the A5

🏛 Parish Church of St Michael 🏛 Waterloo Bridge
🏛 Pont-y-Pair 🏛 Ty Hyll 🏛 Motor Museum
🏛 Conwy Valley Railway Museum 🍃 Swallow Falls
🍃 Gwydyr Forest Park 🍃 Conwy Falls
🍃 Machno Falls 🍃 Fairy Glen Ravine

A sizeable village at the confluence of four beautiful forested valleys, Betws-y-Coed lies on the edge of the **Gwydyr Forest Park** as well as in the Snowdonia National Park. The Forest Park offers horse riding, canoeing, mountain biking and over 20 miles of trails through mountain forests. The stone walls in the park were built by sailors after the defeat of the Spanish Armada to enclose game.

The village first came to prominence with the setting up in 1844 of an artists' colony by

Llanberis Pass

David Cox and other eminent Victorian countryside painters; their work inspired others, and the coming of the railway in 1868 brought the tourists to what soon became a busy holiday centre. The **Parish Church of St Michael**, near the railway station, has been in use since the 14th century and remained the town's major place of worship until the influx of visitors required a larger and more prestigious building. A major attraction is the **Motor Museum**, whose unique collection of vintage and post-vintage cars includes a fabulous Bugatti Type 57. It evolved from the private collection of vehicles owned by the Houghton family, and is housed in an old farm. It is is open daily from 10.30am to 6pm from Easter to October.

As the village is close to the point where the Conwy, Lledr and Llugwy rivers meet, it seems natural that these waterways should play an important role in the development, building and beauty of Betws-y-Coed. Thomas Telford's **Waterloo Bridge**, a marvellous iron construction built in 1815, gracefully spans the River Conwy, and carried an inscription saying that it was built to commemorate the Battle of Waterloo, while the **Pont-y-Pair** ('bridge of the cauldron'),

dating from around 1470, crosses the River Llugwy. Further downstream, an iron suspension footbridge spans the river by the church. However, the main attractions that draw people to this area are the waterfalls: the spectacular multi-level **Swallow Falls** on the River Llugwy, **Conwy Falls**, **Machno Falls** and **Fairy Glen Ravine**.

Next to the railway station is the **Conwy Valley Railway Museum** and shop, a popular place to visit in the summer. The village's most famous, and certainly most curious, attraction is **Ty Hyll**, the Ugly House (now the HQ of the Snowdonia Society), which stands close by the River Llugwy. Apparently this building, which looks as though it was literally thrown together from rough boulders, is an example of hurried assembly (possibly

ANNA DAVIES

Betws-y-Coed, Conwy LL24 0AY
Tel: 01690 710292 Fax: 01690 710433
e-mail: info@annadavies.co.uk
website: www.annadavies.co.uk

In a beautiful village in the heart of Snowdonia National Park, **Anna Davies** sells a wide range of country wear and accessories, home and lifestyle items, gifts, souvenirs and jewellery. The shop was established in 1956 by Anna Davies and it is now owned and run by her daughter Sara and son-in-law Peter. The ground floor is stocked with a wide range of clothing for ladies, gentlemen and children, including outdoor wear, Welsh sheepskin, footwear, hand-knitted garments and accessories. Among the well-known brands are Barbour, Pringle, Bianca, Trespass, Seeland, Schneiders, Ecco and Radley Tula handbags.

On the first floor are Moorcroft and Portmeirion pottery, top-quality ceramics and glass and Clogai Gold, mined deep in the heart of Snowdonia in difficult-to-located veins and therefore very rare – and very desirable. Shop hours are 9 to 6 every day (9 to 5.30 in winter) and most of the goods on display are available by mail order through the excellent website. The distinctive building has many unusual features, including a waterfall that runs from the newest section under the shop and out into the river across the road.

📖 stories and anecdotes   🦜 famous people   🎨 art and craft   🖋 entertainment and sport   🥾 walks

Swallow Falls

superstitious visitor as there are two legends associated with the village inn. The first involves the daughter of a long ago innkeeper, who fell in love with a local farmhand. One night the young man rode up on his white horse and the girl climbed down from her bedroom window and rode off with him, never to be seen again. The second legend concerns a friendly fair-haired lady who watches over all the events here. No one knows for sure whether the two stories are connected.

Close by the village is the **Capel Garmon Burial Chamber**, which dates from around 1500 BC. They are the remains of a long barrow with three burial chambers, one with its capstone still in position.

NANT PERIS
2 miles SE of Llanberis on the A4086

🏠 Parish Church of St Peris   🏛 Well of Peris

Once known as Old Llanberis, the village lies at the opposite end of Llyn Peris from its larger namesake - Llanberis - and at the entrance to the Pass of Llanberis. The **Parish Church of St Peris** dates originally from the 12th century, and is worth visiting because of its 15th century ceiling and chancel screen with a poor box having three locks. It stands on the site of St Peris's original church, was founded in the 6th century. The Pass of Llanberis was once known as Nant y Mynach, or 'valley of the monks', and it may refer to the foundation of the early church. The **Well of Peris**, which lies just north of the village centre, was, until relatively recently, much visited for its healing powers, as well as for wishing. A successful request was said to be signalled by the appearance of a sacred fish.

by two outlaw brothers) in order to obtain freehold on common land in the 15th century. The house was often used as an overnight stop by Irish drovers taking cattle to English markets. The scenery around Betws-y-Coed is truly magnificent, and within minutes of leaving the town centre there are numerous well-marked walks lasting anything from an hour to all day and suiting all energy levels.

CAPEL GARMON
15½ miles E of Llanberis off the A5

🏛 Capel Garmon Burial Chamber

Surrounded by the spectacular scenery of the Snowdonia mountain range, this tiny village has an additional attraction for the

---

🏠 historic building   🏛 museum   🏛 historic site   🔱 scenic attraction   🌿 flora and fauna

SNOWDONIA COAST & INLAND

DOLWYDDELAN

11 miles SE of Llanberis off the A470

🏛 Parish Church of St Gwydellan

🏛 Dolwyddelan Castle

The **Parish Church of St Gwydellan** dates from the 15th century. It was built by a man called Meredydd ab Ieuan, who lived in Cwn Penamnen. However, a band of brigands had taken over an old hospice once owned by the Knights of St John, and were terrorising the area. Rather than leave the place unattended when his household worshipped at the original parish church, some distance away, he had it pulled down, and erected this one nearer where he lived, so that he could rush to

defend it if it were were attacked. It contains St Gwyndellan's Bell, which dates from the 7th century, and was dicsovered in Victorian times on the site of the former church.

Here can be seen the stark remains of **Dolwyddelan Castle**, which is unusual among Welsh castles in that it was constructed by a native Welsh prince rather than by either the English or the Normans. Built between 1210 and 1240 by Llywelyn the Great (who was probably born here in 1173) to control a strategic pass through the mountainous region of his kingdom, the fortress fell to Edward I in 1283. In 1488, the place was acquired by Maredudd ap Levan, who built the village church that now houses his kneeling brass effigy. After Maredudd's death the castle fell into ruin and the modern roof and battlements seen today were added in the 19th century when the core of the castle underwent restoration. However, the beauty of the castle is very much its lonely setting and from here there are stunning mountain views. The Castle is now looked after by CADW - Welsh Historic Monuments. A walk starting at Dolwyddelan provides a succession of glorious views over the surrounding mountains, particularly Snowdon and Moel Siabod. The last part of the walk is along paths and lanes and across meadows by the River Lledr.

PENTREFOELAS

19½ miles SE of Llanberis on the A5

🏛 Parish Church of Pentrefoelas

🏛 Watermill

The **Parish Church of Pentrefoelas** is one of the few in Wales that does not have a dedication. It is Victorian, and

Dolwyddelan Castle

replaced a church built in 1760, which itself was built on the site of an old chapel. Once an upland estate village, Pentrefoelas is now becoming a focal point to the continuation and revival of crafts and skills which were used to maintain the estate; among the attractions is a working **Watermill**.

PENMACHNO
14½ miles SE of Llanberis on the B4406

🏠 Penmachno Woollen Mill	🏠 Penmachno Bridge
🏠 Ty Mawr Wybrnant	🏛 Ty'n y Coed Uchaf

This delightful village of picturesque stone cottages, set in a wooded valley, lies on the River Machno, from which it takes its name. Not only is Penmachno surrounded by glorious countryside but it is also situated within an area that is a stronghold of Welsh culture and here can be found the traditional **Penmachno Woollen Mill**. Visitors to the mill can see the working power looms as they weave the cloth and can also browse through the shop among the finished articles and other Welsh craftwork on display. The sturdy Penmachno Bridge has five arches, and was built in 1785.

To the northwest of the village centre and in the secluded Wybrnant valley lies **Ty Mawr Wybrnant**, the birthplace of Bishop William Morgan (1545-1604) who was the first person to translate the Bible into Welsh (see also St Asaph). Now restored to how it probably appeared in the 16th and 17th centuries, the house (now in the ownership of the National Trust) includes a display of Welsh Bibles, including Morgan's of 1588. A pleasant one-mile walk starts at the house and takes in woodland and the surrounding fields.

To the northeast of the village and approached by a walk alongside the River Machno, lies **Ty'n y Coed Uchaf**, a small farm that gives visitors an insight into the traditional way of life of the Welsh-speaking community in this area.

FFESTINIOG
13½ miles SE of Llanberis on the A470

🏛 Sarn Helen	🏞 Vale of Ffestiniog	🏞 Cynfal Falls

Situated above the **Vale of Ffestiniog**, there is a delightful walk, beginning at the village church, to **Cynfal Falls**, just below the village. Above the falls stands a rock, known locally as Pulpud Huw Llwyd, that recalls a local mystic who preached from here. Three miles to the northeast, **Gamallt** is a remote 300-acre moorland that supports a variety of plant life as well as water beetles, sandpipers, ring ousels, wheatears and meadow pipits. Archaeological remains include a large Iron Age settlement, and the important Roman road known as **Sarn Helen** crosses the property, which is in the care of the National Trust.

BLAENAU FFESTINIOG
12 miles SE of Llanberis on the A470

🏠 Church of the Holy Protection	🏛 Pant-yr-ynn Mill
🏛 Ffestiniog Visitor Centre	🏛 Ffestiniog Railway
🏛 Llechwedd Slate Caverns	
🏛 Gloddfa Ganol Slate Mine	
🏞 Tan-y-Blwch County Park	

This was once the slate capital of Wales. Stretching across from the feet of Manod towards the Moelwyn Mountains, the legacy of the slate industry is visible everywhere - from the orderly piles of quarried slate waste to the buildings in the town.

Today, the industry lives on in two slate mines: **Llechwedd Slate Caverns** and **Gloddfa Ganol Slate Mine.** The Slate

Caverns, the winners of many top tourism awards, take visitors underground to explore the world of a Victorian slate miner and the man-made caverns of cathedral proportions, while, on surface, there is a Victorian village to wander through. The Gloddfa Ganol mine, where digging began in 1818, was once the world's largest, and today slate is still being turned into commercial products. At the foot of Manod Bach, beside the waterfall at Bethania, **Pant-yr-ynn Mill** is the earliest surviving slate mill of the Diffwys Casson Quarry. Built in 1846, it later saw service as a school before being converted into a woollen mill in 1881. It worked until 1964, when it was closed down and the machinery scrapped. The original part of the building has been preserved and the waterwheel restored; it is now home to an exhibition dealing with Blaenau - the town, the communities, the landscape and the changes to it made by the 20 quarries in the vicinity. The exhibition includes drawings and paintings by resident artist and industrial archaeologist Falcon D Hildred.

The town has one of the few Orthodox churches in Wales. The **Church of the Holy Protection** is in Manor Street, housed in a former shop. It was founded in 1981, though there has been Orthodox Christians here since the end of World War II, when Greek women who married Welsh soldiers came home with them. Over the years, many local people have joined the congregation. The church sees itself as the successor to the traditions and saints of the old Celtic Church, which disappeared when Roman Catholicism was introduced.

As well as having a mainline train service, Blaenau Ffestiniog is the end, or the starting point, of the narrow gauge **Ffestiniog Railway**, which runs through the vale to Porthmadog. Built to carry slate down to the sea for shipping off around the world, the railway has since been renovated by enthusiasts and volunteers. There is a comprehensive service giving passengers the chance to admire the scenery of the vale on their journey to the coast. There are many stopping off points so walkers can take advantage, en route, of **Tan-y-Blwch County Park** and other beauty spots.

To the northwest of the town, at First Hydro's power station, is the **Ffestiniog Visitor Centre**, the ideal place to discover the wonders of hydro-electricity. Opened in 1963 by Her Majesty the Queen, the station consists of reservoirs and underwater passages constructed inside the mountains and the displays and exhibitions at the centre explain not only how the electrical power is generated but also the development of electricity over the years.

MAENTWROG
13½ miles SE of Llanberis on the A496

🏛 Plas Tan-y-Bwlch

Lying in the Vale of Ffestiniog, this peaceful and attractive village is home to **Plas Tan-y-Bwlch**, built in the 19th century for the Oakley family. It is now owned by Snowdonia National Park, and is used as a residential centre for courses etc. The 19th century terraced gardens provide glorious views of the surrounding area and picturesque walks through woodland. Here, too, among the magnificent trees and rhododendrons, is an oak wood that provides a small reminder of the vast oak forests that once covered much of Wales.

BEDDGELERT

7¹/₂ miles S of Llanberis on the A498

🏛 Beddgelert Priory   🏛 Parish Church of St Mary

🏛 Llywelyn's Cottage   🏛 Sygun Copper Mine

🏛 Llyn Dinas   🏛 Moel Hebog   🏛 Pass of Aberglaslyn

🏛 Hafod y Llan   🏛 Gelert's Grave   🏛 Dinas Emrys

🏛 Alfred Bestall

The setting of this conservation village in the Snowdonia National Park, surrounded by mountains and, in particular, the 2,566 feet of **Moel Hebog**, is reminiscent of the Swiss Alps. In the 6th century a Celtic monastery was founded here that went on to become one of the foremost religious houses in Wales. Later, in the 12th or 13th century, the monastery was succeeded by a **Beddgelert Priory**, a small Augustinian priory given both

land and support by Llywelyn the Great and Owain Gwynedd. It was destroyed by fire in the late 13th century and rebuilt by Edward I, whose careless troops had originally caused the fire. It was again partially destroyed in the early 16th century, and finally dissolved by Henry VIII at the Dissolution of the Monasteries. Only the chapel was spared, and parts of it are now incorporated into te **Parish Church of St Mary**, which is well worth visiting.

However, Beddgelert was much more than just a religious centre in medieval times. This was thanks to the River Glaslyn being navigable as far as Pont Aberglaslyn, the stone bridge at the narrowest point of the gorge (a distance of six miles). Shipping remained an important mainstay of life here until the

---

LYN'S CAFÉ

Church Street, Beddgelert, Gwynedd LL55 4YA
Tel: 01766 890374

Situated in the heart of Beddgelert, in the foothills of Snowdon, **Lyn's Café & Tea Garden** is a very popular and welcoming establishment, ideal for those who wish to climb Snowdon, the highest mountain in Wales. Open throughout the day for most of the year (weekends only in November and December and, closed in January).

Beddgelert is one of the most beautiful villages in Snowdonia, has long been renowned for the splendid hospitality it offers to visitors. Some come to see the famous landmark, Gelert's Grave, some to see Beddgelert in Bloom in spring and summer, some to shop, some just to stroll

around this delightful village, some for serious hiking and climbing.

The comfortable light and airy interior is complimented by the delightful tea garden at the rear where customers are treated to a menu perfect for walkers after exploring the local area. From the popular Big Breakfast along with sandwiches, soups, morning coffee, lunches, clotted cream teas, and evening meals. The café also holds a table licence. The perfect place for eating at any time of the day.

🏛 historic building   🏛 museum   🏛 historic site   🏛 scenic attraction   🏛 flora and fauna

Porthmadog embankment was constructed in the early 19th century. The **Pass of Aberglaslyn**, through which the racing waters of the salmon river flow, lies to the south of the village; it is a delightful pass with steeply wooded slopes and an abundance of rhododendrons.

Llywelyn's Cottage (NT) lies within the village, and is a 17th century cottage with displays about the area's history and wildlife. Also owned by the National Trust is **Hafod y Llan**, to the east of the village near the A498. This 38,512 acre estate was bought in 1998 following a public appeal. It is being organically farmed by the trust, and sells organically produced lamb. There is a footpath to the summit of Snowdon.

The village's name translates as 'Gelert's Grave' and refers to Llywelyn the Great's faithful wolfhound Gelert, which he left to guard his little son Gruffudd. When he returned, he found the dog covered in blood and the child nowhere to be seen. He concluded that Gelert had killed his son, so in his fury he killed the dog. Only then did he realise that his son was alive, saved by Gelert

from a wolf, whose body lay nearby. It is said that Llewelyn never again smiled, and he buried Gelert with full honours. **Gelert's Grave** is in a riverside meadow, just south of the village, though the stones found here were apparently erected by a local landlord during the 18th century, perhaps hoping to attract more business with the grave as a local place of interest. The land around the grave was bought in 1987 with grants from the Countryside Commission and the Portmeirion Foundation in memory of Sir Clough Williams-Ellis. There's another animal connection: **Alfred Bestall**, the original illustrator of Rupert Bear, lived in Beddgelert. A winner of both National and European Village in Bloom titles, this attractive village is full of flowers in spring and summer.

To the northeast of the village, on the road to Capel Curig, lies the **Sygun Copper Mine**, which was abandoned in 1903. However, today, the former mine has been reopened as a remarkable and impressive example of Welsh industrial heritage where visitors can see the maze of underground tunnels and chambers, the massive stalactites and stalagmites and the copper ore veins that also contain traces of gold and silver. Audio commentaries give details of each stage of the mining process, with lighting and sound effects, which all contribute to this fascinating glimpse of the past.

Just a short distance further along this road lies **Dinas Emrys**, a hill fort that is thought to be associated with the legendary 5th century battle

Beddgelert

Llyn Dinas, near Beddgelert

proved a great defence but was also useful during its blockade by Madog and his men in 1294, when supplies transported in from Ireland enabled the 37 men inside to hold fast. If the use of power and strength to impress and intimidate an indigenous population was ever aided by architecture then Harlech is a prime example. Situated 200 feet above sea level, its concentric design, with lower outer walls, by the architect James of St George, used the natural defences of its site to emphasise its impregnability. However, in 1404 Owain Glyndwr managed to capture the castle and held it for five years while using the town of Harlech as his capital.

between the two dragons - one red and one white - that was prophesised by the young Merlin. The lake nearby, **Llyn Dinas**, is also associated with Merlin the Magician and legend claims that the true throne of Britain is in the lake and will only be revealed when a young person stands on a certain stone.

The song, *Men of Harlech*, has immortalised the siege during the War of the Roses when the castle was held for the Lancastrian side for seven years before it finally became the last stronghold to fall to the Yorkists in 1468. The last time Harlech saw action was 200 years later, during the Civil War, when it again withstood attack and was the last castle in Wales to fall to Cromwell's forces. The panoramic views from the castle's battlements take in both Tremadog Bay and the mountainous scenery behind the town.

Harlech

🏛 Harlech Castle 🏛 Lasynys Fawr 🦅 Ellis Swynne
🏛 Parish Church of St Tanwyg 🌿 Morfa Harlech

Harlech means 'bold rock' and it is an apt description, as the town clings to the land at the foot of its spectacularly sited castle. Another of Edward I's Iron Ring of Fortresses, which was begun in 1283, **Harlech Castle** is perched on a rocky outcrop for added strength and it is, today, a World Heritage Site in the hands of CADW. The castle's situation, close to the sea, has not only

Though not as imposing as the castle, **Lasynys Fawr** is another building worth a visit. The home of **Ellis Swynne** (1671-1734), a clergyman and one of Wales' most talented prose writers, famous for writing

Harlech Castle

the town, to the north, lies **Morfa Harlech**, a nature reserve with woodland trails that occupies the flat land between the town and Llanfihangel-y-Thaethau.

BONTDDU
9 miles SE of Harlech on the A496

Looking at this pleasant village it is hard to imagine that it was, over 100 years ago, a bustling centre of the Welsh gold mining industry. Apparently, there were 24 mines operating in the area around this village, and it was one of these mines that provided the gold for the Royal wedding rings.

Gweledigaetheu y Bardd Cwsc, ('Visions of the Sleeping Bard'), regarded as one of the great works of Welsh literature (see also Llanfair). Dating from 1600, the house is an excellent example of its period. The **Parish Church of St Tanwyg** dates from about 1840, and replaced an earlier church situated south of the town. St Tanwg came to Britanny from Wales in the 6th century.

Some of the scenes in the early James Bond film *From Russia With Love* were shot in Harlech. The famous Royal St David's golf course is just outside the town. Also outside

BARMOUTH
9 miles S of Harlech on the A496

🚲 Barmouth Bridge   🚲 Ty Gywn   ♣ Dinas Oleu

🏛 Lifeboat Museum   ♣ Panorama Walk

Occupying a picturesque location by the mouth of the River Mawddach, Barmouth was once a small port with an equally small shipbuilding industry. As the fashion for

---

CARTWRIGHT UPHOLSTERY
Old Llanfair Store, Llanfair, Harlech, Gwynedd LL46 2SA
Tel: 01766 781030

Jerry Cartwright is a proud member of the Association of Master Upholsterers, and is the driving force behind **Cartwright Upholstery**, a workshop and retail outlet that sells discount fabrics,

leather, vinyl and foam cut to size, and offers an upholstery service in its specialised workshop for antique and modern furniture, caravans, boats etc. Jerry also offers personal tuition in upholstery, and is always on hand to offer help and advice on any products or upholstery problems.

📖 stories and anecdotes   🐦 famous people   🎨 art and craft   🎭 entertainment and sport   🚶 walks

WAVECREST

8 Marine Parade, Barmouth LL42 1NA
Tel: 01341 280330
e-mail: thewavecrest@talk21.com
website: www.lokalink.co.uk/wavecrest

The four-star **Wavecrest** is a superb guest house situated right on the seafront in the lovely small holiday resort of Barmouth - the perfect place for a fun-filled family holiday. It is owned and managed by the husband and wife team of Shelagh and Eric Jarman, and has been open for over 27 years, offering superb B&B accommodation to discerning guests who appreciate comfort, value for money and high standards of personal service.

Shelagh and Eric have tastefully refurbished the Victorian building, keeping many of the original features while not compromising on facilities demanded by today's guests. Many of the nine bedrooms have lovely views out over Cardigan Bay and Snowdonia, and each one is comfortable, decorated and furnished to a high standard, and fully en suite for your comfort. The same care and attention extends to breakfasts with homemade preserves and organic produce being served.

Barmouth and its lovely harbour is at the mouth of a magnificent estuary which is crossed by a famous railway bridge and footpath. It is surrounded by dramatic scenery including "Dinas Olau"; the first land ever owned by The National Trust. The beach has Blue Flag status, so you know you are safe.

LLWYNDU FARMHOUSE HOTEL

Llanaber, Barmouth, Gwynedd LL42 1RR
Tel: 01341 280144   Fax: 01341 281236
e-mail: intouch@llwyndu-farmhouse.co.uk
website: www.llwyndu-farmhouse.co.uk

Llwyndu Farmhouse Hotel is a fine old building at the base of the Rhinog Mountains, overlooking Cardigan Bay, with stunning views over the Lleyn Peninsula. Hosts Paula and Peter Thompson assure guests of the warmest of welcomes, making every visitor feel instantly at home. The exposed stone walls, sturdy old beams, mullion windows, inglenook fireplaces and spiral staircase paint a delightfully traditional scene, and the six en suite bedrooms combine individual character with abundant comfort. Three are in the farmhouse (two with four-posters), three in the converted granary and barn. Peter is a very talented chef, and his 2- or 3-course dinners set great store by top-quality local produce (sea bass, lobster, Welsh Black beef) on Mediterranean-influenced menus that combine traditional and modern

elements. His breakfasts are equally unmissable, with prime bacon and sausages, free-range eggs, juicy kippers and naturally smoked haddock among the options.

seaside resorts grew in the 18th century, the character of Barmouth changed to accommodate visitors flocking here for the bracing sea air. Those suffering from scurvy were even fed seaweed, which is rich in Vitamin C and grew in abundance in the estuary. However, the Barmouth seen today is, like many other resorts, a product of the railway age and the Victorian architecture is still very much apparent. **Ty Gywn** is one of its older buildings, dating from the 15th century. The house, now the home to a Tudor exhibition, is said to have been built for Henry Tudor, Earl of Richmond, later Henry VII. It is thought to have been used as the meeting place where the plot to overthrow Richard III was hatched. The town is also home to a **Lifeboat Museum**.

The town's harbour, host to a regular regatta, is overlooked by **Dinas Oleu**, a small hill that was the first property given to the newly formed National Trust in 1895. It was a gift from the local wealthy philanthropist, Mrs Fanny Talbot, who was a friend of two of the Trust's founding members. **Panorama Walk** is a scenic walk created as a tourist attraction at the turn of the 19th century. There are several viewpoints along its route, the best being the one from the promontory at the end of the path. Built in 1867 and half a mile in length, the **Barmouth Bridge** that carried the railway across the river mouth has a walkway from where there are magnificent views of the town, coast and estuary. The swing bridge section is nowadays only opened for maintenance purposes.

HARBOUR CRAFTS

1a Staffordhire House, Church Street, Barmouth, Gwynedd LL42 1EH
Tel: 01341 280240
e-mail: harbourcrafts@aol.com

One of the most fascinating shops in the popular seaside resort of Barmouth is **Harbour Crafts**. It opened in June 2006, and is owned and managed by Sarah Watson, who was once a nurse but now caters to people who are looking for that extra special souvenir or gift for the home.

From the outside, the shop has a distinctly 'olde worlde' look to it, with its small, neat window panes, its hanging lights and brown facia. Inside it is a cornucopia of gifts for everyone, and a browser's paradise. The shop is the only stockist in town of the world famous Portmerion range of pottery, plus there are many other stoneware and pottery items on show to tempt you. There are also Yankee candles, Lilliput Lane miniature sculptures of buildings and street scenes, a fine range of greetings cards for every occasion, locally made confectionery (which is truly delicious!), Celtic and Welsh-inspired jewellery, Welsh love spoons, local countryside scenes by Colin Williamson, and so on. There is also a range of unique Barmouth souvenirs for you to take home to remind you of your holiday in the town.

Everything is keenly priced, and Sarah or one of her friendly staff is always on hand to help you make that special choice.

LLANABER

8 miles S of Harlech on the A496

🏛 Parish Church of St Mary

Found close to the clifftops, the **Parish Church of St Mary** is said to have been used by smugglers, who hid their booty inside the tombs in the churchyard. Dating from the 13th century and later, this place of worship, which was once the parish church of Barmouth, has an interesting doorway that is one of the best examples of early English architecture. Some people still refer to the church by its ancient dedication, St Bonfan's.

DYFFRYN ARDUDWY

5 miles S of Harlech on the A496

🏛 Arthur's Quoit

Neolithic remains, as well as the remnants of Iron and Bronze Age settlements, abound in this area and in this village can be found two burial chambers. Perhaps the most interesting is **Arthur's Quoit**, the capstone of which is said to have been thrown from the summit of Moelfre by King Arthur.

LLANBEDR

3 miles S of Harlech on the A496

🏛 Parish Church of St Peter   🏛 Maes Artro Centre

🌱 Rhinog Fawr   🌱 Shell Island

This village is an excellent starting point for walks along the lovely valleys of the Rivers Artro and Nant-col and into the Rhinog Mountains. At 2,360 feet **Rhinog Fawr** may not be the highest local peak, but from its summit it commands superb views over the Coed y Brenin Forest to the Cambrian Mountains.

The **Maes Artro Centre** is a privately owned museum that recreates the history and times of the 20th century. There is a Royal Air

Force Museum that traces the history of RAF Llanmbedr and, out in the parkland, there are military vehicles on display. The Rural Heritage Museum explores life in the village in the early 20th century, and the Yester Years Museum recreates the main street of a typical Welsh village. There is also a sea life centre. The **Parish Church of St Peter** ('Bedr' is welsh for 'Peter') is worth visiting to view the Llanbedr Stone, which was brought down to the church from an Iron Age hut circle above the village. It has an unusual spiral decoration.

More correctly described as a peninsula that is cut off at high tide, **Shell Island** is a treasure trove of seashells and wildlife and the shoreline, a mixture of pebble beaches with rock pools and golden sands, is ideal for children to explore. Seals are often seen close by and there is plenty of birdlife; surprising considering the fairly regular aircraft activity from the nearby Llanbedr airfield.

LLANFAIR

1½ miles S of Harlech on the A496

🏛 Parish Church of St Mary   🏛 Llanfair Slate Caverns

Between 1853 and 1906, Llanfair was a prosperous slate mining village and the old, deep quarries, the **Llanfair Slate Caverns**, in use until 1906, are now open to the public, who can don miner's helmets and set out on a self-guided tour. The caverns are accessed from the main tunnel, which opens out into a cathedral-like cavern. It was man-made, like all the tunnels in the complex. The tiny **Parish Church of St Mary,** among sand dunes, is Victorian, and buried in its churchyard is Ellis Swynne (see also Harlech). Though the village is called Llanfair, the parish is called Llanfair juxta Harlech, meaning 'Llanfair next to Harlech', to differentiate it from other parishes in Wales called Llanfair.

Bala

🏰 Tomen y Bala   🌊 Llyn Tegid   🐟 Tegi

🌿 Reverend Thomas Charles

Bala Lake

This agreeable town is a good stopping off point when exploring Snowdonia National Park. Roman and Norman remains have been found here, but the town was really founded in around 1310 by Roger de Mortimer, who was looking to tame the rebellious Penllyn district. The town was, by Tudor times, a small, and by all accounts not very successful, market town, but it later became an important centre for the knitted stocking industry that flourished in the 18th century before the Industrial Revolution put paid to it. Today, though tourism is certainly an important part of the town's economy, it has remained a central meeting point and a market place for the surrounding farming communities.

However, it is perhaps as a religious centre that Bala is better remembered. The **Reverend Thomas Charles**, one of the founders of the Methodist movement in Wales in the 18th century, first visited Bala in 1778 and moved here in 1783 after marrying a local girl. Charles saw the great need for Welsh Bibles and other religious books, and he joined forces with a printer from Chester to produce a series of books and pamphlets. The story of Mary Jones, who walked some 25 miles from Llanfihangel-y-Pennant to buy a bible from Charles, was the inspiration for the foundation of the Bible Society (see also Llanfihangel-y-Pennant). Notable sons of Bala include Thomas Edward Ellis, a Liberal Member of Parliament who worked hard for Welsh home rule, and Owen Morgan Edwards, who was a leading light in the Welsh educational system. There are statues to both these worthies in the town. The son of Owen Morgan Edwards, Sir Ifan ab Owen Edwards, established the Welsh Youth Movement, which has a camp at Bala Lake.

Tomen y Bala is to the north east of the town, and is thought to be the motte of a Norman castle, which would have been built of wood. In the 17th and 18th centuries the knitters of the town congregated here in fine weather to socialise as they knitted. It was also used as a pulpit during open air religious services. To the southwest of the town, Llyn Tegid (Bala Lake) is the largest natural lake in Wales and feeder of the River Dee. Four miles long, nearly three quarters of a mile wide and up to 150 feet deep, the lake is a popular centre for all manner of watersports; it is also the home of **Tegi**, the Welsh version of Scotland's Nessie. Formed during the Ice Age, the lake is an important site ecologically and has been designated a Site of Special Scientific Interest and a Ramsar site (Wetlands of International Importance). Many uncommon wetland plants flourish on its banks, and the birdlife includes coots, mallards, pochards, wigeons and great crested grebes. The fish life is interesting, too, and Bala is the only lake in

🏰 stories and anecdotes   🌿 famous people   🎨 art and craft   🎵 entertainment and sport   🥾 walks

Wales which is home to the gwyniad, a white-scaled member of the herring family that feeds on plankton in the depths of the lake. Along the eastern bank runs the narrow gauge **Bala Lake Railway**, which provides the perfect opportunity to catch a glimpse of the Tegi.

FRONGOCH
2 miles N of Bala on the A4212

🏛 Chapel Celyn   🏛 Llyn Celyn   🏛 Arenig Fawr

Just to the northwest of the village lies the reservoir **Llyn Celyn** on whose banks is a memorial stone to a group of local Quakers who, centuries ago, emigrated to America to escape persecution. The modern chapel close by, **Chapel Celyn**, was built as a reminder of the rural hamlet which was drowned when the reservoir was created in the 1960s.

Overlooking Llyn Celyn is **Arenig Fawr**, which has, on its 2,800 foot summit, a memorial to the crew of a Flying Fortress that crashed here in 1943.

After the Easter Uprising of 1916 in Ireland, a former German prisoner of war camp near the village was used to hold 1,600 Irish prisoners, among them Michael Collins. It earned the nickname of the 'Sinn Féin University', as impromptu lessons were given by some of the prisoners on guerrilla tactics. When Lloyd George came to power in 1916 he closed it down. A plaque marks where it stood.

LLANUWCHLLYN
4 miles SW of Bala on the A494

🌲 Penllyn Forest   🍂 Cwm Hirnant   🍂 Llyn Efyrnwy

This small village at the southern end of Bala

BRYNIAU GOLAU COUNTRY MANOR B&B

Llangower, Bala, Gwynedd LL23 7BT
Tel: 01678 521782
e-mail: katriwalesaux@hotmail.co.uk
website: www.bryniau-goleu.fsnet.co.uk

If you are exploring Snowdonia National Park, and are looking for great B&B accommodation, then look no further. **Bryniau Colau Country Manor B&B** sits right on the edge of the park, and offers superior accommodation at affordable prices. The three spacious rooms, all with double beds, are fully en suite, and overlook Lake Bala. The Berwyn Room and the Arenig Room boast an antique double bed and a luxury bathroom, while the Aran room has a king-sized double bed that can be split into twins, plus a bathroom with spa bath and overhead shower. Each bathroom has under tile heating for your comfort.

The house also has a garden, with terraces overlooking the lake, a guest lounge with TV and a log fire during the chilly months, secure cycle and canoe storage and drying facilities. A hearty cooked breakfast is served in the dining room overlooking the lake, though lighter options are always available as well. All the produce is sourced locally wherever possible to ensure maximum freshness and flavour.

The establishment is perfect as a base from which to explore the area, or to take part in one of the many activities in and around the lake, such as fishing and canoeing. Fishing licenses can be arranged in advance. In addition, there is ample scope for hill walking, pony trekking, white water rafting or just driving around the area exploring its history, heritage and wonderful scenery. Or why not use it as an overnight stop as you drive around Wales, taking in all the country has to offer? You'll be made more than welcome.

🏛 historic building   🖼 museum   🏛 historic site   🍂 scenic attraction   🌿 flora and fauna

Lake is the terminus of the Bala Lake Railway, which follows the lake for four miles with various stops where passengers can alight and enjoy a picnic or a walk. Spreading up from the eastern banks of the lake is the **Penllyn Forest**, which can be reached and passed through via **Cwm Hirnant** on an unclassified road that weaves through the forest to moorland and eventually reaches **Llyn Efyrnwy** (Lake Vyrnwy).

Llanuwchllyn has long been a stronghold of Welsh tradition, and has statues to two eminent Welshmen, Sir Owen Morgan Edwards and his son Sir Ifan ab Owen Edwards, both closely involved in preserving Welsh language and culture.

Dolgellau

🏯 Dollgellau Bridge   🏯 Parish Church of St Mary

🏛 Quaker Heritage Centre   ⛰ Cadair Idris

🐦 Dafydd Ionawr   🏃 Precipice Walk

Meaning 'meadow of the hazels', Dolgellau is the chief market town for this southern area of Snowdonia. Pleasantly situated beside the River Wnion, the town is very Welsh in custom, language and location. Owain Glyndwr held a Welsh parliament here in 1404, later signing an alliance with France's Charles VI. Now, the town's narrow streets can barely evoke those distant times and few early buildings remain. However, the seven-

DOLGELLEY JEWELLERS

Eldon Square, Dolgellau, Gwynedd LL40 1RD
Tel: 01341 422246

Dolgelley Jewellers, owned and managed by Margaret Hughes, is one of the best shops of its kind in Gwynedd. It sells a fabulous range of gold and silver jewellery, fine clocks and watches and superb giftware for both men and women. The shop must be visited to be appreciated. It sits at the heart of the town, right in the town square, and offers good, old-fashioned friendly, personal service coupled with efficiency and value for money prices.

The shop has an 'olde worlde' feel about it, with a double window front and windows crammed with clocks (both traditional and modern), jewellery and a host of other items that would make superb gifts or souvenirs of your visit to the Snowdonia National Park. And the interior is equally as charming, with glass counters, display cases packed with goods that are charming and stylish. Whether it is something with a 'traditional' feel to it, or something that is up to the minute and chic, you'll find it here! So much so that the shop has a loyal customer base, and people who holiday here return to the shop year after year.

Dolgelley Jewellers also offers a watch and clock repair service, and you are sure of getting all the help and advice you need when making a purchase.

📖 stories and anecdotes   🐦 famous people   🎨 art and craft   🎭 entertainment and sport   🏃 walks

Precipice Walk

Distance: *3.4 miles (5.4 kilometres)*

Typical time: *120 mins*

Height gain: *50 metres*

Map: *Outdoor Leisure 23*

Walk: *www.walkingworld.com ID:225*

Contributor: *Ian Morison*

ACCESS INFORMATION:

Car only. A National Park car park (no fee, toilets) is on the left-hand side of the minor road between Dolgellau and the village of Llanfachreth. Go north over the Afon Wnion bridge out of Dolgellau and turn right. After ½ mile fork left, signed Llanfachreth and Precipice Walk. The car park is two miles up the road.

DESCRIPTION:

After a short stretch in woodland, the path reaches open country and to the north, open views of the Coed y Brenin Forest appear. Turning south-west the path runs high above the River Maddach. The ground drops steeply into the valley so that young children will need to be well supervised, but there are no sheer drops. The path is good, but occasionally rocky. At the end of this section, views open out, first to the sea at Barmouth and then over Dolgellau to the northern flanks of the Cader Idris range. Almost certainly one of the most beautiful panoramas in Wales. Finally one returns following the banks of Llyn Cynwch until retracing the final few hundred yards back to the car park.

FEATURES:

Hills or Fells, Lake/Loch, Toilets, Wildlife, Birds, Great Views

WALK DIRECTIONS:

1 | Turn left out of the car park and follow the minor road for 100 yards.

2 | Turn left along the signposted track. Follow it round to the right where the track splits into two, keeping the open field to your left, then keep left as you pass a stone cottage.

3 | Cross a low ladder stile into woodland and turn right along the path.

4 | Cross the stile at the end of the wood into the open country. Follow the path round to

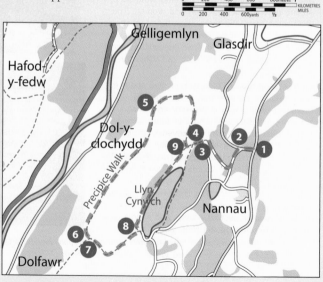

the right - Llyn Cynwch is seen down the valley on the left. Turn right at the corner of the field following the signpost direction and cross the ladder stile. The village of Llanfachreth is seen in the valley to your right. As you follow the stony path round to the left, Coed y Brenin Forest stretches out in front of you.

5 | The narrow, but safe, path takes you along the flanks of Foel Cynwch through heather and bilberry. To the right lies the River Mawddach some 200m below. As you continue, the view opens out with the Mawddach Estuary becoming visible to the right with, ahead, distant views of Cader Idris.

6 | Here is the first superb spot for a picnic. To the west is seen the Mawddach Estuary, the viaduct carrying the railway into Barmouth and the sea beyond. In the valley to the south lies the town of Dolgellau with the northern flanks of the Cader Idris range beyond.

7 | Climb over the ladder stile and follow the path contouring round the hillside to the left. Cross a further ladder stile and follow a soft path of closely cropped grass down towards Llyn Cynwch.

8 | Follow round to the left and drop onto the path alongside the lake. Turn left. Follow the gentle, tree-lined, path beside the lake – another beautiful spot to have a break, particularly if it was windy out on the fellside.

9 | Rejoin the outward route and retrace your steps back towards the car park. Across the field on the right after the woodland you will see Nannau Hall, built in 1693.

arched **Dollgellau Bridge** over the river dates from the early 17th century and, before much of Dolgellau was built in an attempt to lure Victorian holidaymakers to the delights of Cadair Idris, there was a small rural Quaker community here. The **Quaker Heritage Centre** in Eldon Square tells the story of this community and also of the persecution that led them to emigrate to Pennsylvania. North of the town, the seven mile **Precipice Walk** offers superb views. The local gold mines provided the gold for the wedding rings of both Queen Elizabeth II (then Princess Elizabeth) and Diana, Princess of Wales.

Within the **Parish Church of St Mary** there is an effigy of a knight, Meurig ab Ynvr Fychan, who lived in the 14th century. The church itself was built in 1716, and in the churchyard is a monument to **Dafydd Ionawr** (1751-1827 the Welsh poet.

To the southwest of Dolgellau is **Cadair Idris** ('the chair of Idris') which rises to 2,927 feet and dominates the local scenery. On a clear day, a climb to the summit is rewarded with views that take in the Isle of Man and the Irish coast as well as, closer to home, the Mawddach estuary. Much of the area around the mountain became a national nature reserve in 1957. An old legend says that anyone who sleeps on its slopes either wakens up mad or with the ability to write great poetry.

Around Dolgellau

LLANELLTYD
2 miles NW of Dolgellau on the A470

🏛 Cymer Abbey   🏛 Parish Church of St Elltyd

⚜ Kenric Stone

This is the point at which the Rivers Wen and Wnion, boosted by other waters further

upland, meet to form the
Mawddach estuary.
Across the River Wen lie
the serene ruins of
Cymer Abbey, which was
founded by Cistercian
monks in 1198. This
white-robed order was
established in the late
11th century in Burgundy
and they arrived in Britain
in 1128 to seek out
remote places where they
could lead their austere
lives. Cymer was one of
two Cistercian abbeys

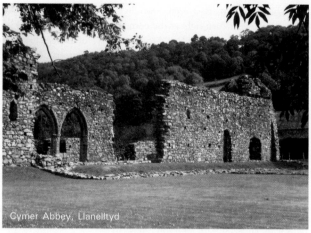

Cymer Abbey, Llanelltyd

created in the Snowdonia region during the
Middle Ages - the other is Conwy Abbey - and
Cymer held substantial lands in this area.
Despite this, the abbey was poor and it also
suffered badly during the fighting between
England and Wales. In fact, by the time of the
Dissolution in 1536 the abbey's income was
just £51. Visitors to this CADW site can see
the remaining parts of the church, refectory
and chapter house set in picturesque
surroundings.

The **Parish Church of St Elltyd** is
medieval, and has a curious stone within it
called the **Kenric Stone**, which has a Latin
inscription and the mark of a footprint.

LLANFACHRETH
3 miles N of Dolgellau off the A470

🏛 Nannau Hall   🏛 Parish Church of St Mackreth

Close to this beautifully located village is
Nannau Hall, the ancient seat of the
Vaughan family, who owned much of the land
in this area. It is said that an earlier house on
the site belonged to Howel Sele, a cousin of
Owain Glyndwr, who, during a dispute with

Glyndwr over Sele's Lancastrian sympathies,
shot at but missed his cousin while out
hunting. Glyndwr was so enraged that he
killed Sele and hid his body in a hollow oak.
This hiding place was later to receive a
mention in Sir Walter Scott's *Marmion* as "the
spirit's blasted tree". The **Parish Church of
St Mackreth** is medieval, but was restored in
the 1820s.

GANLLWYD
5 miles N of Dolgellau on the A470

🏛 Roman Steps   🌲 Dolmelynllyn   🌲 Rhaeadr Ddu

This hamlet gives its name to the attractive
valley in which it is found and which is, in
turn, surrounded by the **Coed y Brenin
Forest Park**, an area of some 9,000 acres
around the valleys of the Rivers Mawddach,
Eden, Gain and Wen. Originally part of the
Nannau Estate, founded by Cadougan,
Prince of Powys, in 1100, the forest was
acquired by the Forestry Commission in
1922, when extensive planting of conifers
took place. Ganllwyd was once a centre for
gold mining and, during the 1880s, the

nearby mine at Gwynfynydd was prosperous enough to attract some 250 miners. The mine had produced around 40,000 ounces of gold by the time it closed in 1917; it re-opened from 1981 to 1989. The mine is on the route of one of the four waymarked trails, which also takes in waterfalls, forest nature trails and an old copper works. Orienteering is a good way to explore the park, which also offers some of the best mountain biking in the UK. Bikes can be hired at the visitor centre, which has a café, shop and exhibitions.

There are also riverside picnic sites and a children's adventure play area. Broadleaved woodlands once covered the land and some of these woodlands still survive at the National Trust's **Dolmelynllyn** estate. On the slopes of **Y Garn**, a path through this expanse of heath and oak woodland leads to **Rhaeadr Ddu** ('Black Waterfall'), one of the most spectacular waterfalls in Wales. Also in the heart of the forest can be found a series of hundreds of steps, known as the **Roman Steps**, which climb up through the rocks and heather of the wild Rhinog Mountains. In spite of their name they are certainly not Roman; they are thought to have been part of a late medieval trade route between the coastal region around Harlech and England.

TRAWSFYNYDD
10 miles N of Dolgellau off the A470

🏚 Trawsfynydd Nuclear Power Station

🦢 Llyn Trawsfynydd 🏛 Roman Amphitheatre

🐦 Hedd Wynn 🐦 St John Roberts

To the west of the village lies **Llyn Trawsfynydd**, a man-made lake developed in the 1930s as part of a hydro-electric scheme. On its northern shores stands **Trawsfynydd Nuclear Power Station**, which opened in

1965 and was the country's first inland nuclear station, using the lake for cooling purposes.

Down a minor road close to the power station are the remains of a small **Roman Amphitheatre** that also served as a fort.

In the village centre is a statue in honour of **Hedd Wynn**, a poet and shepherd who was awarded the bardic chair at the 1917 Eisteddfod while he fought and died in the Flanders fields during World War I. The **Parish Church of St Madryn** was originally dedicated to St Mary, and then to the Holy Trinity before assuming its present dedication when the Church of Wales was disestablished. It was badly burnt in 1978 and rebuilt in 1981. It is connected to **St John Roberts**, who was born in the village to a Protestant family, but later converted to Roman Catholicism. He was hung, drawn and quartered at Tyburn in London in 1610 and canonised in 1970 by Pope Paul VI as one of the 40 martyrs of England and Wales.

DINAS MAWDDWY
8½ miles E of Dolgellau on the A470

🏚 Pont Minllyn 🏚 Meirion Mill

🖼 Gwilliaid Cochion Maeddwy

During the Middle Ages, this now quiet village was a centre of local power but the only surviving building from those days is a packhorse bridge, **Pont Minllyn**. A gateway to the upper Dyfi valley, it was once alive with quarries and mines but all that today's visitors can see of past industry is the traditional weaving of cloth at **Meirion Mill**, where there is also a visitor centre, craft shop and café.

In the 15th and 16th centuries the whole area surrounding the village was plagued by an eighty-strong gang of band of bandits. They were know as the **Gwilliaid Cochion Maeddwy** ('Red Bandits of Mawddwy'). They

🖼 stories and anecdotes 🐦 famous people 🎨 art and craft 🎭 entertainment and sport 🥾 walks stole cattle and sheep, robbed travellers and attacked farmsteads. Eventually they were captured and executed in 1554, their burial place being a mound at Ros Goch ('Red Moor'),two miles from the village. The survivors exacted some revenge by murdering their prosecutor, Baron Lewis Owen.

CORRIS
6 miles S of Dolgellau on the A487

🏚 Railway Museum   🏚 King Arthur's Labyrinth

🌿 Corris Craft Centre

This small former slate-mining village, surrounded by the tree-covered slopes of the Cambrian Mountains, was home to the first narrow-gauge railway in Wales. It was constructed in 1859 as a horse drawn railway, and steam locomotives were introduced in 1878 before the passenger service began in 1883. After closing in 1948, the Corris Railway Society opened a **Railway Museum** that explains the railway's history and also the special relationship with the slate quarries through displays, exhibits and photographs. Part of the line reopened to passengers in 2003.

Industry of a different kind can be found at the **Corris Craft Centre**, which is home to a variety of working craftsmen and women. An excellent place to find a unique gift, the craft centre is also home to the fascinating **King Arthur's Labyrinth** - a maze of underground tunnels where visitors are taken by boat to see the spectacular caverns and relive tales of the legendary King Arthur.

The legend of King Arthur is first told in *The Mabinogion*, a collection of stories which evolved over 1,000 years. Passed from generation to generation from the 4th century onwards, they were not written down in a surviving manuscript form until the 13th century. The *White Book of Rhydderch* and the *Red Book of Hergest* between them contain 11 stories, five of which centre round the exploits of King Arthur and his contemporaries. In these tales we meet Gwenhwyfar (Guinevere), Cei (Sir Kay), Bedwyr (Sir Bedivere), Myrddin (Merlin) and Gwalchmei (Sir Gawain). In the *History of the Britons*, written by the Welsh cleric Nennius around 830, we first read of Arthur's battles, some at least of which took place in Wales, from about 515 onwards. The last great battle, against his nephew Mawdred and his Saxon allies, marked the end of a phase of Celtic resistance to the Saxons. This battle has been dated to 537 and is located by some historians on the Llyn Peninsula. In Welsh tradition, Merlin and the great bard Taliesin took the dying King Arthur to the magical Isle of Avalon, which recent research has identified as Bardsey Island, where St Cadfan established a monastery and where 1,000 Welsh saints are buried. The caverns of King Arthur's Labyrinth are the workings of the Braich Goch Slate Mine, which was operational between 1836 and 1970. At its peak, the mine employed 250 men and produced 7,000 tons of roofing slate annually.

PANTPERTHOG
8 miles S of Dolgellau on A487

🏚 Centre for Alternative Technology

The **Centre for Alternative Technology** has exhibitions and displays on eco-friendly ways of generating power, greenhouses gases and pollution. You can see environmentally friendly ways of building, renewable energy schemes and energy efficiency. There is a visitor centre, a shop and a café.

🏛 historic building   🏚 museum   🏯 historic site   🏞 scenic attraction   🌱 flora and fauna

Tal-y-Llyn

saving for six years for a Welsh Bible, Mary Jones, the 16-year-old daughter of a weaver, walked to Bala in 1800 to purchase a copy from Thomas Charles. As Charles had no copies of the Bible available, he gave her his own copy and the episode inspired the founding of the Bible Society (see also Bala). Mary lived to a ripe old age (88 years) and was buried at Bryncrug, while her Bible is preserved in the Society's headquarters in London. There is a memorial to her in the churchyard of the much-restored **Parish Church of St Michael**.

Close by lie the runs of **Castell y Bere**, a hill top fortress begun by Llywelyn the Great in 1223. Taken by the Earl of Pembrokeshire, on behalf of Edward I, in 1283, the castle stayed in English hands for two years before being retaken by the Welsh and destroyed.

TAL-Y-LLYN

5 miles S of Dolgellau on the B4405

🏛 Parish Church of St Mary   🏞 Tal-y-llyn Lake

This tiny hamlet lies at the southwestern end of the **Tal-y-llyn Lake**, which is overshadowed by the crags of Cadair Idris to the north. A great favourite with trout fishermen, the village has the **Parish Church of St Mary** (at present closed) which some people think is one of the oldest churches in Wales, and has a plaque dating the original building to the 9th century. Some people claim it is even older. It has an unusual chancel ceiling of square panels decorated with carved roses. For the Tal-y-llyn Railway see Tywyn.

LLANFIHANGEL-Y-PENNANT

7 miles SW of Dolgellau off the B4405

🏛 Mary Jones's Cottage

🏛 Parish Church of St Michael 🏛 Castell y Bere

Just to the northeast of this small hamlet lie the ruins of **Mary Jones's Cottage**. After

ARTHOG

6 miles SW of Dolgellau on the A493

🏞 Cregennan Lakes   🐦 Arthog RSPB Nature Reserve

Overlooking the Mawddach estuary, this elongated village is a starting point for walks into Cadair Idris. Beginning with a sheltered woodland path, the trail climbs up to the two **Cregennan Lakes** from where there are glorious mountain views. The lakes are fed by

🎞 stories and anecdotes 🐦 famous people 🎨 art and craft 🎭 entertainment and sport 🥾 walks streams running off the mountains and they have created a valuable wetland habitat that is now in the care of the National Trust. Down by the river mouth, there is the **Arthog RSPB Nature Reserve** protecting the wealth of birdlife and wildlife found here.

FAIRBOURNE
8 miles SW of Dolgellau off the A493

🚂 Fairbourne Railway

This growing holiday resort lies on the opposite side of the Mawddach estuary from Barmouth and, from the ferry that carries passengers across the river mouth, runs the **Fairbourne Railway**. Originally a horse-drawn tramway, now steam-hauled, this 15" gauge railway runs from Fairbourne to the mouth of the Mawddach estuary. Its midway halt was given an invented name that outdoes the 59 letters of LlanfairPG by eight. Translated from the Welsh, it means "Mawddach Station with its dragon's teeth on North Penrhyn Drive by the golden sands of Cardigan Bay". The dragon's teeth are anything but mystical: they are concrete tank traps left over from the Second World War.

LLWYNGWRIL
10 miles S of Dolgellau on the A493

🏛 Parish Church of St Celynin   🚂 Carstell-y-Gaer

The village is named after the giant Gwril, who was supreme in this part of the coast. He was said to be the lowland cousin of Idris, who ruled the mountains, and after who Cadair Idris is named. They spent most of their time throwing rocks at each other. A 'llwyn' is a bush or grove in Welsh, so the name means Gwril's grove. Above the village is **Castell-y-Gaer**, a prehistoric hill fort, and a mile south of the village is the wonderful 16th century **Parish Church of St Celynin** at

Llangelynin, over 600 years old and largely unrestored. Its treasures include wall texts, a rare set of pews named after local families and the grave of Abram Wood, King of the Welsh gypsies.

TYWYN
14 miles SW of Dolgellau on the A493

🚂 Tal-y-llyn Railway   🌳 Dolgoch Falls

🚶 National Trail

This coastal town and seaside resort on Cardigan Bay has long sandy beaches, dunes and a promenade, as well as being the start (or the end) of the famous narrow-gauge (2 feet 3 inches) **Tal-y-llyn Railway**, which takes you as far as Abergynolwyn, seven-and-a-half miles inland. Like most narrow gauge railways in Wales, it was opened (in 1865) to bring slate from the quarries down to the coast. the original two steam engines are still in service.

The area around Tywyn is wonderful walking country, and marked walks include the new **National Trail** that runs between Machynlleth, Welshpool and Knighton. One of the stations on the line is Dolgoch, from which a walk takes in three sets of magnificent waterfalls, the **Dolgoch Falls**. Four walks of varying lengths and difficulty start at Nant Gwernol station and provide an opportunity to enjoy the lovely woodlands and to look at the remains of Bryn Eglwys quarry and the tramway that served it.

ABERDOVEY (ABERDYFI)
16 miles SW of Dolgellau on the A493

This resort at the mouth of the River Dovey (or Dyfi) was once one of the most important ports along the Welsh coast. Shipbuilding flourished here, and records show that on one particular occasion 180 ships were unloading

LINEN AND LACE

Cambrian House, High Street, Tywyn LL36 9AE
Tel/Fax: 01654 711558
e-mail: lorraine@linenandlace.orangehome.co.uk

Tywyn is a popular spot with visitors, set in superb walking country with great views all around. One of the main attractions is the wonderful Talyllyn Railway, but while in town many visitors also make tracks for another destination – **Linen and Lace** on the High Street. It's owned and run by Lorraine Reynolds and Kath Gabriel, who have filled their terrific little shop with a fine selection of household and lifestyle items including bedding, towels, sheets and pillows, quilts, cushions and throws, and bathroom accessories such as bath mats, shower curtains and soap dishes.

There are clothes and bags and costume jewellery, watches, prints and photo frames, mugs, lamps, vases, silk flowers and many other goodies personally chosen by Lorraine and Kath. This is the ideal place to find something to enhance the home or a gift large or small for every occasion. Shop hours are 9 to 5.30 Monday to Saturday (winter 9 to 5.30, half-day Wednesday).

or waiting for a berth. The town has been attracting holiday-makers since Edwardian times, when the railways made such seaside trips possible for many more people. It is a gentle, civilised spot, with all the best attributes of a seaside resort and none of the kiss-me-quick brashness of many larger places. . **The Parish Church of St Peter** is a handsome building constructed in 1837, though the Victorian ballad called *The Bells of Aberdovey* has nothing to do with its peel of ten carrillon bells, which were only installed in 1936. It recounts an old legend that the sea drowned a great kingdom called Cantre'r Gwaelod ('Lowland Hundred') in Cardigan Bay and how on quiet summer evenings the bells can be heard ringing out from beneath the waves.

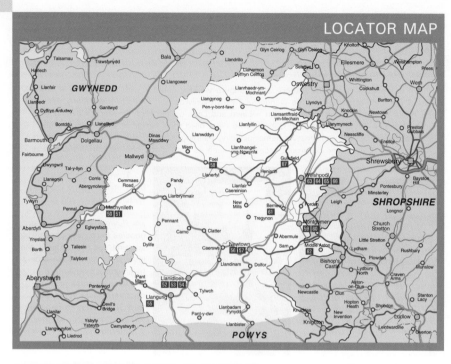

LOCATOR MAP

ADVERTISERS AND PLACES OF INTEREST

🏛 historic building   🏛 museum   🏛 historic site   ⚘ scenic attraction   🐾 flora and fauna

4| North Powys

Once part of the old county of Montgomeryshire, this northern region of Powys is an area of varied landscape and small towns and villages. Situated between the high, rugged landscape of Snowdonia and the farmland of Shropshire, this is a gentle and pleasant region through which many rivers and streams flow. As well as being home to the highest waterfall outside Scotland, Pistyll Rhaeadr (one of the Seven Wonders of Wales), the region has another landmark in Lake Vyrnwy. Built in the 1880s to supply the expanding city of Liverpool with water, this large reservoir is a splendid feat of Victorian engineering that later found fame as a location for the film *The Dambusters*.

The major settlement here is Welshpool, a town situated on the banks of the River Severn and close to the English border. Originally known as Pool, the prefix was added to ensure that the dispute regarding its nationality was finalised once and for all. From the town, leisurely canal boat trips can be taken along the Montgomery Canal, but there is also a narrow gauge steam railway running westwards to Llanfair Caereinion. Near the town can be found the splendid Powis Castle, which is famous not only for the many treasures it houses but also for its magnificent gardens.

Montgomery, a tiny anglicised town that gave its name to the county of Montgomeryshire, not only has a splendidly situated ruined borderland castle but it is also close to some of the best preserved sections of Offa's Dyke (see Prestatyn). Nearby, Newtown which, despite its name, was founded in the 10th century, is another interesting and historic market town. Those who are interested in history, particularly social history, will find the Robert Owen Memorial Museum well worth a visit.

To the west and beyond the quaint town of Llanidloes lies Machynlleth, the home of Owain Glyndwr's parliament in the 15th century. A visit to the Owen Glydwyr Centre, which can be found in the part 15th century parliament house, tells the story of Glyndwr and his struggle against the English.

This is great walking country that takes in some of the finest scenery in Wales. The many marked established trails and walks include a large part of Offa's Dyke Path and Glyndwr's Way, a 123-mile walk that follows a circular route across dramatic landscapes from Welshpool to Knighton by way of Machynlleth.

River Severn, Newtown

Machynlleth

🏠 Parliament House   🏠 Plas Machynlleth

🏠 Parish Church of St Peter   🦅 Owain Glyndwr

This small town is a popular but not overcrowded holiday centre in the shadow of the Cambrian Mountains. It was here that **Owain Glyndwr** held one of his parliaments in around 1404 and, on the site today, stands **Parliament House**, a part 15th century building. It is home to the **Owain Glyndwyr Centre,** which tells the story of the last native prince of Wales and the rebellion he led against the English. The building also has a brass rubbing centre. Glyndwr's aims were independence for Wales, a church independent of Canterbury and the establishing of a Welsh university. After being refused redress when Lord Grey of Ruthin seized some of his land, he laid waste the English settlements in northeast Wales and spent the next few years in skirmishes. He established other parliaments in Dolgellau and Harlech, and sought alliances with the Scots, the Irish and the French, and resisted many assaults by Henry IV's armies. Eventually Henry V seized Aberystwyth and Harlech, and Glyndwr soon disappeared from the scene, dying, it is thought, at the home of his daughter Anne Scudamore. It was while presiding over the parliament that Owain was nearly killed by his brother-in-law Dafyd Gam. The plot failed, and Dafyd was captured. He was granted a pardon by Owain and later fought at the Battle of Agincourt.

🏠 historic building   🏛 museum   🏛 historic site   🏞 scenic attraction   🌿 flora and fauna

I.G.OWENS IRONMONGERS

23-25 Penrallt Street, Machynlleth,
Powys SY20 8AG
Tel: 01654 702317

I.G. Owens is the classic ironmonger, selling everything from screws, nails and wood to garden furniture, DIY products, kitchenware, tools, compost and terracotta pots. Everything is realistically priced, and the service and help you get is second to none. If you live within a five mile radius, there is also a free delivery service. So make I.G. Owens your first stop for all your DIY and garden requirements.

Opposite the house is the entrance to **Plas Machynlleth**, an elegant mansion built in 1653 that was given to the town by Lord Londonderry and which is surrounded by attractive gardens open to the public. This beautifully restored mansion was, up until 2006, home to Celtica, a museum and multi-media centre where the history and the legends of the Celts were uncovered. The **Parish Church of St Peter** was originally dedicated to St Cybi, and was extensively rebuit and enlarged in 1827, though the base of the tower is 15th century. At the centre of the town is an ornate **Clock Tower** dating from 1872 which was built by public subscription to mark the coming of age of Lord Castlereagh, heir to the Marquess of Londonderry.

Around Machynlleth

CARNO
10 miles E of Machynlleth on the A470

🏛 Parish Church of St John the Baptist

🏭 Carno Wind Farm

The dress and interior designer Laura Ashley, who was born in Wales, and her husband moved to Machynlleth in 1963 and later settled at Carno, which became the site of the headquarters of the Laura Ashley empire. It was in the churchyard of the **Parish Church of St John the Baptist**, close to the factory, that she was buried after her death due to a fall in 1985. In the hills of Trannon Moor near the village is the National Wind Power's

Carno Wind Farm

🎞 stories and anecdotes   🐦 famous people   🎨 art and craft   ✒ entertainment and sport   🚶 walks

Carno Wind Farm, a site containing dozens of turbines that generate enough electricity to meet the needs of many thousand homes. The plateau on which the farm is located is visited by over 30 bird species including red kite, hen harrier, buzzard, red grouse, curlew and golden plover. The site access road is located off the A470 at the northern end of Carno village. Visitors can walk along the marked public footpaths that cross the site; there is an information board at the car park.

LLANBRYNMAIR
8½ miles E of Machynlleth on the B4518

🏛 Parish Church of St Mary   🏛 Machinations

🪶 Abraham Rees   🪶 Reverend Samuel Roberts

On the banks of the River Twymyn, this village was the birthplace of **Abraham Rees**, who published an edition of *Ephraim Chambers Cyclopedia* between 1778 and 1788 after having added over 4,500 new pieces of information. Llanbrynmair was also the home for many years of the social reformer the **Reverend Samuel Roberts**, who worked hard for the principles of social equality and was a leader of non-conformist opinion. He was also an advocate of free trade, Catholic emancipation and temperance, and in 1827 he advanced a plan for an inland penny postal service. Between 1857 and 1867 he was in America with his brother Richard Roberts preaching racial equality.

The **Parish Church of St Mary** is essentially 14th and 15th centuries, and stands on the site of an earlier building. It has an unusual bell turret supported by four wood uprights, and there are fragments of medieval glass in one of the windows.

In the village you will find **Machinations**, a museum dedicated to automata - figures driven by clockwork, electricity, wind or hand.

These mechanical models are fascinating, and there are even courses on constructing, painting and carving them.

DYLIFE
8½ miles SE of Machynlleth off the B4518

🏞 Dylife Gorge   🪶 Glaslyn Nature Reserve

Apart from an inn and a few houses, there is little left of this once prosperous lead mining community. A footpath from the settlement passes close to a grassy mound which was once a Roman fort, built to guard the nearby lead mines. The path continues past more redundant lead mines that were last worked during the late 17th century before it meanders through a woodland, following the banks of River Clywedog, and on towards Staylittle. The final part of the route lies close to Bronze Age tumuli which suggest that mining occurred in the area even before the Roman occupation. Close to the village is **Glaslyn Nature Reserve**, a 540-acre tract of heather moorland that is the breeding site for the wheatear, golden plover, ring ousel and red grouse. **Dylife Gorge**, to the west of the village, was gouged from the landscape during the last Ice Age.

STAYLITTLE
11 miles SE of Machynlleth on the B4518

🌲 Hafren Forest   🌲 Plynlimon

A one-time lead mining village, Staylittle is said to have derived its name from the village's two blacksmiths who shoed horses so rapidly that their forge became known as Stay-a-Little. Situated in a remote area high in the Cambrian Mountains, Staylittle is on the edge of the **Hafren Forest**, which has several waymarked trails through the forest, along the banks of the upper River Severn and up to **Plynlimon**, which rises to 2,500 feet.

LLANIDLOES
16½ miles SE of Machynlleth on the A470

🏛 Market Hall 🏛 Llanidloes Castle

⛏ Van Lead Mine 🏛 Parish Church of St Idloes

🏛 Llanidloes Museum ⛏ Bryn Tail Lead Mine

🌊 Llyn Clywedog 🌊 Fan Hill 🎨 Minerva Arts Centre

🚶 Llyn Clyywedog Scenic Trail 🚶 Cascades Trail

🚶 Clywedog Gorge Trail 🚶 Aber Biga Wildlife Walk

This peaceful little market town, which sits at the exact centre of Wales, is certainly one of the area's most attractive, and its adaptability, from a rural village to a weaving town and now to a centre for craftspeople, has ensured that it is likely to remain so for many years to come. John Wesley preached here three times in the mid 1700s and the stone from which he addressed his audience can be seen outside the town's old **Market Hall**, which dates from 1609 and stands on wooden stilts. It was used by Quakers, Methodists and Baptists before those religious groups had their own premises and has also been a courthouse, a library and a working men's institute. The upper floors now house the **Llanidloes Museum**, where there are displays and information on the textile and mining industries that thrived in the area during the 18th and 19th centuries. There is also a natural history exhibition and the red kite centre.

In 1839, the town was a focal point of the bitter Chartist Riots after the Reform Bill of 1832 had failed to meet demands that included universal suffrage and social equality. Cheap labour, cheap wool and efficient new

MINERVA ARTS CENTRE

2 High Street, Llanidloes, Powys SY18 6BY
Tel: 01686 413467
website: www.quilt.org.uk

The Minerva Arts Centre in the friendly market town of Llanidloes is the home of the Quilt Association. Here the Quilt Association stores and cares for its collection of antique quilts. Most of these quilts are Welsh and many have a local connection together with records and reminiscences about them and their making.

As a registered charity, the aims of the Quilt Association are to promote the skills of patchwork and quilting and to encourage others to take up the craft. To this end they hold an annual exhibition during the summer months when quilts both antique and contemporary are on show supported by talks, lectures and workshops. There is a sales area with fabric, threads, books and quilting sundries.

An exciting exhibition space, the Centre has a rolling programme of high quality exhibitions throughout the year. The Christmas Craft Fair featuring local crafts is a particularly popular event.

You will find details of exhibitions and workshops on the website quilt.org.uk, by phone on 01686 413467 or from the Minerva Arts Centre, High Street, Llanidloes, Powys, SY18 6BY.

📖 stories and anecdotes 🗣 famous people 🎨 art and craft 🎭 entertainment and sport 🚶 walks machinery had led to a boom in the wool and flannel trade in Llanidloes, as it had in Newtown, Machynlleth and Welshpool. Workmen flooded in, and in 1858 the population was more then 4,000. But the boom did not last, the factories closed, and unemployment inevitably ensued. Chartist propaganda reached the town and the Llanidloes unions adopted the charter. The crowds started to gather and to arm, the police moved in, and the Chartist leaders were arrested then released by the crowd, The magistrates fled, and the Chartists then ruled for a few days. Mills were re-opened and the prices of goods fixed. Then the Montgomeryshire Yeomanry came on the scene, 32 arrests were made and the Chartist ringleaders put on trial at Welshpool. Three

were transported and the rest served terms of hard labour.

The Chartists originated in London in 1837, when a People's Charter was drawn up by the London Working Men's Association. Their six main demands were: equal electoral areas, universal suffrage, payment for MPs, no property qualifications for voters, vote by ballot and annual parliaments. Support for the Charter spread quickly through Britain, with the Welsh miners especially vociferous. A petition with 1¼ million signatures was rejected by Parliament in 1839, and riots ensued in Lancashire, Yorkshire and Wales. In 1842 another petition, this one with 3½ million signatures, was rejected. The Chartist movement then went into something of a decline, and the repeal of the Corn Laws in

WOOD 'N' THINGS GALLERY

50 Longbridge Street, Llanidloes, Powys SY18 6EF
Tel: 01686 414848
e-mail: bbuckle33@tiscali.co.uk
website: www.llanidloes.com

The **Wood 'n' Things Gallery** is situated in the historic Hamers butcher's shop, 'purveyors to her majesty', with the royal crest above the window, and which still has many of the original features. It is owned and managed by Bernadette and Alan Buckle, and specialises in the promotion of over 50 artists, designers and craftspeople from the locality.

It is truly a guaranteed source of a souvenir, a gift for a loved one, or just something special for your home. There is a wide range of hand-crafted gifts and artwork to suit all tastes, including works from the popular wildlife artist, TV presenter and cameraman 'Dee Doody'. There are also craft items from top class potters, wood workers, painters, jewellery makers, metal workers, workers in glass, and textile/wool designers working in a number of media, including knitting.

You can browse this colourful and fascinating shop at your leisure with no obligation to buy. Or why not enjoy a pot of coffee or tea with home baking as you view the gallery's latest exhibition? They change every month, and Bernadette and Alan are always on hand to offer friendly advice and help when you make your choice.

So come along - you're sure of a warm welcome.

🏫 historic building   🏛 museum   🏛 historic site   ⚘ scenic attraction   ⚘ flora and fauna

1846 helped to better the lot of the working classes.

The town has many arts and crafts shops and galleries featuring the work of local artists and craftspeople. **Minerva Arts Centre**, in the High Street is the home of the Quilt Association and its unique collection of antique Welsh quilts. Exhibitions are held here, as are workshops and other events.

Llanidloes Castle has all but vanished, though there is a portion of the motte still standing. It was built by Owain de la Pole in 1280, when a charter for a weekly market was granted. The tower of the **Parish Church of St Idloes** dates from the 14th century, while the rest of the church is later. It is the only church in the country with a dedication to St Idloes, who was born in the 7th century, the son of Gwyddnabi ab Llawfronedd, described as a 'red-bearded knight'.

The Severn Way and Glyndwr's Way cross in Llanidloes, and an interesting marked five-mile walk covers sections of each. Five miles to the northwest of the town lies **Llyn Clywedog**, a reservoir that was developed in the mid 1960s to regulate the flows of the Rivers Severn and Clywedog. Birds such as buzzards and red kite are frequently seen around the shores of the lake, as are occasional ospreys. Roads follow around both sides of the lake, with the B4518 curving round the slopes of the 1,580 foot **Fan Hill** where the chimneys of the now disused **Van Lead Mine** are still visible. It was once one of the most prosperous mines in this area of Wales, and it is recorded that in 1876 6,850

E. HIGGS & SONS

52 Longbridge Street, Llanidloes, Powys SY18 6EF
Tel: 01686 412369

E. Higgs and Sons has been trading since 1910, offering the very best in bags, shoes and boots. Now owned and managed by Neil Higgs, the founder's grandson, and his wife Pam, it is keeping up the fine traditions of service, a warm welcome and outstanding value for money.

The shop front has a traditional look about it that is reassuring, and the interior is full of footwear and leather goods. You could spend a full afternoon here quite happily! Fortunately, Neil encourages you to browse, and you can take your time as you go round the vast stock. Neil and his wife are always on hand to offer advice and help.

Names such as Betty Barclay, Naot, Wolky, Reiker, Högl, and Ellens feature prominently in the womens'shoes, as well as Dorndorf and Ara in wider fittings. Men can choose footwear from such manufacturers as Camel Active, Merrell, Sebago and Grenson. Plus there is a range of shoes for kids, including Geox and Companucci.

There is also a great range of handbags and accessories for all occasions. If you visit Llanidloes, why not call in a see the wide range for yourself? There is no obligation to buy, and Neil and Pam will give you a warm Welsh welcome.

Llyn Clywedog Reservoir

Scenic Trail, the **Clywedog Gorge Trail** and the **Aber Biga Wildlife Walk** on the lake's shores are short walks suitable for able-bodied families, whereas the **Cascades Trail** in the nearby Hafren Forest is suitable for wheelchairs. A booklet is available that explains cycle routes, including one round the lake. The

tons of lead were produced. The deserted houses and chapels of the village that grew up around the mine add a sombre, evocative note.

There are a number of way-marked routes and walks in the area. The **Llyn Clyywedog**

remains of the **Bryn Tail Lead Mine** sit at the foot of the reservoir's dam, which rises to a height of 237 feet. The lake is well-stocked with rainbow and brown trout, and hosts fishing competitions.

CLOCHFAEN

The Clochfaen, Llangurig, Near Llanidloes, Powys SY18 6RP
Tel: 01686 440687
e-mail: info@theclochfaen.com   website: www.theclochfaen.com

The three-star **Aubrey's at the Clochfaen** nestles in the upper reaches of the Wye valley, and is the natural choice for holiday accommodation in this beautiful part of Wales. The house itself is very old, and was remodelled between 1914 and 1915 by W.A.S. Benson, one of the leading figures in the famous Arts and Crafts Movement.

The house offers superb accommodation, plus a range of sporting activities in the surrounding countryside. There are four stylish and cosy bedrooms (two doubles and two twins), two of which have en suite facilities. Each one has a TV, security safe, radio alarm and tea/coffee making facilities. Here you can enjoy a relaxing break, or you can use the place as an overnight stop as you explore the lovely Wye Valley, an area which has some great facilities for outdoor activities such as walking, fishing and cycling.

Breakfasts are hearty and filling, and served in the morning room. You can choose a full Welsh, or something lighter like a Continental breakfast. Whichever you choose, you'll enjoy it thoroughly.

But the joy of the Wye Valley is its fishing, and Clochfaen has divided its fishing into two beats - Upper Clochfaen and Lower Clochfaen. The upper extends to 3.7 kilometres, with easy wading and very little to snag your casts. The Lower Clochfaen is 3 kilometres of single and double bank fishing, the lower section of which is over bedrock.

🏛 historic building   🏛 museum   🏚 historic site   ⚜ scenic attraction   🌿 flora and fauna

Newtown

🏛 Parish Church of St Mary 🏛 Textile Museum

🏛 Robert Owen Memorial Museum

🏛 WH Smith Museum 🏛 Pryce Jones Museum

🌲 Pwll Penarth Nature Reserve

The name has not been appropriate for centuries, as Newtown's origins date from around AD 973, though it only came to prominence after being granted a market charter by Edward I in 1279. This was a centre for textiles and weaving and, by the 19th century, was the home of the Welsh flannel industry that led it to be referred to as the 'Leeds of Wales'. Some of the brick buildings were built with a third or even fourth storey with large windows to let in light for the looms. One such building now houses the town's **Textile Museum**, which tells the story of this once important industry and also gives a very good impression of the working conditions of the people which Newtown's most famous son, Robert Owen, devoted much of his life to changing. Born in Newtown in 1771, Owen grew from a humble background to become a social reformer and the founder of the co-operative movement who lobbied vigorously for an improvement in the working conditions specifically within the textile industry. He is particularly associated with the New Lanark mills in Scotland, which he ran and partly owned. The workforce at New Lanark numbered 2,000, including 500 children, and Owen provided good housing, cheap goods and an infant's

---

ALAVEN LEATHERSHOP

18 High Street, Newtown, Powys SY16 2NP
Tel: 01686 626665
website: www.alavenleather.co.uk

Established for over 20 years in Newtown, the **Alaven Leathershop** has earned an enviable reputation for the quality of the products it sells and the value for money prices. It is a wonderful shop, and here you can browse to your heart's content, with absolutely no obligation to buy. The shop is located in the High Street, midway between the Town Clock and the Town Hall and close to the main car park by the Oriel Davies Gallery.

The shop specialises in an extensive range of leather goods including handbags, briefcases and folios, wallets and purses, belts, gloves, slippers, sheepskin rugs, jewellery boxes, desk accessories and gift items such as hip flasks. Other complimentary products include travel luggage, umbrellas, and walking sticks. There is also a large range of hand carved love-spoons which would make the perfect gift or souvenir of your holiday in Wales.

Leather brand names include: The Bridge (the finest Italian leather); Marta Ponti; Tony Perotti; the ever popular Radley, Tula and Hidesign (Alaven is the official Radley stockist for Powys); Dents; Smith & Canova; London Clock. Other brand names include Antler; Design Go, Totes and Charles Buyers.

Friendly, knowledgeable staff are always on hand to offer help and advice at the shop, which is open from 10am to 5pm Monday to Saturday.

🎬 stories and anecdotes 🎨 famous people ✏ art and craft 🎭 entertainment and sport 🥾 walks

VANILLA ROSE

Market Street, Newtown, Powys SY16 2PQ
Tel: 01686 623131
e-mail: mail@vanilla-rose.co.uk
website: www.vanilla-rose.co.uk

Vanilla Rose is the perfect place to go to buy that special gift, or a souvenir of your visit to Wales. As well as noted brands such as Cath Kidston, Emma Bridgewater and Bombay Duck, this exclusive boutique also stocks locally crafted products such as cards, soaps and bags. It is a fascinating place, and shoppers can browse to their heart's content among the bright displays. So head for Vanilla Rose for all your gift and souvenir needs in mid Wales.

school. His remarkable life is told at the intimate **Robert Owen Memorial Museum**.

Another interesting visit to consider while in Newtown is to the **WH Smith Museum**, where the shop has been restored to its original 1927 layout and devotes much of its space to the history of the booksellers from 1792 onwards. The people of Newtown must certainly be an enterprising lot as it was here that the first ever mail order company was begun in 1859 by a man called Pryce-Jones. The business started in a small way with Welsh flannel but expanded rapidly, and Pryce-Jones even obtained the Royal seal of approval by having Queen Victoria on his list. In the Royal Welsh Warehosue in Station Road you can visit the **Pryce Jones Museum**, though this is by appointment only.

The former **Parish Church of St Mary** was abandoned in the 1840s due to flooding, and replaced by St David's Church. Its ruined nave originally had a south aisle, and the lower stages of the tower are 13th century. Its 15th century screen was moved to St David's and can be seen there. In the churchyard is the grave of Robert Owen. The grave has magnificent Art Nouveau iron railings, and his monument depicts the man with his workers.

Two miles east of Newtown is **Pwll Penarth Nature Reserve**, a feeding and nesting site for many species of wildfowl. The reserve has a nature walk and two hides, one accessible to wheelchairs.

Around Newtown

TREGYNON
4½ miles N of Newtown on the B4389

🌿 Gregynon Hall Gardens

Just to the south of the village lies **Gregynon Hall Gardens**, which are now part of the University of Wales, and where visitors can wander through the extensive woodlands on waymarked paths. Renowned for its spring bulbs, the sunken lawns before the house are associated with an unfinished design by William Emes. There is also a remarkable golden yew hedge. The hall is the setting for an annual music festival.

LLANFAIR CAEREINION
9 miles N of Newtown on the B4385

🚂 Welshpool and Llanfair Railway

🚂 Great Little Trains of Wales

This village is the western terminus of the **Welshpool and Llanfair Railway**. Passengers at Llanfair can enjoy reliving the days of steam but also relax in the Edwardian style tea rooms at the station. The narrow-

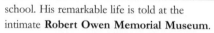

🏛 historic building   📷 museum   🏚 historic site   🌿 scenic attraction   🌱 flora and fauna

BANWY VALLEY NURSERY

Foel, near Welshpool, Powys SY21 0PT
Tel: 01938 820281
e-mail: syd@banwnursery.co.uk
website: www.banwnursery.co.uk

Situated on a north-facing hillside in mid Wales, the Banwy
Valley Nursery offers a wide range of trees, shrubs, climbers and
herbaceous perennials that are all grown within the nursery.
Everything is keenly priced and visitors can browse at their
leisure. A large selection of rhododendrons and azaleas are
always available. The friendly owners and staff are on hand to offer advice. The nursery is open
Tuesday to Sunday from 10am to 5pm, and on bank holidays.

gauge railway was originally opened to carry
sheep, cattle and goods as well as passengers.
It now travels, without the animals and goods
but with happy passengers, along the
delightful Banwy Valley, its carriages pulled by
scaled-down versions of steam locomotives
from Finland, Austria, Sierra Leone, Antigua
and Manchester. There are nine members of
the narrow-gauge **Great Little Trains of
Wales** (GLTOW): Bala Lake Railway; Brecon
Mountain Railway (Merthyr Tydfil); Ffestiniog
Railway (Porthmadog); Llanberis Lake
Railway; Rheilfford Eryri (Caernarfon);
Talyllin Railway (Tywyn); Vale of Rheidol
Railway (Aberystwyth); Welsh Highland
Railway (Porthmadog); and the Welshpool
and Llanfair Railway.

MONTGOMERY

7 miles NE of Newtown on the B4385

🏰 Montgomery Castle ⚔ Robber's Grave

🏰 Parish Church of St Nicholas 🏛 Fridd Faldwyn

🏰 Hen Domen Castle 🏛 Old Bell Museum

Montgomery is an attractive market town with
a pleasant Georgian character, and also some
surviving Tudor and Jacobean buildings that
are worthy of note. Above the town, the ruins
of **Montgomery Castle** stand in affirmation
of this borderland region's turbulent history.
The first castle was built in around 1100 by
the Norman, Roger de Montgomery. Attacked
over the years by rebels, it was rebuilt in 1223
as a garrison when Henry III was attempting
to quell the Welsh, a consequence being that

BUNNERS IRONMONGERS

Arthur Street, Montgomery, Powys SY15 6RA
Tel: 01686 668308 website: www.rhbunner.co.uk

The family run business of **Bunners Ironmongers** in the
heart of Montgomery is a classic ironmongers, and has
been around for over 100 years. There is everything you
will ever need for the home and garden here, from cooking
utensils to lawn mowers and from electrical goods to
Wellington boots! There is also a workshop dedicated to
repairing agricultural machinery, and it still sells paraffin and
petrol on account to loyal clients. So for all your
ironmongery and garden needs, head for Bunners.

🎭 stories and anecdotes 🦅 famous people 🎨 art and craft 🎵 entertainment and sport 🚶 walks

COUNTRY WORKS

Broad Street, Montgomery, Powys SY15 6PH
Tel: 01686 668866
e-mail: countryworks@btconnect.com
website: www.countryworksgallery.co.uk

For over 19 years, **Country Works**, a small, exclusive gallery, has been exhibiting and selling original works of art, including paintings etchings, jewellery, ceramics, glass clothes and cards. It is owned and managed by Barbara Geddes, who brings a wealth of experience to showcasing the work of local artists and craftspeople. She is determined to stock and sell only the best artistic works, and everything is keenly priced so that you, the customer, can own a work of art that you will treasure and admire for many years. The shop was opened in 1987, and Barbara has been here now for four years, offering friendly, helpful advice to people who call in. Country Works has been an award winner in the *Country Living* Small Business Award scheme.

There are two floors, with the upstairs floor being given over to exhibitions of paintings. These exhibitions change every six weeks, and they have featured such local artists as Jenny Jones and Anna Ravenscroft. There have also been exhibitions of pottery, glass and even books.

Country Works is open 10am to 5.30pm from Monday to Saturday and from 1pm to 5pm on Sundays. It closes over Christmas and New Year, but stays open on bank holidays.

Montgomery Castle

the town received a charter from the king in 1227. During the Civil War, the castle surrendered to Parliamentary forces but was demolished in 1649 in punishment for the then Lord Herbert's Royalist sympathies. The remains of the castle are open at all times and entrance is free. Access is up steep paths from the town or by a level footpath from the car park, and the visit is worth it for the views alone. One mile from the town is the motte of yet another ancient castle - **Hen Domen**, again built by Roger de Montgomery.

Offa's Dyke (see Prestatyn) passes close by and is another reminder of the military significance that this area once held. In Arthur Street, the **Old Bell Museum** has 11 rooms of local history including features on civic and social life, Norman and medieval castles, the workhouse and the Cambrian Railway.

🏛 historic building   🏛 museum   🏛 historic site   🝆 scenic attraction   🌿 flora and fauna

The 13th century **Parish Church of St Nicholas** has some interesting features, including wooden carved angels, carved miserere seats and the magnificent canopied tomb of Richard Herbert, Lord of Montgomery Castle. In the churchyard is the famous **Robber's Grave**. John Davis, hanged in public in 1821 for murder, proclaimed his innocence and swore that the grass would not grow above his grave for at least 100 years!

To the west of the town the Iron Age hill fort of **Fridd Faldwyn** tops a 750-foot hill that also provides stunning views to Cadair Idris and eastwards into England.

BERRIEW
7½ miles NE of Newtown on the B4390

🏠 Parish Church of St Beuno 🏠 Glansevern Hall
🏠 Maen Beuno

Over the years, this picturesque village of half-timbered houses beside the River Rhiw has been a frequent winner of Best Kept Village awards. Like a number of other places in Wales, Berriew is associated with St Beuno who apparently heard English voices while communing by the river here and warned the villagers of the imposing threat. A large glacial boulder here **Maen Beuno**, has been named after him. Berriew's **Parish Church of St Beuno** contains fine marble effigies of Arthur Price, Sheriff of Montgomeryshire in 1578, and his two wives, Bridget and Jane. The memorial cross of 1933 in the churchyard is by Sir Ninian Comper, whose work can be seen in churches all over Britain. Though there has been a church on the site for centuries, the present church dates from 1802 and a complete refurbishment of 1875.

The Gardens at **Glansevern Hall** (see panel below), entered from the A483 by the

Glansevern Hall Gardens

Tea Room Gallery Shop Plant Sales

Opening Times
Thursday, Friday, Saturday and Bank Holiday Mondays from first week of May to last week of September. 12 noon - 5 pm

Admission
Entrance fee: £4.00 Children under 16 free
Groups by appointment on other days

How To Find Us
Signposted 4 miles S.W. of Powis Castle on A483

Berriew, Welshpool, Powys SY21 8AH
Tel: 01686 640644 email: glansevern@yahoo.co.uk
for further details: www.glansevern.co.uk

Over 20 acres of mature gardens

GET AHEAD HATS

Middle Aston, near Bishop's Castle, Powys SY15 6TA
Tel: 01588 638246
website: www.getaheadhats.co.uk and
    www.getaheadhats.co.uk/montgomery.php

Special hats for special occasions - that's the proud boast of **Get Ahead Hats**! Nowela Swanson opened her boutique five years ago, selling and hiring out hats exclusively designed by herself and some of the top UK milliners. Elegance and style are the watchwords here, and there are flexible opening hours with evenings by appointment. There is also a wide range of beautiful accessories, such as jewellery, handbags and shoes.

bridge over the River Rhiew, were first laid out in 1801 and now cover 18 acres. Noted in particular for the unusual tree species, they also have lovely lawns, herbaceous beds, a walled garden, rose gardens, a lovely water garden and a rock garden complete with grotto. In the Old Stables are a tea room, a garden shop and a gallery with regular exhibitions of paintings, sculpture and interior design. A wide variety of herbaceous plants, all grown at Glansevern, can be bought. Surrounding a very handsome Greek Revival house, the gardens are themselves set in parkland on the banks of the River Severn. Built for Arthur Davies Owen Glansevern was the seat of the Owen family from 1800 until after the Second World War.

CHURCH STOKE
10½ miles E of Newtown on the A489

🏛 Bacheldre Mill   🏛 Simon's Castle

🏛 Parish Church of st Nicholas

This attractive village, sometimes spelled as 'Churchstoke' lies right on the Welsh-English border. Just to the west can be found some very visible and well preserved sections of Offa's Dyke (see Prestatyn). At Bacheldre, two miles along the A489, **Bacheldre Mill** is a fully restored watermill producing award-

winning organic stoneground flour. Visitors can enjoy a guided tour and even mill their own flour. **Simon's Castle**, to the east of the village, is a motte and bailey site that was probably built in the 12th or 13th centuries. The **Parish Church of St Nicholas** is unusual, as it lies in England, while its parish is in Wales. Its tower is 13th century, and during the Civil War, when Royalist troops took refuge in the building, Parliamentarians set fire to the door to fush them out. The church was rebuilt in the early 19th century, and up until 1881 was dedicated to St Mary.

ABERMULE
4 miles NE of Newtown on the B4386

🏛 Dolforwyn Castle   🎞 Abermule Train Disaster

Across the Montgomery Canal and River Severn from this village, which is also known by its Welsh name Abermiwl, lie the scant remains of **Dolforwyn Castle**, which was built in 1273 by Llywelyn the Last (he was the last native ruler of Wales). This was the last castle to have been built by a native Welsh prince on his own soil, and Llywelyn also tried to establish a small town around the castle to rival that of nearby, and much anglicised, Welshpool. However, the castle was only a Welsh stronghold for four years before it was

🏛 historic building   🏛 museum   🏛 historic site   🔱 scenic attraction   🌱 flora and fauna

taken by the English and left to decay into the haunting ruins you see today. The **Abermule Train Disaster** took place in 1921, when 17 people were killed as two trains collided head on. Human error was later found to be the cause. A double track was later laid, but curiously, as part of the Beeching cuts in the early 1960s, it reverted to single track.

Dolforwyn Castle, Abermule

KERRY

2½ miles SE of Newtown on the A489

🏛 Parish Church of St Michael and All Angels

Situated on the banks of the River Mule, a tributary of the River Severn, this village lies in the heart of sheep rearing country and has given its name to the Kerry Hills breed of sheep characterised by distinctive black spots on their faces and legs. Small, hornless and usually white apart from the markings, the Kerry Hills have very dense fleeces that are particularly suitable for dyeing in pastel shades for knitting yarns. This breed is one of several variants on the Welsh Mountain sheep. Others include Black Welsh Mountain, Badger-faced Welsh Mountain, Beulah Speckle Face, Lleyn and Llanwenog.

The **Parish Church of St Michael and All Angels** dates originally from 1176, though only the nave's north arcade survives from that time. The tower is 14th century, as is the chancel arcade. The rest dates from a rebuild

in the 1880s. It has a chained Welsh Bible of 1690. There was, in former times, a custom at the church that the sexton would 'patrol' the congregation during services and would ring a bell if he found anyone asleep.

LLANDINAM

5½ miles SW of Newtown on the A470

🏛 Parish Church of St Llonio   🪶 David Davies

This quiet village was the home of **David Davies**, an industrialist who was instrumental in founding the docks at Barry in South Wales. Davies' bronze statue, made by the same Sir Alfred Gilbert who was responsible for Eros in Piccadilly, stands in the village. It has been awarded the title of the 'best kept village in Wales, Powys and Montgomeryshire' on a number of occasions. It is well worth visiting to view its black and white timbered buildings. During the Second World War Gordonstoun School was evacuated to here. The **Parish Church of St Llonio** is worth visiting. Though largely rebuilt in the 19th century, it has a 13th century tower, two old tomb recesses and a 17th century reredos and carved choir stalls.

🎭 stories and anecdotes   🪶 famous people   🎨 art and craft   🎭 entertainment and sport   🚶 walks

CAERSWS

4 miles W of Newtown on the A470

🌿 Llyn Mawr Reserve 🐦 John 'Ceiriog' Hughes

The village is built on the site of a 1st century Roman fort that was strategically positioned here by the Rivers Severn and Carno and, to the north, the remains of an earthwork fort can still be seen. In more recent times, Caersws was the home, for some 20 years, of the poet **John 'Ceiriog' Hughes**, who was then the manager of the local Van Railway. Born at Llan Dyffryn Ceiriog in 1833, when he was 17, he took employment on the railways in Manchester. In 1865 he became stationmaster at Llanidloes and six years later took over at Caersws, managing the six-mile railway that ran to the Van lead mines. It is said that many people came to Caersws just for the delight of

having a chat to the affable poet. Hughes lies buried in the graveyard at the nearby village of Llanwnog. Near Caersws, signposted off the A470 Machynlleth road, **Llyn Mawr Reserve** is a 20-acre lake with wetland habitat noted for wetland birds such as the great crested grebe, tufted duck, snipe and curlew.

Welshpool

🏛 Strata Marcella 🏛 Cockpit

🏛 Powysland Museum 🏛 Grace Evans' Cottage

🏛 Montgomery Canal Centre

🚂 Welshpool and Llanfair Railway 🏞 Long Mountain

🌿 Severn Farm Pond Nature Reserve

This bustling market town, which was granted a charter in 1263 by the Prince of Powys, was,

---

ROYAL OAK HOTEL

The Cross, Welshpool, Powys SY21 7DG
Tel: 01938 552217 Fax: 01938 556652
e-mail: relax@royaloakhotel.info
website: www.royaloakhotel.info

The **Royal Oak Hotel** is a 350-year-old Grade 2 listed coaching inn, previously belonging to the Powis Castle estate which is situated less than one mile away. The hotel has recently undergone a spectacular refurbishment and now sets new standards for hotel accommodation in Mid Wales.

It boasts 25 fully en suite Laura Ashley designed bedrooms that offer three levels of accommodation. The Standard rooms offer full facilities at a price more suitable for those with a smaller budget. Contemporary rooms offer a more modern feel and classic rooms and suites can be described as opulence! All rooms appeal to both business travelers and people on holiday or having a weekend break. The hotel is entirely non smoking throughout and offers free wireless broadband.

The food, as you would expect is outstanding. Whether it's a bar snack or a full dinner in the evening, you are sure to be delighted with the menu, which uses fresh, local produce in an imaginative fashion. There is also a popular Sunday carvery, though you are well advised to book in advance.

Why not enjoy a real ale in the new Oak Bar or sit and relax in the snug with a coffee and newspaper and watch the world go by.

 🏛 historic building 🏛 museum 🚂 historic site 🏞 scenic attraction 🌿 flora and fauna

for a long time, known as Pool - the Welsh prefix was added in 1835 to settle the long running dispute concerning its nationality, as it sits no more than four miles from the English border. As is typical with many places in the upper Severn Valley, Welshpool has numerous examples of picturesque, half-timbered buildings, and that alone makes the place well worth visiting..

Housed in a former warehouse beside the Montgomery Canal is the **Powysland Museum**, which was founded in 1874 by Morris Jones. Earlier, many of the artefacts that formed the museum's original collection had been put together by the Powysland Club - a group of Victorian gentlemen who were interested in the history of mid-Wales. The museum covers various aspects of the region:

the development of life in Montgomeryshire from the earliest times to the 20th century; local agriculture and farming equipment; and the building of the first canals and railways in the area.

Along with the museum, the old warehouse is also home to the **Montgomery Canal Centre** where the story of this waterway is told. Completed in 1821, the canal carried coal and food from Welshpool to the upper reaches of the River Severn. Though, as with other canals, its decline came with the arrival of the railways, the section of the canal around Welshpool is once again open, now for pleasure cruises.

Near the town are the scant remains - no more than a few bumps in field - of **Strata Marcella**, the Cistercian abbey founded

THE CELTIC COMPANY

14 Broad Street, Welshpool, Powys SY21 7SD
Tel: 01938 556262
e-mail: sales@celticcompany.co.uk
website: www.celticcompany.co.uk

The **Celtic Company** is the classic gift shop - the perfect place to buy that special gift or souvenir of your visit to Wales. It sells a stunning range of beautiful items, and you could have a truly enjoyable time just browsing the many things on offer. The shop has been open for over 10 years, and is situated right in the centre of Welshpool. There is excellent access to the shop and parking outside for disabled customers. The staff are knowledgeable and always on hand to offer advice and help.

Whether it's the great range of fashion and leather handbags, the Crabtree and Evelyn soaps and fragrances, the decorative tableware or the Storm watches and jewellery, you'll be delighted and amazed at the choice and the outstanding value for money. Children will just love the appealing, stuffed teddy bears and the brightly coloured animal clocks! A popular choice for tourists is the wonderful and ever-popular Portmeirion china and ceramic giftware, or the Sophie Conran range of tableware. One of the latest ranges stocked by shop is a Victorian vintage revival range of jewellery, which harks back to a more romantic time.

So why not call in when you're close to Welshpool? There is absolutely no obligation to buy.

📖 stories and anecdotes   🦅 famous people   ✐ art and craft   ✍ entertainment and sport   🚶 walks

Powis Castle, Welshpool

around 1170 by Owain Cyfeiliog, Prince of Powys. It was one of the largest Cistercian houses in Wales, with a church that was 273 feet long. When Henry VIII dissolved the abbeys in 1536, his men turned up at Strata Marcella to discover that it has already been dissolved by the monks themselves the year before. They had sold it to Lord Powis, who, by the time Henry's men turned up, had stripped it of everything that was of value. Lord Powis had even sold the stones from which it was built, and they ended up in many churches and houses in the area.

The town is also home to two other interesting buildings, the **Cockpit** and **Grace Evans' Cottage.** The only surviving cockpit on its original site in Wales, this venue for the bloodthirsty sport was built in the 18th

ASHMAN'S VINTAGE CLOTHING & ACCESSORIES

7 Park Lane House, Welshpool, Powys SY2 7JP
Tel: 01938 554505
e-mail: ashman-antiques@hotmail.com

Situated in an elegant and pleasantly proportioned townhouse, **Ashman's Vintage Clothing and** Accessories is an Aladdin's cave of unique vintage and retro fashion. The colourful sales areas are cornucopias crammed with colourful clothes, costumes and accessories up to the 1980s, including beaded garments, ball gowns, bags, shoes, embroidered shawls, Oriental costumes, wedding dresses, lace tablecloths, bedspreads, Victorian baby gowns and nightdresses.

She also stocks shoes, gloves and hats, china, umbrellas, bric-a-brac, costume jewellery and an amazing range of accessories for all occasions. It is owned and managed by Diane Ashman, who has been 35 years in the business, and has been in Welshpool since 1991. She is determined to sell only high quality items at amazingly affordable prices, and the shop has a great reputation far beyond the town and its immediate area. There are also many items for men, including braces, cravats, bow ties, bowler hats, top hats and dinner suits. And for children there are dolls and a range of clothing that is sure to delight.

You are free to browse here to your heart's content, and Diane is always on hand to offer friendly advice and help. Next door she has another shop selling antiques, textiles, quilts, linen and lace. Don't forget to call in there as well.

🏛 historic building   🏛 museum   🏛 historic site   🍃 scenic attraction   🌿 flora and fauna century and remained in use until the sport was banned in Britain in 1849. Grace Evans is certainly one of the town's best known citizens as she was instrumental in rescuing Lord Nithsdale (who was in disguise as a lady) from the Tower of London in 1716. As Lady Nithsdale's maid, Grace fled with the couple to France but she returned to Welshpool in 1735 and lived at the cottage, which is said to have been given to her by a grateful Lord Nithsdale, until her death three years later.

At the southern edge of town on Severn Farm Industrial Estate is Severn Farm Pond, one of 13 nature reserves managed by the Montgomeryshire Wildlife Trust. This one is a particularly good site for dragonflies, damselflies and amphibia.

The **Severn Farm Pond Nature Reserve** sits in an industrial estate, however it attracts many birds, animals and insects, especially in the newly cerated ponds and wetland areas. **Long Mountain** stretches four miles along the Welsh side of the border east of Welshpool. It is crossed by Offa's Dyke (see Prestatyn) and on its highest point is an ancient hill fort known as Beacon Ring. It was on Long Mountain that Henry Tudor camped in 1485 before crossing the border, defeating Richard III at Bosworth Field and ascending the throne of England as Henry VII. Henry Tudor had a Red Dragon as his standard and as king he incorporated the Welsh dragon into the Royal arms. There it stayed until James I displaced it with the Scottish unicorn. In 1901 the Red Dragon was officially recognised as

MOORS FARM B&B

Oswestry Road, Welshpool, Powys SY18 6PW
Tel: 01938 583895
e-mail: moors farm@tiscali.co.uk
website: www.moors-farm.com

Moors Farm B&B offers five star bed and breakfast accommodation on a working sheep and beef farm one mile out of Welshpool, right in the heart of one of the most beautiful parts of Wales. It is a gracious and elegant building, well proportioned and full of character, and was once the home farm for Powis Castle, but is now privately owned. It sits on the edge of the Montgomery Canal and has as a stunning backdrop the Rhallt Woods.

There are five fully en suite rooms on offer, each one comfortable and spacious, with individual furnishings and decoration. This is real Welsh farmhouse hospitality, with the B&B tariff including a hearty and filling cooked breakfast, or something lighter if required. The produce is all sourced locally, so you know you are getting quality at competitive prices. The whole area round the farm is ideal for walking shooting and fishing, as well as other country pursuits. It especially welcomes bookings from families and other groups.

Also on the farm is superb self-catering accommodation within a converted barn. This boasts six en suite bedrooms, one of them suitable for the disabled. The accommodation has all mod cons to make your stay a delightful one. Bookings are taken on a daily or weekly basis, and all credit and debit cards are accepted with the exception of Diners and American Express.

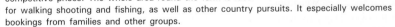

stories and anecdotes   famous people   art and craft   entertainment and sport   walks

OAK INN

Guilsfield, near Welshpool, Powys SY21 9NH
Tel: 01938 553391

The **Oak Inn** is a picturesque 17th century, timber framed, black and white farmhouse within the pretty village of Guilsfield. It retains many original features, and the interior is warm, cosy and inviting, as a good village inn should be. The landlords, David and the two Helens, are proud of their reputation for hospitality, good, honest home-cooking and a great range of drinks. The snack and à la carte menus contain a wide variety of tasty dishes that have earned the pub a reputation far beyond its local area. There is ample car parking, plenty of outdoor seating and a play area for kids.

the Royal badge of Wales and in 1959 the Queen commanded that the Red Dragon on its green and white field should be the official Welsh flag.

Just to the southwest of the town lies one of the best known places in the area - **Powis Castle**. Inhabited for around 500 years, the various alterations which have taken place here over the years now cause the castle to look more like a mansion. The remains of a Norman motte and bailey are thought to be from the original castle which is believed to have been built on this site in the early 12th century and was then destroyed during a dispute between Llywelyn the Great and Gruffydd ap Gwenwynwyn, a local landowner. Edward I granted the family a barony on condition that they renounced their Welsh title, which they subsequently did, and so the castle seen today was built

2002 marked the 50th year of the castle being in the hands of the National Trust, and the occasion was marked by a series of special events, all with a golden theme. From the town, the narrow gauge **Welshpool and Llanfair Railway** takes passengers on a steam train journey through the Powis estates and the delightful Banwy valley to Llanfair Caereinion.

Around Welshpool

GUILSFIELD
2½ miles N of Welshpool on the B4392

Parish Church of St Aelhaiarn Gaer Fawr

The large 15th century **Parish Church of St Aelhaiarn** is well worth a second glance as, not only does it have an unusual upper chamber above the south porch, but there is also a splendid panelled roof from the same date and some fine 19th century vaulting.

Off the B4392 just outside the village, **Gaer Fawr** (it means Great Camp) covers most of a hilltop and includes a scheduled ancient monument. There are great walks through woodland and grassland with some splendid views.

LLANGEDWYN
10½ miles N of Welshpool on the B4396

Sycharth Castle

Just to the northeast of the village and close to the English border, lies one of Wales' most nationalistic shrines, **Sycharth Castle**. A grassy mound is all that remains of one of Owain Glyndwr's principal houses, which was immortalised in a poem by Iolo Goch, which speaks of its nine halls, many guest rooms and a church. The poem appears in a translation by Anthony Conran in the *Penguin Book of Welsh Verse*:

Here are gifts for everyone
No hunger, disgrace or dearth,
Or ever thirst at Sycharth!
Haply the best of Welshmen
Owns the land, of Pywer's kin;
It's a strong, lean warrior owns
This most lovable of mansions.

The **Llangedewyn Millcraft Centre** occupies the site of a former corn mill on the River Tanat, and now has three craft shops as well as a café and offices.

MIDDLETOWN
5½ miles NE of Welshpool on the A458

🏛 Breidden Hill 🏛 Rodney's Pillar

To the north of this village, which stands right on the Welsh/English border, lies **Breidden Hill**, which is thought to have been the venue for a fierce battle between the Welsh and the forces of Edward I in 1292. On the summit stands an obelisk, **Rodney's Pillar**, which commemorates Admiral Rodney's victory over the French off Domenica in 1782.

MEIFOD
5½ miles NW of Welshpool on the A495

🏛 Parish Church of St Tysilio and St Mary

This picturesque village in the wooded valley of the River Vyrnwy is remembered in Welsh literature as being the location of the summer residence of the princes of Powys. The **Parish Church of St Tysilio and St Mary**, which was consecrated in 1155, now mainly dates from the 14th and 15th centuries. is home to an interesting 9th century grave slab that bears old Celtic markings as well as a

Latin cross and a Greek crucifix. According to legend, in AD 550, when St Gwyddfarch was asked where he would like to build his first church, he is said to have replied, in Welsh, "yma y mae i fod" ('here it is to be'). So the village got its name, and after his death the saint is thought to have been buried a short distance away. In the 9th century, while the princes of Powys had their main residence close by, Meifod became a religious centre and it is thought that the grave slab is a memorial to one of the princes.

LLANFIHANGEL-YNG-NGWYNFA
10½ miles NW of Welshpool on the B4382

🏛 Parish Church of St Michael 🐦 Ann Griffith

In the small, Victorian **Parish Church of St Michael** there some old carved stones, and in the churchyard a red granite memorial to the Welsh hymn writer, **Ann Griffiths.** Born at a farm near Dolanog, in 1776, where she lived most of her short life, Ann only ever travelled as far as Bala, where she went to hear Thomas Charles preach. However, despite dying at the early age of 29 years, Ann wrote over 70 Welsh hymns, all dictated to a friend.

LLANWDDYN
14 miles NW of Welshpool on the B4393

🐦 Lake Vyrnwy 🏛 Hirnant Tunnel

The village lies at the southern end of **Lake Vyrnwy** (Llyn Efyrnwy), a four mile stretch of water that was created, in the years following 1881, by the flooding of the entire Vyrnwy Valley, to provide the people of Liverpool with an adequate water supply. Close to the dam, which is 390 yards long, 144 feet high, is a monument that marks the beginning of the **Hirnant Tunnel** - the first stage of a 75-mile aqueduct that carries the water to Liverpool. Another striking

building is the
Gothic tower
designed by George
Frederick Deacon,
engineer to the
Liverpool Water
Board. On higher
ground is an
obelisk that is a
monument to the
44 men who died
during the
construction of the
reservoir.

To construct this,
the first of several
massive reservoirs in north and mid-Wales,
the original village of Llanwddyn, home to
some 400 people, was flooded along with the
valley. On the hill south of the dam stands the
'new' village and the church, built by
Liverpool Corporation in 1887. Photographs
in the Lake Vyrnwy Hotel show the original
village with its 37 houses, all now along with
the church submerged under the lake's 13,000
million gallons of water. The reservoir's
visitor centre not only tells the story of the
construction but is also home to an RSPB
centre; there are four RSPB hides at various
points around the lake and guided tours can
be arranged around the estate for schools and
groups.

A road circumnavigates the lake but walking
around it or on any of the nature trails is an
ideal way to observe the abundant wild and
bird life that live around the shores. Lake
Vyrnwy's sculpture park was started in 1997
and has evolved constantly ever since, using
local timber and on-site materials. Local artists
have worked in partnership with sculptors
from Russia, Estonia, Lithuania and Australia.
The park's key theme is wildlife, and the local

Lake Vyrnwy

artists have been inspired by species found on
the site, while the international artists have
drawn inspiration from their homelands. The
sculpture park is managed jointly by Severn
Trent Water, the RSPB and Forest Enterprise
Wales.

Bethania Adventure, based at the Boat
House, organises activities on and around the
lake, including sailing, windsurfing, kayaking,
canoeing, climbing and abseiling; the lake is
also a favourite spot for anglers. With its
lovely scenery and coniferous forests, the lake
has doubled in films for Switzerland or
Transylvania; it was also used for location
shots in *The Dambusters*.

LLANGYNOG
16 miles NW of Welshpool on the B4391

🏛 Parish Church of St Melangell

🌿 Pennant Melangell

Situated at the confluence of the Rivers
Tanat and Eirth and overlooked by the
Berwyn range, the village's name recalls
Cynog, the son of King Brychan of
Brycheiniog. The **Parish Church of St**

Cynog was built in the late 18th century in fine Georgian style. Further up the wooded valley of the upper River Tanat, in the hamlet of **Pennant Melangell**, lies **Parish Church of St Melangell**, where there can be seen two images that are said to be of a Welsh prince and the 7th century St Melangell. The story goes that a hunted hare took refuge in the saint's cloak and thus she became the patron saint of hares. These creatures were once treated as sacred in this lonely area. A short distance further upstream is a small waterfall that marks the start of the valley.

LLANRHAEADR-YM-MOCHNANT
13 miles NW of Welshpool on the B4580

🏛 Parish Church of St Dogfan

♨ Pistyll Rhaeadr 🎭 Plygeiniau

Despite its relative isolation this village attracts many visitors who pass through on their way to **Pistyll Rhaeadr** (see walk on page 154), which lies up a narrow road to the northwest of the village. This is one of the Seven Wonders of Wales and, with a drop of 240 feet, is the highest waterfall in Britain south of the Scottish Highlands. The English translation of the name is Spout Waterfall, an obvious name as the water drops vertically for 100 feet before running into a cauldron, and on through a natural tunnel in the rock before reappearing.

The **Parish Church of St Dogfan** dates originally from the 14th century, though the tower and parts of the main building are later. It was while vicar here in the late 16th century that Bishop William Morgan made his famous translation of the Bible into Welsh. He was granted permission to carry out this work by Queen Elizabeth I, her father Henry VIII having banned any official use of the Welsh language.

LLANFYLLIN
9 miles NW of Welshpool on the A490

🏛 Parish Church of St Myllin 🏛 Council House

🏛 Pendref Congregational Chapel ♨ St Myllin's Well

This charming and peaceful hillside town lies in the valley of the River Cain where it joins the Abel. It was granted its charter as a borough in 1293 by Llewelyn ap Gruffydd ap Gwenwynwyn, Lord of Mechain. Welshpool is the only other Welsh borough to have been granted its charter from a native Welsh ruler. To celebrate the 700th anniversary in 1993 of the granting of the charter a large tapestry of the town's historic buildings was created, and it can now be seen in the **Parish Church of St Myllin**, a delightful redbrick building dating from 1706.

Overlooking the town is the beauty spot of **St Myllin's Well**. Water from the well has, from the 6th century onwards, been thought to cure all manner of ailments and certainly the view over the town and to the Berwyn Mountains beyond, is uplifting. St Myllin, a 7th century Celt, is traditionally alluded to as the first cleric to baptise by total immersion in his holy well. Opposite the church is the brick **Council House**, which has 13 wall paintings in an upstairs room. These were all done by a Napoleonic prisoner of war, one of several billeted in the town between 1812 and 1814. Ann Griffiths, the famous Welsh hymn writer, was baptised in **Pendref Congregational Chapel**, one of the oldest Non-Conformist places of worship in Wales, established in 1640 (see alsoLlanfihangel-Yng-Nowynfa). The present building dates from 1829.

Two miles southeast of Llanfyllin, off the A490, **Bryngwyn** is a handsome 18th century house by Robert Mylne, surrounded by 18th century and early 19th century parkland.

🎭 stories and anecdotes 🐦 famous people 🎨 art and craft 🎧 entertainment and sport 🚶 walks

Pistyll Rhaeadr

Distance: *3.7 miles (5.9 kilometres)*

Typical time: *210 mins*

Height gain: *230 metres*

Map: *Explorer 255*

Walk: *www.walkingworld.com* *ID:1015*

Contributor: *Jim Grindle*

The falls are a little remote and this is part of
their charm. The easiest access is from the A483
just south of Oswestry. Turn off at the White
Lion onto the A495. After a couple of miles this
becomes the B4396 to Llanrhaeadr-yn-
Mochnant. A well signposted but rather tight
right turn in the village leads to a narrow road
with passing places. The falls are about four miles
along this road. There is some roadside parking,
but parking at the cafe, an old farm, is
inexpensive. The cafe is not open on Mondays
and is not always open in winter.

ADDITIONAL INFORMATION:

The falls are one of the Seven Wonders of Wales
mentioned in a celebrated 18th century verse:

> *Pistyll Rhaeadr and Wrexham Steeple,*
> *Snowdon's Mountain without its people,*
> *Overton Yew Trees, St Winefride's Well,*
> *Llangollen Bridge and Gresford Bells.*

DESCRIPTION:

The waterfall at Llanrhaeadr is well known as one
of the Seven Wonders of Wales and is the
starting point of this walk. Leave the car park by
the cafe at the foot of the falls and go through
the gate to walk the 100m up to the bridge at the
base of the falls. A right turn here takes you
through a beech wood and two gates onto a large
track. Almost at once you turn up on a steep
rocky staircase built by volunteers and leading to
another track.

Turn left and in a few minutes you will see a
signpost indicating a ladder-stile and access to the
top of the falls should you wish to visit them.
The route continues up this quiet valley as far as
a stream with a fence on the far side. Go down to
where two streams meet and cross a gate at the
junction of fences. At this point the route
doubles back on itself towards some huge
sheepfolds after which there is a gradual climb.

When the climb is over there are superb
views of the main peaks of the Berwyns. Height
is maintained for some 2km before a mine track
leads down into the valley on
the left.

The walk is level now and goes through
woodland before once again reaching the bridge
at the base of the falls.

FEATURES:

Hills or Fells, Mountains, River, Toilets, Great
Views, Food Shop, Moor, Tea Shop, Waterfall

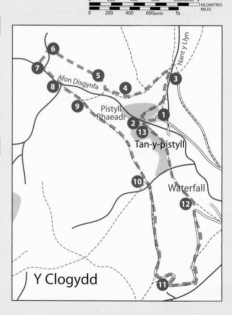

1 | To the right of the entrance to the cafe is a small wooden gate. Go through this and turn right. In 100m you will come to a little iron bridge at the foot of the falls.

2 | Don't cross the bridge when you have admired the falls, but turn right - into the wood. You pass one faint path leading off left and come to a gate. Go through and follow the path slightly left to a stile and gate at the edge of the wood. Beyond this gate is a stony track which you follow for a few metres. You will see a signpost and some rocky steps on the left. Go up these steps to another track at the top.

3 | Turn left. Just over the brow of the hill look for a signpost on the left of the track. It is not very high.

4 | The signpost points towards a ladder stile by some trees over to the left. If you wish to see the top of the falls then turn left and return to continue the walk.   Further up the valley the path divides.

5 | You want the lower path, on the left. The path eventually peters out at a wide, reedy patch - just carry straight through it, picking the best way you can. You will reach a very straight and deep streambed (it sometimes has water in it). On the far side is a wire fence.

6 | Don't cross the stream or the fence but turn left, downhill to where the stream joins the main stream feeding the falls. You will have to cross this stream and the best way to do this is to turn left when you reach it so that you are going downstream. In about 100m you will reach a pebbly shore where the water is shallower. Once across, turn right and make for the corner where the two fences meet.

7 | In this corner are some low gates, the only place that you can get over the fence. Cross and turn left - you have reached the furthest point of the walk in this direction and are now going back

in the direction of the falls. Make for the stone walls of some sheep pens.

8 | Go to the left of the pens and then turn right, following a little stream uphill until you can cross it. The map shows a path here and you may find traces of it. You should aim for the group of conifers which you can just see on the skyline.

9 | When you reach the conifers cross the gate and follow the fence on your left. There is a steady climb here. Eventually another fence comes in from the right and for a short distance you will be between the two. At the top of this first rise there is a gate on your left and good views of the Berwyns.

10 | Keep going with the fence over to your left. The ground drops, you cross a stream, and the grass gives way to a wide, stony track which climbs just a little more to the highest point of the walk. It then drops and takes a sharp turn left in the first of a series of bends into the valley on your left.

11 | The track goes left again before hugging the side of the hill. Just follow the track now until you come to another sharp bend - to the right - 800m away. At this bend leave the track and keep ahead in the same direction as before, using sheep tracks to reach a path alongside a fence below you.

12 | Aim for a rowan tree - it is only a few minutes from the track. Now turn left and follow the path along the fence. Pass a stile on your right and you will come to another one leading into a wood. The path continues on the other side, almost immediately crossing a stream. Follow the path through woodland and some small clearings until you see some fencing below you on the right.

13 | Not too easy to spot but you will be aware of people on the other side at this point. (If you go too far you will be right below the waterfall and know that you have to turn back). Just out of sight is the iron bridge that you came to at the start of the walk. Cross it to get back to the gate and the cafe.

LOCATOR MAP

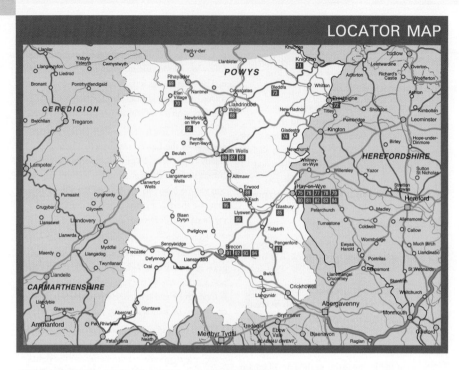

ADVERTISERS AND PLACES OF INTEREST

🏛 historic building   🏠 museum   🏛 historic site   💧 scenic attraction   🌿 flora and fauna

5 South Powys & Brecon Beacons

This southern region of the large county of Powys is steeped in history, and there is evidence aplenty of turbulent times past, from the Romans onwards. The Celtic standing stones and burial chambers and the ruined castles are among the many notable buildings and memorials left by past inhabitants.

In the heart of Wales (the northern part of this region) can be found the four spa towns of Llandrindod Wells, Builth Wells, Llangammarch Wells and Llanwrtyd Wells. Still popular tourist centres today, though no longer primarily spas, these places all grew and developed as a result of the arrival of the railways and the Victorians' interest in health. Although the architecture of these towns suggests that they date mainly from the 19th

and early 20th centuries, there are the remains of a Roman fort (Castell Collen) close to Llandrindod Wells, and Builth Wells saw much fighting in medieval times. As well as the spa towns, the region also has the border settlements of Knighton and Presteigne, the second-hand book capital of the world Hay-on-Wye, and the ancient cathedral city of Brecon.

However, it is perhaps for its varied countryside that south Powys is better known. Close to Rhayader, in the Cambrian Mountains, are the spectacular reservoirs and dams that make up the Elan Valley. Built at the end of the 19th century to supply water to the West Midlands, not only are these a great feat of Victorian engineering but the surrounding countryside is home to one of Britain's rarest and most beautiful birds - the red kite.

Brecon Beacons

Further south lies the Brecon Beacons National Park, which takes its name from the distinctively shaped sandstone mountains of the Brecon Beacons. However, there are two other ranges within the park's 519 square miles. To the east of the Brecon Beacons lie the interlocking peaks of the Black Mountains which stretch to the English border, while to the west is Black Mountain which, though its name is singular, refers to an unpopulated range of barren, smooth-humped peaks.

Llandrindod Wells

🏛 Old Parish Church of Llandrindod	🌿 Bailey Einion
🌿 Abercamlo Bog	🍂 Victorian Festival
🏛 Parish Church of the Holy Trinity	🍀 Radnor Forest
🏛 Radnorshire Museum	🏛 National Cycle Collection
🏛 Castell Collen	🏛 Heart of Wales Line	🍀 Rock Park

The most elegant of the spa towns of mid-Wales, Llandrindod Wells, though not primarily a spa today, is still a popular place that has retained its Victorian and Edwardian character and architecture. This was only a scattering of cottages and two churches until 1749, when the first hotel was built by a Mr Grosvenor and, for a time, until that hotel closed in 1787, the town had a reputation as a haunt for gamblers and rakes.

Llandrindod Wells was, from 1880 up until local government reorganisation in 1974, the county town of the old county of Radnorshire. Despite its chiefly 19th and early 20th century architecture, however, it has ancient roots. To the northwest of the town lies **Castell Collen**, a Roman fort that was occupied from the 1st century through to the

Llandrindod Wells Victorian Festival

*Victorian Festival Office, Wadham House,
Middleton Street, Llandrindod Wells,
Powys LD1 5DG
Tel: 01597 823441
e-mail : info@victorianfestival.co.uk
website: www.vicfest.co.uk*

Each year Llandrindod Wells hosts a Victorian festival. Held in the last full week of August before the Bank Holiday, this popular festival is going from strength to strength and has now become one of the premier Victorian festivals in Britain today.

As Llandrindod was a thriving spa resort in the Victorian era it is natural to base the festival on the Victorian theme. The town's unspoilt architecture provides a perfect backdrop to the celebrations and, on Temple Gardens, there is an ideal venue for the many different types of street entertainment provided free for the visitors and townsfolk throughout the day.

The aim of the festival is to provide a family fun festival and to cater for all ages and tastes, whilst keeping to a Victorian theme. Attracting some 40,000 visitors to a town that has a population of only 5,000 is no mean feat, but the apparent ease with which it is done is largely due to the transformation achieved in the town's reversion to the Victorian era. The effect of horses and carriages, Victorian window displays and the townspeople and some visitors sporting a whole range of appropriate costumes creates an atmosphere, the effect of which is nothing short of miraculous.

At the end of the nine days, the proceedings are closed in the grandest of manners with the moving torchlight procession and fireworks display over the lake - a spectacle not to be missed.

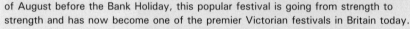

🏛 historic building   🏛 museum   🏛 historic site   🍀 scenic attraction   🌿 flora and fauna

early 4th century and whose earthworks are clearly detectable today. The first castle was of turf and timber, put up by Frontinus in about AD 75, with later versions being made of stone. It was the Romans who first understood the possible healing powers of the country's mineral rich waters, but it was with the coming of the railway in 1867, along with the Victorians' enthusiasm for taking the waters, that Llandrindod Wells really developed into a spa town. People would flock here in their thousands (at its peak some 80,000 visitors a year) to take the waters in an attempt to obtain relief from ailments ranging from gout, rheumatism and anaemia to diabetes, dyspepsia and liver trouble. Special baths and heat and massage treatments were also available.

The most famous of the individual spas in Llandrindod during its heyday, **Rock Park** is a typically well laid out Victorian park where visitors coming to the town would take a walk between their treatments. With particularly fine tree planting and shrubbery, the park is still a pleasant place today, and here and elsewhere in town, visitors can still take the waters or experience some of the more modern therapies.

As well as the evidence of the town's heyday that is all around, visitors can find out more about the spa's history at the **Radnorshire Museum** in Temple Street where not only is there a collection of Victorian artefacts but also relics excavated from Castell Collen. A splendid attraction in the Automobile Palace, a distinctive brick garage topped by rows of white lions, is the **National Cycle Collection**, an exhibition that covers more than 100 years of cycling history, through an amazing collection of over 200 bicycles and tricycles that date back as far

as 1818, and spans every development from the hobby horse and bone-shaker to the high-tech machines of today. Also here are old photographs and posters, historic replicas, the Dunlop tyre story and displays on cycling stars. Each year, Llandrindod Wells hosts a **Victorian Festival** (see panel opposite), swelling the population many times over and culminating in a torchlight procession and a fireworks display over the lake.

There are still two Anglican churches serving Llandrindod Wells. The **Old Parish Church of Llandrindod** ('The Church of the Holy Ttrinity'), just outside the town, is 13th century, though its roof was later removed to encourage people to attend the new church in the town. It was rebuilt in 1894. The **Parish Church of the Holy Trinity** within the town was built in 1871, and is a much larger and grander affair.

Just outside Llandrindod Wells, off the A44 Rhayader road, there is free access to **Abercamlo Bog**, 12 acres of wet pasture that are home to water-loving plants, breeding birds such as the whinchat and reed bunting, and butterflies. Not far away, at Ithon gorge, is **Bailey Einion**, woodland home to lady fern, golden saxifrage, pied flycatchers, woodpeckers and cardinal beetles.

Wales is famous for its amazing little narrow-gauge railways, but it also has some full-size trains, too. One of the most popular tourist lines is the **Heart of Wales Line** that runs from Shrewsbury to Swansea, 'one line that visits two viaducts, three castles, four spa towns, five counties, six tunnels and seven bridges'. Dolau, six miles to the northeast of Llandrindod Wells, is the best starting point on the line to walk to the top of **Radnor Forest**, the highest point in the old county of Radnorshire. Llanbister Road and Llangunllo

Nantmel

Distance: *3.0 miles (4.8 kilometres)*

Typical time: *120 mins*

Height gain: *210 metres*

Map: *Explorer 200*

Walk: *www.walkingworld.com ID:2440*

Contributor: *Pat Roberts*

There is a free carpark in Nantmel, near the telephone box. The village is reached by a slip road off the A44.

After visiting a lovely old church, walk near an unexpected viaduct, a relic of past times. The un-named mountain is only 355 metres high but gives extensive views over a little know area of mid Wales.

Hills or Fells, Church, Wildlife, Birds, Great Views, Butterflies, Public Transport

1 | From opposite the car park walk up the hill signed "Nantmel Church". Walk through the church yard to a stile.

2 | Over the stile and walk right-ish towards the viaduct. Down into the valley to cross a stream and up the other side near to the viaduct . Do not walk through the gateway in front of you.

3 | Left and uphill with the hedge on your right. Soon pass through a gate and ignore a gate on the right after about 30 metres. Continue up the field, fence on your right to reach a gate.

4 | Through the gate to follow a faint track ahead, gradually edging nearer to the hedge line on your right,

5 | Reach this old stile and continue ahead with an old oak wood down to the left, and a fence on the right. Reach the corner of the field and gates in 2 directions.

6 | Go through the gate ahead and bear right to reach another gate near a small coppice. Through the gate and bear right again to walk down the field, hedge line on your right, pass another small coppice and reach another gate.

7 | Through this gate and straight ahead, aim for another gateway on the skyline. Through this gateway and ahead to another gate. (This was fenced when I walked it and I had to climb over). Turn left to walk down with the fence on your left. This track becomes wider and swings right to continue down, a stream on the left. It is now more of a farm track and continues to swing right before going through another gate with fence on the right.

8 | The track divides here but we keep to the left fork which swings left and down to the A44, where right to walk on the wide verge back to Nantmel.

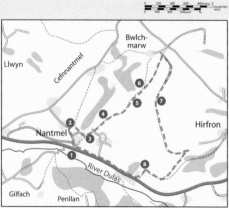

are nearby request halts ideally placed for discovering the remoter scenic delights of the area.

ABBEY-CWM-HIR

6 miles N of Llandrindod Wells off the A483

🏛 Cwmhir Abbey

Cwmhir Abbey, founded by the Cistercians in 1143, is reputed to have been attacked by Owain Glyndwr in 1402 who thought that the monks were English sympathisers, while earlier it had been all but destroyed by Henry III in 1231. It is a place of peace and tranquillity in the lonely Clywedog Valley that is well worth visiting; there is a memorial stone among the abbey ruins to Llywelyn the Last that marks, many believe, the grave of his headless body.

RHAYADER

6½ miles NW of Llandrindod Wells on the A44

🏛 Rhayader Castle 🦅 Gigrin Farm 🎭 Rebecca Riots

🎨 Welsh Royal Crystal 🚶 Wye Valley Walk

Often referred to as the Gateway to the Lakeland of Wales, Rhayader lies at the entrance to the magnificent Elan Valley and the impressive collection of dams and reservoirs it contains. This town, whose name means 'Waterfall of the Wye', dates back to the 5th century, though the waterfall all but disappeared with the construction of a bridge over the river in 1780.

Little remains of **Rhayader Castle**, built here by Rhys ap Gryffydd in about 1177, except some defensive ditches. More recently, Rhayader was the scene of some of the

GIGRIN FARM RED KITE FEEDING STATION

South Street, Rhayaeder, Powys LD6 5BL
Tel: 01597 810248
e-mail: kites@gigrin.co.uk
website: www.gigrin.co.uk

The red kite is one of this country's most beautiful and rare birds. At the **Gingrin Farm Red Kite Feeding Station** you can see them feeding, and wonder at their amazing grace and manoeuvrability. It was founded in 1993, and is now owned and managed by Lena Powell and son Chris. Red kites were roosting at the farm in winter, and were being fed as and when founder Eithel Powell was able.

At that time around a dozen birds visited the farm, and this rose over the years until now over 400 can be seen in winter. In conjunction with the Welsh Kite Trust, Gigrin Farm now also serves as the rehabilitation centre for red kites.

Feeding takes place at 2pm in winter and 3pm in summer, and it is one of the best places to see these magnificent birds swoop down and take the meat in their talons before rising again. So skilful are they at flying they will even eat the meat while flying! Anything up to ¼ tonne of prime meat (which is actually fit for human consumption) is bought in per week, depending on the number of kites visiting. The birds here are all native to Wales, and tests have shown that they are all descended from one female!

There are five hides available and a new area, which allows you to see the kites from above, has been introduced. There is also a nature trail to be explored. There is plenty of car parking space, a shop, a campsite and an interpretation centre.

Rebecca Riots protesting against toll gates (see also St Clears). The men, who dressed up as women and so earned themselves the nickname 'Rebecca's Daughters', destroyed turnpikes in protest at the high toll charges. Many tall stories have grown up around these riots and some of them concern Rebecca herself, who is said to have appeared as an old blind woman at the toll gate and said, "My children, something is in my way."

The first gate to be destroyed was at Yr Efail Wen, where 'Rebecca' proved to be a huge man called Thomas Rees. Many toll gates were demolished by the protesters until, in 1844, the remainder were removed legally.

Welsh Royal Crystal, a manufacturer of hand-crafted lead crystal tableware and gift items, is located in the town and the factory takes visitors on a guided tour to watch the craftsmen at work. Rhayader is at one end of the beautiful **Wye Valley Walk**, which follows the river valley, criss-crossing the border, through Builth Wells and Hay-on-Wye to Hereford, Monmouth and Chepstow.

The area around Rhayader is still very rural and on the outskirts of the town lies **Gigrin Farm**, where visitors can see red kites at close quarters as they are feeding.

ELAN VILLAGE
8 miles W of Llandrindod Wells off the B4518

🌿 Elan Valley   🌿 Caben Coch

The village is close to the beautiful reservoirs of the **Elan Valley** - a string of five dammed

---

ELAN VALLEY HOTEL
nr Rhyaeder, Powys LD6 5HN
Tel: 01597 880448
e-mail: info@lenavalleyhotel.co.uk
website: www.elanvalleyhotel.co.uk

The elegant, whitewashed **Elan Valley Hotel** offers some of the best accommodation, food and drink in mid Wales. It was built in Victorian times as a fishing lodge, and still preserves many original features, while offering everything the modern guest has come to expect from such an establishment. It is a family friendly place, and has ten full en suite rooms, each one furnished and decorated to an exceptionally high standard. One is a single, while the rest are either double, twin or family. All have nine-channel TVs, radio alarm clocks, telephones and internet access.

The hotel places great emphasis on its food. Everything is home cooked to perfection using only the finest and freshest of local produce wherever possible. From good, honest simple dishes to the more exotic, you are sure of a superb eating experience. The restaurant is open each evening between 7pm and 9pm to residents and non-residents alike.

The friendly bar serves a fine range of real ales and malt whiskies, plus there are draught beers, lager, cider, spirits, wines and soft drinks. It's a relaxing place where enjoying a quiet drink is a real pleasure.

The hotel is set in one of the loveliest parts of Wales, with so much to see and do. You can use it as an overnight stop as you explore by car, or as a base. Either way, you will be made most welcome.

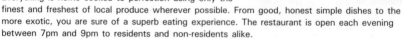

🏛 historic building   🏛 museum   🏛 historic site   ⌬ scenic attraction   🌿 flora and fauna

Elan Valley

the garden can still be seen. In 1814 Shelley left Harriet for Mary Godwin, and soon after Harriet drowned herself in the Serpentine. Shelley married Mary, who was later to write *Frankenstein*. In 1822 Shelley himself drowned off the Italian coast.

lakes that are together around nine miles long and were constructed between 1892 and 1903. Formed to supply millions of gallons of water to Birmingham and the West Midlands, the first of the dams was opened in 1904 by Edward VII and Queen Alexandra and the final dam, the Claerwen Dam, was finished in 1952. Dubbed the 'Lakeland of Wales', the five man-made lakes are surrounded by magnificent scenery and this is a popular area for walkers, cyclists and birdwatchers. The **Elan Valley Visitor Centre**, as well as incorporating a tourist information office, also has an exhibition telling the story of the building of the reservoirs and lots of information about the red kite.

Percy Bysshe Shelley visited his cousin Thomas Grove at Cwm Elan after being expelled from Oxford for writing a treatise supporting atheism. Soon after this visit he eloped with the schoolgirl Harriet Westbrook and married her in Scotland. They returned to Wales and for a brief spell in 1812 stayed at a house in the area called Nant Gwyllt. Like Thomas Grove's house, it is now submerged under the waters of **Caben Coch** reservoir, but when the water level is low the walls of

ST HARMON
8 miles NW of Llandrindod Wells on the B4518

🏛 Parish Church of St Harmon

🌿 Gilfach Nature Reserve

The **Parish Church of St Harmon** is famous for being the church where the diarist Francis Kilvert was vicar in 1876 and 1877 (see also Clyro). It was built in 1821, and is a simple affair with a very short chancel. Kilvert was born near Chippenham in 1840 and was educated at Wadham College, Oxford. He was curate to his father in Wiltshire before taking up a post at Clyro in 1865, where he started his famous diaries. They are detailed, vivid and very personal accounts of life in the remote Welsh countryside in mid-Victorian times. Back to England, then a year here, then back to Bredwardine in Herefordshire, where he married. He died five weeks later of peritonitis, aged only 39.

To the southwest of the village lies **Gilfach Nature Reserve**, a Site of Special Scientific Interest at the mouth of the Marteg Valley. Oak woodland, meadows and upland moorland support a rich diversity of wildlife, and in the ancient longhouse at the heart of the reserve there are exhibitions on the building's history and the surrounding wildlife.

Knighton

🏠 Spaceguard Centre   🏛 Offa's Dyke Centre

🏚 Pinners Hole   🌱 Kinsley Wood   🌲 Glyndwr's Way

Situated in the Teme Valley on the border of Powys and Shropshire and half in Wales and half in England, Knighton lies on the path of Offa's Dyke (see Prestatyn). The Welsh name for the town is Tref-y-Clawdd which means 'town of the dyke' and it is home to the **Offa's Dyke Centre,** where there is information about the long distance footpath that runs from Prestatyn to Chepstow. Here, too, visitors can find out more about the historic background to the 8th century dyke and the bloodshed of the battles that continued in the borderlands for hundreds of years. Knighton and its near neighbour, the border town of Presteigne, saw many battles between the Anglo Saxons and the Celts. 'It was customary for the English to cut off the ears of every Welshman who was found to the east of the Dyke (Offa's), and for the Welsh to hang every Englishman found to the west of it', wrote George Borrow in his 19th century book, *Wild Wales.*

Beginning in Knighton, **Glyndwr's Way** follows the route taken by Owain Glyndwr, one of Wales' famous sons, as he fought the English for Welsh independence in the 1400s. This scenic and important route travels southwest to Abbey-Cwm-Hir, passing by the ancient abbey ruins (see Abbey-Cwm-Hir), before heading northwards into the old county of Montgomeryshire and the market town of Llanidloes. The 128 miles of the path takes in some of the finest scenery in mid-Wales before reaching Machynlleth, from where it heads southeast and finally ends at the border town of Welshpool.

The **Spaceguard Centre** is situated within the former Powys Observatory. It was formed to observe and track comets and asteroids that might collide with our planet, and is open to the public. Beside the banks of the River Teme is **Pinners Hole**, a natural amphitheatre that is strengthened on one side by a superb section of Offa's Dyke where there is a stone that commemorates the opening of the footpath. Across the river lies **Kinsley Wood**, a sizeable area of native oak woodland. Sited on a hillside, trees of different species were planted to form the letters 'ER' to commemorate the Coronation of Elizabeth II.

TOWER HOUSE GALLERY

29 High Street, Knighton, Powys LD7 1AT
Tel: 01547 529530   e-mail: jlr.thg@virgin.net
website: www.towerhousegalleryknighton.co.uk

Situated by the clock tower in the picturesque border town of Knighton, Tower House Gallery provides an exhibition venue for the work of artists and crafts people of the Welsh Marches. The gallery displays work in a variety of media from oils, acrylics and watercolours to ceramics, enamels and wood. They also stock a comprehensive range of materials from artist and student quality paints, pastels, pencils and papers to Fair-Trade buttons. The stock of glass, crystal and semi-precious beads positively entices you to browse through the cabinets. Alternatively, just pop in for a chat with Julia, Jean and John. The Gallery is open 9am-4pm. Closed Sunday and Wednesday.

🏠 historic building   🏛 museum   🏚 historic site   🌀 scenic attraction   🌱 flora and fauna

BLEDDFA

5½ miles SW of Knighton on the A488

The **Parish Church of St Mary Magdalene** is medieval in origin, though its unusual wooden bell turret dates from 1711, when the west tower collapsed and was never rebuilt. The foundations of the tower can still be seen. Inside, the west end is partitioned off, as it was formerly a schoolroom. The communion rails are 17th century.

PRESTEIGNE

5 miles S of Knighton on the B4362

🏠 The Radnorshire Arms 🏠 Duke's Arms

🏠 Parish Church of St Andrew 🏠 Judge's Lodging

Presteigne is a charming and unspoilt place on the southern bank of the River Lugg. A border town distinguished by its handsome black and white half-timbered buildings,

Presteigne grew up around a Norman castle that has long since gone, the site now being occupied by a pleasant park. Presteigne's history is as turbulent as that of most of the region. It was captured by the Mercians in the 8th century, besieged by Llywelyn in 1262 and pillaged by Owain Glyndwr in the early 15th century. By Tudor times the town had got its breath back and had become a peaceful market centre, but it was its position on a major mail coach route between London, Cheltenham and Gloucester and Aberystwyth that brought it prosperity and importance.

One of the town's most outstanding buildings is **The Radnorshire Arms**, which dates from 1616. Originally built as a house for Sir Christopher Hatton, one of Elizabeth I's courtiers, this superb timber framed building became the property of the Bradshaw family before becoming an inn in

THE ROWAN TREE & THE GREEN ROOM

High Street, Presteigne, Powys LD8 2BE
Tel: 01544 260292

The Rowan Tree is undoubtedly the finest and most original gift shop in Presteigne, and is always well worth a visit when you're in the town. It is a cornucopia of colour and craft, with a wide range of gifts, clothes and cards from which to choose the perfect present or souvenir.

There is jewellery by Pilgrim, spongeware from Brixton Pottery, recycled bottle glasses, Essential Care and Earthbound organic cosmetics, soap made in Wales, Moleskine notebooks, children's clothes, toys and books, Jellycat soft toys, Putumayo CDs, kitchenware, Franchi seeds, scarves, bags and a whole lot more. Among the clothes to choose from are Adini, Sandwich, Flax, Fragile, Nomads, Bishopston Trading, Gringo and Pachamama, so there is sure to be something for everyone here.

The shop is owned and personally managed by Gilly Johnstone, who chooses her stock with great care. You are free to browse to your heart's content, and there is no obligation to buy. She and her friendly staff, however, are always on hand to help and advise as you make your choices.

The Green Room, across the road, is a small eco-shop, also run by Gilly, selling permaculture and other green books, and a variety of Fair Trade and recycled products. Make your way to both shops and be prepared to be amazed at the wide selection of gift and souvenir items available.

📖 stories and anecdotes 🐦 famous people 🎨 art and craft ✒ entertainment and sport 🚶 walks

Owain Glyndwr stood here in 1401. The rebuilt inn became a local headquarters for the Roundheads during the Civil War and, in later centuries, was an important coaching inn.

The **Parish Church of St Andrew** is possibly the most handsome church in Radnorshire. It sits in the valley of the River Lugg and is originally from Saxon times, though it was rebuilt in about 1200. The nave and chancel of the present building is from the 14th and 15th centuries.

Although the **Judge's Lodging** only dates from 1829, it is another fascinating attraction in Presteigne. Designed by Edward Haycock and built on the site of the county gaol, this was the judicial centre for Radnorshire and the home of the Radnorshire Constabulary. Today, the house, with its adjoining court, has been furnished as it would have appeared in 1870, and visitors can explore the world of the judges, their servants and the felons.

1792. The best known member of this family was John Bradshaw, who was Lord President of the Parliamentary Commission that brought Charles I to trial. He headed the list of signatories to the King's death warrant, refusing to let him speak in his defence. The town also claims the oldest inn in Radnorshire, the **Duke's Arms**, and records show that an inn which was burnt down by

OLD RADNOR

8½ miles S of Knighton off the A44

🏛 Parish Church of St Stephen

Situated on a hill, Old Radnor was once home to King Harold. The motte by the church was the site of his castle, while the **Parish Church of St Stephen** itself contains interesting

THE 100 HOUSE INN

Bleddfa, Near Knighton, Powys LD7 1PA
Tel: 01547 550333
e-mail: the100houseinn@yahoo.co.uk

Looking for a traditional Welsh inn while touring mid Wales? Then look no further than **The 100 House Inn** at Bleddfa, a few miles west of Knighton on the A488.

This delightful hostelry has been tastefully restored while losing none of its 'olde worlde' charm, and offers three real ales and outstanding food at reasonable prices. Crab salads - smoked salmon - gammon steaks - vegetarian dishes - the place has got the lot. So make your way to the 100 House Inn, admire the Ferrari memorabilia on its walls, and enjoy great food and good drink.

🏛 historic building   🏛 museum   🏛 historic site   🜉 scenic attraction   � flora and fauna examples of 14th century building design, as well as a huge font made from a glacial boulder. Stephen, or Ystyffan, lived in the 6th century, and was a member of the royal family that ruled Powys. The church is the only one in Wales dedicated to that particular saint. Motte and bailey castles were introduced into Britain by the Normans. They basically comprised a ditch or moat surrounding an earth mound with a palisade protecting the tower, or keep. By the tower was a flat area called the bailey, used for stabling and such like.

NEW RADNOR
8½ miles SW of Knighton off the A44

New Radnor Castle   Parish Church of St Mary

Up until the late 19th century this small town was the county town of Radnorshire, and here courts were convened and justice meted out. It is overlooked by the remains of its 11th century motte and bailey Castle. Like many other strongholds in this border region, **New Radnor Castle** suffered at various hands. It was destroyed by King John, rebuilt by Henry III and destroyed again by Owain Glyndwr in 1401.

The **Parish Church of St Mary** sits on a hill overlooking the village, and is totally unlike the one at Old Radnor, having been built between 1843 and 1845. However, a church has stood here for centuries, and the present building incorporates fragments of a medieval screen in its communion rails and two worn effigies, no doubt from tombs in an earlier church built in the 14th century.

New Radnor was the start point in 1187 of a tour of Wales by Archbishop Baldwin, who was accompanied by the scholar and

THE ROYAL OAK

Gladestry, near Kington, Powys HR5 3NR
Tel: 01544 370669
e-mail: theroyaloak@gladestry.co.uk
website: www.theroyaloakgladestry.co.uk

The Royal Oak is a superior inn within the delightful village of Gladestry, near Kinton in Powys. It is a picturesque, whitewashed inn of great charm and character, and is owned and run by Amanda Evans, who has created a place that is renowned throughout the area for the quality of its food, its high standards of service and the comfortable accommodation.

Food is important here. Main courses in the evening range from baked salmon fillet, prime sirloin steak, steak and stout pie and cawl, a traditional Welsh stew of beef, vegetables leeks and parsley. All the produce is fresh and sourced locally wherever possible. The lunch menu has such dishes as delicious three bean chilli, three cheese ploughman's and open sandwiches.

There is a family and a double room available for guests. Each one is furnished and decorated to an exceptionally high standard. The tariff includes a full Welsh breakfast, or something lighter if required. The inn makes the perfect base from which to explore mid Wales, or a stopping off place when you are walking Offa's Dyke Path.

The bar is cosy and inviting, and sells a wide range of drinks, including guest ales. Here you can sit and relax as you plan the following day's outings. There are open fires in all the public rooms in the winter months, ensuring a friendly, warm atmosphere.

stories and anecdotes   famous people   art and craft   entertainment and sport   walks

LLEWELYN & COMPANY DECORATIVE LIVING

19 High Town, Hay-on-Wye HR3 5AE
Tel: 01497 821880   Fax: 01497 821496
e-mail: llewelyn05@aol.com
website: www.llewelynandcompany.co.uk

Llewelyn & Company Decorative Living is one of the leading suppliers of fine furniture and homeware in the region. Hands-on owners John and Anna Llewelyn Funnell are involved in every aspect of the business, from travelling widely to source the stock to creating the eye-catching displays. Anna has always had a passion for blending beautiful antique and pretty vintage items with exciting new crafts by inspirational contemporary designers. Not finding a shop that offers this combination they decided to open a shop of their own, and since starting in 2005 they have steadily built up a loyal band of customers who come here from near and far. Beautiful antique and reproduction French, Scandinavian and British furniture is the main speciality, complemented by well-loved vintage homewares and exclusive new design-led products. Customers old and new are assured of the warmest of greetings, and the owners are always ready with help and advice. Their stock is a harmonious mix of antique,

period and new items for home and garden, all invitingly displayed on two floors of a Grade II-listed Georgian building. On the first floor are the main pieces of furniture, along with mirrors and many other pieces, each piece personally chosen by the owners for individuality and quality.

The second floor is filled with many more equally desirable products in three rooms themed 'Pantry', 'Nursery' and 'Potting Shed', with items ranging from glassware and tableware to jewellery, high quality French garden furniture, toys and baby clothes. The Company also offers an interior design service, a wedding list service and national and international delivery. The shop has two entrances, in High Town at the front and at 10 Market Town at the rear. Style, quality, reliability and personal service have established Llewelyn & Company as one of the leaders in its field, and it could find no more appropriate setting than the marvellous town of Hay-on-Wye.

🏛 historic building   🏛 museum   🏛 historic site   ⊶ scenic attraction   🌱 flora and fauna

Hay Castle

died. Baldwin was the Bishop of Worcester before becoming Archbishop of Canterbury, in which capacity he crowned Richard I.

Hay-on-Wye

- Hay Motte
- Festival of Art and Literature
- Hay-on-Wye Craft Centre
- Hay Castle

churchman Giraldus Cambrensis. They preached the Third Crusade, and after the tour Baldwin, the first archbishop to visit Wales, made a pilgrimage to the Holy Land, where he

This ancient town, tucked between the Black Mountains and the River Wye in the northern corner of the Brecon Beacon National Park, grew up around **Hay Motte**, which still

MIKELL GALLERY

43 Lion Street, Hay on Wye Powys HR3 5AA
Tel: 01497 821806
e-mail: mikellgallery@aol.com

The **Mikell Gallery** in Hay on Wye was opened over four years ago, and since then has become a popular place to buy a gift for a loved one or a souvenir of your visit to the town. Owner Marie Rogers - originally from New York - has lived in Hay on Wye for ten years, and has built up a business that places great emphasis on friendly service and outstanding value for money.

Marie started with stained glass, gaining commissions from many homes in the area, and moved onto other British craft items. The shop sells a wide range of pottery, sculpture, paintings, prints, glass by renowned artists, clocks, tableware, wall hangings, ceramics, jewellery, textiles, bronzes and host of other items that are sure to please. In fact the whole shop is a cornucopia of colour, texture and dazzling craftsmanship.

The shop has a welcoming façade in dark green and white that will attract you immediately, and make you want to enter. The interior is stylish and modern, with plenty of space, and Marie or a member of staff is always on hand to offer help and advice, and you are free to browse with absolutely no obligation.

Opening times are 10am to 5.30pm on weekdays and Saturdays, and 11am to 4pm on Sundays.

OLD BLACK LION

Lion Street, Hay-on-Wye, Powys HR3 5AD
Tel: 01497 820841
e-mail: info@oldblacklion.co.uk
website: www.oldblacklion.co.uk

The three-star **Old Black Lion** is an old, whitewashed inn that dates from the 17th century, though parts of it may even date back to the 1300s! It oozes character and olde worlde charm, and the interior is every bit as picturesque. The bar is cosy and inviting, with its oak timbers and scrubbed pine tables, and the food is renowned throughout the area. In fact, it has received awards and accolades over the years from many organisations. Everything is cooked on the premises from fresh local produce wherever possible, ensuring great taste and outstanding value for money. The menus frequently change to take account of what is in season, and the dishes are cooked and presented with flare and imagination. The wine list is extensive, and there is a range of real ales, including the inn's namesake, 'Old Black Lion Ale'.

The inn also offers ten fully en suite rooms to discerning travellers. They have recently been completely refurbished to an exceptionally high standard, and are both comfortable and spacious. All have direct dial telephones, colour TVs, hair driers and tea/coffee making facilities.

The place makes the perfect base from which to explore Hay-on-Wye, Wales' booktown, and the wonderful Wye Valley. Pay a visit and you're sure to agree.

SIGI LINGERIE

7 Market Street, Hay on Wye, Powys HR3 5AF
Tel: 01497 821944
e-mail: wendy.laurence@btinternet.com
website: www.sigiathay.co.uk

Set in Hay on Wye, **Sigi Lingerie** is a new shopping experience that offers collections of lingerie, jewellery and gifts. In a fun and relaxed atmosphere that froths with colour and texture, women can browse to their heart's content with absolutely no obligation to buy. Wendy Laurence, the owner, founded the company in October 2006, and in a short time has created a boutique that is extremely popular, offering personal, friendly service, a warm welcome and outstanding value for money.

Leading brands such as Lejaby, Fantasie, Freya, Chantelle, Beau Bra and Passionata grace her display units and shelves, and she and her trained staff offer a specialist bra fitting service. In addition, there is a great range of delightful jewellery and gift bags from such makers as Antica Murrina, Troll Beads and Kleshna Crystal, such as heart drop necklaces, bracelets and other items made of glass.

And any woman would be entranced by the range of body and bath products and smokeless candles on offer, as well as the party stockings and hold ups. This is an entrancing shop where the staff are knowledgeable and helpful, and where shopping is a pleasure. So call in, relax, and have a good look round.

survives across the river from the main town centre. This castle was eventually replaced by **Hay Castle**, although this was all but destroyed in the early 1400s by Owain Glyndwr. However, a Jacobean manor house has been grafted on to part of the remaining walls and, close by, there are traces of a Roman fort.

Historic though this town may be, it is as the second hand book capital of the world that Hay-on-Wye is best known. Among the town's many buildings can be found a

---

OSCAR'S BISTRO

High Town, Hay on Wye, Powys HR3 5AE
Tel: 01497 821193

Situated right in the heart of Hay on Wye - with its many bookshops - you will find **Oscar's Bistro**. It offers value-for-money food, and is a popular place with visitors and locals alike, and offers great teas and coffees as well as a range of tasty snacks and meals, such as jacket potatoes, lasagne, baguettes, beef paprika, and so on. During the summer months you can also eat out of doors in the 'street courtyard'. Paintings by local artists adorn the walls, giving the place a colourful, welcoming atmosphere.

"We deserve an Oscar for our food"

THE GRANARY

Broad Street, Hay-on-Wye, Powys HR3 5DB
Tel: 01497 820790
e-mail: info@granaryhay.co.uk

Opposite the clock tower in Hay-on-Wye you will find **The Granary**, one of the best licensed cafés in town. On two floors, you will find good food at affordable prices. You can choose from three soups, plus a range of main courses that make use of local beef, lamb and game. The vegetarian and vegan choices are also very popular, as are cakes and puddings, all baked on the premises. So make it your first stop when visiting Wales' food town.

DOLL'S HOUSE FUN & ART SHOP

19 Brecon Road, Hay on Wye, Powys HR3 5DY
Tel: 01497 821913
e-mail: dollshousefun@dollshousefun.co.uk
website: www.dollshousefun.co.uk

This small, delightful shop was set up 12 years ago by doll's house fan Georgina Abel, and is now one of the best shops of its kind in the country. **Doll's House Fun & Art Shop** also sells art materials, prints and paintings, and a visit here is both fascinating and enjoyable. You can buy 1:12 scale flat pack houses, pre-assembled houses that have been lovingly painted, and a wide range of accessories such as furniture, fittings and even household plants.

📖 stories and anecdotes   🦜 famous people   ✒ art and craft   🎭 entertainment and sport   🚶 walks plethora of book, antique, print and craft shops. The first second-hand bookshop was opened here in 1961 by Richard Booth, owner of Hay Castle, and since then they have sprung up all over the town - the old cinema, many houses, shops and even the old castle are now bookshops, at least 35 in all and with a stock of over a million books. The annual **Festival of Art and Literature**, held every May, draws thousands of visitors to the town.

The impressive **Hay-on-Wye Craft Centre** offers visitors a change from books as well as the opportunity to see craftspeople working at age-old skills such as glass blowing, wood turning and pottery.

THE START

Hay-on-Wye, Powys HR3 5RS
Tel: 01497 821391
e-mail: dawn@the-start.net

The Start is named after the 100 mile raft race from Hay on Wye to Chepstow, and is a delightful B&B establishment that boasts three extremely comfortable rooms with TV and tea/coffee making facilities - a twin and two doubles, all en suite. It sits in a large garden 300 yards from the town centre, and has fine views over the River Wye. All diets are catered for with packed lunches available by prior arrangement. The B&B tariff includes a hearty full Welsh breakfast with free range eggs from the girls in the garden.

NEPAL BAZAAR

Hay on Wye HR3 5AJ
Tel: 01497 820170 e-mail: nancy.nepalbazaar@onetel.net

One of the shops that simply cannot be missed when visiting the book town of Hay on Wye is the **Nepal Bazaar**, nearly opposite the tourist information centre. It is owned and run by Nancy Palmer-Jones, who set up the business in 1991, and it sells an amazing stock of colourful, interesting items from Nepal, Tibet and the Himalayas. She also sells items from Indonesia, Egypt, Peru and India.

The shop is noted for its intriguing and colourful interior, full of clothing, utensils, ornaments, textiles, furnishings and jewellery. There are still many Nepalese craftspeople whose only source of income is from their artistic skills, and Nancy offers employment to some of them at fair wages. She hopes that when you visit this fascinating place, you will buy and enjoy their products, knowing that you are contributing to the wellbeing of a proud and resourceful people.

The shop sells Buddhist artefacts and prayer flags, as well as wood carvings, metal statutes, thankas (paintings with a religious theme), hand-woven wool and cotton jackets, men's shirts, textiles and furnishings, dresses, tops, skirts, silver jewellery, slippers, paintings, books and cards.

The shop opens from 10 am to 5 pm every day including Sunday, and Nancy and her staff are helpful and friendly when you come to choose something to buy. So pay it a visit when in Hay on Wye. See for yourself the intriguing items on offer!

🏛 historic building   🏛 museum   🏛 historic site   🏞 scenic attraction   🌱 flora and fauna

HOLLYBUSH INN

nr Hay on Wye, Powys HR3 5PS
Tel: 01497 847371 website: www.hollybushcamping.co.uk

For fine food, superb accommodation, good drink and a warm welcome, there is nowhere in Wales like the **Hollybush Inn** a few miles south of Hay-on-Wye. The place has a cosy, friendly atmosphere and is a firm favourite with the locals - always a good sign! In fact, it acts as a sort of community centre for the area, and the owner, Barbara Lewthwaite, prides herself on being part of a community that makes tourists and travellers very welcome.

It boasts five fully en suite bedrooms for discerning guests, and each one is furnished and decorated to an extremely high standard. The bar serves a wide range of drinks, including real ales from local breweries and four ciders. The food, which is out of this world, is served all day - everything from tasty snacks such as toasties and omelettes to all-day breakfasts, Irish stew, casseroled cream chicken and lamb shank in a red wine sauce. There are also special vegetarian, vegan and gluten-free options.

The inn boasts a level camping and caravanning site on the banks of the river, with hook ups if required. Supervised canoeing tuition on the river is also available, and there are woodland walks.

So if you're camping, caravanning or motoring through Wales, the Hollybush Inn makes the perfect stopping-off place.

RIVER CAFÉ & B&B AT GLASBURY

Glasbury Bridge, Glasbury on Wye, Nr Hay on Wye, Powys HR3 5NP
Tel: 01497 847007
e-mail: info@wyevalleycanoes.co.uk website: www.wyevalleycanoes.co.uk

With a stylish café and comfortable B&B rooms, **The River Café & B&B** at Glasbury is one of the most popular establishments of its kind in the area. Once the village's post office, it sits right on the banks of the River Wye, at the highest point at which canoes can be launched. The café itself is licensed and serves great food. It is spacious and modern, reflecting its high standards of service and its value for money prices. Everything from fresh crab pasta and sirloin steak with salad and chips to homemade lasagne and fresh grilled sea bass is available, with only the finest and freshest of local produce being used wherever possible.

The four B&B rooms are extremely comfortable, and furnished and decorated to a high standard while still retaining a simple, uncluttered look. There are three doubles and a twin, and TVs and tea/coffee making facilities come as standard. All the rooms are fully en suite. The café and B&B rooms are open from Wednesday to Sunday all year.

The café owns Wye Valley Canoes, where, in the summer months, you can hire canoes and kayaks, and all the accompanying equipment, for a few hours or even a few days on the river. Packed lunches are available.

Whether you're a canoeist, a walker, a cyclist or a motorist, you will be made more than welcome at The River Café & B&B.

stories and anecdotes 🐦 famous people 🎨 art and craft 🎭 entertainment and sport 🚶 walks

CLYRO
2 miles NW of Hay on the A438

🏠 Clyro Castle   🏠 Parish Church of St Michael

🌢 Cwm Byddog

Although little remains of the Roman station that was here, the remains of the motte and bailey of **Clyro Castle**, built by the fiendish William de Braose, can still be seen. The diarist Francis Kilvert was curate in the village between 1865 and 1872 and, in his journal, he describes both life in the village and the surrounding area (see also St Harmon). There are Kilvert memorabilia in his former home, now a modern art gallery. The **Parish Church of St Michael**, where he was vicar, was founded in the 12th century. Apart from the tower, it was rebuilt in about 1853.

A little way north of Clyro, **Cwm Byddog** is a 15-acre ancient woodland with pollarded oaks, bluebells in spring, the remains of a motte and bailey castle and a variety of birds, including the blackcap and the garden warbler.

PAINSCASTLE
5 miles NW of Hay on the B4594

🏠 Castell Paen

🌢 Tawny Owl Animal Park and Craft Centre

Sometimes known as **Castell Paen**, the early castle built in 1130 by Payn FitzJohnon. A motte that still exists was later rebuilt in stone and, by the late 12th century, was in the hands of the notorious William de Braose. The cruelty of de Braose earned him a place in Welsh folklore and he was given the nickname the "Ogre of Abergavenny". This was because he avenged the death of his uncle, the earl of Hereford, by inviting several Welsh princes to Abergavenny Castle for a great feast. Instead of offering them hospitality, he

had them all butchered. His name has also been given to several breeds of cattle in Wales including the de Braose Maud and the de Braose David.

In 1198, the castle was attacked by Gwenwynwyn, Prince of Powys, but William and his English army slaughtered over 3,000 of Gwenwynwyn's men and the prince's dreams of a united Wales died along with them. However, de Braose met his match - for cruelty - in King John, who stripped him of his land. He escaped in disguise to France, where he died. After her husband's death, Maud suggested that John had also killed his nephew Prince Arthur and for this accusation both she and her youngest son were imprisoned in Corfe Castle with little food to keep them alive. So legend has it that when, some 11 days later, the dungeon door was opened, both prisoners were dead and, in an attempt to keep herself alive, Maud had half eaten the cheeks of her son.

Close to the castle remains is an altogether more pleasant place to visit, the **Tawny Owl Animal Park and Craft Centre**, which lies in the shelter of beautiful hills. Opened in 1998, the park is named after the wild owls that live in the broad leafed woodlands surrounding the farm and, as well as the owls (which are not caged), visitors can also see a whole range of farm animals at close quarters. Along with the animals and the farm trails, there are also traditional country crafts on display and for sale which have been made using methods passed down from generation to generation.

The **Parish Church of St Peter** is a simple building with a 14th century nave and a 15th century chancel, though there is plenty of evidence of a substantial restoration in the 19th century. Curiously, the chancel floor is about three feet lower than that of the nave.

🏠 historic building   📷 museum   🏛 historic site   🍃 scenic attraction   🌢 flora and fauna

Builth Wells

🏛 Parish Church of St Mary   🏛 Castle Mound

🏛 Cefn Carn Cafall   ✒ Wayside Arts Centre

✒ Royal Welsh Show Ground   🐟 Groe Park

Another spa town of mid-Wales, Builth Wells lies on the River Wye, which is spanned at this point by a six-arched bridge. The discovery of the saline springs in 1830 helped Builth Wells develop from a small market town into a fashionable spa that became more popular with the arrival of the railways towards the end of the 19th century. As a result, many of the town's original narrow streets are littered with Victorian and Edwardian buildings.

However, the town's history dates back much further than just a couple of hundred years. It grew up around a Norman castle that changed hands many times during the struggles with the English. The inhabitants of Builth Wells earned the nickname 'traitors of Bu-allt' because of their refusal to shelter Llywelyn the Last from the English in 1282 and, as a result, some 20 years later, Llywelyn partly destroyed the Norman stronghold. At the **Castle Mound** only the earthworks remain of the town's 13th century castle that was built by Edward I on the site of the earlier motte and bailey structure. The earthworks can be reached by a footpath from the town centre. The **Parish Church of St Mary** was founded in Norman times, and has a 14th century tower, the rest being Victorian. Above the south porch is a small room.

Since the 1963 opening of the **Royal Welsh Show Ground** at Llanelwedd, on the opposite bank of the Wye, the annual Royal Welsh Show, held in July, has gained a reputation as being the premier agricultural

AUDREY'S

2 High Street, Builth Wells, Powys LD2 3DN
Tel: 01982 552846

Audrey's has been in Builth Wells since 1977, and during that time has offered a wonderful selection of fashion garments and accessories.

If you're looking for an outfit that's a bit different you will find a large range of quirky designs from 'Sandwich', 'Fransa', 'Dranells', 'Intown', 'Adini', and 'Pomodoro'.

When you have found what you need for yourself, why not pop in next door to find an outfit for your little one. On offer you will find ranges from 'Babyface', 'Fransa', 'Du-du', 'Zip-Zap' and 'Abella' also 'Orchard Toys' and lots of books and games.

Audrey, her daughter Sharon, who has now joined the business, and all her staff give a friendly and personal service so why not call in and see for yourself.

🎞 stories and anecdotes   🐦 famous people   ✒ art and craft   ✒ entertainment and sport   🏃 walks

River Wye, Builth Wells

show in the country. Builth Wells is regarded as the centre for farming and agriculture in Wales and the show provides an opportunity for the farming communities to come together at what is considered to be one of the finest and most prestigious events of its kind.

Although spa treatments are no longer available here, Builth Wells remains a popular touring centre and base. As well as the many shops and the weekly market on Mondays, visitors can also enjoy the wide variety of arts and cultural events held at the **Wayside Arts Centre** or take a pleasant riverside stroll through **Groe Park**.

LION HOTEL

2 Broad Street, Builth Wells, Powys LD2 3DT
Tel: 01982 553311
website: www.lionhotelbuilthwells.com

The family-run and family-friendly **Lion Hotel** in Builth Wells offers some of the best hospitality in mid Wales. It is a superb hotel, housed in a building that dates from 1718, elegantly proportioned and of local stone. It looks out over the River Wye, and sits within walking distance of the Royal Welsh Showground. It has recently been refurbished, and boasts 14 fully en suite rooms and two full suites, each one stylishly and sumptuously furnished and decorated. They all have TV, internet access, telephone, tea/coffee making facilities and many other features that make staying here a pleasure that cannot be missed.

The hotel prides itself on its food. The kitchens use only the finest and freshest local produce whenever possible when preparing its many imaginative dishes. Within the spacious restaurant you can choose from such favourites as steak and ale pie, Welsh salmon, rainbow trout, Welsh lamb chops, grilled sea bass and a whole lot more. The hotel is the perfect place for a relaxing dinner accompanied by a bottle of wine form the extensive cellar.

The Lion Hotel has a license for civil weddings, and there is a function suite that can hold up to 60 guests. The bride and groom also offered, on a complimentary basis, the honeymoon suite for the first night of their married life.

There is just so much to do and see around Builth Wells, and the hotel makes an ideal base or an overnight stop when exploring the area. Come and see for yourself!

🏛 historic building   🏛 museum   🏛 historic site   🏞 scenic attraction   🌱 flora and fauna

INITIAL A

9 Broad Street, Builth Wells, Powys LD2 3DT
Tel: 01982 552225
e-mail: pip@mogs7.fsnet.co.uk

There is an elegance and style to **Initial A**, a boutique in Builth Wells that stocks and sells a wide range of footwear for both women, men and children. The shop is owned and personally managed by Alison Morgan, who trained at a West End couturier as a fashion designer, specialising in evening wear. So she brings a wealth of experience to the job, and is always on hand to take you through the process of buying something fashionable and flattering for that special occasion, be it a ball, dinner or party. She is a specialist at made-to-measure outfits, so you know you are in safe hands.

The shop also sells a wide range of accessories to complete the perfect ensemble, including handbags, hats, shoes (her sales staff are all qualified Hush Puppy shoe fitters), sandals, costume jewellery and headpieces. Why not have your unique wedding dress designed and made by Alison? She offers a first class service at reasonable prices, and can even design all the bridesmaids' dresses as part of the overall service. You can even buy lovely fabrics as well as for making your own dresses.

The spacious boutique is a joy to visit. There is plenty of parking round about, and you can browse to your heart's content.

On the summit of the nearby mountain, **Cefn Carn Cafall**, is a cairn that is said to have been built by King Arthur. The stone on top of the cairn bears the imprint of a dog's paw that, according to local legend, was left by King Arthur's dog, Cafall, while they were out hunting. Arthur built the cairn, placing the stone on top, and then named the peak. The story continues that if the stone is removed it will always return to this spot.

Around Builth Wells

ERWOOD

7 miles SE of Builth Wells on the A470

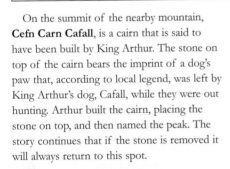 Erwood Station Crafft Centre and Gallery

Pronounced 'Errod', the village's name is actually a corruption of the Welsh Y Rhyd (the ford), a name that harks back to the days when the shallow crossing of the River Wye here was used by drovers. The station at Erwood, closed in 1962, has been turned into the **Erwood Station Craft Centre and Gallery** (see panel on page 178).

GWENDDWR

5 miles S of Builth Wells off the A470

🏛 Parish Church of St Dubricius

The **Parish Church of St Dubricius** has some 14th century features, though most of it dates from a Victorian refurbishment. At one time a small priory, attached to Abbey Dore in Herefordshire.

CILMERY

3 miles W of Builth Wells on the A483

🏛 Memorial to Llywelyn the Last

It was at this village (also called Cefn-y-Bedd)

🎞 stories and anecdotes   🐦 famous people   ✎ art and craft   ✐ entertainment and sport   🐾 walks

ERWOOD STATION CRAFT CENTRE & GALLERY

Llandeilo Graban, Builth Wells, Powys LD2 3SJ
Tel: 01982 560674
e-mail: erwood.station@virgin.net
website: www.erwood-station.co.uk

Once part of the rural Great Western Railway, serving Mid Wales until 1962, Erwood Station has been, for the last 22 years, a Craft Centre and Gallery, promoting the many local artists and craftspeople.

The restoration and development into this most outstanding centre of excellence is the vision of ex-music teacher and master wood-turner, Alan Cunningham and his wife Erika. Alan, on the register of the Worshipful Company of Turners, can often be seen at work in his workshop. He has a well deserved reputation for finely crafted work from Welsh timbers, both functional and decorative, as well as using the skills of his first profession in offering individual courses for beginners or improvers in this fascinating and most satisfying of crafts. (Course leaflet available).

As well as displaying the work of over 70 craftspeople and artists, there are monthly major art exhibitions in the main atrium. Two restored old railway coaches serve as permanent gallery space for the members of 'Platform One Artists and Designer-makers', with David Bellamy as their president.

Freshly ground coffee, tea and home-made cakes in such surroundings is a must. This charming and restorative place has a large picnic site with a River Wye walk and adjacent verge side reserve and signal box information point for Radnorshire Wildlife Trust.

Erwood Station Craft Centre and Gallery is also on National Cycle route 8 and the Wye Valley Walk. For easiest directions, - look for the tourist signs 6 miles South of Builth Wells, leaving the A470 to cross the River Wye above Erwood onto the B4567.

on the banks of the River Irfon, in 1282, that Llywelyn the Last, while escaping after the abortive Battle of Builth, was killed by the English. According to legend, the place where Llywelyn fell and died was once covered in broom which then ceased to grow on the site - in mourning for the loss of the last native Prince of Wales. Thirteen trees have been planted here to represent the 13 counties of Wales. The rough hewn stone **Memorial to Llywelyn the Last** describes him as "ein llyw olaf" (our last leader) while the English tablet beside the monument calls him 'our prince'. Following his death, Llywelyn's head was taken to London and paraded victoriously through the city's streets. His death is still marked every year on

December 11th at the memorial.

LLANWRTYD WELLS
13 miles W of Builth Wells on the A483

🏛 Cambrian Woollen Mill   🌢 Llyn Brianne

🐦 William Williams

🐌 World Bog Snorkelling Championship

Surrounded by rugged mountains, rolling hills and the remote moorland of **Mynydd Epynt**, it was here, in 1792, that the sulphur and chalybeate spring waters were discovered by a scurvy sufferer. As visitors came here in the 19th century to take the waters in relief of numerous complaints, the town developed. Today Llanwrtyd Wells is still a popular holiday centre, particularly with those who

🏛 historic building   📷 museum   🏛 historic site   🌢 scenic attraction   🌱 flora and fauna enjoy bird watching, fishing and walking. However, anyone visiting the town will be surprised that somewhere so small could have so many events and festivals throughout the year. It is the home of the 'Man versus Horse' race in May, a Folk Weekend in spring and a late autumn Beer Festival.

However the most unusual of all the events held here is undoubtedly the annual **World Bog Snorkelling Championship** that takes place each August. Competitors have to swim two lengths of a specially dug 180ft peat bog located a mile from the town. The swimmer's head must be submerged, and the use of the arms is forbidden. The latest variation is bog-snorkelling on mountain bikes!

In the 18th century, **William Williams** the poet, hymn writer and one of the leaders of the Methodist revival lived in the town (see also Llandovery) , while another claim to fame is that the Welsh rugby folk song, *Sosban Fach*, was written here in 1895. It translates into English as 'little saucepan'.

On the outskirts of the town lies the **Cambrian Woollen Mill**, which recalls the rich history of Wales' rural past. The first mill was founded in the 1820s, but its modern form dates from 1918, when it was opened by the Royal British Legion for the benefit of servicemen disabled in the Great War. A tour of the mill allows visitors to see traditional cloths being woven while, in the factory shop, there is a wide choice of beautifully finished items to buy.

On high ground to the northwest of the town is **Llyn Brianne**, the latest of Wales' man-made lakes, which was opened in 1973. The dam that holds the water is the highest of its type in the country - at 300 feet - and the grand scale of the lake has to be seen to be believed.

LLANGAMMARCH WELLS
8 miles W of Builth Wells off the A483

🐦 John Perry 🐦 Theophilus Evans

Situated where the Rivers Irfon and Cammarch meet, Llangammarch Wells was the smallest of the Welsh spas and was renowned for its barium chloride carrying waters that were thought to be useful in the treatment of heart and rheumatic complaints. The old well and pumphouse are contained in the grounds of the Lake Country House Hotel. As well as being the birthplace in 1559 of **John Perry**, who was hanged in London in 1593 for treason, this now sleepy little town was also the home of the wonderfully named Theophilus Evans. He was vicar here, and also wrote a classical historical interpretation of the area entitled *View of the Primitive Age*.

ABERGWESYN
12 miles W of Builth Wells off the B4358

🐦 Abergwesyn Pass

Situated in an isolated spot in the Irfon Valley, Abergwesyn lies on an old drovers' route that twists and climbs through the **Abergwesyn Pass**. Known as the 'roof of Wales', this is a beautiful pathway that, centuries ago consisted of nothing more than dirt tracks, along which the drovers would shepherd cattle and other livestock from one market town to the next. A number of drovers' routes can still be followed - some in part by car. Many of the roads are narrow and, in the south, one such route begins at Llandovery and travels across the Epynt mountain and crosses the ford at Erwood.

NEWBRIDGE ON WYE
4 miles N of Builth Wells on the A470

🏛 Parish Church of All Saints 🗿 Drover's Statue

The **Parish Church of All Saints**, with its

stories and anecdotes 🐦 famous people 🎨 art and craft 🎭 entertainment and sport 🚶 walks

THE NEW INN

Newbridge on Wye, Powys LD1 6HY
Tel: 01597 860211
e-mail: dave@pigsfolly.fsnet.co.uk
website: www.pigsfolly.co.uk

It might be called the **New Inn**, but this former coaching inn dates back to the 16th century, and no doubt got its name because it replaced an even older establishment at that time. It is a delightful whitewashed inn with plenty of character, sitting opposite a statue of an old-time drover, and fits perfectly into the picturesque village of Newbridge on Wye.

Owned and personally managed by Debby and Dave Lang, who have been in the hospitality business for many years, it boasts eight fully en suite rooms to discerning travellers. You can choose from a family room sleeping four and a triple sleeping three, while the rest are doubles and twins. Each one is comfortable, with high quality furnishings and decorations. In addition, there are tea/coffee making facilities and a TV in each room. There is also bunkhouse accommodation sleeping up to 15.

The child-friendly New Inn prides itself on its good, wholesome food, prepared wherever possible from fresh local produce, You can eat in any of the three bars, which are welcoming and friendly, and a firm favourite with the locals, which is always a good sign. There is also a beer garden.

Adjoining the pub they have their own butchers shop selling locally reared meat. They also produce their own award-winning sausages, pork pies, dry cured bacon and hams, all of which are included on the pub menu.

spire, was built in the decorated style in 1883 for the Venables family of nearby Llysdinam. The Revd. Francis Kilvert was chaplain to the Revd Richard Venables, who lived there. The **Drover's Statue** on the village green is a reminder that the village lies on an old drove road that ran from Tregaron and on into England. Droving - the driving of cattle, mainly to the English lowlands for fattening - was one of Wales's main industries until the Industrial Revolution. Drovers needed licenses to ply their trade, and had to be married, over 30 and a householder. This didn't stop them enjoying themselves in inns where they stopped overnight. Newbridge on Wye had 13 inns, and they usually put on dancing, singing, boxing and wrestling to entertain them.

Brecon

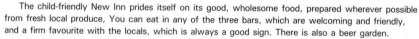

🏛 Brecon Castle	🏛 Heritage Centre
🏛 Captain's Walk	🏛 Brecknock Museum
🏛 Monmouthshire and Brecon Canal	
🏛 South Wales Borderers Museum	🏛 Y Gaer
🏛 Welsh Whisky Distillery and Visitor Centre	

Famous for its ancient cathedral, Georgian architecture and annual Jazz Festival, Brecon lies on the banks of the River Usk, at the confluence of the Rivers Honddu and Tarrell in the heart of the National Park. The first evidence of a settlement in the area are the remains of the Roman fort **Y Gaer** which lie two miles west of the town. First built in around AD 75, the fort was rebuilt twice before it was finally abandoned in about AD 290. A garrison for the 2nd Legion and the Vettonian Spanish cavalry, parts of the fort were excavated by Sir Mortimer Wheeler in 1924 and sections of the outer wall - in places 10 feet high - and traces of gates can be seen.

In the 5th century the daughter of the local ruler was sent to Ireland to marry a local prince. They had a son, whom they named Brychan, and he was sent back to Wales to live with his grandfather. It is from him that the name of the town and the county is derived. Brychan's daughter was Tudful, and she eventually became a holy woman who was killed by Irish invaders in AD 480. It is from her that the town of Mertyr Tydfil, 20 miles to the south, gets its name, 'merthyr' being the Welsh for martyr.

A walk along the promenade beside the River Usk leads to the remains of medieval **Brecon Castle** which can be found partly in the Bishop's Garden and partly at the Castle Hotel. The town grew up around this castle, which was built in the late 11th century by Bernard of Newmarch. It was besieged first by Llywelyn the Last and again during Owain Glyndwr's rebellion in the early 15th century. By the time of the Civil War, Brecon considered its growing cloth trade so important that it remained neutral, and the townsfolk began dismantling the castle.

Close by stands **Brecon Cathedral**, an impressive and magnificent building that originated from an 11th century priory colonised by Benedictine monks from Battle in Sussex. It was founded by the Norman

ST MARY'S BAKERY

4 St Mary Street, Brecon, Powys LD3 7AA
Tel: 01874 624311

St Mary's Bakery in Brecon has been selling cakes and bread rolls for over 105 years across the Brecon area and beyond. Cakes - morning rolls - breads - pies - pasties - the whole range is available here, all baked on the premises using only the finest local flours and other products. It prides itself in being possibly the best bakery in the whole of Brecon and Powys, while still maintaining value for money prices and outstanding service.

The products are either sold in the bakery or through its outside catering service to national parks, schools and other cafes across Brecon and the surrounding areas. It has many, many satisfied customers who appreciate the company's mouth-watering baking, its commitment to quality and its friendly, reliable service.

St Mary's Bakery can also undertake cold buffet catering for all occasions, and this includes business lunches, parties, anniversaries and so on. There is free delivery for its wholesale bread, confectionery, pies and pasties, made-to-order celebration cakes and wedding cakes.

So if you are holidaying in the area, or just passing through, remember to visit St Mary's Bakery for all your baking needs.

📖 stories and anecdotes   🐦 famous people   🎨 art and craft   🎭 entertainment and sport   🚶 walks

EMERALDS ART AND CRAFT SUPPLIES

Coliseum House, 7 Wheat Street, Brecon, Powys LD3 7DG
Tel: 01874 623455

For all your arts and crafts supplies, you just can't beat **Emeralds Arts and Crafts** in Brecon. It is a fascinating shop, with bags of space, colour and light, and is owned and run by Debbie Griffiths, who brings a wealth of experience to the job, having herself been immersed in crafts - especially card making - for many years.

This part of Wales has many craftspeople living there, and the shop is popular with all of them, as well as with people who have craft-based hobbies. It has a huge range of items on sale - in fact, something for everyone. And if Debbie doesn't have it in stock, she can easily order it for you. This is because she believes in the old-fashioned standards of outstanding service, helpful, friendly advice and value-for-money prices.

For the artists, Debbie stocks all the basic art and sketching materials, such as oil paints, acrylics, pastels, pencils, water colours, charcoal, sketch pads and brushes. And the craft items are sure to please everyone. There are materials and tools for stamping, scrapbooks, embossing, decoupage, bead craft, haberdashery, card making, embossing, pergamano, and a whole lot more. You can even make wedding stationery! You will be fascinated by it all.

The shop is laid out logically, so that you can find what you want quickly and easily. But if you want to browse then you are free to do so. There is no obligation to buy, and in fact, Debbie recommends that you take your time. So when in Brecon, make your way to this fascinating shop for al your arts and crafts supplies.

BRECKNOCK MUSEUM & ART GALLERY

Captain's Walk, Brecon, Powys LD3 7DS
Tel: 01874 624121
e-mail: brecon.museum@powys.gov.uk
website: www.powys.gov.uk/museums

Any visit to Brecon, county town of the former county of Breconshire, is incomplete without a visit to the **Brecknock Museum and Art Gallery** in the old Shire Hall. It is one of the liveliest and finest museums in the country - a fascinating place for young and old, and has many exhibits on the country and its landscapes, rural life and towns. The beautiful, porticoed building itself was built in 1842, and is grand and imposing. Not only was it the headquarters of the county council, it also housed the old Assize Court. In fact, one of the exhibits is a recreation of a 19th century court, complete with judge, jury, lawyers and defendant, whose story you can hear. You look down on to it from above, giving a fascinating insight into the workings of a court in Victorian times. Conversion to a museum

took place in 1974, and since then it has been one of the must-see attractions of South Wales. There is a also an art gallery with changing exhibits that you just can't afford to miss, plus a shop selling local craft items - just right to pick up that gift or souvenir.

The town of Brecon itself sits in the stunning Brecon Beacons National Park, and is well worth exploring, with its medieval cathedral, Georgian and Jacobean streets and cruises on the Monmouth and Brecon Canal.

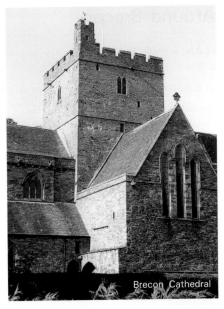
Brecon Cathedral

Brecknock Museum where visitors can see the old assize court as well as take in the extensive collection of artefacts and other items from past centuries including the museum's large collection of Welsh love spoons.

The town's second museum is equally fascinating and the **South Wales Borderers Museum** features memorabilia of the regiment's famous defence of Rorke's Drift. Over 300 years of military history are recorded here through various displays that include armoury, uniforms and medals - the regiment has taken part in every major campaign and war and has won 29 Victoria Crosses and over 100 Battle Honours. However, though its history is long and varied, it is the regiment's participation in the Zulu wars that is best remembered and which

P.F. SWEENEY

9, 10 & 11 Market Arcade, Brecon, Powys LD3 9DA
Tel: 01874 623428

For the very best butcher meat in mid Wales, head for **P.F. Sweeney** in the market arcade in Brecon. It has been owned and personally managed by Paddy Sweeney for the last 29 years, and during that time he has become well known for quality and value, not only in Brecon, but throughout the whole area. It's a traditional butcher's shop like a butcher's shop used to be, and sells home-produced prime Welsh beef, lamb, veal, homemade sausages, hamburgers, faggots, cooked meats, and a host of other products that are sure to please and delight you.

The meat is hung for three weeks before being sold, ensuring great flavour and texture, and all the butchery is done on the premises. Paddy takes a great pride in his realistic prices, the quality of everything he sells, his bright, modern shop and his friendly staff who are always on hand to offer advice and help in choosing a cut that is just right for you.

If you are enjoying a self-catering holiday in the area, why not call in for all your butchery requirements, or for a special cut of meat for a celebratory meal? The premises are immaculately clean, and you can buy with total confidence. So make your way to the market arcade in Brecon and be prepared to be amazed at the high quality and the down to earth prices.

📷 stories and anecdotes   🐦 famous people   🎨 art and craft   🎭 entertainment and sport   🚶 walks was immortalised in the film *Zulu* starring Michael Caine. It recalls the heroic defence of Rorke's Drift in 1879, when 141 men from the regiment were attacked by 4,000 Zulus; nine VCs were awarded here in a single day.

As well as having the River Usk flowing through the town, Brecon is also home to the **Monmouthshire and Brecon Canal**, a beautiful Welsh waterway which used to bring coal and limestone into the town. Work started on the canal in 1797, and a superb viaduct carries it across the River Usk just outside the town. There are attractive walks along the canal towpath as well as pleasure cruises on both motorised and horse drawn barges. The canal basin in the town has been reconstructed and is now proving to be an attraction in its own right.

Anyone thirsty from all the sightseeing can either take advantage of the many pubs, inns, restaurant and cafés in the town or pay a visit to the **Welsh Whisky Distillery and Visitor Centre**. An audio-visual presentation explains the history of whisky making through the ages and, after a tour of the distillery, visitors can sample a tot in the well-stocked gift shop. Well-known natives of Brecon include Dr Hugh Price, founder of Jesus College, Oxford, and the actress Sarah Siddons.

Around Brecon

LLANFRYNACH
2 miles S of Brecon on the B4558

> 🏛 Parish Church of St Brynach   🏛 Canal Museum

Housed in an 18th century warehouse, the **Canal Museum** tells the story of life on the canal. Horse-drawn boat trips start from here, and sometimes a blacksmith can be seen at work. The **Parish Church of St Brynach** is Victorian, though it has a medieval tower. St Brynach was Irish, and came to Wales in the 6th century to preach and spread Christianity. On arriving in what is now Pembrokeshire, he caught the idea of the daughter of a local chieftain. He resisted her advances, and was then attacked and beaten for doing so.

LIBANUS
4 miles SW of Brecon on the A470

> 🏛 Brecon Beacons Mountain Centre   🏛 Twyn y Gaer
> 🔷 Corn Du   🔷 Pen y Fan
> 🏛 Bedd Illtyd   🔷 Brecon Beacons National Park

To the northwest of this attractive hamlet, on Mynydd Illtyd common, lies the **Brecon Beacons Mountain Centre**, where visitors can find out about the **Brecon Beacons**

DAMSON COTTAGE

Alltybrain Farm, Llandefaelog Fach, Brecon LD3 9RB
Tel: 01874 690214 or 07803752989
e-mail: rosevr@talktalk.net
website: www.damsoncottageinwales.co.uk

Situated four miles from the market town of Brecon, **Damson Cottage** is one of the best self-catering five-star cottages in the area. This is a private cottage on a smallholding with its own orchard, stream and various ducks and chickens. The cottage is comfortable, spacious and well-appointed. Every window offers spectacular views and it is perfect for two people wanting a romantic rural holiday. The local pub serves good food and is within easy walking distance.

Breaks are fairly priced for the quality and high standards of the cottage, as any visit will soon prove.

🏛 historic building   🏛 museum   🏛 historic site   🔷 scenic attraction   🌱 flora and fauna

National Park from displays and presentations; there are also some interesting remains to be seen in the area. **Twyn y Gaer**, a Bronze Age burial chamber, and **Bedd Illtyd**, a more modest ancient monument said to be the grave of St Illtyd, the founder of the monastery at Llantwit Major. Brecon Beacons are a small part of the National Park, and were given to the National Trust in 1965. This included the sandstone peaks of **Pen y Fan** (at 2,906 feet, the highest point in southern Britain) and **Corn Du,** and it has become one of the most popular parts of the UK with walkers. The area is also important for sub-alpine plants and is designated a Site of Special Scientific Interest. But the very popularity of the Beacons with walkers has caused great problems, exacerbated by military manoeuvres and the sheep that have grazed here since Tudor times. Erosion is the biggest problem, and the National Trust has put in place an ambitious programme of footpath and erosion repair.

PENCILLI
4 miles SE of Brecon on the B4558

🏛 Parish Church of St Meugan   🏛 Pencilli Castle

The **Parish Church of St Meugan**, which is actually in Llanfeugan, some way out of the village, was built by Ralph de Mortimer of Pencelli Castle in 1272. It is a handsome building with a sturdy tower. Much of the building you see nowadays dates from the 14th century. **Pencilli Castle**, of which there are now only scant remains, was built in the late 11th century by Ralph Baskerville, a Norman knight.

YSTRADFELLTE
12 miles SW of Brecon off the A4059

🏛 Parish Church of St Mary   🏛 Maen Madog

⛰ Fan Llia   ⛰ Fan Nedd   ⛰ Porth-yr-Ogof

The **Parish Church of St Mary** is mainly 16th century, and has a font of the same date. The church is supposed to have been founded by Cistercian monks. The village is a recognised hiking centre and the area of classic limestone countryside around it is one of the most impressive in the British Isles. The narrow road heading north from the village climbs sharply and squeezes its way along a narrow valley between the 2,074 feet high **Fan Llia** on the east side and the 2.176 feet high **Fan Nedd** on the west. The **Maen Madog** is a nine-foot high standing stone with a Latin inscription proclaiming that Dervacius, son of Justus, lies here.

To the south of Ystradfellte is **Porth-yr-Ogof**, a delightful area with a collection of dramatic waterfalls as the River Melte descends through woodland.

Maen Madog, Ystradfellte

🎭 stories and anecdotes   🐦 famous people   🎨 art and craft   🖋 entertainment and sport   🥾 walks

YSTRADGYNLAIS

18½ miles SW of Brecon on the B4599

🔝 Y Garn Goch

Situated at the top end of the Tawe Valley, which stretches down to the city of Swansea, and close to the boundary of the Brecon Beacon National park is Ystradgynlais, a former mining community. A place rich in industrial heritage, iron was produced here as far back as the early 17th century and the legacy of this industrious past can still be seen, although the area surrounding the village is known as waterfall country and is popular with walkers, ramblers and cavers.

A local legend tells of three cauldrons, filled with gold, that are buried beneath **Y Garn Goch** - the red cairn - on the summit of Mynydd y Drum, to the east of the town. The story goes that one day a young girl will come to claim the treasure which, until then, is protected by demons. To prevent anyone trying to take the gold, the legend also tells of a wizard and his apprentice who attempted to overcome the demons with their magic. While the elements raged, a spirit on a wheel of fire swept the apprentice out of the protective circle he had made and gave him a lighted candle, saying that as long as the candle burned his life would last. As soon as the candle was spent the apprentice died and the wizard, terrified, fled from the mountain.

CRAIG-Y-NOS

15½ miles SW of Brecon on the A4067

🏛 Craig-y-Nos Castle   🏛 Dinosaur Park

🏛 Mr Morgan's Farm   🍃 Craig-y-Nos Country Park

🍃 National Showcaves Centre for Wales

🏛 Iron Age Farm

The **National Showcaves Centre for Wales** is centred on the largest complex of caverns in northern Europe, and lies to the north of this village. Discovered in 1912, the caverns have taken 315 million years to create and they include both the longest and the largest showcaves in Britain. The Cathedral Cave, as its name suggests, is like the interior of a great cathedral, and modern lighting and music accentuate the atmosphere. Near the entrance is a display on cave dwellers of the past. Dan-yr-Ogof has a series of lakes connected by passages, and these you can explore as well. Within Bone Cave 42 human skeletons have been discovered, many of them dating back over 3,000 years to the Bronze Age. Deer bones over 7,000 years old have also been discovered.

Exploring the underground caverns is only one aspect of this interesting attraction, as there is also an award-winning **Dinosaur Park**, where life size replicas of the creatures that roamed the earth during Jurassic times can be seen, and **Mr Morgan's Farm**, where Welsh cobs, the wagons they pulled and other farm animals are on show. The replica **Iron Age Farm** gives a realistic idea of how the farmers lived so long ago.

To the east of the village lies **Craig-y-Nos Country Park**, where visitors can enjoy the unspoilt countryside and the landscaped country parkland of the upper Tawe Valley. The mansion in the country park, known as **Craig-y-Nos Castle**, was once the home of the 19th century opera singer Madame Adelina Patti She bought the estate in 1878 as a home for her and her second husband, the tenor Ernesto Nicolini. She installed an aviary, a little theatre modelled on Drury Lane and a winter garden that was subsequently moved to Swansea's Victoria Park. Patti was born in Madrid in 1843, the daughter of a Sicilian tenor, and achieved fame in New York at an early age. Her first husband was the Marquis

🏛 historic building   🏛 museum   🏛 historic site   🍃 scenic attraction   🌱 flora and fauna de Caux, her second Ernesto Nicolini and her third the Swedish Baron Cedarström, whom she married in the Roman Catholic church at Brecon in 1898. The castle is now a hotel.

SENNYBRIDGE

7½ miles W of Brecon on the A40

🏛 Castell Ddu   🏠 Disgwylfa Conservation Centre

Situated along the southern edge of the Mynydd Epynt and on the northern border of the Brecon Beacons National Park, this village is very much a product of the industrial age as it only began to develop after the railways arrived here in 1872, when it became a centre for livestock trading. However, the remains of **Castell Ddu**, just to the west of the village, provides evidence of life here from an earlier age. Dating from the 14th century and believed to stand on the site of an 11th century manor house, this was the home of Sir Reginald Aubrey, trusted friend of Bernard of Newmarch, a Norman knight who was granted tracts of land in the area in the 11th century, and who founded Brecon Priory. Two new waymarked walks have been opened on the Sennybridge army training area, beginning

at **Disgwylfa Conservation Centre** on the B4519. The centre has an interactive learning centre and military and conservation displays. One of the walks is accessible for disabled visitors.

Crickhowell

🏛 Crickhowell Castle   🏛 Parish Church of St Edmund

🏛 Crickhowell Bridge   🏚 Crug Hywell

🌱 Pwll-y-Wrach Nature Reserve

🏄 Welsh Hang Gliding Centre

Situated in the beautiful valley of the River Usk and in the shadow of the Black Mountains that lie to the north, Crickhowell is a charming little town with a long history. The town takes its name from the Iron Age fort, **Crug Hywell** (Howell's Fort) that lies on the flat-topped hill above the town that is aptly named Table Mountain. The remains of another stronghold, **Crickhowell Castle** - once one of the most important fortresses in this mountainous region of Wales - can be found in the town's large park. Built in the 11th century, it is also known as Alisby Castle, after a Norman knight who once owned it. Only the motte and two shattered towers remain of the Norman fortress, which was stormed by Owain Glyndwr and abandoned in the 15th century.

The imposing **Parish Church of St Edmund** was founded in the 12th century by Lady Sybil Pauncefote, whose father Sir Hugh

Crickhowell Bridge

Turberville, owned the castle. Effigies of Sybil and her husband, the wonderfully named Sir Grimbald, can be seen in the sanctuary.

The picturesque and famous **Crickhowell Bridge**, which dates from the 16th century, spans the River Usk in the heart of the town. Still carrying traffic today, the bridge is unique in that it has 13 arches on one side and only 12 on the other! The town, with its fine Georgian architecture, is popular with those looking for outdoor activities such as walking, due to its close proximity to the Black Mountains and the National Park. Close by is **Pwll-y-Wrach Nature Reserve** in a steep-sided valley. Owned by the Brecknock Wildlife Trust, this woodland reserve has a waterfall and also a great variety of flora, for which it has been designated a Site of Special Scientific Interest. The **Welsh Hang Gliding Centre** is to be found in Baoen House in Church Lane.

Around Crickhowell

TRETOWER
2½ miles NW of Crickhowell on the A479

🏛 Tretower Court and Gardens   🏛 Tretower Castle

This quiet village in the Usk Valley is the home of two impressive medieval buildings - **Tretower Court and Gardens** and **Tretower Castle** (both in the hands of CADW). The elder of these historic sites is the castle, though all that remains on the site of the original Norman motte is a stark keep that dates from the 13th century. The castle was built in this valley to discourage Welsh rebellion but, nevertheless, it was besieged by Llywelyn the Last and almost destroyed by Owain Glyndwr in 1403.

Adjacent to the castle remains lies the court, a magnificent 15th century fortified manor house that served as a very desirable domestic residence particularly during the less turbulent years following Glyndwr's rebellion. While the 15th century woodwork here and the wall walk, with its 17th century roof and windows, are outstanding, it is the court's gardens that are particularly interesting. The original late 15th century layout of the gardens has been recreated in such a manner that the owner of the time, Sir Roger Vaughan, would still recognise them. Among the many delightful features there are a tunnel arbour planted with vines and white roses (Sir Roger was a Yorkist), an enclosed arbour and a chequerboard garden. They are all best seen in the early summer.

TALYBONT-ON-USK
7 miles NW of Crickhowell on the B4558

🔾 Talybont Reservoir

Just beyond this attractive village, which won the Powys Village of the Year Award in 2003, the Monmouthshire and Brecon Canal passes through the 375 yard long Ashford Tunnel while, further south, lies the **Talybont Reservoir**. In this narrow wooded valley on the southeast slopes of the Brecons there are several forest trails starting from the car park at the far end of the reservoir.

LLANGORS
8 miles NW of Crickhowell on the B4560

🏛 Parish Church of St Paulinus

🔾 Llangors Lake   🛶 Rope Centre

The **Parish Church of St Paulinus**, dates from the 15th century, though there was much rebuilding in Victorian times. It may have been built on the site of a monastery which was founded in the 7th century and continued up until the 11th century. To the south of the village, which is sometimes spelled Llangorse, lies the largest natural lake in South Wales - **Llangors Lake** (Llyn Syfaddan). Around four miles in circumference and following its way round a low contour in the Brecon Beacons, the waters of this lake were, in medieval times, thought to have miraculous properties. Today, the lake attracts numerous visitors looking to enjoy not only the setting but also the wide variety of sporting and leisure activities, such as fishing, horse riding and sailing, that can be found here. There is also a **Rope Centre**, with climbing, abseiling, potholing, log climbing and a high-level rope course.

Naturally, the lake is associated with a legend and local stories suggest that the land beneath the lake once belonged to a cruel and greedy princess. Though her lover was poor, she agreed to marry him only if he brought her great riches. So the lover set out to accomplish his task and in so doing robbed and murdered a wealthy merchant, giving the riches to his princess. However, the merchant's ghost returned to warn the happy couple that their crime would be avenged, not on them but on the ninth generation of their family. One night, years later, a great flood burst from the hills, drowning the surrounding land and its inhabitants. It is still said today that a city can been seen beneath the water.

Llangors Lake

TALGARTH

10½ miles N of Crickhowell on the A479

🏛 Parish Church of St Gwendoline

🏛 Bronllys Castle 🌱 Hywell Harris

Lying in the foothills of the Black Mountains, Talgarth is an attractive market town with narrow streets that boasts many historic associations as well as some fine architecture. The 15th century **Parish Church of St**

Gwendoline is the burial place of Hywell Harris (1714-73), an influential figure in the establishment of Welsh Methodism. Harris was also instrumental in establishing a religious community, 'The Connexion', which was organised on both religious and industrial lines.

Although this is now a quiet and charming place, Talgarth once stood against the Norman drive into Wales. Some of the defensive structures can still be seen today - the tower of the church and another tower that is now incorporated into a house - though it has also served time as the jail.

On the outskirts of Talgarth lies **Bronllys Castle** a well-preserved centuries old keep built by the Norman baron Bernard of Newmarch. Originally a motte and bailey castle, it was later replaced with a stone edifice and now it is a lone tower standing on a steep mound that is in the hands of CADW - Welsh Historic Monuments.

LLANGOED HALL

Llyswen, Nr Brecon, Powys LD3 0YP
Tel: 01874 754525
e-mail: enquiries@llangoedhall.com
website: www.llangoedhall.com

Llangoed Hall is different. Here, they have created, not the ambience of a country house hotel, but of a great country house, and all that implies. On your arrival you will be greeted by a butler.

It sits in mid Wales, on the banks of the River Wye, and has wonderful views out towards the Black Mountains.

The hotel was created by its founder, Sir Bernard Ashley, husband of the late Laura Ashley, and his dream of comfort combined with a quiet efficiency has been more than fulfilled. They are proud of the place, and want to invite you to visit and see for yourself just how exceptional it is. The open fireplaces, the grand staircase, the panelled library and upstairs gallery, all adorned with fresh flowers, antiques and paintings, speak of the elegance and simplicity of former days. The house itself is a dignified Jacobean mansion whose earliest parts date back to 1632. Most of the building as you see it today was the work of the renowned Sir Clough Williams-Ellis, who finished rebuilding it in 1919.

There are 23 outstanding bedrooms, each one individually designed and furnished with antiques and paintings by such artists as Sickert, Augustus John and Whistler. The fabrics are from Elanbach, Sir Bernard's own company, which has premises in the grounds.

They are particularly proud of their cuisine, which has won no less than two rosettes. The resident chef, Sean Ballington, firmly believes in fresh, local produce, and this is reflected in the outstanding menu, which combines simplicity and fine flavours with imagination and flair. Welsh lamb, salmon, and his signature dish, Black Beef, are classics - but with a subtle twist or two! The wine list is award winning, and guests can order anything from the wine list from a bottle of Chateau Miraval House Wine at a very reasonable £18, to a bottle of Dom Perignon at £975!

Llangoed Hall has two rooms specially licensed for civil wedding and civil partnership ceremonies, and they can undertake all the arrangements. In the past they have catered for weddings with up to 200 guests in a marquee on the grounds, and up to 80 within the building itself. It is the very epitome of a romantic setting, and their attention to detail makes the whole day pass smoothly and efficiently.

They can also make all the arrangements for conferences and seminars, and have function rooms so that parties may be divided into separate working parties. All the latest presentation equipment is on hand, and they can even arrange entertainment or guest speakers!

CWMFFOREST RIDING CENTRE & GUEST FARM

Cwmfforest Farm, Pengenford, Talgarth, Brecon LD3 0EU
Tel: 01874 711398
e-mail: riding@transwales.com
website: www.transwales.com

One of the best ways to see Wales is on horseback, and one of the best riding centres is the **Cwmfforest Riding Centre and Guest Farm**. It is situated deep in the Black Mountains of mid Wales, and these can be explored at a pace that is gentle and appealing, with riders losing none of the wonderful panoramic views and the spectacular scenery for which the country is famous. This takes you far away from the hustle and bustle of modern life, and offers an enriching experience that will long be remembered.

The centre is owned by the Turner family, who have been offering full inclusive riding holidays since 1970. Six and seven day trails offer comfortable accommodation on the way, as well as all food and drinks (except alcoholic drinks). In addition, there are three-day trails, weekend trails, day trails and half-day trails.

You don't need to be a proficient rider to enjoy this way of experiencing Wales. Anyone who is reasonably competent and feels easy around horses can take part. The trails offer good, traditional fare, comfortable accommodation, trustworthy Welsh cobs and, in the winter months, roaring logs fires in the guest house attached to the riding centre and on the stopping off points on the trails.

LLANGYNIDR
4 miles W of Crickhowell on the B4558

🏛 Chartists' Cave

Rising to the south of this riverside village on the open moorland of Mynydd Llangynidr, lies the **Chartists' Cave**, where members of the movement stored ammunition during their active years in the mid 19th century.

LLANGATTOCK
1 mile SW of Crickhowell off the A4077

🏛 Parish Church of St Catwg

🌿 Craig-y-Cilau Nature Reserve

The **Parish Church of St Catwg**, which was founded sometime during the early 6th century, is dedicated to one of Wales' most honoured saints. Born in around AD 497, by the end of his life, in around 577, he had become a bishop and taken the name Sophias. The church's large tower is from the 16th century, while the rest of the building dates from the 14th century and later. It was restored in Victorian times, but most of the medieval features can still be seen.

To the southwest of the village, towards the boundary of the Brecon Beacons National Park lies the **Craig-y-Cilau Nature Reserve**. With over 250 plant species and over 50 kinds of birds breeding within the reserve, this is one of the richest in the National Park.

🎭 stories and anecdotes 🐦 famous people 🎨 art and craft 🎭 entertainment and sport 🚶 walks

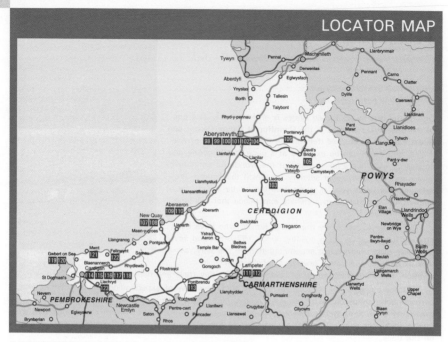

LOCATOR MAP

ADVERTISERS AND PLACES OF INTEREST

🏛 historic building   🏛 museum   🏛 historic site   💧 scenic attraction   🌿 flora and fauna

6| Ceredigion

Ceredigion's countryside features some of the most beautiful landscapes in Wales and also attracts many rare species of birds, animals and plants. In particular, it is home to the graceful red kite, and keen birdwatchers are well served by nature reserves around the Teifi and Dyfi estuaries and at Llangranog, New Quay and Cors Caron.

Ceredigion means the land of Ceredig, son of the Celtic chieftain Cunedda. Dating from around AD 415, the region is steeped in history and tradition. It is renowned for its unique brand of Welshness and, within Wales, its inhabitants are affectionately known as 'Cardis', as Ceredigion encompasses most of the former county of Cardiganshire. The patron saint of Wales, St David, was born in Ceredigion and many famous Welsh princes are buried in the ruins of Strata Florida Abbey. The region is not as well endowed with castles as the counties further north, but Aberystwyth and Cardigan castles both saw fighting before they were left in ruins, and Cardigan is credited with being the venue for the first recorded Eisteddfod in 1176.

Perhaps, though, this county is best known for its coastline on the great sweep of Cardigan Bay. Many of the one-time fishing villages have now become genteel resorts, but few seem to have attained the great degree of brashness that is associated with other seaside holiday destinations. In the north of the county and close to the mouth of the River Dyfi is the great expanse of sand at Borth while, further south, the coastline gives way to cliffs and coves - once the haunt of smugglers.

Much of Ceredigion can be classed as very Welsh and very rural, and it is also an important area of learning. St David's College at Lampeter, a world renowned ecclesiastical establishment, is now, as University College, part of the University of Wales, while Aberystwyth is home not only to the first university in Wales, founded in 1872, but also to the National Library of Wales.

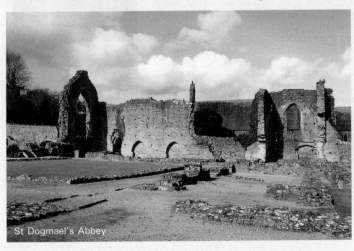

St Dogmael's Abbey

Aberystwyth

🏛 Aberystwyth Castle 🏛 War Memorial 🏛 Pier

🏛 Old College 🏛 Ceredigion Museum

🏛 Welsh Christian Heritage Centre 🚋 Cliff Railway

🏛 National Library of Wales

🐾 Aberystwyth Camera Obscura

🏖 Aberystwyth Harbour and Marina

Aberystwyth is the largest town on Cardigan Bay, the seat of local government and the home of the University of Wales Aberystwyth and the National Library of Wales. It is not only the unofficial capital of mid-Wales but also a cosmopolitan coastal resort that, at its peak, attracted many thousands of tourists each year. Although there is evidence that the town is older, Aberystwyth as we know it can

certainly be traced back to the late 13th century when, in 1277, Edward I began building **Aberystwyth Castle** and also granted a charter that made the settlement around the new fortification a free borough with a ditch and wall, a guild of merchants, a market and two fairs. Constructed to subdue the Welsh, the castle withstood a siege in 1282 but in 1404 it fell to Owain Glyndwr during fighting that destroyed the surrounding town. Glyndwr made the castle his base for four years and it became an important seat of government until, in 1408, it was recaptured by Prince Henry (who later went on to become Henry V). In 1637, Thomas Bushell was given permission to set up a mint within the castle, and during the Civil War the silver coins minted here for Charles I were needed to pay the Royalist soldiers, as Cromwell had

DOTS

6+8 Market Street, Aberystwyth, Ceredigion SY23 1DL
Tel: 01970 626333 website: www.dots-gifts.co.uk

Aberystwyth is one of Wales' most beautiful and popular seaside resorts, and if you are holidaying there - or simply just passing through - then you must visit **dots...** for all your gift solutions. This fascinating shop is very definitely 'design led', as all its goods have a stylish, modern look that is sure to please. There is a huge range of household gifts and accessories from clocks, vases and cushions to toiletries, jewellery and a wonderful range of children's gifts.

The owner, Lowri Steffan opened the shop in 2001 and was the winner of the Welsh young people's Award for Business Enterprise in 2003. She and her team of staff are always available to give a helping hand in choosing that perfect gift. Whether it's a driftwood mirror, some Carrie Elspeth jewellery or a beautiful Melin Tregwynt throw, you truly will be spoilt for choice at **dots...**

Lowri also offers a design consultancy service for both private and business customers, helping them furnish and accessorise an individual room or even a whole house with stylish solutions to fit any budget. Not forgetting the Wedding Hire Service - here customers have an opportunity to buy or hire large artificial topiaries, display vases or smaller table decorations or favours for a wedding reception or for any celebration. A range of her most popular products are also available to buy online.

So don't delay... make straight to **dots...** in Aberystwyth - a one stop gift shop.

dots... anrhegion trawiadol i ti ac i'r ty

🏛 historic building 🏛 museum 🚋 historic site 🐾 scenic attraction 🌿 flora and fauna taken control of the mints in London. However, the castle finally fell to the Parliamentarians in 1646 and Cromwell destroyed the building some three years later. Today, the ruins, standing on the rocky headland, remain an impressive sight. Also on Castle Point can be found the town's **War Memorial**, a splendid monument that was commissioned the year after World War I ended. It is the work of the Italian sculptor Mario Rutelli.

In the years following the turmoil of the Civil War, and before the arrival of the railways, Aberystwyth remained essentially a fishing town, but with a growing shipbuilding

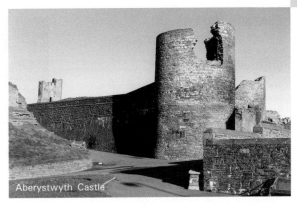
Aberystwyth Castle

industry. Although much of this industry has now ceased, **Aberystwyth Harbour and Marina** is still a bustling place that can accommodate over 100 vessels and, at the town quay, all manner of fish and seafood are landed.

FURNITURE CAVE

3 Cambrian Street, Aberystwyth, Ceredigion SY23 1NZ
Tel: 01970 611234
e-mail: thecave@btinternet.com
website: www.furniture-cave.co.uk

The Furniture Cave, in the heart of the seaside town of Aberystwyth, is aptly named, as it is an Aladdin's cave of stripped pine and reproduction furniture, antiques, ceramics, garden statuary, carpets and rugs, maps, modern silver and jewellery, fireplaces and pictures. As soon as you enter, you will be astonished at the quality and low prices of what is on offer.

It is housed in a former tea warehouse, and has two whole floors of goods, making this a fascinating place to visit. You are free to browse, and the owner, Phil David, advises that you take your time when you do so, as there is just so much to see and admire. He has been in the antiques trade for over 25 years, and is knowledgeable about everything he has on offer, as are his two staff members. They will be only too glad to point you in the direction of something that suits your tastes and price bracket.

Most of the antiques on show are new to the trade, as they have usually come from private houses and collections. Some of the smaller objects would make delightful souvenirs or gifts, and if it's something larger you're after, Phil can arrange to have it delivered anywhere in the country. He also undertakes valuations and house clearances. So pay the Furniture Cave a visit when you're in Aberystwyth - but set aside plenty of time for it, as you're sure to stay longer than you intended in this fascinating shop.

SLATERS BAKERS

9 North parade, Aberystwyth, Ceredigion
SY23 2JH
Tel: 01970 612658

Wales is justly famous for its breads and cakes, and nowhere is this more in evidence than at Slaters Bakers in Aberystwyth. This shop has a reputation for its traditional baking, using only the finest ingredients and made in the traditional way. There is also a fine range of foreign breads, and the smells as you enter the shop will send your taste buds tingling! If you're staying in the town, or just passing through, then head for Slaters.

The arrival of the railways in the 1860s saw the town expand rapidly as first the Victorians and then the Edwardians made their way here to enjoy the sea air and the beauty of the great sweep of Cardigan Bay. The town's 700 foot long **Pier** was constructed in 1864 and the Pavilion at the end was added in 1896 to provide a capacious venue for light entertainment. Great Victorian and Edwardian villas were built along the seafront, and these still exist, converted now to hotels and guest houses. Just to the north, along the coast from the town centre, lies the longest electric **Cliff Railway** (see panel opposite) in Britain. It was

TY BELGRAVE HOUSE

Y Prom/Marine Terrace, Aberystwyth,
Ceredigion SY23 2AZ
Tel: 01970 630553
website: www.tybelgravehouse.co.uk

A warm welcome awaits you at **Ty Belgrave House**, an exquisite boutique guest house situated right on the promenade at Abersystwyth. It boasts nine delightful en suite rooms with stylish, contemporary furnishings and sea views. This is holiday accommodation at its very best, and fully warrants the four stars it has been awarded by the Welsh Tourist Board. Morning coffee, snacks and afternoon teas are served in the lounge and bar, which also serves a wide range of beers and spirits.

The three-star Four Seasons Hotel in Portland Street (01970 612120) is another splendid establishment, and offers 16 extremely comfortable en suite bedrooms to discerning guests. It, too, has a lounge bar that serves coffees, snacks and evening meals, and its restaurant is renowned for its high standard of cuisine.

The two-star Queensbridge Hotel in Victoria Terrace (01970612343) sits on a quieter part of the promenade, just five minutes form the town centre. Fifteen en suite rooms - and the hearty Welsh breakfasts, ensure that guests enjoy a comfortable stay. It is in an unrivalled position, as it overlooks a panoramic sweep of Cardigan Bay. There is a large TV lounge and bar area where you can enjoy a quiet drink.

All three hotels are part of the same group, and offer outstanding value for money and service. If you come to Aberystwyth, be sure to book into one of them.

🏛 historic building　🏛 museum　🏛 historic site　🔾 scenic attraction　🌿 flora and fauna

opened in 1896, when it was powered by an ingenious water balance system. In 1921 it was converted to electricity, and it still carries passengers up the slope of Constitution Hill at a sedate four miles an hour. From the summit there are panoramic views over the bay and, inland, to the Cambrian Mountains. Also on the summit is the **Aberystwyth Camera Obscura**, housed in an octagonal tower. A faithful reconstruction of a popular Victorian amusement, the huge 14 inch lens - the biggest in the world - gives visitors an even better view from this excellent vantage point. It was originally built in 1880 within Aberystwyth Castle, and rebuilt on Constitution Hill in 1896, the year the Cliff railway opened. However, by the 1920s it had gone. The present camera was built in 1985.

While the town today certainly seems to cater to holidaymakers' every need, Aberystwyth is also a seat of learning. The **Old College** was originally built to JP Seddon's design in the 1870s as a hotel designed to accommodate the influx of Victorian visitors. However the venture failed and in 1872 the high Gothic building was sold, becoming the first university in Wales and now home to the departments of Welsh, Education and Theatre, Film and Television. The great crowds of holidaymakers may have gone, but the town still has over 7,000 students living in it during term-time, adding greatly to its economy.

With such an intellectual heritage it is not surprising that the town is also the home of the **National Library of Wales**, one of only

CONSTITUTION HILL

Constitution Hill Ltd, Cliff Railway House, Cliff Terrace,
Aberystwyth SY23 2DN
Tel/Fax: 01970 617642
e-mail: manager@aberystwythcliffrailway.co.uk
website: www.aberystwythcliffrailway.co.uk

Constitution Hill in Aberystwyth can lay claim to not one but two unique attractions – the longest electric Cliff Railway in Britain and the largest Camera Obscura in the world. The railway opened in 1896 to ferry Victorian holidaymakers up to the top of the hill and the varied attractions and amusements that awaited there. The railway was originally operated on the water balance system but today a powerful electric motor hauls the carriages along the 778ft track at a steady 4 mph, allowing the passengers ample time to enjoy the views on the way up. Those views are naturally at their finest at the summit, from where on a fine day 26 mountain peaks, 100 miles of coastline and 1,000 square miles of land and sea can be seen – with the naked eye and also reflected by a 14" lens onto a circular screen in the viewing gallery.

There are various other activities and attractions at the top, including a licensed restaurant serving a range of drinks, snacks and meals every day in the summer, Wednesday to Sunday off season. On Thursday, Friday and Saturday the Steak House is the place to go for a choice of succulent steaks and grills, scrumptious puddings and well-chosen wines. Also on the summit are gift shops, a bouncy castle, quad bikes and Frisbee golf.

📖 stories and anecdotes   🦅 famous people   🎨 art and craft   🎭 entertainment and sport   🚶 walks

BRYNARTH COUNTRY GUEST HOUSE

Lledrod, Aberystwyth, Ceredigion
SY23 4HX
Tel: 01974 261367
e-mail: bookings@brynarth.co.uk
website: www.brynarth.co.uk

Brynarth Country Guest House is different. It's not often that you come across an establishment that puts such emphasis on high standards of service and comfort. This is thanks to its hands-on owners Cathy and Ian Campion. Brynarth nestles in the shelter of a circle of small hills, and looks more like a peaceful village than a guest house. It is situated eleven miles south east of Aberystwyth within some stunningly beautiful countryside, yet close enough to the holiday resort to enjoy all its amenities. It is a friendly, informal place, and the 17th century farmhouse and its outbuildings have been converted into some of the best accommodation available in Ceredigion, while still retaining their period features.

Brynarth boasts five double rooms and two singles, all en suite, and two doubles with shared bathroom, though these are being converted into a family suite. They are all individually furnished and decorated, as well as being comfortable and spacious. All are centrally heated, and have tea/coffee making facilities, with fresh milk always being available from the kitchen. Two of the double rooms are in the farmhouse itself, and have en suite facilities and vaulted ceilings. One has a sitting

area, while both of them have access to an extra, separate bathroom. The other rooms are in a long, whitewashed barn which is close by.

The dining room and lounge are within the main farmhouse and boast exposed beams, stone walls and an inglenook fireplace. The dining room is where hearty breakfasts and evening meals are enjoyed and there is a cosy licensed bar off the living room. Special dietary needs are catered for by prior arrangement. Within the barn there is a games room where you can enjoy table tennis, pool, darts and bar billiards. Well behaved and sociable dogs are welcome but please phone to discuss before booking.

Within the grounds of Brynarth there is a two-and-a-half acre wood that has a blanket of bluebells in May, and all around you can hear owls, pheasants and many other birds. To the front of the farmhouse is a large pond with goldfish, frogs and lilies. Dragonflies hover over the water, and at night bats swoop down looking for insects. The whole place seems far away from the hustle and bustle of modern life. Cathy and Ian would like to welcome you to their haven of peace and tranquillity - so come along and experience the place for yourself.

🏛 historic building   🏛 museum   🏛 historic site   ♨ scenic attraction   🌿 flora and fauna

SBRI

5a Market Street, Aberystwyth,
Ceredigion SY25 1DL
Tel: 01974 261259

West Wales has long been a fertile source of antiques, and the many outlets attract not only local customers but collectors coming to the area on holiday and dealers from many parts of the UK and overseas. In the centre of Aberystwyth, off Great Darkgate Street, the husband-and-wife team of Steven and Jean Ainsworth own and run **SBRI**, which specialises in Welsh country and fine furniture, pine and collectables.

When the weather is fine, one or two pieces are displayed outside the shop on the broad pavement to tempt passers-by to browse and buy. The old-world interior is filled with a hand-picked selection of furniture, clocks, lamps, brass ornaments, china, porcelain and paintings by Jean and other local artists.

SBRI undertakes commissions for paintings and offers a full restoration service for furniture; they also offer the best prices for buying antiques. Opening hours are 10.30 to 5 Tuesday to Saturday (half-day Wednesday).

six copyright libraries in Great Britain, and the keeper of the majority of materials that relate to the Welsh people and their culture. Founded in 1909, the foundation stone of the building was laid by George V in 1911. In 1916 the librarians and books moved in, and in 1937 it was officially opened by George VI, though work on the building didn't officially finish until 1955. The library holds many early Welsh and Celtic manuscripts, among which is the *Black Book of Carmarthen*, a 12th century manuscript that is the oldest written in Welsh. An enhanced visitor centre and other new facilities opened in 2002. Housed in a beautifully restored Edwardian music hall, right in the centre of the town, on Terrace Road, is the **Ceredigion Museum**, opened in 1982. It is housed in a former theatre, and has been described as 'probably the most beautiful museum interior in Britain'. It tells the history of Cardiganshire through an interesting collection of materials: the history of seafaring, agriculture and silver and lead mining are all well chronicled. Within the Parish Church of St Michael, built in Victorian times, you will find the **Welsh Christian Heritage Centre**, with displays and artefacts about the history of Christianity in Wales.

Around Aberystwyth

DEVIL'S BRIDGE
10 miles SE of Aberystwyth on the A4120

🏛 Hafod Arch   🚂 Vale of Rheidol Railway

💧 Devil's Bridge Waterfalls   🚶 Pwllpeiran Trail

The eastern terminus of the **Vale of Rheidol Railway**, the narrow gauge railway that runs

🕮 stories and anecdotes   🐦 famous people   🎨 art and craft   🎭 entertainment and sport   🚶 walks

Devil's Bridge Falls

from Aberystwyth through the Rheidol valley, Devil's Bridge attracts many people who come here to see the splendid **Devil's Bridge Waterfalls** that drop some 300 feet through this breathtaking gorge. While the scenery is marvellous, there are also three interesting bridges here - dating from the 11th, 18th and 20th centuries - which were built one on top of the other. An iron bridge built in 1901 straddles the top of the falls and, just below it,

there is a stone bridge of 1708 while, further down stream again, lies the original **Pont-y-gwr-Drwg** (Bridge of the Devil), thought to have been built by the monks of Strata Florida Abbey. Local legend suggests, however, that the bridge was built by the Devil and that he would claim the first soul to cross to the other side. However, an old woman, wanting to retrieve her stray cow, outwitted the Devil by throwing a crust across the bridge which her dog chased after. The Devil had to make do with the soul of the dog and the old lady safely retrieved her cow. The legend goes on to say, however, that if you cross the bridge by night, the devil is likely to push you off in a fit of pique for being denied the old woman's soul.

Along with the footpaths and nature trails that descend the 94 steps of Jacob's Ladder to view the falls, other paths lead to another vantage point - the **Hafod Arch**. It was erected by Thomas Johnes, the squire of Hafod, in 1810 to honour the Golden Jubilee of George III, the farmer king. Johnes also transformed the area with forestation, planting the surrounding countryside with over four million trees, as if in anticipation of the Forestry Commission who now own the land. The Arch, which marks the highest point on the former Hafod Estate, is one of many points of interest on the **Pwllpeiran Trail**, a

---

HAFOD HOTEL

Devil's Bridge, nr Aberystwyth, Ceredigion SY23 3JL
Tel: 01970 890232
Email: hafodhotel@btconnect.com
Website: www.thehafodhotel.co.uk

Standing alone at the head of the world-famous Mynach Falls, the **Hafod Hotel** offers all that is best in great Welsh hospitality. It is a delightful building, and boasts 23 rooms, most of which have spectacular views, and the restaurant has an enviable reputation for the quality of its food, which is all home cooked. The Victorian Tea Room also offers home-baked cakes, bara brith and light snacks in the summer. It sits close to the Hafod Forest, which offers many splendid walks, as well as the Rheidol Railway, running from Devil's Bridge to Aberystwyth.

🏛 historic building   🏛 museum   🏛 historic site   🌢 scenic attraction   🌿 flora and fauna four-mile trail that affords exciting views over Hafod and the Upper Ystwyth Valley and provides information on the agriculture, forestry, wildlife and history to be seen along its route. One section of the walk joins the Cambrian Way Long Distance Path through Myherin Forest. On its way it passes through Gelmast farmyard, which was Thomas Johnes' original experimental farm. Elsewhere on the trail, below some new oak woodland, is the **Bwlch yr Oerfa**. The remains - no more than some bumps in the ground nowadays, are thought to be part of the former Cwmystwyth Grange of the Old Cistercian Abbey at Strata Florida, possibly a raised garden.

YSBYTY CYNFYN
10½ miles E of Aberystwyth on the A4120

🏛 Parish Church of St John

Found in the circular wall of the Victorian **Parish Church of St John**, are five stones from a Bronze Age stone circle. Only one of the stones is now in its original position, and two of them have been used as gateposts at the entrance to the churchyard. This is an excellent example of the early Celtic church 'Christianising' pagan sites.

PONTERWYD
10 miles E of Aberystwyth on the A44

🐦 George Borrow   🦋 Kite Country Centre

🦋 Nant yr Arian Visitor Centre

An inn called the Borrow Arms remembers **George Borrow**, who came here to dry out after falling into a peat bog. Norfolk born, Borrow was a noted philologist and linguist who travelled widely overseas, acting for a time as an agent for the British and Foreign Bible Society. Later, he tramped around England and Wales, sometimes with his step-daughter, and in 1862 published his best-

known work *Wild Wales*. Close by is the **Nant yr Arian Visitor Centre**, a Forest Enterprise centre with forest walks and trails, a mountain bike trail, orienteering course, tea room, local crafts and picnic and play areas.

Here, too, is the **Kite Country Centre** and feeding station. Designated the Bird of the Century in 1999, the red kite was a fairly common bird in the Middle Ages, seen even in London scavenging in the streets. It was at that time considered useful and was even protected by the Crown, but with the passing of the Enclosures Act in the 16th century this impressive bird was among many species thought to be a threat to agriculture. Persecuted as vermin, they disappeared entirely from England and Scotland, but a few pairs remained in mid-Wales. With care and conservation efforts from individuals and organisations, the numbers gradually increased, so that now there are more than 300 breeding pairs. At 2 o'clock each afternoon throughout the year the kites swoop down to be fed, joined by other species looking for an easy meal, including crows, buzzards and ravens. Other red kite feeding stations in Wales are at Gigrin Farm near Rhayader, Powys, and Tregaron in Ceredigion, the latter feeding in winter only.

LLYWERNOG
9 miles E of Aberystwyth on the A44

🏛 Llywernog Lead & Silver Mine

Just to the north of the village lies the **Llywernog Lead & Silver Mine** (see panel on page 202), a museum that covers the history of this major rural industry in mid Wales. This mine opened in 1740 and had its most prosperous period between 1850 and 1879. In the slump that followed most of the mines closed for good, but Llywernog refused to die and was briefly reopened in 1903 as a

Llywernog Lead & Silver Mine

Ponterwyd, Aberystwyth,
Ceredigion SY43 3AB
Tel: 01970 890620
e-mail: enquiries@silverminetours.co.uk
website: www.silverminetours.co.uk

The mining of silver-rich lead ore was an important industry in the Plynlimon Mountains of mid-Wales in the 1860s. Most of the mines were later abandoned but **Llywernog Lead & Silver Mine** survived and was saved from dereliction by the late Dr Stephen Harvey and his son Peter, who now run this seven-acre heritage site. Visitors can follow the Miners Trail, take the underground tour to the Great Chasm and see the working water wheels, mining machinery and mineral displays. The site, which has a souvenir shop and tea room, is open from mid-March to the end of October; closed Mondays except Bank Holidays and July/August.

zinc prospect. It was saved in 1973 by the present owners.

LLANBADARN FAWR
1 mile E of Aberystwyth on the A44

🏛 Parish Church of St Padarn

Although this village has now become a suburb of Aberystwyth, it was once a town in its own right and, in the 6th century, St Padarn established a small monastery here. For over 600 years, the monastery and the church were dominant despite the merging of the bishopric at Llanbadarn - the oldest in Wales - with that of St David in the 8th century. The present **Parish Church of St Padarn** dates from a rebuild of 1257 after a fire destroyed the older church, and two Celtic crosses that are associated with St Samson, Padarn's brother.

PENRHYNCOCH
4 miles NE of Aberystwyth off the A487

🦋 Penrhyncoch Lakes

This is another village associated with one of Wales' great poets: Dafydd ap Gwilym, who was born just a short distance from

Penrhyncoch (see also Pontrhydfendigai). Although little remains of Gwilym's house except a small pile of stones, his medieval poetry lives on. Situated above the village is a series of five lakes known as the **Penrhyncoch Lakes** that offer fishing.

TRE TALIESIN
7½ miles NE of Aberystwyth on the A487

🏛 Bedd Taliesin

This village was the home, in the 6th century, of one of the earliest recorded British poets, Taliesin. The standing stone behind the village, **Bedd Taliesin** ('Taliesin's Grave'), actually dates from the Bronze Age (around 15000 BC) and while it marks a burial chamber it is unlikely to be that of the poet. An old legend says that if anyone is to sleep on his grave for one night, he or she will waken up either a poet or a fool.

TRE'R-DDOL
8 miles NE of Aberystwyth on the A487

🏛 Lodge Park

The former medieval deerpark, **Lodge Park**,

🏛 historic building   📷 museum   🏛 historic site   🦋 scenic attraction   🌿 flora and fauna is now managed by Forest Enterprise, which has restored this semi natural woodland and has also preserved its northern boundary that comprised a ditch and bank. The Wesleyan chapel in Tre'r-ddol was bought, in 1961, by a Mr RJ Thomas to house his folk object collection. He left this collection to the National Museum of Wales and it is now administered by Aberystwyth's Ceredigion Museum.

FURNACE
10½ miles NE of Aberystwyth on the A487

🏭 Dyfi Furnace   🌿 Cwm Einion

This quaint old village was, in the 18th century, home to an iron ore smelting foundry and, today, **Dyfi Furnace** is an important early industrial site that has one of the country's best preserved charcoal burning blast furnaces. The bellows that pumped the air into the furnace were powered by a huge waterwheel driven by the River Einion and visitors here can see the wheel (now restored to working order) as well as tour this industrial heritage site and museum.

The road opposite Dyfi Furnace leads up the **Cwm Einion** - Artists' Valley - which is so called because it was once a favourite haunt of 19th century watercolourists. As well as seeing the remains of a silver lead mine, walkers climbing up the valley will find pleasant woodland trails and picturesque picnic spots.

EGLWYS FACH
11 miles NE of Aberystwyth on the A487

🐦 Ynyshir RSPB Nature Reserve

Found in the sheltered waters of the Dovey estuary, the **Ynyshir RSPB Nature Reserve** is the home of a great many species of birds, in particular waders. It has an extensive

network of walks, with bird watching hides, where visitors in winter can observe the reserve's unique flock of Whitefronted Geese from Greenland and also the smaller flock of Barnacle Geese. It is the most important breeding site in Wales for lapwings and redshanks. The nature reserve's visitor centre has much information on the various species of birds found here.

The poet RS Thomas was the vicar of **St Michael's Parish Church** from 1954 until 1967 (see also Rhiw).

BORTH
5½ miles N of Aberystwyth on the B4353

🐾 Animalarium   🐾 Borth Bog   🏛 Cantre'r Gwaelod

The original settlement of this now popular seaside resort lies on the slopes of Rhiw Fawr and it is there that some of the older fishermen's and farmer's cottages can still be seen. The growth of the village began with the arrival of the railway linking it with Aberystwyth in the 1860s and its long, safe, sandy beach, along with the spectacular views out over Cardigan Bay and inland to the mountains, have ensured that it is still a much used holiday destination. Within Borth is the **Animalarium**, a collection of animals that includes wild animals, endangered species, domestic animals and farm varieties.

At a very low tide it is possible to see the remains of a submerged forest that, according to local legend, once formed part of the dynasty of **Cantre'r Gwaelod** (the Lower Dynasty) which extended out into the bay and was protected by a huge sea wall. It was ruled by King Gwyddno Garanhir, and flourished in the 6th century. It was said to be very fertile, and one acre of land in Cantre'r Gwaelod grew as much as four acres anywhere else.

One night the gatekeeper is said to have had

too much to drink and forgot to close the gates against the rising tide so that, with the help of a storm, it drowned the forest and the dynasty.

To the east of the village lies **Borth Bog** (Cors Fochno), an important area of raised coastal peat mire (one of only two such areas in Europe) that supports an abundance of wildlife.

YNYSLAS
7½ miles N of Aberystwyth off the B4353

🗘 Ynyslas Sand Dunes and Visitor Centre

Situated at the northern end of Borth beach, Ynyslas - the name means Green Island - extends to the Dovey (Dyfi) estuary, where there are broad expanses of sand, particularly at low tide, although the swimming is unsafe. The **Ynyslas Sand Dunes and Visitor**

Centre explains the natural beauty of the Dovey in wildlife displays and slide shows. There is also a conservation shop selling books, stationery and "green" pocket money gifts. From the centre there are glorious views over the river mouth to Aberdovey.

New Quay

🏛 New Quay Heritage Centre   🗘 New Quay Head

🗘 Cei Bach   🐦 Bird and Wildlife Hospital

🗘 Treath Gwyn   🐦 Bird Rock

🐦 Cardigan Bay Marine Wildlife Centre

🖉 New Quay Yacht Club

This small yet busy resort, whose harbour now boasts more yachts than fishing boats, built its economy on fishing, smuggling,

---

PLAS-Y-WERN COTTAGES

New Quay, Ceredigion SA45 9ST
Tel: 01545 580156
e-mail: milesgtr@aol.com
website: www.westwales-cottages.com

The 70-acre Plas-y-Wern estate is set in a wooded valley two miles from the picturesque old fishing village of New Quay, on Cardigan Bay, and half a mile from Cei Bach beach. The listed, grade II manor house of the estate was where Henry II rested his army on route to the battle of Bosworth in 1485, and brims with history. Now you can rest here too - as the estate boasts the **Plas-y-Wern Cottages**, superb self-catering accommodation that counts as some of the best in the country. They have been lovingly converted from 18th century stone buildings to create cottages that are warm and welcoming, and which retain many of their original features, such as old beams and stone fireplaces.

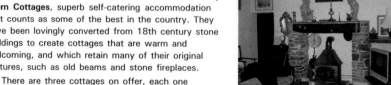

There are three cottages on offer, each one representing outstanding value for money. One sleeps two to four people, one sleeps two people, and a third, larger one, sleep six to eight. They have all been fitted out to a high standard, ensuring comfort and convenience for everyone. There is plenty of car parking, and a guests' garden where you can relax and admire the flowers and plants. The cottage owners, Ann and Thomas (who live in the manor house), have lived here for 60 years, and are keen to offer you the very best in self-catering accommodation in an area where there is so much to do and see.

🏛 historic building   🏛 museum   🏛 historic site   🗘 scenic attraction   🐦 flora and fauna

New Quay

fishing industry, smuggling was also rife and, in 1795, New Quay was described as a place of "infamous notoriety" and the headland was reputedly riddled with a network of caves where contraband was stored.

New Quay's natural surroundings as a port and harbour of refuge led to its being considered, at one time, as a suitable place from which direct sailings could be made to Wicklow and Dublin. Today's visitors will find charter boats operating out of the harbour offering a wide range of trips including deep sea and inshore fishing outings. The **New Quay Heritage Centre** has displays on the town's history, including local characters, shipbuilding, smuggling and fishing. It also details what is being done to protect the area's bottlenose dolphins, grey seals and porpoises.

shipbuilding and coastal trading. However, although these traditional ways of life declined in the 19th century as the rail links developed, New Quay has retained much of its maritime charm. The first vessel to be built here was the 24 ton sloop *William and Mary*, launched in 1779, and the subsequent shipping boom brought a great deal of employment to the area, causing the population to rise to 2,000. Hand in hand with the shipbuilding and

The sands and boating facilities at New Quay have long been an attraction for holidaymakers and the **New Quay Yacht Club** welcomes all visitors. The north beach leads to the rocky headland, **New Quay Head**, where an invigorating path follows the

BLACK LION HOTEL

Glanmor Terrace, New Quay, Ceredigion SA45 9PT
Tel: 01545 560209
e-mail: blacklionnewquay@btconnect.com
website: www.blacklionnewquay.co.uk

Reputed to be Dylan Thomas' favourite watering hole, the **Black Lion Hotel** is a picturesque inn overlooking the harbour and beautiful Cardigan Bay. There are nine large, well furnished and extremely comfortable bedrooms, most of which are en suite and many with spectacular sea views out over the bay. The menu offers something for everyone, with many home-made dishes and a children's menu. The bar offers a wide range of drinks including real ales. There is a residents' car park and large beer garden with panoramic views across the bay.

📖 stories and anecdotes   🦜 famous people   ✐ art and craft   🖊 entertainment and sport   🚶 walks line of the sheer cliffs to **Bird Rock**, the home of many sea birds. Inland, lies the **Bird and Wildlife Hospital** which treats and returns to the wild any birds or mammals needing veterinarian treatment and particularly birds involved in oil spillages. The **Cardigan Bay Marine Wildlife Centre**, overlooking the harbour, has interpretive displays on marine life in Cardigan Bay, especially the bottlenose dolphins.

The coast to the south of New Quay is best described as rugged and there is a Heritage Coastal path that threads its way along the clifftops down through Cwmtudu to Llangranog and beyond. Whilst, to the northwest of the town are the long sandy beaches of **Treath Gwyn** (White Beach) and **Cei Bach** (Little Quay) that were once a hive of shipbuilding activity and are now peaceful and secluded places.

Along with Laugharne in Carmarthenshire, New Quay lays claim to being the original Llareggub in Dylan Thomas' *Under Milk Wood*. Thomas had an ambiguous relationship with New Quay: it is said that he was disliked in the town, not least for his failure to pay his bills. It would seem he had his revenge, however, as Llareggub reveals its true meaning when spelled backwards!

Around New Quay

LLANINA
1 mile E of New Quay off the A486

🏛 Parish Church of St Ina 🏛 Cerrig Ina 🎭 King Ina

This tiny village, with a long tradition of fishing, is also associated with the legend of **King Ina**, king of the West Saxons, who succeeded to the throne in AD 688. One day, in the early 8th century, a ship was wrecked on the

rocks close to the village during a violent storm, and a local fisherman and his wife and daughter, having seen the disaster, rowed out to rescue the stricken sailors. Once safe, the family, unable to understand the language spoken by the shipwrecked strangers, sent for a monk who told them that they had saved King Ina. In thanksgiving, the king built a church from which the present **Parish Church of St Ina**, built in 1850, takes its name. **Cerrig Ina** (Ina's Stones) can be seen offshore and mark the spot where the original church stood.

ABERAERON
4½ miles NE of New Quay on the A487

🏛 Alban Square 🐾 Aberaeron Wildlife Park
🎨 Craft Centre

Situated at the mouth of the River Aeron, this is a delightful small town with charming Georgian houses, particularly around **Alban Square**. These are the result of astute town planning initiated in the early 19th century by the Reverend Alban Gwynne, who was happy to spend his wife's inheritance on dredging the Aeron estuary and creating this new port. He was thus instrumental in turning the settlement from a small fishing hamlet into a bustling port that also became famous for its shipbuilding.

Just inland from the town lies **Aberaeron Wildlife Park**, the home of llamas, red deer, parrots, owls and Jimmy, who is believed to be the world's only albino crow and who starred in the television series *Gormenghast*. As well as the animals at the park, there are natural trails, a miniature railway and plenty of other activities to keep all the family amused.

Although animals, birds and fish abound in this area, Aberaeron also has a **Craft Centre**, housed in traditional farm buildings, where visitors can not only see the beautiful products

OWAIN'S BUTCHERS

3 Bridge Street, Aberaeron, Ceredigion SA46 0AP
Tel: 01545 570242
e-mail: cigows@fsmail.net website: www.owainsbutchers.co.uk

Situated in the heart of the village of Aberaeron, **Owain's Butchers** is owned and managed by Owain Peckover, and has gained many awards over the years for the quality of its fine meats. This is a traditional shop, where service, high standards and value for money are still top of the agenda. The skilled staff have an in depth knowledge of lamb, pork and beef, and ensure that everything they sell has been raised and slaughtered within 15 miles of the shop, ensuring the very best in flavour.

Customers come from up to 40 miles away to buy Owain's cuts of meat, as well as the traditional sweetbreads, sheeps' hearts, kidneys, ox tails, tongue, tripe, mutton and cooked meats. His beefburgers have won silver and bronze awards, and in 2006 he won the coveted Daily *Telegraph* Traditional Business Award, which was presented to him at the House of Lords in London. He also sells cheese and free range eggs which he sources locally.

Owain buys champion beef from Smithfield shows so that his discerning customers know they are getting the very best. He is also a qualified meat inspector, with a diploma from the Royal Society of Health, so you know that the shop is always clean and immaculate.

LLYS AERON GUEST HOUSE

Lampeter Road, Aberaeron, Ceredigion SA46 0ED
Tel: 01545 570276
e-mail: enquiries@llysaeron.co.uk website: www.llysaeron.co.uk

Llys Aeron dates from the early 1800s, and is one of the most impressive Georgian houses in Aberaeron. Now it houses one of its best guest houses - four star **Llys Aeron Guest House**. The building has been sympathetically refurbished, and now offers comfortable accommodation that combines elegance with all the modern conveniences that guests expect nowadays. High standards of service and comfort come together in a perfect fusion, creating a B&B that will long be remembered.

The three rooms (a double, a twin and a double/twin) are spacious yet inviting, and all are fully en suite. In addition, they each boast a TV, central heating and tea/coffee making facilities. The double room has a 6' 6" bed where you are assured of a good night's sleep! There is also a self-catering unit on offer, situated within the main building that sleeps up to six people in absolute comfort. This makes the perfect base from which to explore Ceredigion - one of the most beautiful parts of Wales.

The guest house sits in half an acre of grounds, which are well tended, and a walled garden as well as a spacious conservatory can be enjoyed by guests at all times. Breakfasts are prepared from only the finest and freshest of organic and free range local produce, and indeed the place has a reputation for its cooking. You can choose from a full Welsh cooked breakfast or something lighter - but in both cases you won't be disappointed. This is B&B accommodation at its very best. Here Georgian elegance and informality combine to make a place where you can stay overnight, or have a relaxing break away from the hustle and bustle of modern life.

📖 stories and anecdotes 🦜 famous people 🎨 art and craft ✐ entertainment and sport 🚶 walks

Llanerchaeron

stones from the 9th and 10th
centuries. The scant remains of
Deinerth Castle can be seen a little
way inland from the village. It was
probably built by Richard de la Mare
in about 1110, though it was later
destroyed by Gruffydd ap Rhys in
1116. It was then substantially
rebuilt, only to be razed to the
ground again by Owaibn Gwynedd
20 years later, when it was finally
abandoned. It was rebuilt yet again,
but was finally abandoned in about
1202.

being handmade but have the opportunity to
buy a unique reminder of their time in the
town.

LLYSWEN
*4½ miles NE of New Quay
on the A482*

🏛 Llanerchaeron

Llanerchaeron sits to the east of the village,
and is a small 18th century estate and house,
now owned by the National Trust that was
typical of that owned by minor Welsh gentry.
The house was designed by John Nash and
built between 1794 and 1796. In the courtyard
you can see a brewery, laundry, dairy and
salting house. It was bequeathed to the
National Trust in 1989 by JP Ponsonby Lewes.

ABERARTH
6 miles NE of New Quay on the A487

🏛 Parish Church of St David   🏛 Deinerth Castle

This former shipbuilding village is often
bypassed because of the charm of its more
illustrious neighbour Aberaeron, but it is a
picturesque village overlooked by the **Parish
Church of St David**. Founded in the 6th
century, the church was rebuilt in 1860 but
still contains three early Christian inscribed

LLANRHYSTUD
11½ miles NE of New Quay on the A487

🏛 Caer Penrhos   🏛 Castell Bach   🏛 Castell Mawr

To the south of the village, which lies near the
confluence of the Rivers Wyre and Carrog,
are the two former hill forts of **Castell Bach**
and **Castell Mawr** which are separated by a
vale known as 'the dell of slaughter' - a
reference to an ancient battle. More remains
can be found to the east, this time of **Caer
Penrhos**. Built in around 1150 by Cadwaladr
ap Gryffydd, the castle was razed to the
ground some 50 years later to avoid it falling
into a rival's hands.

PENNANT
4 miles NE of New Quay on the B4577

🏛 Mari Berllan Piter

In the 19th century, this village was the home
of a recluse named Mari Berllan Piter (Mary
of Peter's Orchard). Supposedly granted
magical powers, her exploits were legendary.
When a miller refused to grind her corn she
made his mill wheel turn the wrong way, a
young girl who stole an apple from Mari's
orchard was forced to walk home backwards

and sometimes, it is said, Mari turned herself into a hare. The ruins of Mari's cottage, known locally as The Witch's Cottage, can still be seen surrounded by her now overgrown orchard.

LLANARTH

2½ miles E of New Quay on the A487

🏛 Parish Church of Llanarth 🏚 Cross of Girhiret

The **Parish Church of Llanarth** was built between 1870 and 1872 on the site of a much older building. Within it is an old stone inscribed with a cross, known as the **Cross of Girhiret**, name after an Irish nobleman of the 9th century. A local story tells that one night the Devil tried to steal the bell from the former church. However, he made such a noise that he woke the vicar who, armed with bell, a book and a candle, climbed up into the belfry to

The Cross of Girhiret, Llanarth

investigate. By solemnly repeating the name of Christ, the vicar managed to drive the Devil to the top of the tower and forced him to jump off. In the graveyard is a strangely scarred gravestone that is said to bear the marks made by the Devil when he landed.

CROSS INN

2 miles S of New Quay on the A486

🍯 New Quay Honey Farm

To the south of the village lies **New Quay Honey Farm**- the largest honey farm in Wales, and housed in an old chapel.

Lampeter

🏛 University of Wales, Lampeter 🎭 Elen Lloyd

Lampeter, with a population of just over 1,900, has long been the centre for this part of the Teifi Valley and an important meeting place for drovers. It was given its royal charter in 1284 by Edward I, and today is best known as being the home of a college of the University of Wales. Founded in 1822 by Bishop Thomas Burgess of St David's, St David's College, as it was first known, was Wales' first institution to award degrees, and only the third in England and Wales. It now predominantly teaches the liberal arts and theology. The main university buildings include CB Cockerell's original buildings round a stuccoed quadrangle dating from 1827, which were designed to mimic an Oxbridge College and, underneath these buildings, lies the town's old castle motte. Since 1971, the college has been integrated with the University of Wales - hence its new name **University of Wales, Lampeter** - although the campus still retains its own unique atmosphere.

While the 1,500 students add a certain bohemian flavour to Lampeter, during term

CALICO KATE

36 High Street, Lampeter, Ceredigion SA48 7BB
Tel: 01570 422866
e-mail: kate@calicokate.co.uk
website: www.calicokate.co.uk

In a fine building full of charm and character, you will find **Calico Kate**. Here you can wander through eight rooms of fabric, haberdashery and yarn, in a relaxed and homely atmosphere to the sound of gentle music. Welsh woollen fabric and costumes from local mills,

cottons for dressmaking, patchwork and curtains, velvets, satins, fleece and more – you will delight in the selection. Knitting yarns from Sirdar, Opal and Elle, from the traditional to the latest novelty yarns; cross-stitch and tapestry kits for all abilities and ages, beads, books, feathers, and gifts from Norfolk Lavender... come and see for yourself!

Lampeter is a traditional Welsh market town surrounding the handsome buildings of the university, and has a selection of shops no longer found in many high streets. There is an excellent variety of good eating places, a free car park and easy, level access to the shops.

Calico Kate is open Monday, Tuesday, Thursday, Friday 10am – 5pm; Saturday 10am – 4pm.

FACE OF FLOWERS

Unit 20, Llambed Business Park, Tregaron Road,
Lampeter SA48 8LT
Tel: 01570 423523
e-mail: info@facepfflowers.com   website:www.faceofflowers.com

On the outskirts of Lampeter, in a small trading estate, you will find **Face of Flowers**, your one stop shop for all things organic and natural. This fascinating shop, which is owned and managed by mother and daughter Jo and Liz Lawrence, is a fascinating place that sells a wide range of ecologically sound products that are sure to please.

Organic food (such as soups from the Knobbly Carrot Soup Company), skincare products such as soaps, oils and creams, bedding, children's clothes, towels, adult underwear, pet food and baby goods, toys, jewellery, candles - they're all here, at amazingly realistic prices. Great emphasis is placed on locally produced Welsh goods, and the place is ideal for picking up that special gift or souvenir of your visit to Wales.

The beef sold here has a Soil Association 2006 silver award, and the cheeses and the Llanfynydd-based Pencae Mawr Traditional Farm Food chutneys are all award-winning as well. The website contains a full list of the products on sale, most of them being available through home delivery. Jo and Liz are convinced of the benefits of organic produce and chemical-free beauty products. Why not come along and see the wide selection of goods on offer? You won't be disappointed.

JEN JONES WELSH QUILTS

Pontbrendu, Llanybydder, Ceredigion SA40 9UJ
Tel: 01570 480610
e-mail: quilts@jen-jones.com   website: www.jen-jones.com

For a wonderful gift or souvenir of your visit to Wales, head for **Jen Jones Welsh Quilts**. She has over 1,000 genuine, hand-crafted quilts mostly made between 1820 and 1939. Each one is unique, and many were made in one of the little woollen mills that used to dot rural Wales. Though the prices are very reasonable, these quilts are all antiques, and will be passed down through your family and cherished for many years to come.

time, this is essentially a genteel and very Welsh town with a pleasant mixture of Georgian and Victorian buildings. Back in the 17th century, on what is now Maesyfelin Street, stood the home of the Lloyds of Maesyfelin. When the only daughter of the family, **Elen Lloyd**, became engaged to Samuel Pritchard, the son of a poet priest from Llandovery, her four brothers, fearing the loss of their inheritance, tied her lover underneath a horse and galloped him from Lampeter to Llandovery. Samuel died of his injuries and the brothers threw his body in nearby River Teifi. On hearing what had happened, Elen was driven mad with sorrow and died soon afterwards. Samuel's father, Rhys, put a curse on the family and, just a short while later, their family house caught fire and burnt to the ground. The eldest brother, out of remorse or perhaps due to the curse, killed his brothers and then himself.

Around Lampeter

LLANDYSUL
11 miles SW of Lampeter on the A486

🖊 Cnapan Folk Festival 🐓 Christmas Evans

Set in the deep and picturesque valley of the River Teifi, this traditional little Welsh town

was another centre of the woollen industry and it was also the birthplace, in the early 19th century, of the wonderfully-named Christmas Evans, a Baptist minister who was famed for his fiery, emotional sermons. The son of a cobbler, he was orphaned early in life, and became a Baptist minister instead of a Presbyterian minister because the Presbyterians required qualifications which he did not have. Today, this tranquil little town is renowned for its outstanding scenic views, fishing and white water canoeing as well as for the delights of its Victorian town centre.

A few miles up the A486, Ffostrasol is the setting for the annual **Cnapan Folk Festival**, the largest Celtic folk music event on the British mainland.

CAPEL DEWI
8½ miles SW of Lampeter on the B4459

🏭 Rock Mills Woollen Mill

Close to the village lies **Rock Mills Woollen Mill**, which was established in 1890 by John Morgan, whose descendants still weave here today. The machinery is powered by a waterwheel which also drives a small alternator to provide lighting. The mill once provided power to the neighbouring church, From pure new wool, the mill produces all

🖼 stories and anecdotes   🐓 famous people   🖊 art and craft   🖊 entertainment and sport   🚶 walks manner of woollen goods, including bedspreads, blankets and rugs, and it is one of the last traditional mills where the entire process, from fleece to fabric, may be viewed.

LLANDDEWI BREFI
7 miles NE of Lampeter on the B4343

🏛 Parish Church of St David   🏚 Llanfair Clydogau

This traditional country village was host, in AD 519, to a synod which was attended by St David. The meeting was called to debate the Pelagian heresy, a doctrine advocating freedom of thought rather than the Biblical version of original sin that determined the morality of the time. The **Parish Church of St David** stands on a mound said to have risen up as St David preached during the synod. The church itself dates from the 13th century and contains some old inscribed stones. One is known as St David's Staff and another has an inscription in the obscure Ogham language thought to commemorate a heretic of the type that St David was denouncing.

Close by are the sites of several hill forts including **Llanfair Clydogau**, where the Romans mined for silver, and which sit beside the Sarn Helen, a military road that once connected a gold mine in the south, at Dolaucothi, with a fort at Bremia in the north.

TREGARON
9 miles NE of Lampeter on the A485

🏛 Tregaron Kite Centre and Museum   🏛 Cors Caron

🐦 Henry Richard   🏛 Rhiannon Welsh Gold Centre

🖉 Festival of Harness Racing   🏇 Old Railway Walk

This small market town - a meeting place for 19th century drovers - still serves the remote farming communities in the Teifi valley. The surrounding land is sheep country and Tregaron also became famous for its woollen industry and, in particular, hand-knitted woollen socks. While many of the socks were transported to the mining communities of South Wales, David Davies, an engineer from Llandinam, found another use for the wool - he used it to form a stable bed on which to lay the railway across Cors Caron bog. In the town's main square stands a statue of **Henry Richard** (1812-1888), the Liberal MP and son of Tregaron, who was a vociferous supporter of disarmament and an advocate of arbitration in international disputes; he became known as the 'Apostle of Peace'.

Housed in the Old National School, which opened in 1873, the **Tregaron Kite Centre**

Tregaron

🏛 historic building   🏛 museum   🏚 historic site   🏞 scenic attraction   🌱 flora and fauna

and **Museum** is an interesting and informative place which is dedicated to the red kite. With the dual aims of providing people with a better understanding of these beautiful birds of prey and with ensuring their survival in this part of mid Wales, visitors to the centre can also see the kites being fed daily here during the winter months. Also at the museum are artefacts from Ceredigion Museum that relate specifically to Tregaron and the surrounding area.

Although Tregaron is chiefly associated with sheep and wool, it is also the location of the **Rhiannon Welsh Gold Centre**, in the centre of the town. And in August each year is held the popular **Festival of Harness Racing** held at the Tregaron Trotting Club grounds at Neuadd Brenigg

To the north of the town lies **Cors Caron**, an ancient bog that is home to rare flora and fauna. The land was originally covered by a glacier and, at the end of the last Ice Age, this glacier melted to create a natural lake which gradually filled with sediment and vegetation. The peat grew in thickness, creating three distinctive domes above the original lake bed level. The **Old Railway Walk**, along the track bed of the old Manchester-Milford Haven railway, provides visitors with the chance to observe some of the over 170 species of bird recorded here, including red kites, buzzards and sparrow hawks. The walk starts from the car park near Maesllyn Farm on the B4343, two miles north of Tregaron.

PONTRHYDFENDIGAID
15 miles NE of Lampeter off the B4343

🏛 Strata Florida Abbey

Just a short distance from this village, the name of which translates as the 'bridge across the blessed ford', lies **Strata Florida Abbey**, a Cistercian house founded in 1164 by Robert Fitzstephen. This austere order was renowned for seeking out remote and isolated sites for its religious establishments and Strata Florida - the vale of Flowers - is one such site. Even though the abbey is in ruins today, it is still an evocative place. Just two years after its foundation the abbey's lands were overrun by Rhys ap Gryffyd but, in 1184, he refounded the abbey, and most of the buildings date from this time. During the 12th and 13th centuries, Strata Florida became not only one of the most important religious centres in Wales, but also a place that influenced Welsh culture, as it was patronised by both royalty and poets. Some of the last native princes and princesses of Wales were buried here, as was Dafydd ap Gwilym, probably the most famous of all Welsh medieval poets, who was born near Aberystwyth (see also Penrhyncoch). In 1238, the Welsh princes swore their allegiance to Llywelyn the Great's son, Dafydd, at the abbey. This was also the time when the abbey became very wealthy, mainly through wool from the sheep that grazed its vast lands.

After the Dissolution in the 16th century, the abbey and its lands passed through various hands and the ruins today, which are now in the ownership of CADW, consist mainly of the cloister, the chapter house and the church. In the north transept stands a memorial to the poet Dafydd ap Gwilym. The yew tree that stands amidst the abbey's remains is thought to mark his grave. One legend associated with the abbey suggests that the Holy Grail, which was given to the monks at Glastonbury by Joseph of Aramathea, later ended up at Strata Florida. When the abbey, which formed part of the Nanteos estate, was left to fall into ruins, the cup, which had pieces bitten out of its sides by pilgrims convinced of its healing powers, was stored at Nanteos mansion.

CASTLE CAFÉ & CELLAR BAR

25-26 Quay Street, Cardigan SA43 1HU
Tel: 01239 621621
website: www.middleearthenterprises.co.uk

Situated near the castle ruins in the picturesque old town of Cardigan, the **Castle Café and Cellar Bar** is a must-visit place fpr any one seeking good food, a quick snack or a relaxing drink. It is owned and run by April and Stephen Greenhalgh, who are already well known in the town for Middle Earth, a shop for people with an interest in the Wiccan way of life, as well as a number of other shops that sell everything from armour to hand-crafted furniture.

The café, which is housed in an interesting old stone building over 200 years old, is open from early to late seven days a week. Upstairs is the café, a delightfully atmospheric place with bare stone walls and dark wooden furniture. It sells uncomplicated but hearty food (all prepared on the premises) and drinks, all served by a staff that is enthusiastic, eager to please, friendly and efficient. There is a fixed menu each day that takes advantage of wholesome, fresh local produce wherever possible. There is always a vegetarian option, and by prior arrangement a vegan option can also be made available.

During the daytime, the café does three different sizes of all-day breakfast, and also sells a range of delicious home-baked cakes. The place is also licensed. Downstairs you will find the Cellar Bar, which is welcoming and atmospheric, with comfortable seating that includes soft sofas. The bar itself is well stocked, and is surrounded by bar stools to give the place the genuine stylish ambience. Here you can choose drinks form a wide range of beers, wines, spirits, soft drinks should you be driving, and delicious coffees.

Most evenings there is live musical accompaniment ranging from rock to jazz, from acoustic to folk and from soul to blues. At least four nights a week you can take part in such events as poetry nights and quizzes. Tickets cost no more than £5, and for that you get great music, a plate of food and entry into a raffle.

The Castle Café and Cellar Bar website contains details of forthcoming gigs, and you can also sign up for the mailing list that will keep you up to date with what's happening. This is Welsh hospitality at its very best, so make sure to come along if you're ever near Cardigan.

🏠 historic building   🏛 museum   🏚 historic site   🌳 scenic attraction   🌿 flora and fauna

Cardigan

🏛 Cardigan Castle 🏛 Shire Hall 🏛 Shire Hall

🏛 County Gaol 🏛 Parish Church of St Mary

🏛 Teifi Bridge 🏛 Cardigan Heritage Centre

🌱 Welsh Wildlife Centre 🎭 Theatr Mwldan

Once the busiest port in Wales, Cardigan is an ancient borough which received its first charter in 1199 and it was, in the 12th century, a power base of Lord Rhys, one of the last Welsh princes to rule an independent principality. The few remains of **Cardigan Castle**, which stand beside the river, conceal a turbulent history. The first castle was built in the 11th century, then rebuilt by Gilbert Fitzrichard in the early 1100s. Gryffydd ap Rhys took the castle in 1156 and rebuilt and

strengthened it. It then passed into the hands of the Earl of Pembroke in 1240. Thought to be the site of the first Eisteddfod in 1176, the castle fell to Parliament in 1645 during the Civil War.

The **Shire Hall** was built in 1763, and housed the courtroom and council chamber, which has previously been within the castle. In the 19th century these functions passed to the newly-built Guildhall. Prisoners who had been convicted at the Shire Hall were paraded through the street to the County Gaol, being pelted with rotten fruit and eggs as they went. The **County Gaol** itself still stands, and was built in 1793 to the designs of John Nash. In 1881 it was converted into a police station and private house. The **Parish Church of St Mary** was originally built in the 12th century

APRICOT

29 Priory Street, Cardigan SA43 1BZ
Tel:01239 621771

Owned and managed by Alison Rowley-James, **Apricot** is a stunning shop selling a wide range of smart and casual women's fashions. It sits in the centre of Cardigan, and no one visiting the picturesque old town can afford to miss it. Alison took over the shop ten years ago, and since then has created a boutique which is known and respected for its quality and keen prices not just in the town, but throughout the whole area as well. She knows women's clothing intimately, as she has a diploma in fashion and textiles which gives her the experience to stock only the best made, most fashionable items at affordable prices.

The interior of the shop is welcoming and colourful, with racks of fine clothing and bare wooden floors to give it that modern, stylish look. Famous names such as Gold, Emreco, Poppy, Elton, Brandtex and many, many more are featured in her stock, so you are sure to find something that is just right as fashionable, every day wear or for that special occasion. Apricot also stocks a wide range of accessories, such as handbags, purses, scarves, gloves and eye catching jewellery.

Alison is always on hand to offer advice about what suits you best, and you are assured of her best attention at all times.

🎞 stories and anecdotes 🍗 famous people 🎨 art and craft ✒ entertainment and sport 🚶 walks

GO MANGO WHOLEFOODS

4-6 Black Lion Mews, High Street, Cardigan,
Ceredigion SA43 1HJ
Tel: 01239 614727

Go Mango Wholefoods is a busy and very popular vegetarian store in a delightful little mews just off the High Street. Founded 25 years ago, it has constantly expanded its range and enhanced its standing within the community – as shown by winning Cardigan Trader of the Year awards. This achievement is the recognition of the efforts of the owner Ray Hasler and his hard-working staff, who show a very real understanding of their product and their valued customers.

The shop offers the widest choice of top-quality, locally sourced food in west Wales, including a huge range of certified organic fruit and vegetables. Lunchtime snacks, cakes and organic bread and rolls baked fresh every morning especially for Go Mango are also available. The shop also stocks an impressive array of environmentally friendly household products, supplements and herbal remedies, fresh herbs and spices, pulses, legumes, cereals and chilled and frozen foodstuffs. An important recent addition is a juice bar serving revitalising smoothies and juices, and Go Mango's go-ahead owner's plans for 2007 include a café serving the very best vegetarian, vegan and raw meals. Go Mango also stocks 25 varieties of organic wines and has the largest selection of dried herbs and spices in west Wales.

TIGER'S EYE LTD

1-2 Black Lion Mews, High Street, Cardigan SA43 1HJ
Tel: 01239 615498
e-mail: jude.tigerseye@ukonline.co.uk

For the very best in special souvenirs and gifts, head to **Tiger's Eye Ltd** in the heart of the lovely old town of Cardigan. It is owned and run by Jude, who set it up in over 14 years ago after running a shop in Bristol. She hankered after a more rural way of life, so settled here to sell eco-friendly gift items that are sure to please.

The shop itself is in a picturesque old black and white Tudor-style building in a small courtyard just off the town's main street, and houses a marvellous array of items from all over the world. Choose from crystals, healing crystals, candles (from the Yankee Candle Company), aromatherapy oils, jewellery and body jewellery, ceramics, wall hangings, chimes, gemstones and even didgeridoos from Australia.

In addition, there is a marvellous range of clothes from Fairtrade companies in sizes ranging from small to extra large, each one hard wearing and keenly priced. Step inside and be delighted by the bright interior, crammed with gifts and craft items of all shapes and sizes. Take in the sights, sounds and smells that greet you. Incense mixes with perfumed candles, and the whole place is a cornucopia of delights, all with an eco-friendly emphasis.

🏦 historic building   🏛 museum   🏛 historic site   ⚘ scenic attraction   🌱 flora and fauna as the chapel of a Benedictine priory. It now dates mainly from the 19th century, and. was once a place of pilgrimage, as it housed a fine statute of Our Lady which was destroyed at the Reformation.

The River Teifi, which provides Cardigan with its Welsh name Aberteifi, continues to be fished for trout and some still use the traditional coracle. Dating from pre-Christian times, coracles were once common on many of Britain's rivers and they have changed little over the centuries. The silting up of the Teifi estuary, along with the arrival of the railway, were the main causes of Cardigan's decline as a major port which had, at one time, over 300 ships registered there.

Cardigan Castle and Bridge

However, while the river is no longer at the centre of the town's economy it is still a place of charm enhanced by the six-arched **Teifi Bridge** - an ancient structure which was rebuilt in 1726. Housed in a warehouse built in 1745 on Teifi Wharf, the **Cardigan Heritage Centre** tells the story of this

CLEO

28 High Street, Cardigan, Ceredigion SA43 1JG
Tel: 01239 621465
e-mail: info@cleo-of-cardigan.co.uk
website: www.cleo-of-cardigan.co.uk

Cleo is a fabulous women's clothes shop at the heart of the small, attractive town of Cardigan. It has been owned and run by Sara Edwards (who has lived all her life in the area) for the last ten years, and before that by her grandmother. So there is a wealth of experience about high quality women's fashions and accessories here, as well as friendly, helpful service and outstanding value for money.

The interior of the shop is much bigger than it looks from the outside, and is elegant, spacious and welcoming. You are free to browse to your heart's content, though it is the kind of establishment where the staff are friendly, always eager to help and full of good advice. So don't be afraid to ask.

The shop stocks fashions and accessories that are essentially day-wear for the discerning woman, from such well-known names as Lucia, Delmod, Hauber, Evalinka, Jocavi, Escorpion, Gina B, Doris Streich, Sommermann, Jackpot and Fisser.This is elegance with a twist, and Sara certainly has an eye for what is fashionable and yet classic - things that will never date. She offers an alterations service, and if you step through her door you are never under any obligation to buy. So if you're looking for clothes that are smart, wearable, casual or elegant, of high quality and yet reasonably priced, then head for Cleo.

CARDIGAN BAY HOLIDAYS

Blaenwaun, Mwnt, Cardigan, Ceredigion SA43 1QF
Tel: 01239 613456
e-mail: eleri@cardiganbayholidays.co.uk
website: www.cardiganbayholidiays.co.uk

Cardigan Bay Holidays presents Golygfa Deg ('Fair View'), a beautiful self-catering bungalow at Gwbert-on-Sea, on the eastern shore of the Teifi Estuary. It is an attractive place, and has a WTB five star rating, meaning that its facilities are superb. It sleeps up to six people in two double bedrooms (with views of the sea from one) and one twin which overlooks the garden and benefits from the morning sun.

The lounge diner is spacious yet cosy and inviting, and boasts two settees, occasional furniture, digital TV, video and DVD player, CD stereo system and a table seating up to eight people. French doors open onto an attractive patio area - just right for those warm summer days, and where amazing sunsets over Cardigan Bay can be seen and appreciated. There is also a small patio at the back of the bungalow, and steps lead from it to a lawn where children can safely play.

The kitchen is fully equipped with modern conveniences, such as oven and hob, microwave, fridge freezer, dishwasher, washer dryer, plus all crockery, cutlery and cooking utensils. There is a large main bathroom with w.c., bath and shower, and a separate shower room. The cottage is a short walk from bars and restaurants, plus there is an 18-hole championship golf course within half a mile and a 9-hole cliff top course nearby.

THE GWBERT HOTEL

Gwbert-on-Sea, Cardigan, Ceredigion SA43 1PP
Tel: 01239 612638 Fax: 01239 621474
e-mail: gwbert@enterprise.net website: www.gwberthotel.net

The **Gwbert** is a family-run hotel close to the cliff path and a short stroll from Cardigan Golf Club. The owners offer high standards of accommodation, with lifts to all floors and wonderful views from most of the rooms. All the spacious bedrooms have en suite facilities, TV, radio, telephone and hot drinks tray, and among the amenities at the hotel are a gym, sauna, jacuzzi, pool table and PCs with internet access. Smart modernisation in 2006 included an attractive glass-fronted bistro (Flat Rock) with views of the Teifi estuary and the Pembrokeshire National Park to accompany an extensive menu that caters for all tastes.

Open all year, the Gwbert offers autumn/winter breaks for 2 or 3 nights to include dinner, bed and breakfast, as well as golfing and walking packages. The owners also have three handsome detached houses sleeping 8, 10 and 12 for self-catering holidays, with breathtaking views over Cardigan Bay, just 100 yards from the clifftop and a few steps from the hotel. Golfing discounts are available, and guests who don't want to cook can take their meals in the hotel. There's always plenty to do hereabouts, including exploring the cliffs and shingle bays, enjoying the glorious scenery and looking out for the rare choughs and Cardigan Bay's bottle-nosed dolphins.

🏛 historic building   🏛 museum   🏛 historic site   🌣 scenic attraction   🌿 flora and fauna former county town, from prehistoric times through to the present day. From its origins in the medieval age to its heyday in the 18th and 19th centuries, the port, in particular, is explored through the eyes of those who lived here. In addition to the permanent exhibitions, there is a programme of temporary exhibitions covering a range of topics. Those looking for performing arts and other cultural events will also not be disappointed as the **Theatr Mwldan**, in the town, is one of Wales' leading theatrical venues.

Beside the river, just outside the town, lies the **Welsh Wildlife Centre**, a nature reserve that provides a variety of habitats, including reed beds, woodland and meadow. As well as an extensive network of footpaths and, being home to a surprisingly wide variety of flora and fauna, the reserve also has an excellent visitor centre.

The cardigan as an item of clothing was named after the 7th Earl of Cardigan, John Thomas Brudenell (1797 - 1868), who commanded the Light Brigade during the Crimean War. He did not invent the cardigan (they had been around in the 17th century) but he did popularise them.

Around Cardigan

GWBERT-ON-SEA
2½ miles NW of Cardigan on the B4548

🦀 Cardigan Island

🌿 Cardigan Island Coastal Farm Park

This small resort on the eastern banks of the River Teifi estuary is an excellent place for cliff walking and for looking out over the estuary and observing its wildlife. To the north of the village, and lying some 200 yards offshore, is **Cardigan Island**, a nature reserve

to which there is no unauthorised access and which is inhabited by a flock of wild Soay sheep.

Back on the mainland, **Cardigan Island Coastal Farm Park** is an ideal place from which to look out over the island from the headland and also to observe the rare choughs colony of seals breed and some lucky visitors may also spot Cardigan Bay's bottlenose dolphins. The farm is also home to friendly farm animals, including goats, sheep, pigs, ponies and ducks, as well as a llama, a wallaby and rare breed cows.

FELINWYNT
3½ miles NE of Cardigan off the A487

🌿 Felinwynt Rainforest and Butterfly Centre

This village is home to the **Felinwynt Rainforest and Butterfly Centre** (see panel on page 220) where, in a large tropical house, visitors are transported to the jungle to see the beautiful free-flying butterflies that live amidst the exotic plants. There is also a rainforest exhibition, which explains the delicate ecology of this interesting habitat, a tea room and a gift shop.

MWNT
3½ miles N of Cardigan off the A487

⛪ Parish Church of the Holy Cross

This beauty spot was on the Pilgrims' Route to Bardsey Island off the Lleyn Peninsula. The tiny **Parish Church of the Holy Cross** dates from around 1400 and stands on the site of a much earlier Celtic church, originally built in a hollow to hide it from view and protect it from possible raiders coming by sea.

Much of the coastline here, including the cliffs, the rocky headland and the safe family beach, is owned by the National Trust. This

BLAENWAUN CARAVAN PARK

Blaenwaun Farm, Mwnt, Cardigan, Ceredigion SA43 1QP
Tel: 01239 613456
e-mail: info@blaenwaun.com
website: www.blaenwaunfarm.com

As they say in Wales - croeso! Welcome to the four star **Blaenwaun Caravan Park**, located four miles north of Cardigan. It is an organic working beef and arable farm, and offers the very best facilities in the area for caravaners.

It has flush toilets, hot and cold water hand basins, baby changing facilities, free hot showers, fully equipped disabled shower room, laundry, indoor dishwashing facilities, shop and all the other things that make a good site superb. Camping and Calor Gas is available for exchange, and electric hook-up points are provided on request. Pets are very welcome, but, as the site is on a working farm, they must be kept under control at all times and exercised off the field. In addition, there is a play area for kids and a coarse fishing lake which is well stocked with tench, carp and rudd, and is ideal for beginners.

This part of Wales is perfect for those contemplating a caravan or camping holiday. The whole of the Ceredigion coastline is on your doorstep, including the award winning Mwnt Beach, which has a coveted place among the ten cleanest and best family beaches in the United Kingdom. You can also enjoy a leisurely stroll along the cliff tops, or climb Foel-y-Mwnt, a conical mound that soars to over 250 feet high. From here you can see the dolphins and seals at play in Cardigan Bay.

In short - it is a caravaner's paradise, and should not be missed.

The Felinwynt Rainforest Centre

Rhosmaen, Felinwynt, Cardigan,
Dyfed SA43 1RT
Tel: 01239 810882
website: www.butterflycentre.co.uk

Felinwynt Rainforest Centre has become one of Ceredigion's chief attractions with thousands of visitors every year. The highlight of any visit is the Mini-Rainforest created by owner John Devereux. Wander through a jungle among tropical plants, exotic butterflies, waterfalls, pools and fish, with the soothing sounds of the Peruvian Rainforest.

The Video room show films of rainforests and butterflies. The Visitor Centre houses the gift shop with an extensive range of gifts for everyone, the café where you can have fresh cooked meals and snacks all day including Dorothy's homemade cakes and the exhibition based on the Tambopata region of Peru.

All the facilities are suitable for disabled. Entrance Charge to Tropical House only.

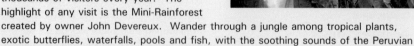

🏚 historic building 🏛 museum 🏚 historic site 🐾 scenic attraction 🌱 flora and fauna

area is a geological SSSI (Site of Special Scientific Interest) and is part of the Ceredigion Heritage Coast; it is especially rich in maritime flora. The bay was the site of a battle in 1155, when Fleming invaders were repelled by the local forces.

ABERPORTH
6 miles NE of Cardigan on the B4333

🌾 Penbryn

The original village of Aberporth consisted of small, single storeyed cottages with thick mud walls and thatched roofs that reflected the simple and hard lives of those living in this fishing and farming community. At one time Aberporth became famous for its herring industry as great shoals of the fish came to feed and spawn in the shallow waters of this sheltered part of the Cardigan Bay coast. Today, and particularly in the summer months, the village is a small yet thriving resort that is popular with yachtsmen.

A little way up the coast is the National Trust's beach at **Penbryn**, an SSSI, part of the Ceredigion Heritage Coast and a good spot for insect, bird and dolphin spotting.

The approach to this popular, sandy beach is by way of Hoffnant Valley from the Trust's car park at Llanborth Farm, where a shop, café and WCs are open in season. The valley is known locally as Cwm Lladron, Robbers Valley, probably because of old-time smuggling connections.

LLANGRANOG
9½ miles NE of Cardigan on the B4334

🏫 Parish Church of St Caranog   🏛 Carreg Bica

🌾 Walled Garden at Pigeonsford   🐟 Sarah Jane Rees

Lying in a narrow valley and rather reminiscent of a Cornish fishing village,

Llangranog (sometimes spelled Llangrannog) is not only one of the most attractive villages along the Ceredigion coast but also one of the most popular resorts in the area. The headland and cliffs to the north of the village (now the property of the National Trust) offer excellent walks and dramatic scenery (see walk on page 222). The sheltered coves around Llangranog once helped to sustain a thriving shipbuilding industry but they also proved perfect landing and hiding places for contraband and the area was rife with smuggling activity. On the beach there is a rock known as **Carreg Bica** ('Bica's Rock'). Legend says it is the tooth of the giant Bica, who spat it out when he had toothache. The **Parish Church of St Caranog** is dedicated to a saint who was the grandson of Ceredig, from which Ceredigion gets its name. The church was founded in the 6th century, though the persent building fates from 1885. In the churchyard is the grave of **Sarah Jane Rees** (1839 - 1916), master mariner and poet. She was the daughter of a ship's captain, and taught navigation and mathematics in her native Wales, as well as Liverpool and London. She was also a leading member of the Band of Hope and a supporter of the Temperance Movement.

To the east of the village lies the privately-owned **Walled Garden at Pigeonsford**, a Georgian walled garden which has been replanted with botanical collections of herbaceous plants and shrubs as well as vegetables and fruits. Maintained as a working garden, the walled garden is set in large and less formal grounds that include shrubbery, woodland and riverside walks.

Llangranog

Distance: *2.8 miles (4.5 kilometres)*

Typical time: *90 mins*

Height gain: *100 metres*

Map: *Explorer 198*

Walk: *www.walkingworld.com ID:1451*

Contributor: *Pat Roberts*

There is a free car park at the top of the hill down to Llangranog. It is signed left at the post office. There is parking at the cafe and pub down at the coast if you are using these facilities. For Llangranog, follow signs from the A487 from New Quay to Cardigan.

DESCRIPTION:

Not a long walk, but it can be rewarding if you wish to see dolphins and choughs. However, like all wildlife they do not appear to order. The spectacular views are always available.

FEATURES:

Sea, National Trust/NTS, Wildlife, Birds, Flowers, Great Views, Butterflies

WALK DIRECTIONS:

1 | From the car park, walk left down to the post office and at the junction go left for about 150 metres. Look over the wall on the left to see a magnificent waterfall and if you are lucky, some dippers.

2 | Just as the road starts to descend to the sea, take this "No Through Road" on the right. There are wnderful views of the coast on the left.

3 | Here where the road divides, we take the left or lower path to contour around the mound ahead. The return is through the upper gate.

4 | When you reach the farmhouse of Lochtyn, take this gate to the right of the buildings; there is a footpath sign on it.

5 | After about 40m the path is signed to the left to follow the coast. After a while, it is joined by the coast path coming up from the left.

6 | Take the left, lower path to walk down to the headland of Ynys-Lochtyn, usually the home of the choughs, but return to this point to continue on the top path, which is the coast path, for views on up the coast towards Cwmtudu.

7 | The path ahead is the coast path, but we leave it here to climb up to the ridge to the right.

8 | At the top join a tarmac track. If you wish to climb to the top, walk right and up. Otherwise, go left through the kissing-gate and follow the track down to rejoin the outward route at Waymark 3 (the upper path in the photo). Walk down the road to the more main road where turn left and at the post office right, up to the car park.

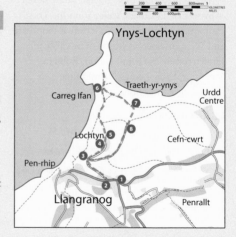

ST DOGMAELS
1 mile W of Cardigan on the B4546

🏚 St Dogmael's Abbey   🏚 The Mill   🏖 Poppit Sands

Situated on the western banks of the mouth of the River Teifi, it was here that the Lord of the Manor, Robert Martyn, founded **St Dogmael's Abbey** in the 12th century for the monks of the the Tironensian order brought over from Tiron in France. An earlier Welsh abbey on the site was sacked by the Vikings. Adjacent to the abbey ruins is a church which features an inscribed Sagranus stone whose markings and Latin inscriptions provided the key to deciphering the ancient Goidelic language. Close to the abbey is **The Mill** (Y Felin), a water-powered flour mill. To the west of the village is the **Poppit Sands**, a beautiful Blue Flag beach, and one of the most popular in the area.

HENLLAN
11½ miles SE of Cardigan on the B4334

🚂 Teifi Valley Railway

This village is home to the **Teifi Valley Railway**, another of Wales' famous little trains. This narrow gauge railway, which originally served the slate quarries, was created from a section of the Great Western Railway (also known as God's Wonderful Railway) that served the rural areas of West Wales. Today's passengers can enjoy a 40-minute steam train journey through this delightful valley while, at the Henllan terminus, there are plenty of attractions to keep the whole family amused: woodland walks, crazy golf, the station tearooms and a gift and souvenir shop.

CASTELL MALGWYN HOTEL
Llechryd, Cardigan Ceredigion SA43 2QA
Tel: 01239 682382
e-mail: reception@malgwyn.co.uk
website: www.castellmalgwyn.co.uk

Castell Malgwyn is an elegant, classical mansion, situated in an eight acres estate in the beautiful Teifi valley, which was built by Sir Benjamin Hammett in 1795. Now it is a charming country house hotel that boasts the best of everything, and offers its guests high standards of service and an informal yet efficient friendliness that is hard to find nowadays. The hotel has 17 delightful en suite rooms that combine taste, informality and comfort, each one individually furnished and decorated. Here you can relax completely, and rise the following morning to sample one of the hotel's excellent breakfasts. In fact Castell Malgwyn is renowned for its food. 'Lily's' restaurant seats up to 40, and is stylish yet restrained, combining local and international cuisine on its imaginative menu, prepared by its superb chefs. And there is sure to be a fine wine on the hotel's wine list that complements your meal perfectly. Afterwards, you can relax in the Lounge or Library Bar over a quiet drink, contemplating your next day's activities.

There is plenty to see and do in the area, from sightseeing to sporting activities. The River Teifi runs through the hotel's grounds, and its sea trout and salmon are renowned. Plus it is the perfect place for a wedding or special celebration, with the hotel doing all the arranging and the hard work. So if it is elegance and high standards of service you are after, Castell Malgwyn fits the bill.

📖 stories and anecdotes   🐦 famous people   🎨 art and craft   🎭 entertainment and sport   🥾 walks

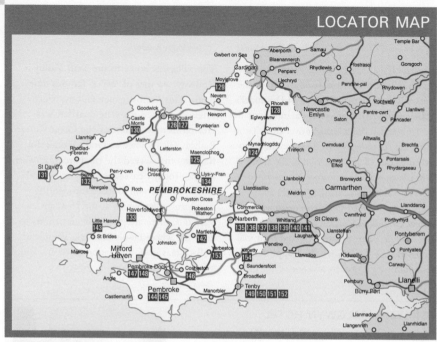

LOCATOR MAP

ADVERTISERS AND PLACES OF INTEREST

🏠 historic building   🏛 museum   🏚 historic site   ◔ scenic attraction   ❦ flora and fauna

7| Pembrokeshire

Pembrokeshire, which is known as Sir Benfro in Welsh, is home to Britain's only coastal national park - the Pembrokeshire Coast National Park. Visitors flock to this leading European holiday destination to see the spectacular grandeur and tranquil beauty of the countryside and walk some of the 186-mile coastal cliff top path. The coastal region is also a paradise for bird-watchers. Incorporating one of the most fantastic stretches of natural beauty in Europe, the Pembrokeshire Coast National Park begins (or ends) on the south-facing shoreline near Tenby. Running right around the ruggedly beautiful south western tip of Wales, around St Brides Bay and up along the north facing coast almost to Cardigan, the Park also includes quiet fishing villages, the huge cliffs at Castlemartin, sweeping golden beaches and small, often busy harbours.

Although not strictly on the coast, the labyrinthine Cleddau river system also lies within the Park's boundaries and here there are delightful little villages such as Cresswell and Carew, as well as the superb sheltered harbour of Milford Haven.

Offshore there are various islands, including Grassholm, Ramsey, Skokholm and Skomer, which have changed little since they were named by Viking invaders. Many are now bird and wildlife sanctuaries of international importance. Grassholm is home to thousands of gannets, Skokholm has Manx shearwaters, Skomer has shearwaters and puffins. In addition, Ramsey harbours such species as choughs and the red-legged crow, and is also the resting place of many Welsh saints. One island, Caldey has, for over 1,500 years, been the home of a religious community which continues today to live a quiet and austere life. Between their devotions, the monks of Caldey scrape a living from the land and are famous for their range of perfumes and toiletries inspired by the island's wild flowers. Pembrokeshire is the home of the corgi, which was brought to the notice of the Kennel Club by Captain Jack Howell. He presented Princess Elizabeth with her first corgi, and the rest, as they say, is history.

In Pembrokeshire you will also find the Preseli Hills, sometimes known as the Preseli Mountains, though in fact the highest point, Foel Cymcerwyn, is only 1,759 feet high. Though the range of hills is inland, it forms part of the Pembrokeshire Coast National Park, which takes a swing to the east to form a bulge before rejoining the coast near Cardigan. It is excellent walking country, and it was from here that the bluestones for the inner circle of Stonehenge were quarried.

There is one place in Pembrokeshire which is sacred to all Welsh people - the city of St Davids. City status was officially granted in 1994, though in truth people had looked on it as a city long before that, thanks to its cathedral. It is near here that the country's patron saint, St David (Dewi Sant), was born, and it was in what was then called Rose Vale that he founded a monastery that later became St Davids Cathedral. In AD 589 he died, and his bones lie here to this day.

Preseli Hills

Preseli Hills and the Bluestone Country

Walking in the Preseli Hills it feels like time stands still - the magic and mystery of the millennia are there for you to discover. The area has had a spiritual significance for thousands of years and it lingers in the atmosphere. There are many standing stones, cromlechs and Iron Age Forts.

This range of attractive hills forms part of the Pembrokeshire Coast National Park, though they lie many miles inland. The highest point is Foel Cymcerwyn, at 1,759 feet, and they stretch from the east of the county (Crymych) and to the north (Newport).

There are a series of peaks which can be approached from a variety of places and some people walk the whole range which is a wonderful experience. The hills are ideal walking country, and the Pembrokeshire Coast National Park website lists six recommended walks, ranging from the Foel Eryr walk, which is 4¾ miles long, and takes you past Bronze Age burial sites and an observation beacon, to

the Golden Road walk, which is just under 7½ miles long. This takes you along the Preseli ridge and across moorland. The track dates back to prehistoric times, and during the Iron Age it was a favourite route for people travelling to and from Ireland. The views from the ridge are spectacular. The Rosebush walk takes you past flooded slate quarries, testimony to one of the main industries in the Preseli Hills in Victorian times.

Perhaps one of the most important connections is that concerning Carn Meini and the bluestones. Why did our ancestors consider these stones so important to be used in building the inner ring of Stonehenge, one of the worlds greatest monuments. The stone was quarried from Carn Meini ('Rock of Stones'), locally known as the Dragons back. The bluestone glistens blue when wet, known as spotted dolerite. From the village of Mynachlogddu there is a bridal path from which a track leads up to Carn Meini.and further along the ridge is a stone- circle known as Bedd Arthur. (which translates as 'Arthur's Grave'). The circular walk takes you up onto Carn Sian from which there is a beautiful view to the coast and down into the valley.

MYNACHLOG-DDU
14 miles SE of Fishguard off the A478

🏛 Gors Fawr Stone Circle   🏛 Carn Menyn

🏛 Bedd Arthur

Mynachlog-ddu lies to the southeast of the Preseli Hills and, on the moorland below, close to the village, is another important site,

TRALLWYN COTTAGES & ASHERA POTTERY

Mynachlogddu, Preseli Hills, Pembrokeshire SA66 7SE
Tel: 01994 419278
e-mail: trallwyn@clara.co.uk
website: www.simplystonecottages.com

Located in a magical setting by moor and mountain and an ancient stonecircle in the midst of the bluestone country, **Trallwyn** offers idyllic cottages retaining many original features which have been renovated with care by local crafts people. This is wonderful wild country for those who are truly looking to get away from it all.

Trallwyn Converted Cowshed is a unique and beautiful building with curvy stone walls and beams and heaps of charm. It comprises an open plan kitchen, diner and living-room with oak flooring and woodstove and sleeps five in three bedrooms plus cot. With its simple use of natural materials and it's strong Steiner-influenced architecture it is a real fairytale cottage. Trallwyn Farmhouse is 300 years old and is full of character complete with original inglenook, woodstove, thick stone-walls and a conservatory. It sleeps six in three bedrooms. For couples and smaller families Trallwyn Cottage sleeps three and Bach sleeps two. In the warmer months Trallwyn also offers a Yurt which sleeps two-four and a Lodge which sleeps five.

If you feel like a creative break **Ashera Pottery** in the gardens of Trallwyn offers optional pottery tuition to all guests, whether experienced or beginners. Both adults and children are welcomed.

the 5,000 year-old stone circle at **Gors Fawr**. Built at a similar time to Stonehenge and made up of 16 stones, there are two outlying stones which are aligned to the Summer solstice. One of these outlying stones is called The Dreaming Stone. It is a magnetic rock with a slight seat and is a beautiful place to rest a while.

From here you can join the lane back to the village of Mynachlogddu passing by Ashera Pottery where beautiful pottery and crafts can be found.

Artists and photographers love to portray the ever changing moods of the Preselis with colours and light changes, shadowy clouds or clear blue skies, curves of the hills, purple

of the heather and the bright yellow of the gorse.

There are also castles aplenty and celtic crosses and churches to be found in this area steeped in legend. One such legend tells of St Brynach, a friend and contemporary of Wales

Gors Fawr Stone Circle

[fi] stories and anecdotes   famous people   art and craft   entertainment and sport   walks

patron Saint David, who communed with angels on Carn Ingli, a summit high above Newport with a breathtaking view and the gateway to the Bluestone country.

CRYMYCH
17 miles E of Fishguard on the A478

🏛 Crymych Wayside Barrow

This village lies to the east of the Preseli Hills, but is not within the national park. It is sometimes referred to as Crymmich (with two 'm's) and grew around a former railway station that lay on the line that ran from Whitland to Cardigan. The **Crymych Wayside Barrow** dates from the Bronze Age, and actually sits in someone's back yard.

ROSEBUSH
8½ miles SE of Fishguard off the B4313

Lying in the shadow of **Foel Cwmcerwyn**, the highest point in the Preseli Hills, Rosebush lies on the southern edge of the Preselis. It is full of memories of the old slate quarries and, now that the stone extraction has ceased, the village and surrounding area has returned to being a peaceful rural community surrounded by lovely natural scenery. The local quarrymaster in the 1870s was one Edward Cropper, and it is said that he had a special siding for his own railway carriage so that his wife did not have to mingle with the riff-raff! Rosebush slate was renowned, and used in many grand buildings, including the

---

TWMPATH GUEST HOUSE

Maenclochog, Pembrokeshire SA66 7RL
Tel: 01437 532990
e-mail: twmpath@hotmail.com
website: www.twmpathguesthouse.co.uk

Twmpath Guest House is one of the best places to stay while touring beautiful Pembrokeshire. The house itself is over 200 years old, and is set among stunning countryside with wonderful views of the Preselli Mountains, and boasts three fully en suite rooms that are comfortable, well furnished and spacious. They are all fully centrally heated, and have a colour TV, clock radio, hair dryer and tea/coffee making facilities. One of the rooms - on the ground floor - has been specially equipped to accommodate the disabled.

The guest house is owned and run by Diane Davies, who is determined to make your stay at her establishment as enjoyable as possible. You can use it as an overnight stopping place or as a base form which to explore all the history, heritage and marvellous scenery that is on the doorstep. Breakfast and evening meals are served at times convenient for the guests, and served in a beautiful dining room. Diane uses only fresh, local produce wherever possible, so guests know they are getting a culinary treat.

There is ample parking space, plus storage for bicycles if required. There are even drying facilities, and packed lunches can be made to order. If guests arrive by train, they can be picked up from Fishguard or Haverfordwest stations. Stay here and you will remember it for all the right reasons.

🏛 historic building   🏛 museum   🏛 historic site   🐾 scenic attraction   🌿 flora and fauna

Palace of Westminster. Rosebush is thought to have been the first Welsh village with piped water.

BRYNBERIAN

8½ miles E of Fishguard on the B4329

🏛 Bedd-yr-Afanc

This village sits to the north of the Preseli Hills, surrounded by prehistoric remains. **Bedd-yr-Afanc** ('the water monster's grave') is a Bronze age barrow grave from 1500BC. According to local legend, the afanc lived in a pool in the water beneath Brynberian bridhe. It was killed and buried within this mound.

CROSSWELL

10 miles E of Fishguard on the B4329

🏛 Pentre Ifan Burial Chamber

To the west of this village, on the northern slopes of the Preseli Hills, is the Bronze Age **Pentre Ifan Burial Chamber**, one of the grandest megalithic remains in Wales, thought to be 3,500 - 4,000 years old. An ancient chamber with a huge 16-foot capstone, the monument is made of the same Preseli bluestones that somehow found their way - though no one has yet come up with a fully convincing explanation - to Stonehenge on Salisbury Plain. The site is managed by CADW.

PONTFAEN

4½ miles SE of Fishguard off the B4313

🍃 Foel Cwmcerwyn   🍃 Gwaun Valley

🌱 Penlan Uchaf

The village lies on the western edge of the Preseli Hills, whose highest point, **Foel Cwmcerwyn** (1,759 feet) lies to the southeast. It has views stretching as far as Snowdonia to the north and the Gower Peninsula to the

south. These hills have seen many inhabitants come and go, and they are littered with prehistoric sites. There are Iron Age hill forts, Bronze Age burial cairns and standing stones scattered along the 'Golden Road', the ancient bridleway across the range.

In the foothills of the Preseli Hills is the **Gwaun Valley**, a truly hidden place that runs from the hills to Fishguard. Some of the locals in this area still celebrate New Year on 12th January, in keeping with the custom that predates the introduction of the Gregorian calendar in 1752.

Located in the heart of the Gwaun Valley, **Penlan Uchaf** is the place to see an abundant display of miniature plants, dwarf conifers and alpines that are all set in attractive landscaped surroundings through which runs a fast flowing stream.

The Rest of Pembrokeshire

Fishguard

🏛 Parish Church of St Mary   👤 Jemima Nicholas

🏛 The Last Invasion Embroidered Tapestry

Situated at the mouth of the River Gwaun, from which the town takes its Welsh name Abergwaun, the geography of Fishguard can be somewhat confusing to visitors. The picturesque old harbour, a pretty little quayside lined with fishermen's cottages, is Lower Fishguard, which was the location for the fictional seaside town of Llareggub used in the filming in the 1970s of Dylan Thomas' play, *Under Milk Wood*, starring Richard Burton. The new harbour, built at the beginning of the 20th century, lies across the bay at Goodwick and it is from here that the ferries depart for Ireland. On the high ground between the two harbours lies the main town of Upper Fishguard, a bustling place packed with shops, restaurants and pubs.

It was here, in February 1797, that the last invasion of Britain took place when a poorly equipped band of Frenchman landed at Carregwastad Point. Under the command of an American officer, Colonel William Tate (who hoped to start a peasants' rebellion), the 1,400-strong French expeditionary force, who were mainly ex-convicts, stole drinks and looted the local farms. Unchecked by the local militia, the unruly invaders set up headquarters at a nearby farm and, according to local tradition, several local women, dressed in red cloaks, advanced on the French soldiers. The women were led by **Jemima Nicholas**, who carried a pitchfork, and the drunken invaders fled in terror mistaking the ladies for the British army. The French retreated to the beach below Goodwick, where they formally surrendered to Lord Cawdor just two days after landing. Jemima Nicholas, who is said to have captured 12 Frenchmen single handedly, became famous as the 'General of the Red Army'. She died in 1832 and is buried in the **Parish Church of St Mary**. Though there has been a church here for centuries, the present church dates from 1857.

The Last Invasion Embroidered Tapestry, which was created in 1997 to mark the bicentenary of this bizarre event, hangs in the church hall. Designed by Elizabeth Cramp

---

ORIEL GLAN Y MÔR GALLERY

West Street, Fishguard, Pembrokeshire SA 65 5AE
Tel: 01348 874787
e-mail: beth@orielglanymor.wanadoo.co.uk
website: www.orielglanymorgallery.co.uk

Pembrokeshire has always been popular with artists and craftspeople. In Fishguard you will find one of the best studio/galleries in the county - one selling original and affordable paintings of north Pembrokeshire. It is the **Oriel Glan y Môr Gallery**, run by Beth Robinson, former opera singer and now a highly talented and respected artist in her own right. Since the gallery opened five years ago, many, many people have called in to admire and buy the paintings on show. They are an interesting blend of styles, with prices ranging from a modest £15 right up to £1,500.

It sits in the centre of the town, just off the roundabout on Market Square, so you can't miss it. Beth showcases not only her own work, but the work of many exciting artists who now live and paint in one of the most beautiful parts of Wales. The fine character studies and intimate landscapes of Evan Jon, for instance, attract many appreciative comments, as do the accessible landscapes of Sheila Craft. Also on offer are prints, cards, jewellery and craft items made by locally based craftspeople. As Beth's husband is a picture framer, the gallery also offers a framing service at affordable prices.

The gallery is intimate and welcoming, with Beth's studio and a small exhibition area on the ground floor, and a small gallery above. The shop is open Monday to Saturday 10am to 5pm, though out of season it occasionally closes on Monday or Wednesday afternoons.

🏛 historic building 🏛 museum 🏛 historic site 🍃 scenic attraction 🌾 flora and fauna

FISHGUARD GARDEN CENTRE

Glasfryn, Fishguard, Pembrokeshire SA65 9QS
Tel: 01348 874034
e-mail: info@fishguardgardencentre.co.uk
website: www.fishguardgardencentre.co.uk

Conveniently situated on Cefn Road, the **Fishguard Garden Centre** is your one-stop shopping experience for all your gardening needs. It is run and managed personally by Gill and Nick Chilton, who between them have over 23 years experience in the horticulture and landscaping industries.

Here you will find an impressive range of bedding plants, shrubs, trees, perennials, ornaments, pots and garden sundries. They specialise in summer and winter bedding plants and also produce hanging baskets for both private and business customers. Even though everything sold is of the highest quality, the prices are always keen and the staff are always friendly, knowledgeable and helpful. You are free to browse to your heart's content, and there is no obligation to buy. The centre has a simple ethos - it likes to take care of its customers, and it likes to take care of its 'green friends' - in other words, plants! So you know you are getting the very best of everything.

So if you're ever in Fishguard, call in at the Fishguard Garden Centre, and see for yourself.

RWS and worked by more than 70 embroiderers, the 100-foot long tapestry is in the style of the famous Bayeux Tapestry and depicts scenes from the invasion. The tapestry has its home here, but sometimes goes on tour.

Around Fishguard

DINAS

3½ miles NE of Fishguard on the A487

🌱 Dinas Island 🌱 Dinas Head

The village is situated at the base of **Dinas Island** which is, in fact, a promontory that culminates in the cliffs of **Dinas Head**, which are 463 feet high. Now no longer a true island, the land was given this name because at the end of the Ice Age it was indeed separated

from the mainland. In the care of the National Trust, the headland is an important nesting site for sea birds, and grey and Atlantic seals can often be seen swimming offshore.

NEWPORT

6½ miles E of Fishguard on the A487

🏰 Lords' Castle 🏛 Carreg Coetan Arthur

As its name would suggest, Newport was once an important port. It had a brisk wool trade until the time of the great plague, when trade was diverted to Fishguard. Newport was also the capital of the Marcher Lordship of Cemaes - the only one not to have been abolished by Henry VIII - and the **Lords' Castle**, which was built in the 13th century, and has now been incorporated into a mansion house (not open to the public).

🎭 stories and anecdotes 🐦 famous people ✏ art and craft 🖌 entertainment and sport 🚶 walks

PEMBROKESHIRE RETREAT

Rhos-y-Gilwen Mansion, Rhoshill, Cilgerran,
Pembrokeshire SA43 2TW
Tel: 01239 841387
e-mail: enquiries@retreat.co.uk
website: www.retreat.co.uk
www.rhosygilwen.co.uk

Rhosygilwen Mansion - a **Pembrokeshire Country
Retreat** is a delightful, sophisticated country guest
house set in 55 acres that offers guests the very
best in Welsh hospitality. Whether its business or
pleasure, time spent here in this restored Welsh
Gothic mansion (called Rhos-y-Gilwen) is sure to
recharge your batteries. It boasts seven en suite
bedrooms and two that share a very grand
bathroom. When restoring the mansion, great
attention was paid to marrying all the
conveniences expected of a modern establishment
with the tone and ambience of earlier, more
leisurely times. The guest house is able to
accommodate couples, family groups and business
parties, and it can tailor its catering to individual
needs.

The food is, or course, outstanding. While the
restaurant does not cater for the general public,
the chefs have a fine reputation for the
imaginative use they make of fresh local produce.
They are dedicated to preparing food that suit's
the needs of guests and groups, and this is one of
the Mansion's many pluses.

One of Rhosygilwen Mansion's glories is its
gardens. The Walled Garden is reached via a path
through an area of grass deliberately left uncut to
encourage insects (particularly butterflies) and wild
flowers. It was laid out in Victorian times, and up
until recently lay neglected. Now it has been
restored, and not only flowers and shrubs are grown

here, but organic vegetables and herbs which are used in the mansion's kitchen. The Arboretum was
also laid out and planted in Victorian times, and has fine specimens of many trees from both Wales
and around the world. Both gardens are a haven of tranquillity in a world of hustle, bustle and noise,
and are the perfect places for thoughtful reflection as you stroll through them.

Rhos-y-Glwen is ideally suited for meetings of like-minded people who are interested in such
activities as music, literature or art. It can be a memorable venue for music concerts (featuring
both Welsh and classical music), poetry and literature readings, exhibitions, either in the
mansion itself or in its lovely grounds. In the past there have been opera recitals in the garden,
readings from Shakespeare (accompanied by the music of Vaughan Williams), garden open days
and a literature festival. Special pre-concert dinners, plus themed dinners, can be arranged to
round off an evening perfectly.

Visit Rhosygilwen Mansion, and be prepared to have your batteries recharged.

🏛 historic building   🏛 museum   🏛 historic site   ◔ scenic attraction   🌱 flora and fauna

Today, this is a pretty little seaside town with a fine beach that still retains the charm of its fishing port. An excellent place from which to explore the Preseli Hills to the south. Just to the north of the town is **Carreg Coetan Arthur**, a collapsed burial chamber that reputedly held the remains of King Arthur.

NEVERN

10 miles E of Fishguard on the B4582

🏛 Parish Church of St Brynach   🏛 Nevern Castle

🏛 Mynydd Carn Ingli   🏛 St Brynach's Cross

🏛 Mounting Block

The village of Nevern's most interesting features can be found at the **Parish Church of St Brynach**, which is dedicated to the 5th century Irish saint whose cell was on nearby

Mynydd Carn Ingli - the Mount of Angels. Inside the church are two carved stones: the Maglocunus Stone, dating from the 5th century, commemorates Maglocunus, the son of Clutor, and it bears both Latin and Ogham inscriptions, and the Cross Stone, which bears a Viking cross and dates from the 10th century. Outside in the churchyard, near the entrance to the church, stands one of the finest Celtic crosses in Wales - **St Brynach's Cross**. Dating from the 10th or 11th century, the cross stands some 13 feet tall and, according to tradition, the first cuckoo to be heard each year in Pembrokeshire sings from the top of the cross on St Brynach's Day (7th April). In the road outside the chruch can be seen the **Mounting Block**, used as a 'leg up' when riders were mounting their horses. It is

---

PENRALLT GARDEN CENTRE

Moylgrove, nr Cardigan, Pembrokeshire SA43 3BX
Tel: 01239 881295
e-mail: penrallt.nursery@virgin.net
website: www.penralltnursery.co.uk

Situated in Moylgrove, a village a few miles southwest of Cardigan, the **Penrallt Garden Centre** is the perfect place to buy all your gardening needs. It is set with 70 acres of woodland, farmland and coastal walks, and its three-acre site has a vast expanse of greenhouses and tunnels that make the perfect environment for growing plants, from a sapling to a tree and from a seed to a flower. In fact, the garden centre prides itself on having the largest selection of plants in Wales.

There is also a tremendous range of accessories to make your garden much more enjoyable, from greenhouses and barbecue supplies to tools, hanging baskets, furniture and decking. The staff are all knowledgeable and friendly, and your queries and questions will be answered promptly. Take your time wandering round, as there is no obligation to buy. Visit the licensed Pavilion Café for snacks, an evening meal or a relaxing cup of tea or coffee. Make your way along one of the coastal or woodland walks, or visit Pet's Corner, where you can see such things as dog kennels and wooden dovecotes.

The whole place is so much more than a garden centre. It is, in many ways, a tourist attraction, as you could spend the whole day here, in this fascinating cornucopia, not just for the committed gardener, but also for the beginner. Come along and see for yourself.

📖 stories and anecdotes   🦜 famous people   🎨 art and craft   🎣 entertainment and sport   🚶 walks one of only two left in Pembrokeshire.

To the northwest of the village are the remains of **Nevern Castle**, which was originally a local chieftain's fortress until, in around 1100, the Marcher Lord of Cemaes, Robert Martyn, built a motte and bailey castle on the site. The castle came into the hands of Rhys ap Gryffydd at the end of the 12th century and he added the stone castle, parts of which can still be seen today among the overgrown ruins.

EGLWYSWRW
11½ miles E of Fishguard on the A487

🏛 Parish Church of St Cristiolus   ⛏ Castell Henllys

To the west of the village lies **Castell Henllys**, an Iron Age settlement that is still being excavated by archaeologists. While the dig is continuing throughout the summer months, visitors to this late prehistoric site can also see the thatched roundhouses and outbuildings created to give as true as possible an insight into the lives of Iron Age man. Events throughout the season help to portray the wide spectrum of Celtic culture, from story-telling and craft demonstrations to the celebration of ancient festivals.

The name of the village refers to St Eirw, a minor female saint who was said to have been buried in a small chapel that stood in Elizabethan times next to the persent **Parish Church of St Cristiolus**.

CILGERRAN
15 miles NE of Fishguard off the A478

🏛 Cilgerran Castle   🏛 Parish Church of St Llawdogg
🏛 Coracle Centre   ❦ Welsh Wildlife Centre
⛏ Princess Nest   🔷 Sir William Edmond Logan

The remains of **Cilgerran Castle**, one the most picturesque in Wales, sits on a rocky promontory overlooking the River Teifi. A tranquil site today, this land was once hotly disputed territory and the castle's defences reflect this - there are almost sheer drops on two sides of the building, while the 13th century twin round towers and curtain walls protect the flank away from the cliff. The building of the castle is thought to have begun around 1093 but it was strengthened by Gerald de Windsor, to whom it was granted by Henry I. Thereafter it changed hands many times, being partially sacked by Rhys ap Gryffydd in 1164, retaken by the Earl of Pembroke in 1204 and finally falling to Llywelyn the Great in 1233.

The castle is forever associated with the legend of **Princess Nest**, the Welsh Helen of Troy, who, in 1109, was abducted by the besotted Owain, son of the Prince of Powys. Nest's husband, Gerald of Pembroke, escaped by slithering down a chute through the castle walls. One of the first major tourist attractions in Wales - in the 18th and 19th centuries it was fashionable to take a river excursion to the ruins from Cardigan - today, these romantic ruins still provide inspiration to artists, as they have done for centuries, and both JMW Turner and Richard Wilson are known to have

Welsh Wildlife Centre, Cilgerran

🏛 historic building   🏛 museum   ⛏ historic site   🔷 scenic attraction   ❦ flora and fauna

visited here. Tourist signs lead from the point where the A478, A484 and A487 meet to the **Welsh Wildlife Centre**, an excellent place for spotting birds and animals, wild flowers and butterflies. Wild footpaths pass through woodland, reed beds, meadows, marsh and riverside, providing the chance to see a vast variety of wildlife in different habitats. More than 130 species of birds have been recorded, and more than 20 mammals, including otter, red deer, voles, badgers and bats. The River Teifi is one of the few rivers in Britain where fishing from coracles can still be seen. The **Coracle Centre** in Cilgerran tells the history of the town and its river down the centuries.

In the churchyard of the **Parish Church of St Llawdogg** is the grave of **Sir William Edmond Logan** (1798 - 1875,) who was born in Montreal of Scottish parents, and became director of the Geological Survey of Canada. He produced the first geological survey of South Wales, and Canada's highest mountain, Mount Logan, is named after him.

LLANFAIR-NANT-GWYN
12½ miles E of Fishguard on the B4332

🐦 Bro-Meigan Gardens

Bro-Meigan Gardens, to the east of the village, is a delightful place to spend a few hours meandering through the carefully designed gardens. With panoramic views over the Preseli Hills, the backdrop to the gardens,

Bro-Meigan Gardens

visitors to Bro-Meigan will see an incredible range of plants from all over the world, all grown from seed. While enjoying the superb horticultural displays, visitors can also rest at the gardens' traditional tea rooms housed in a 300-year-old barn, enjoying homemade cakes and scones served on bone china.

LLANGOLMAN
11½ miles SE of Fishguard off the A4313

🏠 Penrhos Cottage   🎨 The Slate Workshop

Slate has been quarried in this area for centuries and, housed in a renovated 18th century corn mill, **The Slate Workshop** is a place where the art of handcrafting quality Welsh slate items continues. A wide range of articles are made here, including high quality plaques, sundials, clocks and objets d'art, and many illustrate the great skill required to work and carve the slate. To the south of the village lies another interesting building, **Penrhos Cottage**, which is one of the few lasting examples of an 'overnight' house. If a man, with the help of his friends, could build a dwelling between sunset and sunrise, he was entitled to all the land that lay within, literally, a stone's throw from the door. This particular 'overnight' house dates from the 19th century and still contains the original furnishings.

GOODWICK
1 mile W of Fishguard off the A487

🏠 Oceanlab   🐦 Manorowen Garden

This once-small fishing village is now effectively the base for Fishguard harbour, which was built here between 1894 and 1906 by the Fishguard and Rosslare Railways and Harbours Company to provide a sea link between southwest Wales and Ireland. Still offering a much-used ferry service today, Goodwick is older than it first appears. The

MELIN TREGWYNT WOOLLEN MILL

Castle Morris, nr Fishguard, Pembrokeshire SA62 5UX
Tel: 01348 891288
e-mail: info@melintregwynt.co.uk
website: www.melintregwynt.co.uk

Glorious countryside surrounds the **Melin Tregwynt Woollen Mill**, one of the must-visit places in Pembrokeshire. It is a picturesque, white-washed building that speaks of tradition and history, though nowadays it has added high standards of service and value for money to its many attributes. It sits in a remote wooded valley close to the coast, and sells craft-based products from all over Wales.

From the 18th century onwards, local farmers would bring their fleeces here to be washed, spun and woven into fine woollen blankets. Now it is tourists and local people who make the pilgrimage, attracted by its colourful displays of fabrics, soft furnishings, cushions, blankets clothing, socks, footwear, bags, hats, purses, and so much more. The whole interior is inspiring, combining modern, chic design with traditional methods. You can browse to your heart's content with absolutely no obligation, as this is the perfect place to buy a loved one that special gift, or indeed a souvenir for yourself to remind you of your visit to Pembrokeshire. They can gift-wrap the item you choose and put in a personal card.

The products woven here are exported all over the world, especially Japan, Europe and America, and there are many satisfied customers. The items are timeless in design and simple in spirit, qualities held in high regard in Wales.

The mill has been in the same family since 1912, and you can still admire the huge waterwheel, driven by the waters of the river, which powered the many machines housed here long ago through pulleys, leather belts and cogs. In fact, the mill is a "Quality Assured Visitor Attraction", an award which has to be earned the hard way from the Wales Tourist Board.

The coffee shop is the perfect place to relax over a cup of coffee or pot of tea. It sells locally baked sponge cakes, bara brith (traditional Welsh fruit bread) and light snacks.

Why not send away now for a catalogue (Tel: 01348 891644), and when you arrive at the mill in person, you will have a great idea of what is in stock as well as the prices? The staff are friendly and knowledgeable, and will make you more than welcome!

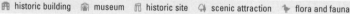 historic building 🏛 museum 🏛 historic site 🍂 scenic attraction 🌱 flora and fauna

settlement was known to ancient inhabitants as Gwlad hud a Lledrith - the Land of Mystery and Enchantment. The surrounding countryside certainly lives up to this name, although the tales told by James Wade, one of Pembrokeshire's best known storytellers, are rather far fetched, but nonetheless delightful. On one occasion Wade, who died in 1887, recounted that, while he was fishing on Goodwick beach, a great carrion crow swooped out of the sky and carried him, in its beak, across the sea to Ireland. On reaching land, the crow dropped Wade and he landed in a cannon where he spent the night. As he was waking the next morning, the cannon was fired and Wade was rocketed across St George's Channel and he landed beside his fishing rod in the exact spot from which he had been plucked!

Strumble Head

The **Oceanlab** has hands on exhibitions about marine life, and displays explaining how marine creatures defend themselves from predators. There is also a dolphin buzzer, a feel box and a food chain puzzle. Just a mile to the south of Goodwick lies **Manorowen Garden**, an interesting walled garden which has an historic gazebo. The garden was also involved in the French invasion of the 18th century, with a skirmish taking place between Colonel William Tate's invading army and the local militia.

LLANWNDA
4 miles NW of Fishguard off the A487

🏠 Parish Church of St Gwyndaf   🏛 St Gwyndaf Stones

The **Parish Church of St Gwyndaf** is Victorian, though there has been a church here for centuries. The **St Gwyndaf Stones** are a series of early Christian carved stones

now incorporated into the churchyard wall. Giraldus Cambrances (Gerald the Welshman), the 12th century historian and writer, was rector of the church at one time (see also Manorbier and St Davids).

STRUMBLE HEAD
3 miles W of Fishguard off the A487

🏛 Good Hope   ⚓ Carregwastad Head

This huge headland, with its lighthouse warning ships off the cliffs on the approach to Fishguard harbour, offers some spectacular coastal scenery as well as an outlook over the great sweep of Cardigan Bay. Just to the east lies **Carregwastad Head**, a remote headland which was the landing place of the ill-fated French invasion of Britain in the 18th century. Also to the east is **Good Hope** (National Trust), a traditional farmed landscape with an unusually wide variety of plant life.

CASTLE MORRIS
7 miles SW of Fishguard off the A487

🏠 Castle Morris   🏠 Melin Tregwynt

Situated on the southern bank of the River Cleddau are the scant remains of **Castle Morris** itself. It was once a motte and bailey fortification, though the motte itself (the conically shaped hill on which the Norman

---

🎞 stories and anecdotes   🐦 famous people   🎨 art and craft   🎭 entertainment and sport   🥾 walks castle stood) has long since disappeared. The bailey, or courtyard, still survives. The castle was an outpost of the much grander castle at St David's, but was soon abandoned, and there is no evidence that the timber castle was everreplaced by a more permanent stone one.

Melin Tregwynt was built in the 18ᵗʰ century as a corn mill, and was the mill for the nearby Tregwynt Estate. It later became a fulling, or 'pandy' mill, where hammers (driven by water) beat the finished cloth to soften it.

PORTHGAIN
10 miles SW of Fishguard off the A487

🏛 Brickworks

As well as being a natural beauty spot the sheltered harbour at Porthgain ('Chisel Harbour') has added interest, as the harbourside is dominated by the shell of the 19th century **Brickworks**. This monument to the village's industrial heritage stands close to remnants from Porthgain's heyday as a slate and granite exporting port. Many buildings, as far afield as London and Liverpool, have Porthgain granite in their construction. Nowadays, it is difficult to imagine the hectic scenes on the quayside a century ago when the harbour was packed with boats queuing for their cargoes of stone and brick needed for Britain's building boom. The harbour's unique personality has led it to being used as a location by film-makers.

ST DAVIDS
16 miles SW of Fishguard off the A487

🏛 St Davids Cathedral   🏛 Bishop's Palace

🎬 St Elvis   🌿 Ramsey Island   🏛 St Non's Chapel

🏛 St Non's Well   🔱 St Justinian's

🌿 Marine Life Centre   🌿 Oceanarium

To Welsh people everywhere, St Davids is a special place. Named after Wales' patron saint,

St Davids is the smallest and the oldest cathedral settlement in Britain. It was here, in the 6th century, that St David founded a religious order and, on this site in 1176, the magnificent **St Davids Cathedral** was completed. Situated in a deep hollow below the streets, so that not even its square tower can be seen above the rooftops, the cathedral contains several treasures that include saintly bones which are believed to be those of St Caradog. The undoubted highlight of the cathedral's interior is the oak roof, which displays wonderful ornate carvings by 15th century craftsmen. In 1120, Pope Calixtus II decreed that two pilgrimages to St Davids were equivalent to one to Rome and successive monarchs, from William the Conqueror to Queen Elizabeth II, have worshipped here. The Queen also has a special seat reserved for her in the cathedral and it was from here that Maundy Money was distributed for the first time in Wales. Within the cloisters is the Refectory, where locally sourced food is available.

Adjacent to the cathedral, in the same grassy hollow, lie the ruins of the **Bishop's Palace**, a once imposing building which, even though now in a ruined state, still conveys the wealth and influence of the Church in medieval times. Most of the Palace's construction was overseen by Bishop Henry de Gower in the mid-14th century, and he spared no expense on creating this lavish residence, which he felt befitted a leader of both church and state. There were two complete sets of state rooms at the palace set around a courtyard. De Gower used one for his private business and the other for ceremonial entertaining. The palace fell into disrepair in the 16th century after the incumbent bishop stripped the roof of its lead in order to pay for his five daughters' dowries.

🏛 historic building   📷 museum   🏛 historic site   🔱 scenic attraction   🌿 flora and fauna

Unlike other national saints of the United Kingdom, we know something about David, thanks to biographies written in the 11th century by a man called Rhygyfarch, though what he wrote may be no more than a hagiography. Giraldus Cumbrances (see also Manorbier and Llawnda) also wrote a book in the 12th century about David's travels throughout Wales. He was born near what is now the city of St Davids, his father being Sandde, grandson of the king of Ceredigion and his mother being Non, a lady 'of noble birth', who is also said to have been a niece of King Arthur. She dedicated herself to the religious life, but caught the eye of Sandde. He could not be denied, and the inevitable happened after they were married. Non fell pregnant, and David was born in March 1st, which is celebrated to this day as St David's

Day. He was canonised in AD 1120 by Pope Callactus II.

He was said to be a gentle person who ate only bread and herbs and drank only water, though he was well-built and muscular. Not only did he travel through Wales, he also visited Southwest England, Cornwall and Brittany. Along with two companions, he once went on a pilgrimage to Jerusalem. One curious fact is that he was baptised at Solva, a few miles south east of the city, by his cousin, a man called **St Elvis**. Because of this, some people have tried to claim that Elvis Presley was descended from Welsh stock (see also Solva), and that Presley is a corruption of Preseli, as the Preseli Hills are close by.

St David is a central figure in one of the many legends concerning how the leek came to be adopted as the national emblem of

PEBBLES YARD GALLERY & ESPRESSO BAR

The Pebbles, St David's, Pembrokeshire SA62 6RD
Tel/Fax: 01437 720122
email: pebblesyard@tesco.net
website: www.pebblesyard.co.uk

At the heart of the historic city of St Davids, the very popular and unique **Pebbles Yard Gallery & Espresso Bar** is situated on the picturesque old street that leads directly to the bell tower and Cathedral. The street level gallery is the domain of the accomplished photographer and writer Jacki Sime and a wide cross section of her work hangs on the walls along with other inspiring designer led contemporary art including, original paintings, prints, sculptures, ceramics, lighting, glass, metalwork and the largest collection of contemporary jewellery in Pembrokeshire.

Situated above the gallery is the friendly, comfortable, organically-orientated coffee bar where a variety of wholemeal sandwiches, filled pitta breads, soups and salads are made fresh to order. Soft drinks include pressies, smoothies and fresh juices and along with a selection of teas and home-baked cakes is a superb selection of coffees. All food and drink can be purchased to eat in or take away. Outside in spring and summer the espresso bar garden yard seating area is in great demand. The espresso bar also run a monthly changing exhibition of contemporary artists work.

RAUL SPEEK GALLERY

The Old Chapel, Main Street, Solva, SA62 6UU
Tel: 01437 721907
Websites: www.raulspeek.co.uk   www.thepassioncollection.com
www.speeksalsa.co.uk and www.heatherbennett.co.uk

Opening times:

April to September – daily 11am to 6pm;
October to March – Wednesday to Sunday 11am to 4pm
Outside these times please ring 01437 721907 as the owners
live on the premises and may be available.

Solva is a beautiful small coastal village lying between two hills
and opening out into a tidal harbour.   It is an ideal place for
short or long holidays and safe for children with plenty of good
food and places to stay.   See the village website
www.solva.net for details.

The Old Chapel houses the studio gallery of internationally
known Cuban artist Raul Speek and photographer Heather
Bennett. Raul came to the UK in 1991 having a gallery initially in
London's Spittalfield Market; he moved to Solva on the west
coast of Pembrokeshire in 1995.   Cuban energy is vibrant and
life giving and so is that of Wales – within the gallery the art
work and music seeks to explore this fusion. Come along and
enjoy!

The main websites www.raulspeek.co.uk and
www.heatherbennett.co.uk give details and news of exhibitions
and workshops both in Wales and elsewhere. The gallery is an
ever changing tapestry of colours, shapes and styles where Raul
can often be found painting and talking to visitors.   He teaches
individuals and groups at the Chapel and also acts as visiting
tutor in local schools, libraries, art societies etc. He accepts
commissions for paintings, sculptures and murals from private
and public sources.

Workshops in art, creativity, photography, creative writing
and self development are available both by demand and on a
scheduled basis. These are run by Heather, Raul and other local
folk.

This summer, on fine days, tea, coffee, juices and cakes will
be available in the garden.

Wales. The legend states that just before a battle against the Saxons he advised the Britons to wear a leek in their caps to distinguish them from the enemy. St David's Day, March 1st, is the traditional national day of the Welsh, when Welsh people all over the world wear the leek, or the other national emblem, the daffodil. The Welsh words for leek and daffodil are the same (*cenhinen* means leek, *cenhinen pedr* means daffodil), which could explain why both are national emblems.

Apart from the religious sites, there are various other attractions at St Davids and two in particular relate to the sea and the wide variety of creatures found there. The **Marine Life Centre** offers a diver's eye view of the deep, without getting wet and, set within the simulated caves, visitors can come face to face with creatures found in the local waters. For bigger and more exotic fish, the **Oceanarium** with its sharks and rays, is also well worth exploring. In August 2002, St Davids hosted the National Eisteddfod, one of the highlights of which was the induction of the Archbishop-designate of Canterbury, Dr Rowan Williams, into the Gorsedd of Bards, a historic order of Druids. The ceremony was held in a circle of standing stones fashioned, like the stones at Stonehenge, from Pembrokeshire rock. The ceremony involved the singing of Welsh Christian hymns and the Welsh National Anthem, the reading of a citation by the Arch-Druid and the wielding of a giant ceremonial sword - a burdensome task entrusted to Druid Ray Gravell, a former Welsh rugby international. Dr Williams is the third Archbishop to be a member of the Gorsedd. Speaking Welsh is a prerequisite for consideration for nomination, with one exception - the Queen.

Just outside the city, in a stunningly beautiful spot overlooking the sea, are **St Non's Well** and the ruins of **St Non's Chapel**, thought to be built on the actual site of David's birth. The bay is named after St David's mother and legend has it that he was born during a great storm in around AD 520. The waters of St Non's Well are said to have special powers for healing eye diseases and it was much visited during the Middle Ages by pilgrims.

Another coastal beauty spot, which is also steeped in legend, is **St Justinian's**, a rock-bound harbour that is home to the St Davids Lifeboat Station. Justinian was a 6th century hermit who retreated across to **Ramsey Island**, a short distance offshore, to devote himself to God. A strict disciplinarian, he must have been too severe with his followers as they eventually rebelled and cut off his head! Justinian is then said to have walked across the waters of Ramsey Sound, back to the mainland, with his head in his arms. Ramsey is a Norse name, a legacy of the time when this part of the coast was terrorised by Viking invaders. Today, the island is an RSPB reserve, and home to an abundance of wildlife. Boat trips round the island offer visitors the chance to observe the numerous sea birds and the colonies of grey seals.

SOLVA
16 miles SW of Fishguard on the A487

🏛 St Elvis's Cromlech 🧶 Solva Woollen Mill

🌱 Pumpkin Shed Organic Walled Garden

Situated at the end of a long inlet and well protected from the sometimes stormy waters of St Bride's Bay, Solva harbour is one of the most sheltered in Wales. Green hills roll down to the quayside and this picturesque view was the last sight of Wales for many 19th century emigrants who sailed from Solva to America for 10 shillings - the price of a one way ticket.

Now no longer such a busy port, Solva is a charming old seafaring village that boasts a good range of craft shops. **Solva Woollen Mill** , in the beautiful valley of the River Solfach, has been in continuous production since it opened in 1907. It now specialises in carpets and rugs, and visitors can usually see weaving in progress.

The **Pumpkin Shed Organic Walled Garden** has fruit and vetebale gardens as well as herb and flower gardens. Some distance from Solva is the delightfully named St Elvis' Farm, where St David is supposed to have been baptised by his cousin St Elvis of Munster. There is also a Neolithic burial chamber called **St Elvis' Cromlech** (see also St Davids). Near to it used to stand St Elvis' Church.

Haverfordwest

🏛 Haverfordwest Castle	🐦 Christian Bale
🏛 Parish Church of St Martin	🐦 'Suggs'
🏛 Priory Church of St Thmas the Martyr	
🎭 Landsker	🏛 Parish Church of St Mary
🏛 Haverford Town Museum	
🐦 Gwen and Augustus John	

This old county town, with its pleasant rural surroundings, lies on the banks of the labyrinthine Cleddau river system and is more or less in the centre of Pembrokeshire. Lining the steep streets of this hilly town there can be found some fine Georgian buildings that date back to the days when Haverfordwest, even though it is several miles inland, was a

---

THE FURNITURE DIRECTORY

Freystrop Cross, Haverfordwest,
Pembrokeshire SA62 4LD
Tel: 01437 890390   e-mail: ryandavis@aol.com
website: www.pinedirectory.com

For stylish pine wood furniture in Pembrokeshire, head for **The Furniture Directory** at Freystrop Cross, a short drive south of Haverfordwest off the A4076. It is owned and run by Andy and Ryan Davis, who bring a wealth of experience in the furniture industry to the company. It is probably the finest furniture warehouse in the country, and has a huge stock in the warehouse, which covers two floors and has recently seen yet another extension. And it's not just pine that is sold. There's a great range of furniture in other woods, both soft and hard.

The Furniture Directory imports from around the world, placing special emphasis on oak and pine. Everything is keenly priced, and deliveries can be arranged to anywhere in the country. Feel free to browse with no obligation. Whether it's dining tables and chairs, dressers, cupboards, beds, wardrobes, chests, shelf units and so on, you will find a huge range of styles and sizes. In addition, the warehouse also stocks smaller items such as reclaimed mirrors, stools, occasional tables, paper racks, umbrella stands, coat racks, carved figures and animals, and a fine range of soft furnishings and design led accessories that will complement any purchase perfectly. If it's garden furniture you're after, then The Furniture Directory also stocks that. The staff is friendly and knowledgeable, and a member of staff is always on hand to offer help and advice. The company can arrange delivery to most parts of the country.

🏛 historic building   🏛 museum   🏛 historic site   🌿 scenic attraction   🌸 flora and fauna

prosperous port trading largely with Bristol and Ireland. Its name means 'ford used by bucks', and the town is known locally as 'Harford'.

However, the town predates this trading boom by several centuries and its unusual name is a legacy of Viking raids. Set on a hill overlooking the River Cleddau is the striking landmark of **Haverfordwest Castle**, which was built around 1120 by the Englishman Gilbert de Clare, Earl of Pembroke. The town grew up around the fortress and throughout the 12th and 13th centuries it saw various inhabitants including Henry II and Edward I, who gave it to his wife, Queen Eleanor. Throughout its history it was held continuously by the English, but by the late 16th century had become ruinous. During the Civil War it was hastily rebuilt, and for a while it was held by Royalists. A story is told of how the garrison mistook a herd of cows for Parliamentary soldiers, so hastily abandoned it. General Laugharne then took it in 1645 without a shot being fired. He ransacked the place, and today the former governor's residence is home to the **Haverford Town Museum**, which houses the oldest letter box in Wales, dating to 1857.

The **Priory Church of St Thomas the Martyr**, founded by Augustinian Canons in the early 13th century, can be found by the Western Cleddau river. Excavations of the priory land have revealed that there were gardens here in the cloister and also between the priory buildings and the river. The riverside gardens, which were laid out in the mid 15th century, provide a rare example of the sort of garden that is often seen in medieval manuscripts and

Haverfordwest Priory

the narrow raised beds have been replanted with plant species appropriate to the period.

The **Parish Church of St Martin**, the oldest in town, dates from rebuilding in the 14th century. The west window is perpendicular, and there is a priest's room over the porch. The **Parish Church of St Mary** is the town's other church, and has one of the best collections of monumental brasses in Pembrokeshire. It has a fine panelled Tudor roof, reckoned to be the best in Wales.

Close by is a strange, ghostly border that cannot be seen: known locally as the **Landsker** (or land scar) it divides the English speaking 'little England beyond Wales' of south Pembrokeshire from the Welsh speaking north. This abrupt division of the county can be traced back to early medieval times when Norman invasions into these parts paved the way for Anglo Saxon and Flemish immigrants.

A line of castles was built from Amroth right across to Roch and, although the Landsker is an invisible border, its significance has been profound in the past. It was unthinkable that a marriage should take place between a man and a woman from different sides of the line even though they may have lived only a short distance apart.

📖 stories and anecdotes　🐦 famous people　🎨 art and craft　🎭 entertainment and sport　🚶 walks

The Landsker borderlands feature delightful countryside and fascinating villages and hamlets with a rich heritage and many stories to tell. **Christian Bale**, who played Batman in *Batman Begins* (released in 2005), was born in Haverfordwest, and **Gwen John**, the sister of the artist **Augustus John**, was also born in here. She and her brother were brought up in the town. Graham McPherson (also known as Suggs), the lead singer with the group Madness, attended school in Haverfordwest.

Around Haverfordwest

SCOLTON
4½ miles NE of Haverfordwest on the B4329

🏛 Scolton Manor House   🌶 Visitor Centre

🏛 Pembrokeshire's County Museum

The early Victorian **Scolton Manor House**, which dates from around 1840, along with its

grounds is, today, a museum and country park that makes an interesting and enjoyable visit. The house, stable block and exhibition hall, as **Pembrokeshire's County Museum**, features a number of displays that illustrate the history of this southwest region of Wales. While the past is concentrated on here, at the award-winning **Visitor Centre** there is an exhibition which looks to the future and, in particular, green issues and the wildlife of the surrounding park. The country park itself has lovely landscaped grounds, nature trails, picnic areas and a play area.

LLYS-Y-FRAN
7½ miles NE of Haverfordwest off the B4329

🌶 Llys-y-fran Reservoir

The impressive dam built to form **Llys-y-fran Reservoir** in the 1960s has been constructed in sympathy with the surrounding countryside and, when it was officially opened in 1972 by

LLYS-Y-FRÂN COUNTRY PARK
Visitor Centre, Llys-y-Frân, Nr Haverfordwest, Pembrokeshire SA63 4RR
Tel: 01437 532273

Situated to the north of Haverfordwest off the B4329, **Llys-y-Frân Country Park** is one of the most popular tourist attractions in Pembrokeshire. It is centred on the Llys-y-Frân reservoir, a man made sheet of water that provides drinking water for Pembrokeshire. There is so much here for the family to do that everyone will enjoy themselves. You can walk, cycle, row, fish and do so many things in a setting not far from the beautiful Preseli Hills. Or you can just enjoy spectacular views of the impressive 100 feet high dam and the surrounding countryside.

Entry to the park is normally free, but when a special event is taking place, such as a speed hill climb, then a small fee is payable. There is also a restaurant/ cafe open from March until October) that serves wonderful foods and snacks and you should phone the above number if you want details or to book. They have beautiful views out over the water, and a sun patio which is open during the summer.

There is also a gift shop (just right for buying that special souvenir or gift) and the park is open from dawn until dusk 365 days of the year. There is plenty of parking, plus facilities for the disabled, including two specially adapted boats for anglers.

🏛 historic building   🏛 museum   🏛 historic site   🌶 scenic attraction   🌶 flora and fauna

Princess Margaret, the reservoir was able to meet the growing needs of the county's population and of the oil refineries at Milford Haven. Surrounded by a glorious country park, which lies in the shadow of the Preseli Hills to the north, there is a seven-mile perimeter path around the reservoir that provides an opportunity to see some of the local inhabitants, including foxes, badgers, mink, squirrels and otters. The fishing is some of the best in Wales, with the waters regularly stocked with rainbow trout and with a steady population of brown trout. Anglers can fish from boats or from the banks.

CANASTON BRIDGE
7 miles E of Haverfordwest on the A40

🏰 Blackpool Mill 🖉 Oakwood

To the south of the village can be found two very different attractions. **Blackpool Mill,**

beside the Eastern Cleddau river, dates from the early 19th century and it is one of the finest examples of a water powered mill in Britain. Further south and hidden among trees lies **Oakwood**, Wales' premier theme park that is home to Europe's longest watercoaster, biggest wooden rollercoaster and largest skycoaster. As well as the outdoor rides there is an all-weather complex with a multitude of games, puzzles and rides. An area called Playtown is aimed at younger children.

NARBERTH
9½ miles E of Haverfordwest on the A478

🏰 Narberth Castle 🏛 Narberth Museum

This small old town, sited on a steep hill, is said to have been the legendary court of Pwyll, Prince of Dyfed. It is, however, a historical fact that Narberth grew up around its early Dark Ages' castle and that the town

---

FABRIC HOUSE SIXTHEHIGHSTREET
6 High Street, Narberth, Pembrokeshire SA67 7AR
Tel: 01834 861063

The **Fabric House, SixTheHighStreet** is a fascinating and colourful shop selling a wide range of gorgeous homeware, gifts, fashion and accessories at prices that are realistic and affordable. Here you can browse to your heart's content knowing that the friendly, knowledgeable staff will offer all the advice and help that you might need.

Lovely canteens of cutlery, dinner sets, bedding, jewellery, curtains, bed linen, plate racks - they're all here, and more. There are many famous names to choose from, from Burleigh blue and white ware and dinner services by Culinary Concepts of London, Monsoon and Ditton Hill co-ordinated bed linen, fabrics and wallpaper by Sanderson, Harlequin and Romo amongst others.

The jewellery is especially attractive, as are the collectable teddy bears by Steiff and Deans. Why not buy one of the delightful candles, or pamper yourself with a 'Heaven Scent' bathroom product? There is a great range to choose from. Upstairs you will find a huge range of contemporary womens and menswear, which adds to the attractiveness of the place.

The place is owned and managed by Jenny Thomas, who has a wealth of experience in soft furnishings, giftware and other items, and she is always willing to share that experience with you as you buy a gift for a loved one or a souvenir of your visit to Wales. So call in, and be prepared to be delighted.

📖 stories and anecdotes   🦜 famous people   🎨 art and craft   🖉 entertainment and sport   🚶 walks

GOLDEN SHEAF GALLERY

25 High Street, Narberth,
Pembrokeshire SA67 7AR
Tel: 01834 860407
e-mail: suzanne@thegoldensheaf-gallery.co.uk
website: www.thegoldensheaf-gallery.co.uk

Welcome to the most unique collection of quality products outside London! The **Golden Sheaf Gallery** can be found in an attractive Georgian building in the small attractive town of Narberth in Pembrokeshire, and is owned and managed by Suzanne Somers, who brings a wealth of experience in selling fine, unique products that make the ideal gift or souvenir.

The inside of this shop is a treasure trove of colours, textures and shapes, and all are beautifully displayed to delight and enthral everyone who enters. Jewellery - textiles - ceramics - innovative gifts - books - lifestyle products - they're all here, and a whole lot more besides. Approved by the Crafts Council for quality, customers are invited to browse at leisure, or relax on one of the comfy sofas in the first floor gallery as they marvel at the oil paintings, watercolours, limited edition prints by local artists, ceramics, bronze sculptures and textiles.

Or how about the ground floor, where you could really treat yourself by buying from the large range of women's textiles, hats, superior quality leather bags, delicious toiletries by Neal's Yard, Green people, L'Occitane, Burt's Bees and a fantastic selection of handmade contemporary jewellery with a special emphasis on diamond and gold wedding and engagements rings by Stephen Tyler and Dower & Hall?

Elsewhere in the building you will find rooms of carefully chosen products that are sure to

delight. A light and airy room displays kitchenware by Cath Kidston, Emma Bridgewater ceramics and Linum Textiles with accessories ranging from the 1950s styles to retro kitchen utensils, tea towels, aprons and tablecloths. Venture further and you will discover a boudoir room, a real treat for any gentleman wondering what to buy his lady. For those special occasions, there is also a room devoted to the best in handmade and everyday cards and wrapping paper.

Last, but definitely not least, is something for the children. One whole room of fabulous toys awaits exploration. John Crane, Brio, puzzles, games, baby gifts and the sensational Groovy Girl range of dolls and accessories. The stock is constantly changing and the list of products endless. No matter how many times you look in on this splendid place, you will always find that browsing is rewarded with something new, original or unusual as a personal treat or a gift for a friend. When visiting Pembrokeshire, a trip to the Golden Sheaf Gallery is simply unmissable.

 historic building   museum   historic site   scenic attraction   flora and fauna was burnt down by Norsemen in 994. **Narberth Castle**, in the southern part of the town, is one successor to the original fortification here; built in the 11th century, it was destroyed by the Welsh in 1115. Today, only a few fragments still stand of the castle rebuilt in 1264 by Sir Andrew Perrot and dismantled following the Civil War.

The **Narberth Museum** (formerly the Wilson Museum) has displays and exhibits on the social history of the town. It was founded in 1982 when Desmond Wilson, managing director of a local wine merchants, donated the building, a former bonded store.

PLAS FARMHOUSE B&B

Church Street, Narberth, Pembrokeshire SA67 7BH
Tel: 01834 869089
e-mail: julie@plasfarmhouse.narberth.co.uk

The picturesque **Plas Farmhouse B&B** sits next to the parish church in Narberth, and has been tastefully refurbished to create some of the best B&B accommodation in Pembrokeshire. There are two bedrooms, one en-suite and one with private bathroom, both are comfortable and inviting, having been decorated and furnished to an extremely high standard. Full farmhouse breakfasts are served each morning, or something lighter if required, with most of the produce being organic and sourced locally. It's the ideal place to stay.

SUSIE'S SHEEPSKIN BOOTS

Wild and Woolly Workshop, Spring Gardens, Narberth,
Pembrokeshire SA67 7BT
Tel: 01834 861047
e-mail: info@susiesheepskinboots.co.uk
website: www.susiesheepskinboots.co.uk

Make a fashion statement in Pembrokeshire! Buy a pair of **Susie's Sheepskin Boots**, and be ahead of the game! These superbly hand-crafted boots are made in the county by Susie Lincoln and her dedicated staff, and had their origins in the Australian surfing community, where they are known as ugg boots. They are highly fashionable, while at the same time being warm and cosy, and have proved to be a real hit in Pembrokeshire, where young and old have discovered the benefits of chic, modern style coupled with comfort and durability. As Susie herself says, cherish your feet and let them breathe properly!

The company was established 25 years ago and is one of the county's most successful cottage industries. You can buy from stock or you can have them made to measure. Even if you can't visit Narberth, all you have to do is send an outline of your feet and Susie will do the rest! There are many styles, from the original boots to mules and slippers, with a wide range of colours to choose from. You can give them a ring, visit the workshop by appointment and buy some then and there or order from a brochure or the company's website. Prices always reflect Susie's commitment to value for money and you get outstanding personal service.

THE NARBERTH GALLERY & THE GALLERY COFFEE SHOP & BISTRO

11-13 Market Square, Narberth, Pembrokeshire SA67 8AU

Situated on the Original Town Square, adjacent to Town Memorial you will find two complementary businesses, sharing a common entrance to a building steeped in history.

THE NARBERTH GALLERY

Tel: 01834 869955
wwebsite: ww.thenarberthgallery.co.uk

The **Narberth Gallery** is owned and managed by accomplished painter Desmond Leeke. For 20 years he has lived and worked with the landscape and the people of Pembrokeshire, which inspire him when he picks up his brushes and paints. He works in various styles, though each painting shines through with his commitment to his art and craft. But it is not only his own work that is shown

in the gallery, local artists exhibit there as well, each one working in their own style, be it figurative or something more challenging. There are superb paintings of coastal Pembrokeshire, the superb etchings of David Beattie who has 30 years experience, together with numerous other well known artists of Pembrokeshire and beyond.

The gallery also sells exquisite contemporary jewellery crafted locally and on the premises by such craftspeople as Phillipa Lawrence and Sarah Lloyd Morris. There are bracelets, necklaces, earrings, and many of the craftspeople undertake commissions. Des will also frame any work purchased in house or general framing undertaken. And that's not all - you can see and appreciate superb examples of stained glass work, wood turning and felt work, all created locally and all at prices that won't break the bank! Des himself accepts commissions for portraits, and pricing starts from £100.

THE GALLERY COFFEE SHOP & FAMILY BISTRO

Tel: 01834 869111

Deceptive from the front is the Coffee Shop selling fairtrade coffees, homemade breads, cakes and pastries, light lunches and snacks. Recently refurbished to a high contemporary standard the rear of the building houses:

- 50 seater restaurant. The bistro serves traditional affordable homemade meals.
- Early Bird meal deals are available between 6 & 7pm.
- A la carte menu is available evenings from 7pm.
- Group bookings and parties are welcome.
- Set Menu's and Buffets.
- Organic menu available to compliment main menu.
- Most meals gluten free and all allergy or dietary requirements catered for.
- Childrens menu including healthy eating options available.
- Coffee Shop & Restaurant fully licensed and wide selection of wines & spirits available.
- Fresh & local produce used whenever possible.
- Appreciate local artwork extensively displayed on the walls whilst you enjoy your meal.

Hours of opening vary seasonally so it is advisable to phone for information.

Why not take the time to visit this unique corner of Narberth, browse through the multi levelled Gallery and then relax with a coffee or a glass of wine before taking a walk to the recently restored Narberth Castle.

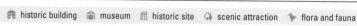

🏛 historic building   🏛 museum   🏛 historic site   ⌘ scenic attraction   🌿 flora and fauna

CONTEMPORARY JEWELLERY BY SARA LLOYD-MORRIS

14 Market Square, Narberth, Pembrokeshire SA67 7AU
Tel: 0845 634 4057
e-mail: sara@saralloyd-morris.co.uk
website: www.saralloyd-morris.co.uk

Hidden away in Narberth, between the sea and Preseli hills of Pembrokeshire, overlooking her tropical courtyard garden, you will find Sara Lloyd-Morris working in her studio. Inspired by her travels and her seascape surroundings, Sara designs and makes her own distinctive style of jewellery, full of fun and colour.

Taking a piece of silver or gold, Sara skillfully brings it to life giving it form and texture, adding colour in a variety of ways, then giving it those special touches such as a gold highlight, a freshwater pearl, a beautiful semi-precious stone or foundling.

When you buy Sara's distinctive jewellery you are unlikely to see anyone wearing a similar design, but you are likely to be asked where you got yours from. Whether you're looking for a gift, something to wear every day, or for a special occasion, jewellery by Sara Lloyd-Morris will make you look and feel great.

A changing range of contemporary jewellery is available on her website, along with a list of galleries stocking her work, or you can visit her studio which is open by appointment.

HOTEL PLAS HYFRYD

Moorfield Road, Narberth, Pembrokeshire SA67 7AB
Tel: 01834 869006
e-mail: info@plashyfrydhotel.com   website: www.plashyfrydhotel.com

At **Hotel Plas Hyfryd** they are justly proud of the three stars from the Wales Tourist Board. The hotel was once a rectory, and is an imposing, well proportioned building that gives great views out over the village green of this delightful village, which sits only a short distance from the popular seaside resorts of Tenby and Saundersfoot.

It is a family owned hotel, where friendliness, informality and a great atmosphere combines with what people today expect of an inn or hotel - value-for-money, great standards of service and quiet efficiency. There are 14 superb no-smoking rooms, which include family suites, twins and doubles. All are fully en suite, and all extremely comfortable and furnished and decorated to a high standard. Children are most welcome, and they can supply travel cots should you need them. Each room has a colour TV and hospitality tray.

Why not enjoy a quiet drink in the spacious yet inviting lounge bar? It is extremely comfortable, selling a great range of drinks. The à la carte menu in the restaurant features many fine dishes, prepared with flare and imagination by the resident chef. All the produce is sourced locally wherever possible, and it is open to non-residents. There is also a function suite that has all the modern facilities you'll ever need. Business conferences, seminars, wedding receptions, parties and anniversaries can be accommodated here. The owners are proud of their hotel, and want to invite you to sample the traditional Welsh hospitality, which is second to none.

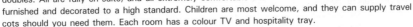

🎭 stories and anecdotes   🦅 famous people   🎨 art and craft   🎵 entertainment and sport   🚶 walks

THE RHOS
3½ miles SE of Haverfordwest off the A40

🏛 Picton Castle   🌱 Woodland Garden

East of the Cleddau toll bridge lies the tidal estuary formed by the confluence of the Western and Eastern Cleddau rivers, into which also flow the Rivers Cresswell and Carew. Beside the river banks are some of the Pembrokeshire Coast National Park's most beautiful treasures. However, this area is so often overlooked by visitors that is has become known as the Secret Waterway.

The Rhos, the only village in the ancient parish of Slebach, overlooks the Eastern Cleddau and here, close to the river, lies **Picton Castle**, the historic home of the Philipps family, still lived in by the direct descendants of Sir John Wogan, who had the castle built in the 13th century. The family, over the centuries, has had its ups and downs. They were awarded their coat-of-arms by Richard the Lionheart following their exploits during the Crusades, and they supported Parliament during the Civil War. In the 18th century, they took on prominent roles in the economic, educational and social life of Wales. Although the principal rooms were remodelled in the mid 18th century, some medieval features remain and, in the 1790s, the 1st Lord Milford added the wing that now includes the superb dining room and drawing room.

The castle is also home to an art gallery with a permanent exhibition of paintings by Graham Sutherland. Outside, the gardens are

---

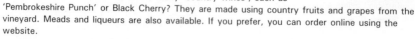

🏛 historic building   🏛 museum   🏛 historic site   ⌀ scenic attraction   🌱 flora and fauna

equally impressive and include a walled garden with fish pond, rosebeds, culinary and medicinal herbs and herbaceous borders. In the extensive **Woodland Garden** there is a fine collection of woodland shrubs in among the ancient oaks, beeches, redwoods and other mature trees.

MARTLETWY
6 miles SE of Haverfordwest off the A4075

🏛 Parish Church of St Marcellus

🌿 Cwm Deri Vineyard

Cwm Deri Vineyard, to the south of Martletwy and set in the Valley of the Oaks, is the ideal place to see vines growing from spring through to the autumn harvest. At the vineyard shop not only can visitors purchase estate grown vintage wines but also fruit

wines and liqueurs produced here. Wine tastings, of course, are always very popular and, for younger members of the family, the vineyard is home to some rescued donkeys plus a teddy bears' hideaway. The **Parish Church of St Marcellus** dates from a rebuilding of 1848 - 1850, though the chancel arch is thought to be 13th century and the south porch to be 16th century.

MILFORD HAVEN
6½ miles SW of Haverfordwest on the A40

🏛 Parish Church of St Katharine

🏛 Hubberston Priory   📷 Milford Haven Museum

📷 Kaleidoscope Discovery Centre

As well as being the name of the town, Milford Haven is also the name of the huge

---

THE CASTLE

Little Haven, Pembrokeshire SA62 3UF
Tel: 01437 781445
e-mail: bar@castlelittlehaven.co.uk
website: www.castlelittlehaven.co.uk

Clustered round an inlet of St Bride's Bay are the picturesque cottages of Little Haven, and it is here that you will find **The Castle**, a pub that has been expanded to become so much more. Thanks to the efforts of owners Mary and Malcolm Whitewright, it also offers superb food and overnight accommodation. The interior is open plan, though there is still the Black Bar, where you can relax over a drink and meet the local people, and the lounge bar, where evening meals are served.

The whole place speaks of tradition, as the premises were first opened in 1871. The interior boasts exposed stonework, modern beams and polished, bare wooden floors. The service, the accommodation, the food and the drink, however, are most certainly up to date. There are two en suite, spacious rooms with satellite TV and tea/coffee making facilities. Room one has twin beds, while room two has a double bed and a view out over the beach.

The food is outstanding, and, of course, features many fine seafood dishes, such as monkfish wrapped in bacon and fillet of local wild sea bass. Plus you can order rack of Welsh lamb, chicken schnitzel, even fish and chips, and other dishes both traditional and imaginative. All the produce used in the kitchen is sourced locally wherever possible.

The Castle makes the perfect base for a quiet seaside holiday, or you can stop overnight as you explore this wonderful part of Wales. You'll be made more than welcome.

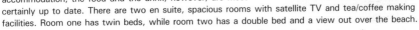

🎭 stories and anecdotes   👤 famous people   🎨 art and craft   🎵 entertainment and sport   🚶 walks

natural harbour here. Described by Nelson as "the finest port in Christendom", the harbour offers some of the best shelter in the world to large ships, as it is some ten miles long by up to two miles broad. Norsemen used the harbour, as did both Henry II and King John, who set sail from here to conquer Ireland. However, it was Sir William Hamilton (husband of Lord Nelson's Lady Emma) who, having inherited two nearby manors, saw the potential of the haven as a major harbour. Hamilton was in Naples as an Envoy Extraordinary, so he appointed his nephew RF Greville to establish the town around the harbour. Greville contracted a Frenchman, J-L Barrallier, to lay out the town and dockyard in a square pattern that can still be seen today Although the docks, completed in 1888, failed to attract the hoped for larger ships, the Neyland trawler fleet moved here and, by the beginning of the 20th century, Milford Haven had become one of the country's leading fishing ports. During both World Wars, the Haven was busy with Atlantic convoys but after 1945 there was a decline and trawling also began to disappear. However, since the 1960s Milford Haven has developed as a major oil port and is still used by the leading oil companies.

Aptly housed in a former whale oil warehouse that dates from 1797, the **Milford Haven Museum** at the Old Custom House has a range of displays that follow the fortunes of the town and dockyard including hands-on exhibits tracing the town's history from a Quaker whaling port to a premier oil terminal. A seal hospital is located on the quayside opposite the museum. The tomb of Sir William Hamilton can be seen in the graveyard of the **Parish Church of St Katharine** (on which work started in 1802),

while inside the church are a bible and prayer book presented by Lord Nelson. **Hubberston Priory** once stood to the west of the town. It was founded in 1170 as a Benedictine house, but was dissolved by Henry VIII. Only scant remains are left.

SANDY HAVEN
8 miles W of Haverfordwest off the B4327

The sheltered creek in this lovely village has been described as truly idyllic and, particularly at low tide in the spring and autumn, many birds can be seen feeding here. The picturesque banks of the creek are heavily clad with trees and a path from the village provides walkers with an excellent view of the entrance to Milford Haven harbour.

ST ISHMAEL'S
9 miles SW of Haverfordwest off the B4327

🏯 Parish Church of St Ishmael   🏛 Long Stone

This small village, known locally as 'Tish', sits on the Marloes and Dale Peninsula and is named after a colleague of the 6th century St Teilo. Close by is evidence of early inhabitants of the area as, on the village outskirts, lies a motte that is Norman if not earlier while, just half a mile away, is the **Long Stone**, the tallest standing stone in the Pembrokeshire Coast National Park. During the 14th century, Sir Rhys ap Thomas of Carew Castle is said to have promised Richard III that if Henry Tudor passed through Pembroke it would be by riding over his body. When Henry landed at Mill Bay, to salve his conscience, Sir Rhys lay under Mullock Bridge (between St Ishmael's and Marloes) as Henry rode over the river and then Sir Rhys rode quickly to Carew Castle to welcome Henry.

The **Parish Church of St Ishmael**, hidden in Monk Valley is very picturesque. It has a

Marloes Sands and Gateholm Island

MARLOES
11 miles SW of Haverfordwest off the B4327

Wooltrack Point Gateholm Island

Skomer Island Skokholm Island

This inland village, on the road to **Wooltack Point**, has a sandy bay to the southwest with **Gateholm Island** at its western extremity. Only a true island at high tide, the name comes from the Norse for Goat Island and there are traces here of a possible monastic settlement.

Right up until the end of the 19th century the ancient custom of hunting the wren, which was supposed to embody the evils of winter, was followed throughout Wales. In Pembrokeshire, the hunting took place on Twelfth Night and the captured bird would be placed in a carved and beribboned 'wren house' and paraded around the village by men singing of the hunt. A particularly fine example of a wren house from Marloes can be found in the Welsh Folk Museum, at St Fagans, near Cardiff.

Close by, at Martin's Haven, boats leave for **Skomer Island** and **Skokholm Island**. Skomer Island National Nature Reserve and Skokholm and Grassholm provide some of the best and most spectacular birdwatching anywhere in Britain.

double bellcote and was built in Victorian times on a site that is much older. There is a walk from the church to Monk Haven beach.

DALE
11 miles SW of Haverfordwest off the B4327

Dale Study Centre St Ann's Head

A delightful little sailing and watersports centre, Dale lays claim to being one of the windiest places in Britain, as gusts have been known to exceed 100 miles an hour. However, on the other side of the climatic coin, Dale is also one of the sunniest places in the country with an annual average of 1,800 hours a year - or five hours a day! To the south of the village, on the southern tip of the peninsula, is **St Ann's Head**, where a lighthouse and coastguard station keep a close watch over the dangerous rocky shores at the entrance to Milford Haven. The **Dale Study Centre** at Dale Fort is an excellent place to learn about the ecology and wildlife of the local coastline.

NOLTON HAVEN
6½ miles W of Haverfordwest off the A487

The village sits at around the centre of St Brides Bay and the coastline here has steep, undulating cliffs and sandy beaches which have remained completely unspoilt despite

THE OLD CROSS SAWS INN

109 Main Street, Pembroke,
Pembrokeshire SA71 4DB
Tel: 01646 682475
Fax: 01646 688041
e-mail: oldcrosssawsinn@btconnect.com
web: www.victorrees.btconnect.com

When widely-travelled Victor Rees bought the **Old Cross Saws Inn** in 2001 he gave it a new lease of life. He has made it one of the most sociable and convivial places for miles around, a pleasure to visit whether it's for a drink, a meal or an overnight stay. Behind a cheerful and inviting red facade, the 16th century inn has a single bar that runs the length of the building. Two real ales are always on tap, along with specials announced on a blackboard outside, and a very wide selection of other draught and bottled beers, wines and spirits. In the dining area, the food served ranges from sandwiches and light snacks to a full à la carte menu featuring pub classics such as steaks and sizzling platters. Victor is very much a hands-on proprietor, being involved with all the inn's many activities; there's something going on most nights of the week, with live music on Saturday, regular jazz and quiz nights, and a number of events that help to raise money for charity. Pool is particularly popular here, and both ladies' and gentlemen's teams compete in the local leagues. The historic town of Pembroke has much to attract the visitor, including the well-preserved medieval town walls and the magnificent castle, one of

Britain's most imposing medieval monuments. A few days are needed to see all the sights, and the Old Cross Saws Inn makes an ideal base for exploring. The inn has seven neat, practical letting bedrooms for bed & breakfast, including a family room; all the rooms have en suite or private bathrooms, TV and tea/coffee trays. The inn has a beer garden with tables and chairs set out on the decking and a barbecue for the summer evenings.

On the approach to Pembroke, take the A4075 to the one-way system round the town. The Old Cross Saws Inn is on the right just before the road rejoins the A4075.

🏛 historic building   🏛 museum   🏛 historic site   ♨ scenic attraction   🌿 flora and fauna being within easy reach of Haverfordwest and Milford Haven. As part of the Pembrokeshire Coast National Park, the coastline here is rich in outstanding natural beauty with a wide variety of natural amenities available to the holidaymaker including various short and longer distance footpaths from where an abundance of wildlife, sea birds and wild flowers can be seen. This area is a Mecca for walkers, bird watchers, surfers, swimmers and sailors.

ROCH
5½ miles W of Haverfordwest off the A487

🏰 Roch Castle   📖 Adam de la Roche

Found on a rocky outcrop overlooking the village and the surrounding plain, are the remains of **Roch Castle**, which was originally built in the 13th century by the feudal Lord of Roch, **Adam de la Roche**. A local story tells that de la Roche was told by a witch that he would be killed by a snake, but that if he could pass a year in safety, then he need never fear the prophecy. Accordingly, de la Roche had the castle built in such a way as to be out of reach of any snake and so the fortress was constructed on this particularly well-defended site. His year free from snakes began and de la Roche moved into the top floor of the castle and remained there, in constant fear, for a year. The very last night of his self-enforced imprisonment was bitterly cold and someone sent a basket of firewood to the castle to help Adam pass the night in comfort. The basket was taken to his room and, as de la Roche was putting the logs on the fire, an adder crawled out from among the logs and bit him. The next morning, Adam de la Roche was found dead in front of his hearth.

Pembroke

🏰 Pembroke Castle   🏛 Museum of the Home

🏰 Parish Church of St Nicholas and St John

🏰 Monkton Priory

This historic town, with its long and unbroken line of well-preserved medieval town walls, is dominated by the mighty fortress of **Pembroke Castle**. It was founded in the 11th century by the Montgomerys, who established the first timber castle on a rocky crag above the River Cleddau. The later stone castle was built between 1189 and 1225. In 1457 Henry VII was born in the castle.

Found opposite the castle, at Westgate Hill, is the charming **Museum of the Home,** which houses a unique collection of household utensils, appliances and toys and games that span three centuries. Also on display are Welsh costumes from the 19th century.

Just half a mile from the castle, and across Monkton Pill, stood **Monkton Priory**, founded in 1098 by Arnulf de Montgomery for Benedictine monks. It was given to St Albans in

Pembroke Castle

🎭 stories and anecdotes   🦅 famous people   🎨 art and craft   ✒ entertainment and sport   🚶 walks

THE CORNSTORE

Quayside Café and Interior Furnishings
North Quay, Pembroke,
Pembrokeshire SA71 4NU
Tel; 01646 684290
e-mail; info@vintage-interiors.net
website: www.vintage-interiors.net

Standing in the shadow of Pembroke Castle on the North Quay of the town, **The Cornstore** is an imposing three storey building, which is a physical reminder of the important maritime history of the town. It has recently won a national award for the quality of its' renovation, being a truly historic Eighteenth Century property built upon the foundations of much earlier commercial buildings. Indeed commerce has been conducted upon this site for many hundreds of years. Large schooners would moor at the quayside using the mooring rings set in the walls of the building to exchange cargo for onward transport to Ireland and England.

Today The Cornstore is still a commercial centre featuring a quayside café and innovative accessories for you and your home. Here at The Cornstore we have a simple philosophy, we want to supply superbly designed and made objects for the home, and our customers tell us we have succeeded admirably. By designing and commissioning those items directly from our makers we can maintain high quality and reasonable price. So today instead of coming to The Cornstore to purchase Coal, Ale, Grain or Potatoes our customers visit us for inspiration and purchase solid wood, full-hide leather furniture, ceramics, textiles, lighting, jewellery, handbags, images and accessories. Where possible we stock products from local artists which change every season.

The Quayside Café is famed locally for its' Coffee, home cooked Light Lunches and snacks. Our Cakes and Desserts are simply 'TO DIE FOR' We use locally sourced ingredients for the daily changing menu which is prepared on the premises. We are proud to have been awarded the Pembrokeshire Produce Mark for the quality of our menu which you can enjoy inside our Café or sit on the quayside to enjoy the enviable views of the Castle as you dine.

The Cornstore is open Monday – Saturday 10.00 am until 5.00 p.m. and we look forward to offering you something a little different!

🏠 historic building   🏛 museum   🏛 historic site   ⌬ scenic attraction   🌿 flora and fauna

1473. The priory church, now the **Parish Church of St Nicholas and St John**, with its long narrow barrel-vaulted nave and monastic chancel, was rearranged in the 14th century and, after lying in ruins for many years, was restored again in the late 19th century.

Around Pembroke

UPTON
3 miles NE of Pembroke off the A477

🌿 Upton Castle Gardens

Set in a secluded valley running down to the River Carew, **Upton Castle Gardens** have three raised formal terraces that drop down from the medieval castle. Along with the rose gardens and herbaceous borders, there are 40 acres of wooded grounds containing some 250 species of trees and shrubs. There's also a medieval chapel from which the walled garden can be seen.

CAREW
4 miles E of Pembroke on the A4075

🏰 Carew Castle

🏰 Carew Cheritan Control Tower

🏚 Carew Tidal Mill   🎞 Celtic Cross

Located on the shores of the tidal mill pond, **Carew Castle** is one of the few such buildings to display the development from Norman fortification (it was built between 1280 and 1310) to Elizabethan manor house. However, this site is much older, as archaeological excavations have found remains which go back some 2,000 years. Various remarkable individuals have connections with the castle, and the Great Tournament held here in 1507 was attended by 600 nobles. The castle also gives an insight into the lives of servants, craftsmen, priests and common

soldiers of the time. During the summer months a wide variety of events is held in the castle grounds, including drama, school projects, holiday activities, battle re-enactments, country fairs and concerts.

Here, too, can be seen one of only three restored tidal mills in Britain. **Carew Tidal Mill** still retains its original machinery. The Story of Milling exhibition traces the history of milling through the ages and the mill's role in the local community. While touring this lovely four-storey building, visitors are given explanations of each stage of the milling process. As well as the castle and the mill, the Carew site also incorporates a causeway, a medieval bridge and an 11th century **Celtic Cross** that is one of the best examples of its kind in Wales.

The **Carew Cheritan Control Tower** is on a World War II airfield near the village, and

Carew Castle and Celtic Cross

has been restored by a group of enthusiasts. It is sometimes open to the public in summer, especially at weekends.

MANORBIER

5½ miles SE of Pembroke off the A4139

🏛 Manorbier Castle

Manorbier is charmingly situated at the head of a valley that reaches down to the shore in a beautiful bay with a safe bathing beach. The village's name is thought to have been derived from Maenor Pyr (Manor of Pyr) and Pyr is believed to have been the first Celtic abbot of Caldey who lived in the 5th century. Overlooking the bay of the same name, **Manorbier Castle** was founded by Odo de Barri in 1095 when he built a wooden hall within a defensive structure. However, it was his son William who began building the stone fortification in the early 12th century.

Famous for being the birthplace, in 1146, of

Giraldus Cambrenses (Gerald of Wales), a monk and chronicler who wrote the first account of life in medieval Wales, the castle was described by him as being "the pleasantest spot in Wales" (see also St Davids and Llanwnda).

Today, life size wax figures placed at various points, including the impressive great hall, the turrets and the chapel, bring the history of this ancient building to life as atmospheric music captures the castle's spirit. The castle gardens were laid out by J R Cobb in the late 19th century and there is also a late Victorian cottage with appropriate herbaceous borders lining the castle walls.

LAMPHEY BISHOP'S PALACE

1½ miles SE of Pembroke on the A4139

🏛 Bishop's Palace

🏛 Parish Church of St Faith and St Tyfai

Just northwest of the village, in the 13th century, the medieval bishops of St David's

BREWERY INN

Cosheston, Pembrokeshire SA72 4UD
Tel: 01646 686678

Cosheston is an attractive village lying to the northeast of Pembroke, and it is here that you will find the **Brewery Inn**, a picturesque old coaching inn that dates back 400 years. Some people claim that it is the most picturesque pub in all of the county, and anyone who sees it usually agrees! But it is not only extremely pretty, it offers the very best in food, drink and convivial company, as it is a popular place with locals and visitors alike. The interior is equally as appealing, with its warm and welcoming bar and restaurant, its natural slate floor, exposed stone walls and wooden bench type seating. There is a comfortable 'snug' area where you can really relax and unwind after a hard day sightseeing!

The restaurant is noted for its good food, and uses fresh local produce wherever possible in its dishes, including locally caught fish and Welsh black beef. Plus the friendly bar serves real ales and a great range of beers, wines, spirits and soft drinks.

The Brewery Inn boasts five self-catering apartments contained within the old brewery building itself, and they are fully equipped so that families can have a comfortable holiday in an area that is rich in history and heritage. One apartment sleeps six, and is fully accessible for the disabled.

🏛 historic building   🏛 museum   🏛 historic site   🏛 scenic attraction   🌿 flora and fauna built the magnificent **Bishop's Palace** as a retreat from the affairs of Church and State. Though improved over a period of 200 years, the major building work was undertaken by the dynamic Bishop Henry de Gower between 1328 and 1347 and he was responsible for the splendid great hall. Although now in ruins, this is a peaceful and tranquil site where successive bishops were able to live the life of country gentlemen among the estate's orchards, vegetable gardens and rolling parkland. The **Parish Church oif St Faith and St Tyfai** has a fine late 14th/early 15th century tower and one of the best Norman fonts in the county.

HODGEASTON

3 miles E of Pembroke on the B4584

🏛 Parish Church of Hodgeston

The **Parish Church of Hodgeston** has a 14th century chancel built by Bishop Gower of St Davids and a fine Norman font. Its tower is early medieval, and close to the chancel are the stairs to a former rood loft. It is one of the few churches in Wales without a dedication to a saint (though it had at one time), and is owned by the Friends of Friendless Churches.

ST GOVAN'S HEAD

5 miles S of Pembroke off the B4319

🏛 St Govan's Chapel

The cliff scenery is at its most spectacular at St Govan's Head, where the tiny, **St Govan's Chapel** huddles among the rocks almost at sea level. It is thought to have been built in the 11th century, though some experts say it may got back to the 6th century. Accessible by climbing down approximately 74 stone steps, the chapel was built on the site of a holy well that once attracted pilgrims who believed the well's waters to have miraculous healing

powers. There is a legend which says that the number of steps cannot be accurately counted, and indeed people who use them usually come up with different answers. However, there is a simple explanation. The steps have been cut irregularly, so some of them are 'half steps' which many people fail to count.

Inside is a vertical cleft in the rock which, according to legend, first opened so that St Govan could hide inside and escape his enemies. Closing behind him, the rock did not reopen until the danger had passed. Accordingly, a wish made while standing in the cleft and facing the rock will come true provided the person making the wish does not change his or her mind before turning round. Although many miracles have been credited to St Govan he remains a mysterious and little known man. Some believe him to have been a disciple of St David while others claim that he was a thief who, having miraculously found the hiding place, became a convert. St Govan is also thought by some to have been a woman named Cofen - the wife of a 5th century chief - who became a recluse.

PEMBROKE DOCK

1½ miles NW of Pembroke on the A477

Once an important naval dockyard, Pembroke Dock sits on the southern shore of the Cleddau, at the point where modern development ends and the gentler hinterland of the river system begins. At one time the town relied on its naval dockyard for employment and 263 Royal Navy vessels were built here between 1814 and its closure in 1926. Also built here were the royal yachts *Victoria and Albert I, II* and *III*.

In 1930 the site was taken over by the Royal Air Force, and became the home of Squadron

DORINA

Lower Meyrick Street, Pembroke Dock, Pembrokeshire SA72 6JD
Tel: 01646 683174
e-mail: angelina.rees@tesco.net

Owned and managed by sisters Angelina and Giovanna, **Dorina** is a shop dedicated to wearable fashion. It was once a children's fashion shop owned by the sisters' parents, and now that they have taken over they have created one of the most popular shops in the area. It caters for all sizes from 8 to 20, and carries a wide stock of outfits and fashion that are sure to please.

The exterior of the shop has recently undergone a complete renovation to give its façade a traditional feel with just a hint of modern styling. The interior is a cornucopia of clothes, and you are welcome to browse here to your heart's content.

Dresses, blouses, tops, trousers, woollens, scarves, lingerie, underwear, gloves - it's got everything for the woman who cares about fashion and about her appearance. The whole place has been well fitted out to show off its range of fashions and accessories to perfection. Gaze at the free-standing glass cases with their wonderful displays of jewellery, or their bags, purses and scarves. Admire the racks full of desirable fashion items. Take your time - there's no hurry, and both Angelina and Giovanna are always on hand to offer help and advice about your choices. In addition, they offer a bra fitting service, as they are both qualified to fit and measure.

So if you're in Pembroke Dock, you can't afford to miss this exciting, colourful shop, where the service is always friendly and the prices always reasonable.

PEMBROKESHIRE STAINED GLASS LTD

Units 11 & 12, Pier Road, Hobbs Point, Pembroke Dock,
Pembrokeshire SA72 6TR
Tel: 01646 612333
e-mail: cbale@clara.co.uk

Discover the beauty of stained glass at **Pembrokeshire Stained Glass Ltd**, situated at Hobbs Point in Pembroke Dock, close to the town of Pembroke itself. This ancient and time consuming craft is being carried out here at their workshops. Using traditional methods to produce individual works of art, they can create leaded lights for doors, windows and conservatories, mirrors and sun catchers.

Repairs and restoration of stained glass windows, leaded lights and all aspects of ecclesiastical are undertaken by experienced craftsmen. The company has carried out many projects within Wales, including Castlemartin, Ferryside and a spectacular, complete rose window in Porthcawl.

Treat yourself to a small souvenir of your visit to Wales by taking away a special piece of leaded glass. You can choose from a selection of handcrafted mirrors and suncatchers available at the workshop, or be inspired and commission a larger piece of work.

Call in and see for yourself, but to avoid any disappointment, please phone before you visit to confirm opening times. (Credit card facilities are unavailable).

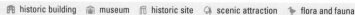

🏚 historic building   🏛 museum   🏛 historic site   🔱 scenic attraction   🌿 flora and fauna

261

210, which consisted of flying boats. It grew to become the largest flying boat base in the world, its most famous aircraft being the Short Sunderland. It supported airt crews from not only the UK, but Canada, Australia and New Zealand. So important was the base that it was continually bombed in 1940, with over 200 houses in thr town being destroyed. The air base closed in 1959.

BOSHERSTON
4½ miles SW of Pembroke off the B4319

🏛 Parish Church of St Michael and All Angels

🌱 Stackpole Gardens

The **Parish Church of St Michael and All Angels** dates from the 13th century and later, and replaced an even earlier church that stood on the site. The font is medieval, and there is a 14th century tomb in the south transept, thought to be that of a Duchess of Buckingham. There is an old preaching cross in the churchyard. The building was restored in 1855 by the then Earl of Cawder, who owned the nearby Stackpole estate. To the east of the village and occupying part of estate, are **Stackpole Gardens**, which were landscaped in the 18th century. Romantic in style and containing some interesting and well-engineered water features, including an eight arched bridge, these are intriguing gardens to explore and, although the original manor house has gone, the 19th century terraces, woodland garden and summer house remain, along with a grotto, an ice house and three walled gardens.

ART MATTERS GALLERY
South Parade, Tenby, Pembrokeshire SA70 7DG
Tel: 01834 843375
e-mail: info@artmatters.org.uk   website: www.artmatters.org.uk
Partners: Margaret Welsh and John Faulkner

This extensive gallery shows original art by some of the best Welsh and British artists in a uniquely relaxed and welcoming environment. Exhibitions change every four weeks or so in the large ground floor space whilst the five upstairs rooms display a rotation of work by regular exhibitors. There are hundreds of paintings on show at any time, ensuring a wide choice of styles from traditional watercolours and oils to abstracts, in every medium and a huge range of subject matter. Art Matters Gallery was established in 2001 and has become best-known for paintings, wood-

engravings and etchings but also shows a variety of sculpture, ceramics and wood.

With comfortable sofas, and tea and coffee always available, the gallery offers a warm welcome to all. It is open all year from mid-February to early January, from 10am to 5pm daily, except Wednesdays (and Sundays November to Easter).

Art Matters Gallery is situated in Tenby town centre opposite the medieval town walls and next to the fire station. All the work on show can be viewed on the gallery website which is updated frequently.

🎦 stories and anecdotes   🐦 famous people   🖌 art and craft   📖 entertainment and sport   🚶 walks

JAGO

Athol House, Tudor Square, Tenby, Pembrokeshire SA70 7AJ
Tel: 01834 842674
e-mail: jaogokg@onetel.com

If it's style you're after when in Tenby, then look no further that **Jago**, which sits right in the heart of the town, and attracts not just residents and tourists, but people from all over the area. In fact, it has the reputation of being one of the most popular shops in town - one that has made Tenby what it is today - one of the best holiday resorts in the United Kingdom! You know as soon as you see the shop's distinguished and attractive blue and white exterior and its fabulous window displays that it stocks stylish, chic fashions that are founded in tradition, great workmanship and value for money, plus some of the best designed and colourful kitchenware available.

The shop has been in the same family for over 20 years, and is run by Kate Davies and her attentive staff, who are anxious to offer you a warm Welsh welcome to their shop. The interior is as delightful as the exterior, full of warm, inviting colours, attractive textures and intriguing fashions. If it's a gent's pullover you are after then look no further. If it's jewellery that makes a certain statement, then the shop has it too. If you are looking for a gift for a newly-born child, then you've come to the right place. And if you want to find colourful and practical gifts for the kitchen, then this is the place for you as well!

Downstairs there is an eclectic mix of household items that are sure to please, from kitchen goods and bowls to mugs, scales, oven gloves and cooking pots. You are almost spoiled for choice, though Kate and her staff are always on hand to give all the help you need to make your choice. They are very knowledgeable about everything they have in stock, and their advice will be impartial and directed towards your own particular needs. Upstairs is a spacious and light sales area where you will find the clothing and fashion accessories. Famous brand names such as Pepe Jeans of London, Fullcircle men's and women's wear and so on can be found here. Plus there are display cabinets full of

costume jewellery such as necklaces, bracelets and earrings, and accessories such as handbags. There's even an area given over to children's clothing, playsuits, toys and stuffed toys such as teddy bears. Again, the advice and help you will get in making a purchase will be second to none.

And we're not finished yet! You can also buy toiletries, fragrances, candles and scents, all at affordable prices. This is indeed an Aladdin's cave of colour, texture and fragrance. Why not come along and browse? There is no obligation to buy, and you will receive a warm welcome from Kate and her staff.

🏠 historic building   🏛 museum   🏯 historic site   🐦 scenic attraction   🌱 flora and fauna

Tenby

- 🏛 Tenby Castle
- 🏛 Tudor Merchant's House
- 🏛 Five Arches
- 🏛 Parish Church of St Mary
- 🏛 Belgrave House
- 🏛 Tenby Museum
- 🏛 South Parade
- 🪶 Richard Recorde
- 🐟 Silent World Aquarium and Reptile Collection

Tenby's Welsh name, Dinbych y Pysgod, means "Little Fort of the Fishes" and certainly its most photographed scene is the pretty harbour with its pastel coloured Georgian houses. However, the whole place is a real delight, prompting many eulogies such as this from the artist Augustus John: 'You may travel the world over, but you will find nothing more beautiful: it is so restful, so colourful and so unspoilt.' The artist was born in Tenby at **Belgrave House**, where a collection of his works, and those of his sister Gwen, can be found. The town still retains its charming medieval character together with the crooked lanes that are enclosed within its surprisingly well-preserved 13th century town walls. On one particular stretch, **South Parade**, the walls are still at their full height and the two tiers of arrow slits are very much visible. The **Five Arches**, a fortified gateway on the walls, is perhaps the most famous feature.

Unfortunately, the same is not true for **Tenby Castle**, the scant remains of which can be found on a small headland. However, the ruins are well worth a visit for the spectacular views out across Carmarthen Bay and along the Pembrokeshire coast. A statue to Prince Albert can also be found on the headland, along with **Tenby Museum,** which was founded in 1878, and is the oldest independent museum in Wales. As well as having archaeological and historical material relating to the area, the museum has a fascinating maritime section and an impressive art gallery.

Close to the quay lies the **Tudor Merchant's House** (NT), a relic of Tenby's prosperous sea-faring days and a fine example of a comfortable townhouse of the late 15th century. Narrow and built with three storeys, the house has been furnished to recreate the atmosphere and environment in which a wealthy Tudor family would have lived. With a Flemish chimney, early floral frescoes on some of the interior walls and a small herb garden outside, there is plenty at the house to evoke the times of around 600 years ago. The large and lavish **Parish Church of St Mary** is another testament to the town's illustrious maritime past. The tower was built in the early 14th century, and

IVYBANK GUEST HOUSE

Harding Street, Tenby, Pembrokeshire SA70 7LL
Tel: 01834 842311
e-mail: steve@ivybanktenby.co.uk
website: www.ivybanktenby

The **Ivybank Guest House**, situated in a quiet residential street only five minutes from the sea front and three minutes from the town walls, is a four star establishment that offers the very best in holiday accommodation. All the fully en suite rooms are extremely comfortable and inviting, meaning that you can enjoy a superb holiday in one of the best holiday resorts in Wales. There is a residents' lounge, a table license, and is open all year round except Christmas. This is the place to stay when you're in Tenby.

Tenby

served as a place of sanctuary and a lookout point in times of trouble. The tower is topped by a small spire, which itself is over 500 years old. The whole thing is 152 feet high. The chancel is 13th century as well, and its barrel roof has over 75 carved bosses. A wall plaque commemorates the 16th century mathematician and alchemist **Richard Recorde** (1510 - 1558), who invented the 'equals' sign (=). After a distinguished career in London, he eventually died a pauper in King's Bench Prison, Southwark.

Perhaps of more interest to younger visitors to the town is the **Silent World Aquarium and Reptile Collection** housed in an attractive 19th century chapel. In these interesting, if somewhat unusual, surroundings there is a wide range of exotic fish, amphibians and invertebrates on display, as well as fish and other creatures that live around the shores of Pembrokeshire. Upstairs are the reptiles, and here visitors can see a fascinating collection

AUDREY BULL ANTIQUES & JEWELLERY

Upper Frog Street, Tenby, Pembrokeshire SA70 7JD
Tel: 01834 843114

Audrey Bull opened her first antiques shop in Cheltenham in 1956 along with her mother Blanche Beck. This shop in Tenby, **Audrey Bull Antiques**, opened in 1957, and in 1998 she opened a branch in Carmarthen.

These two delightful shops just have to be visited. They are now owned by Jane and Jonathan Bull, ably assisted by their daughter Quita, while their son Matthew manages the restoration workshop. Here you are free to browse with absolutely no obligation, while at the same time you will be given all the help and advice you need should you choose to buy an item. The owners are general antique dealers who specialise in 19th and 20th century furniture, Welsh oak pieces, silver, porcelain and jewellery, which includes antique pieces, gem-set and modern designer creations. Everything is realistically priced, so why not buy a souvenir of your trip to Wales, or a special piece that will surely be treasured down through the years?

The workshop prides itself on repairing and polishing in a way that preserves the original patination. They do not follow the fashion for making the furniture match the repair - they make the repair match the furniture. The shop is open from 9 am - 5 pm Monday to Saturday, and on Sunday during the summer months.

🏚 historic building   🏛 museum   🏛 historic site   ♧ scenic attraction   🌱 flora and fauna of snakes and lizards from around the world. Gifts for all ages, some made by local craftsmen, are on sale in the shop, where grown-ups can enjoy coffee, tea and a snack while the youngsters play with toys, draw, do a brass rubbing or try one of the quizzes. It is open all year.

Around Tenby

ST FLORENCE
4 miles W of Tenby off the B4318

🏛 Parish Church of St Florence   🏛 Flemish Chimneys

🐦 Manor House Wildlife and Leisure Park

🧀 St Florence Cheese

A small and quiet village located on the border of the National Park, St Florence is noted for its **Parish Church of St Florence**, which is

Norman. Inside the church is a memorial to Robert Ferrar, Protestant Bishop of St David's, who suffered a martyr's death in Carmarthen in 1555 at the instigation of Mary Tudor. To the northeast of the village lies **Manor House Wildlife and Leisure Park** where the original village manor house provides the perfect backdrop for the park's collection of birds, animals, fish and reptiles. Snake handling, bottle feeding and animal handling sessions all take place undercover in the Close Encounters Barn, while the wooded grounds and formal gardens are ideal places for both exploration and picnics.

Ivy Tower Farm is the home of **St Florence Cheese**, where traditional cheese is made from both cows' and goats' milk. Also here are a farm shop, meadow walk and several mazes. Up until the early 19th century, the

YERBESTON GATE FARM SHOP

Yerbeston, Pembrokeshire SA68 0NS
Tel: 01834 891637
e-mail: info@farmshopfood.co.uk
website: www.farmshopfood.co.uk

For the very best in local produce, head for the **Yerbeston Gate Farm Shop** in lovely Pembrokeshire. It is owned and run by husband and wife team Debbie and Andy Eastwood, who have been here since 2004. In that time they have built on the shop's already fine reputation, and people come from near and far to browse and buy.

The range of fresh produce is astonishing, as it the great value-for-money. The farm won the True Taste of Wales gold award in 2005/2006 for its Welsh Black beef from a herd reared on the farm, and a commended from the same organisation for its beer-fed pigs that produce succulent beer-cured gammon. It also stocks Welsh cheeses, free range eggs, locally made breads and cakes, locally made chocolate and a host of other products that are sure to set your mouth watering! The beef is traditionally hung and dry-aged, and prepared on the premises. Plus the shop is licensed, and you can buy from a fine range of Welsh ales and meads, whiskies, wines and liqueurs. Why not buy mail order via the shop's website? Everything will arrive at your door especially packed to seal in the freshness and flavour.

The farm shop is open seven days a week from April to September, and closed on Monday during the winter months. Opening times are 9am to 6pm Monday to Saturday and 9am to 12 noon on Sunday. It can be found about two miles south of Oakwood on the A4075 just past the Yerbeston/Jeffreyston crossroads.

🎞 stories and anecdotes   🦜 famous people   🎨 art and craft   🎭 entertainment and sport   🏃 walks

River Ritec was tidal as far as the village at high tide, and it had a small port. You can still see the stone where the boats tied up. The so-called **Flemish Chimneys** attached to some 16th and 17th century cottages in the village are reminders of the Flemish immigrants to the area, though in truth they predate their coming.

SAUNDERSFOOT
2½ miles NE of Tenby on the B4316

🌿 Stammers Gardens

This picture postcard fishing village is centred around its harbour which, during the summer months, is packed with colourful pleasure craft. The harbour was constructed in the 1820s primarily for the export of anthracite, which was mined a short distance away then brought to the quay by tramway. Today,

however, the industry has all but ceased and this resort, which has an attractive sandy beach, is probably one of the busiest watersports centres in South Wales. In the heart of the resort is a lovely surprise in the shape of **Stammers Gardens**, eight carefully developed acres with shrubberies, ponds, woodland and a bog garden.

AMROTH
4½ miles NE of Tenby off the A477

🌿 Colby Woodland Garden

Lying at the south eastern most point of the Pembrokeshire Coast National Park, this quiet village has a lovely beach overlooking Carmarthen Bay. As well as the delightful surroundings, the village is home to the enchanting **Colby Woodland Garden**, an

---

BEGELLY ARMS HOTEL

New Road, Begelly, Kilgetty, Pembrokeshire SA68 0YF
Tel: 01834 813285 e-mail:begelly.arms@btconnect.com
website: www.begellyarms.co.uk

The **Begelly Arms Hotel** is the perfect base from which to explore Pembrokeshire, in southwest Wales. It sits on the A478 north of Tenby, and offers the very best in Welsh hospitality. It has 24 extremely comfortable rooms on offer in a variety of sizes - double, twin and single - all with en suite shower and WC. One room is disabled friendly, and there is also a honeymoon suite with jacuzzi and a wonderful view out towards Begelly Church.

The hotel wants to put the comfort and convenience of the guest at the top of its priorities, and is proud of its part-conservatory restaurant, which has a coveted accreditation from *Taste of Wales*. Here you will find excellent food, all prepared on the premises by the hotel chefs from fine, fresh, local produce wherever possible. Meals are served throughout the day and in the evenings, when fine dining is to the fore. There is a carvery each evening and at Sunday and Wednesday lunch. Choose from two Welsh meats, freshly carved from the joint, and a selection of potatoes and locally grown vegetables. Lighter lunches and snacks are also available. All the meals represent amazing value for money, and are so popular that you are well advised to book in the evening and Sunday lunchtime.

The bar and lounge bar serve a great range of beers, wines and spirits. Relax over a drink or two as you plan your next day's outing, or mull over the places you visited that day. A stay at the Begelly Arms hotel is an enjoyable experience not to be missed, as a warm welcome always awaits you.

🏛 historic building   🏛 museum   🏛 historic site   🗿 scenic attraction   🌿 flora and fauna eight-acre area of woodland set round a Nash-style house in a secluded valley that is home to one of the finest collections of rhododendrons and azaleas in Wales. The carpets of bluebells follow the displays of daffodils in the spring and there is a mass of colour during the summer when the hydrangeas flower, before the garden is taken over by the rich colours of autumn. The garden is part of the National Trust's Colby Estate, which takes its name from John Colby, a 19th century industrialist.

STEPASIDE
4 miles N of Tenby off the A477

🏛 Victorian School Museum

Between 1849 and 1877 this village, set in a wooded valley, had a thriving colliery and an iron works. In 1877, the village school in Kilgetty Lane opened to provide education for the workers' children. Finally closing in 1992, the school has been reopened as the **Victorian School Museum**, and provides

today's visitors with the chance to taste 19th century school days. Sitting at 100-year-old desks with slates and pencils, visitors can relive the austere school world of over a century ago. However, the life of a Victorian school child was not only work and, outside, the playground has been recreated to match the environment where Victorian children would let off steam. Also at the museum is a display that brings the mining history of the village back to life and, along with the reconstructed mine shaft, visitors can see the hardships of the children as young as six who worked in the collieries.

CALDEY ISLAND
2½ miles S of Tenby off the A4139

🏛 Caldey Abbey 🏛 St Illtyd's Church 🏛 Old Priory

🏛 St David's Parish Church

This peaceful and tranquil island, which along with its sister island of St Margaret's, lies just a short distance off the coast of Tenby, has been the home of monks for some 1,500 years.

As well as **Caldey Abbey**, a modern working monastery that is home to a community of 20 monks of the Reformed Cistercian Order, there are the remains of a 13th century monastery which was also founded by the Cistercians. **St Illtyd's Church** (still a consecrated Roman Catholic church), along with the **Old Priory** ruins, can be visited, and a small museum on the island tells the history of this beautiful island. **St David's Parish Church** is Notrman, though some of its foundations may date back to the 7th century. There are some fine, modern stained glass windows within it.

Today's monks live their lives according to the austere Rule of St Benedict which necessitates them attending seven services a day - the first beginning at 3.15 am.

📖 stories and anecdotes   🐦 famous people   🎨 art and craft   🎭 entertainment and sport   🥾 walks

LOCATOR MAP

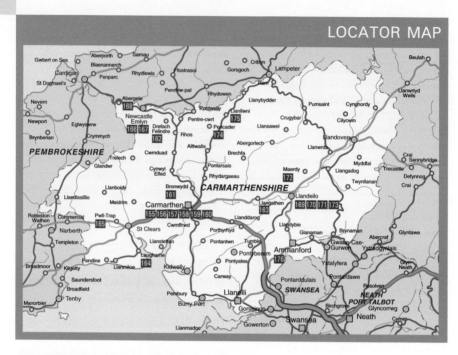

ADVERTISERS AND PLACES OF INTEREST

🏤 historic building 🏛 museum 🏚 historic site 🛝 scenic attraction 🌢 flora and fauna

8| Carmarthenshire

Carmarthenshire has a wealth of interesting places and superb countryside to enchant the visitor. There are coastal strongholds at Laugharne and Kidwelly, abbey ruins at Talley and Whitland and the famous rugby and industrial centre of Llanelli. Covering some 1,000 square miles, the county also has beautiful clean beaches, seaside towns and villages and rural idylls. A place of myths and legends, Carmarthenshire has remained essentially Welsh in most aspects.

The coastline, which is over 50 miles long, includes the award-winning Pembrey Country Park and beach, once the site of a munitions factory, and Pendine, whose long stretch of sand saw many land speed world records established. Of the seaside villages, Laugharne is certainly the most famous, due mainly to the fact that it is the place where Dylan Thomas lived for the last years of his short life. But the village does not rely solely on its literary links, as it also has one of the country's most handsome castles and offers wonderful views over the estuary of the River Taf.

Inland lies Carmarthen, the county town, whose origins lie back in Roman times. The town is a centre for the agricultural communities of West Wales, and to the east is an area associated with the legends and mysteries of Merlin the magician. Also in this part of Carmarthenshire is one the country's most recent important projects - the National Botanic Garden of Wales. Dedicated to conservation, horticulture, science and education, and boasting the largest single-span glasshouse in the world, this is one of the country's newest gardens, while close by lies Aberglasney, one of the oldest, first mentioned in 1477. Evidence of the Roman occupation of Carmarthenshire is most striking at the Dolaucothi Goldmines, to the northwest of Llandovery. At Cenarth, visitors can see salmon fishermen on the River Teifi still using the coracle, a tiny round boat whose origins are lost in the mists of time. A fascinating museum tells the story of these distinctive little craft.

Kidwelly Castle

Carmarthen

🏛 Carmarthen Castle 🏛 Guildhall 🏛 Trinity College

🏛 Parish Church of St Peter 🏛 Caer Maridunum

🏛 Carmarthen Heritage Centre 🏛 Merlin's Hill

🏛 Picton Monument 🐦 John Nash 🌿 Oriel Myrddin

One of the oldest Roman towns in Wales, Carmarthen (or Caerfyrddin in Welsh) is now the county town of Carmarthenshire and lies at the centre of the West Wales agricultural community. The name means 'fort of Myrddyin', and some people have linked this Myrddyin with Merlin the Magician. One particular story associated with the town has, thankfully, so far turned out not to be true. Carmarthen's inhabitants are eternally grateful that, when Merlin's Oak was removed during a road widening scheme, the town remained unharmed, and the prophecy, 'When Merlin's Oak shall tumble down, then shall fall Carmarthen town' was not realised. According to another tradition, the magician is said still to live in a cave on **Merlin's Hill** (Bryn Myrddin) just outside Carmarthen where he is kept in perpetual enchantment by Vivien, the lady to whom he taught all his spells.

At the site of **Caer Mari Unum** (built about AD 75), the most westerly Roman fort in Britain, the remains of the amphitheatre can still be seen, and the Roman town walls were known to have been visible in the 12th century. However, the historic old part of Carmarthen grew up around **Carmarthen Castle**, which was originally built around 1109 by Henry I. Overlooking the River Tywi, little

---

KING STREET GALLERY

30 King Street, Carmarthen SA31 1BS
Tel: 01267 220121
e-mail: gallery@kingstreetgallery.co.uk
website: www.kingstreetgallery.co.uk

The **King Street Gallery** is a cornucopia of paintings, sculpture, stained glass, ceramics and craft items such as greeting cards and turned bowls. It is situated on the two floors above an art shop called Community Crafts in the old, picturesque town of Carmarthen, and is owned and managed by the local artists and craftspeople who exhibit there. Over 23 such artists are in the collective,

There are three display galleries within the complex, one of them - the small gallery - being used to display works by visiting artists working in all media. You may be surprised and delighted with the range and quality of what is exhibited. Payment can be made by credit card, debit card, cheque or, of course, cash, and thanks to the interest-free Principality Collectorplan scheme, buyers can now buy through this unique loan scheme.

Everything on show is keenly priced while still maintaining each particular artist's unique vision, and you can choose from the traditional right through to the abstract and avant garde. Feel free to browse before making a choice, and be assured that there is always someone on hand to offer knowledgeable help and advice. A piece of artwork, or a craft piece, makes a memorable souvenir of your visit to Wales, and the King Street gallery is the ideal place to purchase it.

🏛 historic building   🏛 museum   🏛 historic site   🌿 scenic attraction   🐦 flora and fauna

remains of the castle today except the early 15th century gatehouse. The **Guildhall**, which was built in 1767 to replace the hall of 1583, is in Nott Square - named after Major General Sir William Nott, victor of the First Afghan War in the 1840s and a native of Carmarthen.

The town's Victorian Old Art College has, since 1991, been the home of **Oriel Myrddin**, a contemporary craft gallery and regional art venue. Focusing on the present and the future, the work of some of the most innovative and interesting craftspeople in Wales is displayed here and, in the retail area, there is a wide range of crafts for purchase. By contrast, housed in a new development on the banks of the River Tywi is the **Carmarthen Heritage Centre** which,

through displays, multi-media and video presentations, tells the story of the town from the time of the Roman occupation in AD 75 through to the present day.

Carmarthen is home to **Trinity College**, which, since 2005, has been part of the University of Wales. After lampeter, it is the second oldest higher education institution in the country. It was originally a teacher training college, but has now widened its curriculum.

The Ivy Bush Royal Hotel in Carmarthen has notable literary connections. A stained glass window and stone circle commemorate the 1819 Eisteddfod, when Iolo Morganwg introduced the Gorsedd (society of bards) to the Eisteddfod (see also St David's). The essayist and dramatist Sir Richard Steele

HAMILTON'S RESTAURANT

The Queen's Hotel, Queen Street, Carmarthen, Carmarthenshire SA31 1JR
Tel: 01267 235631

Adjacent to the Queens Hotel you will find one of the best restaurants in Carmarthen - **Hamilton's Restaurant**. It served superb food, and people come from miles around to sample the cuisine and have a relaxing, enjoyable time. The produce used in the kitchens is sourced locally wherever possible to ensure maximum freshness and flavour, with fish and juicy steaks being the speciality. It is open seven days a week for lunch and dinner. Accommodation within newly furnished rooms is available in the Queens Hotel.

🎞 stories and anecdotes   🦜 famous people   🎨 art and craft   🎵 entertainment and sport   🚶 walks

UNO GIFTWARE

Jackson's Lane, Carmarthen,
Carmarthenshire SA31 1QD
Tel: 01267 220685

History abounds in Carmarthen, and visitors will always find a wealth of interesting shops in which to spend a happy hour or two browsing and buying, especially in the old town, near the castle, where there are many small, independent shops to discover and explore.

One of the most interesting is **Uno Giftware** (Uno Home and Gift), which occupies a building in a prime location close to the main car park and the town centre. It opened in 2004, and is owned and run by Susan and Jonathan Faull, a very professional and enthusiastic couple whose eye for quality and style is evident in everything they display on the two floors of their shop.

Behind the double-fronted window, display cabinets, carousels, shelves and gondolas are filled with an amazing variety of contemporary art, crafts and giftware. The range extends from cushions and soft furnishings to lamps and lighting accessories, bowls and glasses, pots and vases, mirrors, potted plants, toiletries and fragrances, executive toys, games, books and cards.

There are also displays of women's scarves and handbags for all moods and al occasions, many of them with matching purses. Uno Giftware specialises in amber and silver fashion jewellery, and you will be amazed at the wide and comprehensive range on offer.

Among the well-known designers and manufacturers featured in the shop are SIA UK, Parlane International, One World, Celtic Herbal, Bomb Cosmetics, David Westnedge, Jane Shilton, Nici and Doudou. You can also choose from a wide selection of the famous Yankee Candles, and the shop also carries a great range of Diddle children's toys and gifts, all at affordable prices.

🏛 historic building   🏛 museum   🏛 historic site   🦢 scenic attraction   🌷 flora and fauna

STEMS FLOWER SHOP, JEWELLERY AND COFFEE SHOP

16 Queen Street, Carmarthen, Carmarthenshire SA31 1JT
Tel: 01267 231821/238300

Say it with flowers, they say, and if this is true, then **Stems Flower Shop, Jewellery and Coffee Shop** is the place to buy the flowers. This delightful emporium offers innovative and traditional floral services, having flowers such as the tropical and vibrant anthurium to the comforting carnation. There is also a wide range of contemporary jewellery from makers such as *Pilgrim* and *Robin Rive,* plus a wonderful coffee shop where you can enjoy marvellous coffee or a pot of tea as you rest your weary legs after a hard day's shopping.

stayed at the Ivy Bush in the later years of his life. Steele is best known for his periodical essays and for his collaboration with Joseph Addison. Educated, like Addison, at Charterhouse and Oxford, Steele published his first work in 1701, when he was 28. It had the far from catchy title of *The Christian Hero:*

An argument proving that no principles but those of religion are sufficient to make a great man. Steele had two wealthy wives and several children. Bad health and pressing debts forced him to move to Wales, and he died in Carmarthen in 1729. A brass plaque on the wall of the **Parish Church of St Peter** commemorates him.

LICKLEY'S MOUNT ANTIQUES

16 Queen Street, Carmarthen,
Carmarthenshire SA31 1JR
Tel: 01267 220005

Lickley's Mount Antiques is situated right next to County Hall, and has a wide and fascinating range of antiques set over three floors and nine rooms. Here you can browse to your heart's content as you examine the many treasures on offer, all at amazingly affordable prices. From Victorian and Edwardian fireplaces to blankets from Wales, and from Eastern rugs to pine cottage and Welsh oak furniture - it is all here for you to discover.

You will be amazed at the impressive collection of mining memorabilia that is sure to capture the attention of any collector, and you will be impressed by the ceramics and china, as well as the EWWNNY, Clay Pits, Swansea and Lanelli pottery. If you are furnishing a holiday cottage, for instance, you can chose from traditional or funky, contemporary furniture, and you can find wall hangings and plates that give the place that authentic feel. There is also original art, lighting and textiles, plus those quirky items found in all antique shops that you can't quite categorise but you know you must have.

The shop is open Monday to Saturday from 10 am to 5 pm, except Thursday (9 am to 4 pm). On Sunday it is open between 9 am and 4 pm. So come along and see the vast range of quality antiques for yourself. The owner, Robert Lickley, or one of his staff, will offer all the help and advice you need to make a choice.

📖 stories and anecdotes   🐦 famous people   🎨 art and craft   🎭 entertainment and sport   🥾 walks

AUDREY BULL ANTIQUES

2 Jacksons Lane, Carmarthen SA31 1QD
Tel: 01267 222655

Audrey Bull opened her first antiques shop in Cheltenham in 1956 along with her mother Blanche Beck. This shop in Carmarthen, **Audrey Bull Antiques**, opened in 1998, following the success of the Tenby branch which opened in 1957.

These two delightful shops just have to be visited. They are now owned by Jane and Jonathan Bull, ably assisted by their daughter Quita, while their son Matthew manages the restoration workshop. Here you are free to browse with absolutely no obligation, while at the same time you will be given all the help and advice you need should you choose to buy an item. The owners are general antique dealers who specialise in 19th and 20th century furniture, Welsh oak pieces, silver, porcelain and jewellery, which includes antique pieces, gem-set and modern designer creations. Everything is realistically priced, so why not buy a souvenir of your trip to Wales, or a special piece that will surely be treasured down through the years?

The workshop prides itself on repairing and polishing in a way that preserves the original patination. They do not follow the fashion for making the furniture match the repair - they make the repair match the furniture. The shop is open from 9 am - 5 pm Monday to Saturday, and on Sunday during the summer months.

This church, which dates back to the 12th century, has many interesting features, including an organ thought to have been built in the reign of George III for Windsor Palace, and the impressive tomb of Sir Rhys ap Thomas, who led an army to fight for Henry Tudor at the Battle of Bosworth Field, where Richard III was killed and Henry crowned as King Henry VII on the battlefield.

The **Picton Monument** at the west end of the town commemorates Sir Thomas Picton (1758 - 1815), who was killed at the Battle of Waterloo. He had the rank of Lieutenant General, and was the Member of Parliament for Pembroke. His body lies in St George's Church, Hanover Square, London.

Carmarthen has a thriving food market, where one of the local specialities on sale is Carmarthen ham, which is air-dried, sliced and eaten raw, like the Spanish Serrano ham.

Around Carmarthen

BRONWYDD
2 miles N of Carmarthen on the A484

🚂 Gwili Steam Railway

From Bronwydd Arms Station (just off the A484 Carmarthen to Cardigan road) the **Gwili Steam Railway** offers visitors the opportunity to step back in time and take a short steam train journey through the Gwili Valley on part of the old Great Western Railway line connecting Carmarthen to Aberystwyth. This line originally opened in 1860 and, although it finally closed in 1973, it

CWMDWYFRAN FARM COTTAGES

Cwmdwyfran Farm, Bronwydd, Carmarthen,
Carmarthenshire SA33 6JF
Tel: 01267 281419
e-mail: info@cwmdwyfran.co.uk
website: www.cwmdwyfran.co.uk

Situated on a farm among some of the most picturesque scenery in Wales, the Cwmdwyfran Farm Cottages are one of the best self-catering establishments in the area, and offer the ideal base from which to explore this historic and beautiful part of Wales. It is open from the beginning of March until the end of December, and though there are two steps up into it, it is all on one level so would suit someone with limited mobility.

The cottages sleep four each in two bedrooms - a double and a twin, and have been awarded four coveted stars from the Welsh Tourist Board. The interiors are comfortable and stylish, with central heating, though supplementary heating is available if required. The kitchens boast a microwave, fridge/freezer, cooker and all crockery, cooking utensils and cutlery. There is a car park, and children and dogs are most welcome. Cots and highchairs are available on request and all linen and towels, except beach towels, are included. There is a spacious decked area for those relaxing summer evenings. As well as breaks of a week or longer, short breaks of two days or more are also available during off-peak times.

The cottages make a relaxing place to stay in beautiful Wales, and you can spend as hectic or as relaxing a time as you wish here, deep in the Welsh countryside. Come along and see for yourself. You won't be disappointed.

has since the late 1970s been run by volunteers. Trains run on timetabled days between April and October and in December. The station has a souvenir shop and sells hot and cold refreshments. Visitors can enjoy the train journey through a

beautiful wooded valley, and the other end of the line, Llwyfan Cerrig, is the perfect place for a picnic by the river. Unusually, the village takes its name from an inn that once stood here, the Bronwydd Arms. A plaque now marks the spot where it stood.

DREFACH
12 miles N of Carmarthen off the A484

🏛 National Woollen Museum

🏚 Woollen Mill Trail

Many of the water driven mills of this area still continue to produce flour and distinctive woollen goods, and this important part of the region's industrial heritage is explored in

Gwili Steam Railway

📖 stories and anecdotes   🐦 famous people   🎨 art and craft   🎭 entertainment and sport   🚶 walks

CLYN GLAS COTTAGES & WOODTURNING CENTRE

Cwmhiraeth, Drefach Felindre, nr Llandysul SA44 5XL
Tel: *01559 371997*
e-mail: *hilaryhizzard@tiscali.co.uk*   website: *www.clynglascottages.co.uk*

With 150 clean, welcoming beaches within 50 miles, the picturesque, stone-built **Clyn Glas Cottages and Woodturning Centre** makes the ideal place to have a wonderful holiday in beautiful Wales. They are owned and run by Hilary and Tony Hizzard, and have earned four coveted stars from the tourist board. There are two cottages - one with one bedroom and one with two, and each has stunning views of the Hiraeth Valley. They come fully equipped, with wood burning stoves, colourful gardens and BBQ areas, and are comfortable and welcoming. The whole area is criss-crossed with footpaths - just right for walking - and the National Welsh Woollen Museum is a mile away.

Tony is a wood turner, and since 1991 has offered residential and non-residential courses in this fascinating craft. He sells his products on site and in local galleries. So why not combine a restful holiday with easy-to-learn courses on wood-turning? They are suitable for novices, and are very enjoyable. Of course, you don't have to take part in the courses. You could just have a marvellous, relaxing holiday in one of the most beautiful areas of Wales. The place is renowned for

  bird watching, walking, sight seeing, golf and many other activities.

Even if you're not staying at Clyn Glas, why not call in and buy one of Tony's hand-turned products as a gift or souvenir? You won't be disappointed.

the **National Woollen Museum**. One of the most traditional and rural industries, the processes involved in the spinning, weaving and dyeing of wool are explained here, and there are also demonstrations of cloth making and dyeing carried out on 19th century machinery. As well as trying their hand at spinning, visitors can stroll around the sites of the old woollen mills in the village, which still produce flannel cloth and tweeds, and follow all or part of the **Woollen Mill Trail** through the scenic Teifi Valley. There are 24 miles of waymarked trails from the museum, the longer ones taking in the seven so-called flannel villages.

PONTARSAIS

5 miles N of Carmarthen on the A485

🏵 Gwili Pottery

The village is best known as the home of

Gwili Pottery. To the west of the village lies Llanpumpsaint, whose name literally means 'the church, or enclosure, of the five saints'. The five saints are Ceitho, Celynen, Gwyn, Gwyno and Grynnaro, who all lived in the 6th century, and were all brothers from the semi-royal Cunedda family. However, the present parish church is dedicated to just one saint - St Celynyn.

ABERGWILI

1½ miles E of Carmarthen off the A40

🏛 Carmarthenshire County Museum

🏛 Merlin's Hill Centre

Carmarthenshire County Museum occupies a lovely old house that was a palace of the bishop of St David's up until 1974, and visitors can still see the bishop's peaceful private chapel. Concentrating on Carmarthenshire's past, the museum's displays range from Roman gold through to Welsh furniture and there is also a reconstruction of a school room. The palace's grounds, too, are open to the public, and the delightful parkland is ideal for a stroll and a picnic.

Found on land that has been farmed for over 2,000 years, the **Merlin's Hill Centre** at Alltyfyrddin Farm explains the history and legends of the surrounding area and its connections with Merlin the Magician. As well as listening out for the wizard's wailings - he is supposed to be imprisoned under an Iron Age hill fort on the farm - visitors can also explore this dairy farm and learn about farming, past and present.

LLANARTHNE

7½ miles E of Carmarthen on the B4300

🏯 Paxton's Tower   🏯 Parish Church of St David

🏛 Caercastell Cross

🌱 National Botanic Garden of Wales

To the southwest of the village lies **Paxton's Tower**, designed by SP Cockerell and built in the early 19th century on the Middleton estate for William Paxton, who dedicated it to Lord Nelson. Constructed so that it could be seen from the main house, it affords panoramic views from the tower over the estate and the Tywi valley. The **Parish Church of St David** dates mainly from the 13th century, though the base of the tower may be earlier. In the porch can be see the **Caercastell Cross**, which dates from the 10th or 11th century.

To the south of Llanarthne, and set in the 18th century parkland of the former regency estate of Middleton Hall (which no longer exists), is the **National Botanic Garden of Wales** - a Millennium project that covers an amazing 568 acres on the edge of the beautiful Towy Valley. Dedicated to conservation, horticulture, science and

education, this national botanic garden, the first to be constructed in Britain for over 200 years, is centred around a great glasshouse that is the largest single span house of its kind in the world. Among the many delights to be found within this old parkland are one of Europe's longest herbaceous borders, the recently restored Double Walled Garden, a Japanese garden, lakeside walks and the Physicians of Myddfai, an exhibition that pays tribute to the legendary Welsh healers of the Middle Ages. Tribute is also paid to the Welsh botanist Alfred Russel Wallace, whose theories of natural selection paralleled those of Charles Darwin. However, this is also very much a garden of the future and, in the Energy Zone, there is a biomass furnace using salvaged or coppiced wood for heating the site, and the Living Machine sewage treatment system.

National Botanic Garden of Wales

🎭 stories and anecdotes   🦅 famous people   🎨 art and craft   🎟 entertainment and sport   🚶 walks

DRYSLWYN

8½ miles E of Carmarthen
on the B4300

🏰 Dryslwyn Castle

By the side of the River Tywi lie the remains of **Dryslwyn Castle**, built on the hill by one of Lord Rhys' descendants in the mid-13th century. An ideal location for a stronghold, the castle throughout its life suffered several savage attacks that contributed to its present ruined condition.

LLANGATHEN

11 miles E of Carmarthen off the A40

🏰 Parish Church of St Cathen

🌿 Aberglasney

The village is home to **Aberglasney** (see panel below), one of the oldest and most interesting gardens in the country. The first recorded description of Aberglasney House and Gardens was made by the bard Lewis Glyn Cothi in 1477 when he wrote of "a white painted court, built of dressed stone, surrounded by nine gardens of orchards, vineyards and large oak trees". At a later date, at the beginning of the 17th century, the estate was sold to the Bishop of St Davids and it was Bishop Anthony Rudd who improved both the house and gardens in a manner befitting a bishop's palace. At the heart of the nine acres is a unique and fully restored Elizabethan/Jacobean cloister garden and a parapet walk, the only surviving example in the UK.

The **Parish Church of St Cathen** is medieval, worth visiting to see the tomb of Bishop Anthony Rudd, who became Bishop of St David's in 1594 and died in 1615. It is in the south aisle, and dates to the early 17th century.

Aberglasney Gardens

Llangathen, Carmarthenshire SA32 8QH
Tel/Fax: 01558 668998
e-mail: info@aberglasney.org.uk
website: www.aberglasney.org.uk

Aberglasney is one of the country's most exciting garden restoration projects, and the gardens are well on the way to becoming one of the leading garden attractions in the UK. The recovery and restoration are taking place under the aegis of the Aberglasney Restoration Trust, set up in 1995, and the nine acres contain six different garden spaces including three walled gardens. At the heart is a unique, fully restored Elizabethan/Jacobean cloister and parapet walk giving wonderful views over the site. The gardens have already won many awards from the Wales Tourist Board and other prestigious bodies. There's a café in the gardens.

As well as the magnificent gardens, the house is also undergoing restoration. Its history dates back over many centuries and, through scant recorded details, is thought to have been originally owned by the Lords of Llangathen, before passing into Tudor hands.

🏰 historic building   🏛 museum   🏚 historic site   🍃 scenic attraction   🌿 flora and fauna

GOLDEN GROVE
11 miles E of Carmarthen off the B4300

🐾 Gelli Aur Country Park

To the east of the village lies **Gelli Aur Country Park** (Gelli Aur means 'golden grove') on part of the estate of the ancestral home of the Vaughan family. Containing remnants of a 17th century deer park (where the deer still roam), the landscaped parkland was laid out in the 18th century and the country park also includes a Victorian arboretum planted by Lord Cawdor. Other attractions include nature trails, a new adventure playground and a cafeteria. The original mansion, now part of an agricultural college, was the work of the architect Joseph Wyatville.

LLANSTEFFAN
7 miles SW of Carmarthen on the B4312

🏰 Llansteffan Castle   ⛲ St Anthony's Well

🏰 Parish Church of St Ystyffan

This village, near the mouth of the River Tywi, is dominated by the ruins of **Llansteffan Castle** on a headland above the estuary. The successor to an earlier defensive earthwork, the castle dates from the 12th century and the main remaining feature is the impressive gateway dating from 1280. To the southwest of the castle lies **St Anthony's Well**, the waters of which were thought to have medicinal properties. The **Parish Church of St Ystyffan** dates from the 13th century and later. In AD 1170 the church was given to the Knights Hospitaller by the local lord of the manor, Geoffrey de Marmoin.

Llansteffan, along with Ferryside, its neighbour across the river mouth, is a paradise for walkers as well as sailors and the

waymarked walks around the estuary take in some truly breathtaking coastal scenery. The promontory of Wharley Point, in particular, affords stunning views across the Taf and Tywi estuaries to Carmarthen Bay.

LAUGHARNE
9 miles SW of Carmarthen on the A4066

🏰 Laugharne Castle   🏰 The Boathouse

🏰 Parish Church of St Martin

This pretty rural town of Georgian houses on the estuary of the River Taf is home to one of the country's most handsome castles. Originally an earth and timber fortress, **Laugharne Castle** was built in stone around the 13th century and, although much of the fortification still remains, it is the transformations undertaken by Sir John Perrot in the 16th century that make this a particularly special site. Granted Laugharne by Queen Elizabeth I, Perrot, an illegitimate son

Dylan Thomas' Boathouse

Laugharne

Distance: *3.5 miles (5.6 kilometres)*

Typical time: *240 mins*

Height gain: *180 metres*

Map: *Explorer 177*

Walk: *www.walkingworld.com ID:2718*

Contributor: *Pat Roberts*

There is a large free car park next to the castle. There is only a small sign for it but there is plenty of space. Toilets are up the road on the right as you leave the car park, opposite the doctor's surgery.

DESCRIPTION:

Laugharne was the home of the poet Dylan Thomas and this walk visits many of the places made famous by him. There is plenty of information in the village itself and there are information boards at the places of note.

FEATURES:

Sea, Pub, Toilets, Church, Castle, Wildlife, Birds, Flowers, Great Views, Butterflies, Cafe, Woodland

WALK DIRECTIONS:

1 | From the car park walk over the footbridge and follow the path under the castle.

2 | Take this track l ft, signed to the Boathouse, and over rocks at first before climbing steps to a tarmac track. Right and soon come to the garage used by Dylan as his writing Shed. After about 45 metres see the Boathouse down on the right, there are steps down to it should you wish to visit it. Continue, cross over a road and on into the trees.

3 | There is a track own to the right but we keep to the upper main track to reach a stile.

4 | Over the stile an follow the obvious track fairly near the right hedge. Through some trees

into the next field and on to another stile behind a large tree trunk.

5 | Over the double stile and head for the farmhouse. Over another stile and round to the left of the farmhouse to continue up the drive. It is quite a long drive with a gate (usually open) at the top, here it is joined from the right by another driveway to go forward for 20 metres to a road.

6 | At the road go le t. The road soon swings right and continues to lose height. At the end of a wall look for a metal Kissing gate into the churchyard. The old graves are particularly interesting. Go to the front of the church and up steps over a footbridge into the new part. Left and up to reach another kissing gate halfway across the top hedge. Dylan Thomas' Grave is in the centre of the new grave yard and is a large white cross. Through the gate and turn right to follow this old bridleway to the road.

7 | Reach the road at the entrance to a caravan park. Cross the road and follow a footway signed "The Boat House" until reaching a white building with double black doors.

8 | Right to walk bac down the steps and path we ascended on the outward route. Walk on round below the castle to the car park.

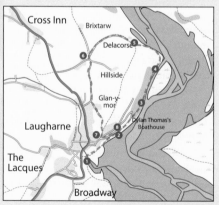

of Henry VIII, turned the castle into a comfortable mansion that, after seeing action in the Civil War, declined into the ruins seen today.

However, romantic though the castle ruins are, this is not all Laugharne Castle has to offer, as the Victorian garden has been splendidly restored. Both the castle ruins and the superb surroundings have provided inspiration for artists over the centuries and, in particular, they are the subject of a dramatic watercolour by JMW Turner.

Writers, too, have found this an inspiring place and both Dylan Thomas, who wrote in a gazebo in the grounds, and Richard Hughes, author of *A High Wind in Jamaica*, are associated with Laugharne Castle. This coastal town is today a shrine to its most famous

resident, Dylan Thomas, who spent the last four years of his life living at **The Boathouse** set in a cliff overlooking the Taf estuary. Discovering this small out-of-the-way place in the 1940s, Thomas famously 'got off the bus and forgot to get on again', and it was while in Laugharne that he wrote some of his best works, including *Under Milk Wood*, a day in the life of his imaginary village of Llareggub (read the name backwards to find why it has this odd name). Thomas, notoriously prone to destructive drinking sprees, died in The White Horse Bar in New York in 1953, at only 39 years of age. The Boathouse is now a heritage centre dedicated to the writer and, as well as the fascinating memorabilia on display here, there is also an interpretation centre, bookshop and tea room.

THE STABLE DOOR RESTAURANT AND WINE BAR

Market Lane, Laugharne, Carmarthenshire SA33 4SB
Tel: 01994 427777

The **Stable Door Restaurant and Wine Bar** enjoys a wonderfully atmospheric location behind the clock tower and up a pretty cobbled lane off the main street of the town where Dylan Thomas spent the last years of his life. It is owned and run by Wendy Joy, who trained at Pru Leith's School of Food and Wine and ran a restaurant and catering company in London. She brings a wealth of experience to the establishment, which has earned a bronze Eating Out in Wales award.

The sturdy stone walls of the original stables, the intimate lighting and the many interesting decorative touches make a splendid backdrop to a meal here, and when the weather is fine, the garden is a particularly quiet, pleasant spot for a drink. The menu makes excellent use of fresh, local produce in dishes that are inspired by British, Mediterranean and Eastern cuisines. Typical choices might include fillet of Welsh beef en croute with a sauce of locally picked wild mushrooms cooked in cream and brandy, roast panga fish fillet wrapped in prosciutto, organic chicken breast filled with pesto and mozzarella, then wrapped in Parma ham, and chilli ban burritos flavoured with coriander and lime.

There is an excellent wine list to accompany the food, with an emphasis on New World bottles, so you are sure to find something which will complement your meal.

🎞 stories and anecdotes   🦆 famous people   🎨 art and craft   🎵 entertainment and sport   🥾 walks

The **Parish Church of St Martin**, in the churchyard of which Thomas is buried, contains a replica of the plaque to his memory which can be seen in Poets' Corner, Westminster Abbey. The church itself dates mainly to the 13th century, and has a magnificent reredos and a carving of St Martin of Tours.

PENDINE
13½ miles SW of Carmarthen on the A4066

🏛 Museum of Speed

The vast, seven mile long expanse of sand which makes Pendine a popular place with families was used in the 1920s by Sir Malcolm Campbell and others for attempting land speed records. In 1924, Sir Malcolm broke the World Motor Flying Kilometre Record here by averaging 146 miles per hour. He later raised that to 174 mph, and went on to achieve speeds in excess of 300 mph on the salt flats at Bonneville, Utah. In 1927, while attempting to beat Sir Malcolm's record, Welshman J G Parry Thomas was decapitated in an accident on the beach and his car, Babs, lay buried in the sand before being unearthed in 1969 and restored by Owen Wyn Owen, a lecturer from Bangor. Babs can now be seen in all its gleaming glory at the **Museum of Speed**, which explores the history of this stretch of sand where so many records were broken. However, not all the speed attempts involved land vehicles as it was from these sands in 1933 that the intrepid aviatrix Amy Johnson and her husband Jim Mollinson set off on a de Havilland Dragon Rapide for a non-stop flight across the Atlantic. In 2004 all vehicles were banned from the beach because of possible bombs lying on it, as at one time it was owned by the MOD.

The **Parish Church of St Margaret**, with its saddleback tower, has a cast iron gravestone

in its churchyard. The building largely dates from the 14th century, though it was restored in Victorian times. No one knows which St Margaret the church is dedicated to, so one of the windows features three of them - St Margaret of Antioch, St Margaret of Scotland and the shadowy local saint St Margaret Marloes. As the lord of the manor at the time of the dedication, Sir Guy de Bryan, claimed descent from St Margaret of Scotland, this is the likeliest candidate.

ST CLEARS
8½ miles SW of Carmarthen on the A40

🏠 Parish Church of St Mary Magdalene

This small market town was the site of the defeat of Owain Glyndwr by Pembrokeshire's army in 1406. Later, in the 1840s, St Clears was involved in more trouble when it featured in the Rebecca Riots (see also Rhayader) during which the rioters destroyed toll gates. All that remains of **St Clears Castle** is its motte. It was founded in the 11th century, but we know little about its early history.

The large **Parish Church of St Mary Magdalene** had its origins in a Clunaic priory established here in the 12th century. It was a daughter house of St Martin des Champs in Paris, but supported only two or three monks at a time. As an 'alien' (i.e. foreign) priory it was always viewed with suspicion, especially when England was at war with France. So much so that it was finally dissolved in 1414.

WHITLAND
13 miles W of Carmarthen on the B4328

🏠 Whitland Abbey　🏠 Holy Cross Abbey

🏛 Hywel Dda Centre

This small market town and centre of the dairy industry is historically important as the meeting place of the assembly convened by Hywel Dda

GLYN-COCH CRAFT CENTRE

Ffynnongain Lane, Pwll-Trap, nr St Clears,
Carmarthenshire SA33 4AR
Tel: 01994 231867
e-mail: glyncoch@btinternet.com
website: www.glyn-coch.com

In a picturesque rural setting excellently sign-posted from the A40, **Glyn-Coch** is a Welsh craft centre with a wide variety of attractions for all the family. It was a commercial farm until 1995, and was managed by a family who appreciated wildlife. The present owners, Thelma and Huw Jones, share that appreciation, and have developed a woodland walk that takes in an amazing diversity of animals, birds, insects, trees and plants. The plants were the inspiration for the famous Glyn-Coch Design china, that was decorated here until 1995. They still hand paint bone china, and visitors can see the pottery and make or decorate pots themselves.

In the traditional stone barn is a huge range of beautiful, locally-made items both ornamental and useful. These include wool and woollen garments from the fleeces of resident Norfolk Horn sheep, personalised bone china with local scenes and the Thelwen range of pottery, made on the site. There are also unique collections of jewellery and seasonal decorations.

The tea room serves hot and cold drinks, delicious snacks, local ice cream and cream teas. There is a campsite for Caravan and Camping Club members. Glyn-Coch is open all year round, and has plenty of parking space. Open 10am-6pm everyday, closed Tuesdays.

---

in the 10th century. Born towards the end of the 9th century, Dda made a pilgrimage to Rome in AD 928 and, some 14 years later, he was ruler of most of Wales. Summoning representatives from each part of Wales to Whitland, Dda laid down a legal system that became known for its wisdom and justice and which remained in force in Wales up until the Act of Union with England in 1536. This system and its instigator are remembered at the Prince of Wales Design award-winning building the **Hywel Dda Centre**. Here, too, is a memorial in the form of six gardens representing the six separate divisions of the law: Society and Status, Crime and Tort, Women, Contract, the King, and Property.

Just north of the town lie the remains of the once great **Whitland Abbey**, which was

founded in 1140 by Bernard, the first Norman Bishop of St David's. It moved to its present position in 1151 and, at one time, was the premier Cistercian house in Wales. Nearby is **Holy Cross Abbey**, a modern foundation, having been set up in 1991 for Cistercian nuns.

LLANBOIDY
12 miles NW of Carmarthen off the A40

🎨 Welsh Chocolate Farm   🎨 Llanboidy Cheeses

In old stone farm buildings to the north of the village is a chocoholic's dream - the **Welsh Chocolate Farm**, where chocolates of all shapes, sizes and flavours are made. As well as watching chocolate making demonstrations and touring the factory to see just how the chocolate is produced, visitors can buy gifts and treats for family

---

🎬 stories and anecdotes   🐦 famous people   🎨 art and craft   🎭 entertainment and sport   🚶 walks

RUBYS

8 Sycamore Street, Newcastle Emlyn SA 38 9AJ
Tel: 01239 711545

New clothes deserve new shoes. After being dressed by Scallywag those in the know just cross the street to Ruby's. Also owned by Sue Kind, and with an unusual interior of old floorboards and pink and purple curved display counters, Ruby's stocks shoes, boots and sandals for most

occasions and to suit all ages. Some of the brands include Dr Martens, Tamaris, Oxygen, Rocket Dog, Bronx, Crocs and Art Shoes. The emphasis is on different but eminently wearable. Open for one year Ruby's has already made a positive impact on the feet of people visiting Newcastle Emlyn. Definitely worth a visit.

Both shops are open from 9.30 to 5.30 Monday to Saturday.

SCALLYWAG

Sycamore Street, Newcastle Emlyn SA38 9AJ
Tel: 01239 711118
e-mail: suekind@btinternet.com

The imposing ruins of the Castle, overlooking the river and the valley, bring many visitors with a sense of history to Newcastle Emlyn. But for women with a sense of fashion, and the unusual, two shops on the main street are high on the list of places to visit. Sue Kind moved to the area 35 years ago and started trading with a market stall in various local towns before opening Scallywag in 1987. Behind its lilac and purple frontage the shop is stocked with an excellent selection of smart-casual and fun clothes as well as hand picked accessories including jewellery and bags. Brands sold include Noa Noa, Ou Soleil, Desert Design and Angel Circle. Knitwear is provided by Pachamama and fashionable hemp bags by Sativa. There is a large selection of silver jewellery with many one off designs by Siren Silver. The costume and funky jewellery is mostly by Mint Designs or Goose Island. The dragon of the logo relates to the legend of the last dragon slain in Wales. She was driven from the town and took refuge in the river which twisted and turned to accommodate her curves. It is believed she lives there still and her breath can be seen on the surface of the river in early morning.

🏛 historic building   🏠 museum   🏛 historic site   ♨ scenic attraction   🌱 flora and fauna

and friends (and selves) at the farm shop, which has the largest selection of chocolates in Wales. And, as this is rich dairy country, there are also farmhouse cheeses and other dairy delights at the shop along with a wide range of hand-roasted coffee beans prepared daily. Don't even try to resist the homemade fudge! Another gastronomic treat is in store at **Llanboidy Cheeses**, made since 1985 on Cilowen Uchaf farm by Sue Jones from local organic milk. She took the gold medal for cheeses in 2001.

CENARTH
16 miles NW of Carmarthen on the A484

🐟 Salmon Leap Museum   🐟 Cenarth Mill

🐟 Old Smithy   🏠 National Coracle Centre

🐟 Salmon Leap Waterfalls

This ancient village, first mentioned by Giraldus Cambrenses (see also St David's and Manorbier) in the late 12th century when he passed through on his journey with Archbishop Baldwin to drum up support for the Crusades, has for centuries been a centre for coracle fishermen. Situated on the banks of the River Teifi, famous for its **Salmon Leap Waterfalls**, and the accompanying **Salmon Leap Museum**, the conservation village is home to **Cenarth Mill**. Dating from the 18th century, the watermill, which has two

Coracle on the River Teifi, Cenarth

pairs of stones (one for barley, the other for oats) is powered by the river close to the salmon leap. Now restored and producing wholemeal flour, the mill complex also houses the **National Coracle Centre**, where visitors can see a unique collection of these ancient boats from around the world. Dating back to the Ice Age, these little round boats, once covered in skins, are still used for salmon fishing and at the Centre visitors can see demonstrations of coracles at work. The **Old Smithy** can be found within an 18th century blacksmith's workshop that still has some of the old tools used by a blacksmith. There is also a craft shop.

NEWCASTLE EMLYN
14 miles NW of Carmarthen on the A484

🐟 Newcastle Emlyn Castle   🐟 Old Cilgwyn Gardens

In Newcastle Emlyn, the first printing press in Wales was set up by Isaac Carter in 1718. The town grew up around **Newcastle Emlyn Castle**, which was built in 1240 by Maredudd ap Rhys beside the River Teifi. Like that of many other castles in Wales, Newcastle Emlyn's turbulent history is in some ways confirmed by the present condition of this now ruined fortress, as it changed hands several times until it was destroyed during the Glyndwr rebellion in the early 1400s. Having fallen into disrepair, the castle was granted to Sir Rhys ap Thomas by Henry VII in the late 15th century and became a country residence before being all but demolished during the Civil War for harbouring Royalist sympathisers. On the B4571, a mile north of Newcastle Emlyn, lie **Old Cilgwyn Gardens**. This is a 14-acre mixed garden set in 900 acres of parkland that includes a 53-acre Site of Special Scientific Interest. It contains the site of the last duel fought in Wales.

🎦 stories and anecdotes   🐦 famous people   🎨 art and craft   🎭 entertainment and sport   🥾 walks

CAWS CENARTH

Abercych, nr Newcastle Emlyn,
Carmarthenshire SA37 0LH
Tel: 01239 710432
e-mail: cenarth.cheese@virgin.net
website: www.cawscenarth.co.uk

Organic Cheese from an Organic Farm.
Caws Cenarth, now run by Carwyn
Adams, who has taken over from his
parents, Gwynfor and Thelma Adams,
continues to make headlines inspired
by premium quality cheese. In 2006,
Carwyn entered five competitions and
won five Gold Awards: Best Caerffili
and Best Welsh Cheese at the British Cheese Awards, Best Organic and Best Producer at the
True Taste Awards, and from the Soil Association, the Best Organic Cheese in the UK - all in
addition to the Top Awards at the Royal Welsh Show.

Being deeply interested, HRH Prince Charles visited the farm, on a private visit. Other visitors
include famous chefs, broadcasters and Rick Stein who nominated the firm a Superhero. Harrods
in London have been selling Caws Cenarth for 20 years.

Come and visit Caws Cenarth to see cheese being made and to enjoy the free tastings.
Admission is free. During the summer, you can also enjoy a cup of tea and delicious food in the
delightful setting of the vegetarian and organic cafe. Try the yummy home-made icecreams!

The shop is open Monday to Saturday, 10am - 5pm. Closed Sundays. The cheese is made
several days a week, but please check before hand.

Llandovery

🏛 Llandovery Castle

🏛 Parish Church of St Mary on the Hill

🏛 Dolauhirion Bridge   🏚 Twm Sion Catl's Cave,

🏛 Llandovery Heritage Centre

🎭 Physicians of Myddfai   ♞ Rhys Pritchard

As it is situated at the confluence of the
Rivers Bran, Gwennol and Tywi, Llandovery's
Welsh name, Llanymddyfri (meaning the
church amid the waters), seems particularly
apt. Evidence suggests that the area around
Llandovery has been important since Roman
times. **Rhys Pritchard**, known as a preacher
and as the author of the collection of verses
The Welshman's Candle, lived here in the 17th
century, as did the renowned Methodist poet

and hymn writer William Williams in the 18th
century (see also Llanwrtyd Wells).

Llandovery Castle, the remains of which
overlook the cattle market, was the most
easterly Norman castle within
Carmarthenshire, constructed in 1116 by
Richard Fitzpons only to be captured and
destroyed some 42 years later. Although it
was repaired in the late 12th century by Henry
II, the castle was left to decay after 1403 and
only the tumbledown remains are visible
today. Within the ruins is a monument to
Llewelyn ap Gruffydd Fychan of Ceao who, in
1401, was executed for refusing to betray
Owyn Glyndwr.

Visiting in the 19th century, the author
George Borrow called Landover 'the
pleasantest little town in which I have halted'.

🏛 historic building   🏚 museum   🏚 historic site   ♘ scenic attraction   🌱 flora and fauna

Llandovery Castle

The history of this town, which delighted many people before and since George Borrow, is told at the **Llandovery Heritage Centre** where the legends surrounding the hero Twm Sion Cati - the Welsh Robin Hood - and the local **Physicians of Myddfai** are also explored. The legend concerning the physicians is that a lady appeared one day from a lake in the Black Mountain. A local farmer's son fell in love with her and she agreed to marry him on condition that he did not hit her three times without cause. Over the years he had given her three light taps for what he thought was poor behaviour and sure enough she returned to the lake. But before disappearing she passed on her herbal healing secrets to her three sons, who became the first of the famous Physicians of Myddfai, a line of healers who practised from the 12th to the 18th centuries. A new

venture among a group of farmers in Myddfai (a short drive south of Llandovery) is bringing together this age-old legend and the growing modern interest in the properties of herbs. They hope to establish a centre where visitors can learn more about the legend and modern practices and where the farmers would sell their own brand of herbal products. The **Parish Church of St Mary on the Hill** was built within the ramparts of a Roman fort that once stood in the town, and some Roman tiles can be seen in the walls of the church. Also of note are the barrel-vaulted chancel and tie-beam roof.

The attractive **Dolauhirion Bridge** spanning the River Tywi was built in 1173 by William Edwards, whilst the village's chapel is said to have been the first meeting place of Methodists in Wales. North of Llandovery, near Rhandir-mwyn, is all that remains of **Twm Sion Catl's Cave**, the hideout of the 16th century "Robin Hood of Wales". A poet whose youthful escapades earned him the title, Twm Sion later curtailed his activities and settled down after marrying the heiress of Ystradffin and even became a magistrate. He died in 1620.

CILYCWM
3½ miles N of Llandovery off the A483

🏛 Capel Bwlchyrhiw   🏛 Parish Church of St Michael

The village's **Capel Bwlchyrhiw** is said to have been the first meeting place of Methodists in Wales. The **Parish Church of St Michael** dates from the early 14th century, and the nave has delightful wall paintings.

LLANGADOG
5 miles SW of Llandovery on the A4069

🏛 Llangadog Castle   🏚 Carn Goch   🎭 Bethlehem

This small town in the Vale of Towy was once home to **Llangadog Castle**, although all that

🎭 stories and anecdotes   👤 famous people   🎨 art and craft   🎟 entertainment and sport   🥾 walks

BARITA DELI & COFFEE SHOP

139 Rhosmaen Street, Llandeilo, Carmarthenshire SA19 6EN
Tel: 01558 823444
e-mail: rita@barita.co.uk website: www.barita.co.uk

In the attractive small town of Llandeilo you will find one of the best delis in South Wales - **Barita Deli and Coffee Shop**. This is owned and run by Rita Morgan and Nigel Williams, and it stocks the finest fare, not only from Wales, but from all over Britain and Europe. This is the place to stock up on all those savoury and sweet delicacies we love so much.

Welsh ham from Carmarthenshire - the best sea salt (Halen Mor) - honey from Talley - and Llanfaes dairy ice cream, made by a Welsh family in the Brecon Beacons National Park from an old Italian recipe. There is also plaits of French garlic (white, pink and smoked), as well as herbs from Provence, succulent German sausages, Italian salami, Belgian chocolates and marzipan, superb Italian Illy coffee, and a whole lot more.

You can enjoy much of the produce - including superb home-baked organic bread - in the coffee shop. Let it accompany a bowl of tasty soup, or super sandwiches. You can take away many of the items on the menu, including quiches and savoury pies with fillings such as laver bread and leek or brie.

In the near future, the shop is going to expand and diversify to bring you even more superb foodstuffs, so keep calling in. The owners also have a pharmacy which is close by (01558 823556).

RIG OUT

105 Rhosmaen Street, Llandeilo,
Carmarthenshire SA19 6HA
Tel: 01558 822853

On the main street of Llandeilo, **Rig Out** is a wonderful shop specialising in elegant women's fashions. Owner Gwenda Lloyd Davies started her working life as a primary school teacher, but she was always interested in fashion, so opened the shop in 1984. She has loved it ever since, and her professionalism and enthusiasm have earned the shop a customer base that extends all over south and west Wales.

The display area on the ground and first floors of a delightful town centre Victorian building, features clothes from many of the top British and Continental fashion houses, including Bandolera, Jocavi, Hucke, Rosies, Sandwich and Persona. The shop also offers a bespoke tailoring service on site (by Gwenda's mother, a trained seamstress) and sells many delightful accessories, including jewellery and hats.

🏛 historic building   🏛 museum   🏛 historic site   ⚜ scenic attraction   🌿 flora and fauna remains today is a mound, as it was destroyed by its owners in 1277 rather than let it fall into the hands of the English. A few miles to the southwest lies **Carn Coch**, the largest hill fort in Wales, whose earthworks and stone ramparts cover some 15 acres. Also southwest of the town is the village is **Bethlehem**. Thousands of people from all over the world send cards to the Post Office here at Christmas time to be franked and sent on elsewhere, a practise which is known locally as 'franking sense'.

TRAPP
12 miles SW of Llandovery off the A483

🏛 Carreg Cennen Castle

🎨 Trapp Arts and Crafts Centre

Situated on the top of a precipitous limestone crag on the Black Mountain and with a vertical drop to the River Cennen below, **Carreg Cennen Castle**, to the east of Trapp, enjoys one of the most spectacular locations of any Welsh castle. Although the present castle dates from the late 13th or early 14th century, there was undoubtedly a fortress here before that; some attribute a castle here to Urien, a knight of Arthur's Round Table. Despite its origins being shrouded in obscurity, the castle is known to have been hotly fought over. Carreg Cennen fell to Owain Glyndwr's Welsh insurgents and, during the War of the Roses, it became a base for bandit Lancastrians. Taken on behalf of the Yorkists in 1462, the fortress was dismantled on the orders of Edward IV, leaving the romantic ruins seen today. A visit is well worth the effort to enjoy the impressive views and to appreciate what a daunting task attacking the castle must have been. There is only one way up - a steep, grassy hill protected by a complicated system of defences.

One local legend tells of a narrow underground tunnel which leads from the castle to a wishing well where visitors used to throw corks into the water to make their dreams come true. The well's waters were also thought to have special powers, particularly in curing eye and ear complaints. Trapp itself has a connection with water as the village is the source of Brecon Carreg mineral water. In the converted barns of Llwyndewi Farm is **Trapp Arts and Crafts Centre**, which specialises in Welsh crafts. The shop stocks an interesting range of quality items including stained glass, lovespoons, pottery and jewellery, and the art gallery on the first floor shows the work of local artists. Demonstrations and exhibitions run throughout the summer months, and the centre has a coffee shop.

LLANDEILO
11½ miles SW of Llandovery on the A483

🏛 Tywi Bridge 🏛 Parish Church of St Teilo

🏛 Dinefwr Castle 🌳 Dinefwr Park

The former ancient capital of West Wales, Llandeilo's hilltop position shows off to best advantage this pretty little market town. Pastel coloured Georgian houses line the main road, which curves elegantly up from the **Tywi Bridge** (its central span is said to be the longest in Wales) to the Victorian **Parish Church of St Teilo**, which was designed by the well-known architect Sir Giles Gilbert Scott. St Teilo lived in the 6th century, and was a companion of St David. He founded a monastery at Llandeilo, where he later died, on the site of the church. It is best known for producing the beautiful *Gospel of St Teilo*, one of Wales' best-known manuscripts. It was later known as the *Lichfield Gospels* and Book of St Chad. Serving the rich agricultural land which surrounds it, Llandeilo was one of the original founders of the Welsh Rugby Union.

To the west of the town lies **Dinefwr**

SALVADOR DELI

3 Carmarthen Street, Llandeilo, Carmarthenshire SA19 6AE
Tel: 01558 824609

The **Salvador Deli** was originally a pub dating from 1625, and it still has
its original beams and open stone fireplace. It stands in the centre of
Llandeilo, and its small shop front belies the large interior, which is
packed with goods. In fact, it is a fascinating place inside, quirky and
delightful, with displays of foodstuffs that show off local, British and
European foodstuffs to perfection. Pickles - cheeses - cold meats -
sausages - organic bread - herbs - garlic bulbs - sauces - marinades -
it's got the lot!

It is owned and managed by Sarah Shore-Taylor, who, since she
opened the deli in 2006, has created an establishment that is
becoming well-known beyond Llandeilo and the surrounding area.
Sarah, a former social worker who comes from a family with catering
and foodstuffs in its blood, imports many delicious items, especially
from Italy and Spain,

Among the popular items that are offered for sale are the award-
winning Hawkshead relishes and pickles from Cumbria, which are
delicious, Bernadini sauces from Tuscany, and, on Friday, fresh fish
from the fishing ports of Wales. Sarah is determined to build on her
already fine reputation for great foodstuffs and value for money, and
she invites you to pay her a visit and see for yourself.

MAERDY HOLIDAY COTTAGES

The Maerdy, Taliaris, Llandeilo,
Carmarthenshire SA19 7DA
Tel: 01550 777448
e-mail: enquiries@maerdyholidaycottages.co.uk
website: www.maerdyholidaycottages.co.uk

Owned and run by Margaret Jones, the four and five star
Maerdy Holiday Cottages opened in 1980, and since then have
been providing superb self-catering holiday accommodation on
the edge of the Brecon Beacons, one of Wales's most scenic
areas. The Maerdy sits in a glorious setting with the 300-year-
old farmhouse and its stone buildings being beautifully and
sympathetically converted into six cottages that sleep up to
ten people, enabling groups of up to 30 to visit.

They enjoy a tranquil setting among mature and naturally
wooded gardens, with a stream running through it. Each cottage comes furnished with many
antiques, and is well equipped throughout. All have a TV set, CD player, radio cassette, central
heating, washing machine and microwave, and some even boast a dishwasher, telephone and
open fire. An initial supply of logs is free, and thereafter they are supplied at cost. Being cool in
summer and cosy in winter, they make the perfect retreat for any time of the year. Catering
services are available, as well as B&B accommodation. Well-behaved dogs are accepted for a
small extra charge, and high chairs and cots can be supplied by prior arrangement. Extra china,
cutlery and glasses are available for larger parties. Maerdy Cottages offer some of the finest
self-catering accommodation in Wales, and they make a perfect base from which to explore the
many attractions and facilities Wales has to offer.

🏠 historic building   🏛 museum   🏛 historic site   🐿 scenic attraction   🌿 flora and fauna

JH COOPER

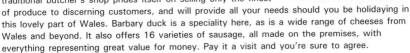

Smithfield House, 4 Carmarthen Street, Llandeilo, Carmarthenshire SA19 6AE
Tel: 01558 823463
e-mail: jhcooper@btconnect.com

For the very best in local beef, pork, lamb, sausages, cured bacon and poultry, you just can't beat **JH Cooper**! This traditional butcher's shop prides itself on selling only the finest of produce to discerning customers, and will provide all your needs should you be holidaying in this lovely part of Wales. Barbary duck is a speciality here, as is a wide range of cheeses from Wales and beyond. It also offers 16 varieties of sausage, all made on the premises, with everything representing great value for money. Pay it a visit and you're sure to agree.

Castle, the ancient seat of the Princes of Deheubarth, one of the three ancient kingdoms of Wales. The fortress was built on the site of an Iron Age fort and legend has it that Merlin's grave is in the area. Overlooking the River Tywi, the first stone castle here is believed to have been built by Rhys ap Gryffydd in the 12th century and, seen as an important target, it was dismantled by Rhys Grug in 1220 to prevent Llywelyn from taking this strategic position. The castle ruins are surrounded by **Dinefwr Park** (NT). Extensive areas of parkland were landscaped by Capability Brown in 1775 and incorporated the medieval castle, house, gardens and ancient deer park into one breathtaking panorama. Footpaths through the parkland lead to the castle, bog wood and beech clumps and offer outstanding views of the Tywi valley. The site is one of international importance for wintering birds, including white-fronted geese, curlews and lapwings. There is a small herd of white cattle.

TALLEY

8½ miles W of Llandovery on the B4302

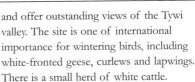

Talley Abbey   Parish Church of St Michael

This village, with its backdrop of rolling hills, takes its name from Tal-y-llychau, meaning Head of the Lakes. Between two lakes lies **Talley Abbey**, founded in the late 12th century by Rhys ap Gryffyd, and the only Welsh outpost of the austere Premonstratensian canons who, ejected by the Cistercians in the early 13th century, had

HOLLYVILLE COTTAGE B&B & SELF-CATERING

Maesyerugiau, Pencader, Nr Lampeter SA39 9DL
Tel: 01559 395301
e-mail:bizzylizzy_hollyville@btinternet.com
website: www.dreamwales.com

For the very best in B&B and self-catering accommodation, you must make your way to **Hollyville Cottage B&B and Self-Catering**, set among some of the most beautiful scenery in Wales. The four star B&B accommodation consists of two lovely, comfortable rooms and, on choosing either the double or the twin, you will also have a private bathroom. The two rooms are also let together to accommodate families in which case the bathroom is shared. The five star cottage is cosy yet spacious, open planned, with two en suite bedrooms and wood burning stove.

GOETRE FARM TRADITIONAL PORK AND POULTRY

Llanllwni, Llanybydder Carmarthenshire SA40 9SG
Tel: 01570 480671
website: www.goetrefarm.co.uk

Goetre Farm grows and produces free range ducks and pigs – with top-of-the-range turkeys at Christmas. All are reared on the farm in the traditional way.

Michael and Jennifer have been running their small Welsh hill farm on the side of Llanllwni Mountain since 1990 when just a few dressed chickens were sold to local farmers. They have since expanded the range of products and now sell to discerning, loyal, local customers as well as supplying farm shops and restaurants. Since launching a website in 2006 sales by overnight courier have also become increasingly popular.

The saddleback pigs roam freely on natural pasture and are fed a cereal diet and forage on root crops. The pork is butchered on farm and made into joints and sausages, dry-cured into bacon and gammon. The ducks are a speciality, benefiting from grazing on the Welsh mountain grass to improve succulence. Traditional bronze and white free range turkeys are available at Christmas.

Produce is available Wednesday to Saturday morning throughout the year. However, customers are advised to ring before calling at the farm.

appealed to the Archbishop of Canterbury and were granted their own religious rights in 1208. Of the few remains to have survived, an immense tower still overshadows the peaceful abbey lawns. The nearby 18th century **Parish Church of St Michael** is something of an oddity: it was built with no aisle and its interior was entirely taken up with box pews.

CRUGYBAR
7 miles NW of Llandovery on the B4302

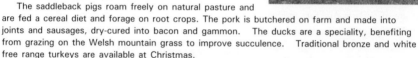

Just to the northeast of the village, and nestling in the beautiful foothills of the Cambrian Mountains, lies **Felin Newydd**, a 200-year-old working watermill believed to have been constructed on the site of a grist mill used by Roman soldiers working on the nearby gold mines. Restored in the 1980s, when fascinating graffiti on the mill walls

linked the building with 19th century Welsh colonists of South America, the mill is now capable of grinding flour once more.

The land around the mill

Felin Newydd

is quiet, unspoiled and ideal for discovering all manner of wild plant and animal life. Lucky visitors have been known to see red kite circling overhead although there are also more friendly ducks and chickens to amuse young children. A renovated byre has been converted into a cosy tearoom that also includes an interesting selection of local crafts for sale.

🏛 historic building   🏛 museum   🏛 historic site   🍃 scenic attraction   🐑 flora and fauna

PUMSAINT
8 miles NW of Llandovery on the A482

🏛 Dolaucothi Goldmines

Near this hamlet, whose names means Five Saints, is the **Dolaucothi Goldmines** (NT), which date back some 2,000 years to a time when the open-cast gold workings were secured by the Roman army. Once a likely source of gold bullion for the Imperial mints of Lyons and Rome, the mines are still in a remarkable state of preservation despite being abandoned by the Romans in AD 140. They were reopened for a short time between 1888 and the late 1930s. Visitors can see both the ancient and modern mine workings, including a number of the horizontal tunnels dug into the hillside for drainage and access. There is also the opportunity to try gold panning, to see an exhibition of vintage mining machinery and to tour the surrounding woodland on a waymarked trail. The site also has a shop selling Welsh Gold and tearoom serving delicious home-cooked food.

Llanelli

🏛 Parish Church of St Elli   🌳 Pembrey Country Park

🏛 Llanelly House

🌱 National Wetlands Centre of Wales

🖼 Parc Howard Museum and Art Gallery

🌳 Millennium Coastal Park and Cycleway

Essentially an industrial town with tinplating, steel, chemical and engineering works, Llanelli was named after the Celt St Elli, to whom the **Parish Church of St Elli** is dedicated. It has two naves, one dating from Norman times and one built in the 15th century. The stained glass windows commemorate the traditional industries of the town - iron making and

mining. While heavy industry certainly put the town on the map, Llanelli is perhaps more famous as the home of the Scarlets, one of the most famous rugby teams in Wales. The saucepan tipped rugby posts at Stradey Park and the Scarlets' anthem, *Sospan Fach* ('little saucepan'), are both reminders of Llanelli's industrial heritage. In Stepney Street, the Stepney Wheel was made in the early 20th century; this was an inflated spare tyre on a spokeless rim, to be fixed over a punctured wheel. In India, the term Stepney Wheel is still sometimes applied to any spare tyre. Housed in a former mansion set in a large civic park, **Parc Howard Museum and Art Gallery** has a collection of local paintings and 19th century Llanelli pottery as well as displays on the history of the town. However, Llanelli is not all industry and rugby as the town is home to one of the country's newest attractions, the **Millennium Coastal Park and Cycleway**. Providing all manner of leisure activities and peaceful wildlife havens, the park incorporates wetlands, gardens, woodlands, a golf course and both sailing and watersports. **Llanelly House**, built in 1714, opposite the church, is a good example of an early 18th century house. The local council has purchased the property, and will be restoring it.

To the east of Llanelli lies the **National Wetlands Centre of Wales**, which is one of the eight centres established by the Trust founded by Sir Peter Scott at Slimbridge in 1946. Also a haven for wild plant and animal life throughout the year, the centre's 200 acre saltmarsh is home to flocks of curlew, lapwing and redshank, which visitors can observe from secluded hides. The Discovery Centre has hands-on activities to help visitors find out about conservation.

🏛 stories and anecdotes   🐦 famous people   🎨 art and craft   🎭 entertainment and sport   🚶 walks

Around Llanelli

GORSLAS
9 miles N of Llanelli on the A476

🏛 Mynydd Mawr   🏞 Llyn Llech Owain Country Park

Legend tell us that on **Mynydd Mawr**, a mountain to the north of the village, there was a well that was long ago given to the shepherds by the fairies to water their flocks. The only condition of the gift was that the shepherds had to replace the well slab after they used it. This the shepherds did, and everything remained peaceful. Some time later, King Arthur had sent his knights out to seek the Holy Grail, and one of them, Sir Owen (Sir Gwain on the Arthurian legends) met and slew a pagan knight who lived near Gorslas. Weary and parched, he rested by the well, and both he

and his horse drank from it. But so tired was he that he forgot to place the slab over the well before falling asleep, and when he wakened he found that the water had created a great lake at the foot of the mountain.

Not only that, shepherds were running towards him, angry that he had robbed them of good farmland. He had to think of something to tell them, so he calmly explained that he had created a great lake at the foot of the mountain, and that they need not climb it any more to get good, fresh water. Placated, the shepherds left him in peace. The lake of water which was left is known today as Llyn Llech Owain - the 'Lake of Owain's Stone Slab'.

Today, **Llyn Llech Owain Country Park** includes the lake, as well as the peat bog which surrounds it, an area of largely coniferous woodland and dry heath. The lake and peat

---

STITCH BY POST

9 Colonel Road, Betws, Ammanford,
Carmarthenshire SA18 2HB
Tel: 01269 591538
Mobile: 07799851965/07940574231
e-mail: info@stitchbypost.co.uk website: www.stitchbypost.co.uk

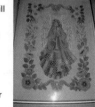

For all your stitching needs and specialist hand-crafted x-stitched cards for that special occasion, visit **StitchByPost** in Colonel Road, Betws. This fascinating establishment has everything you will need. A special new mail ordering system is fully operational too.

StitchByPost is owned by Sharon Walker a mother of nine children who is also a writer and poet laureate too. She is an experienced stitcher and can offer expert help and advice where needed. She may even be able to help with a stitching problem. Mrs Walker sells a vast variey of specialist hand crafted X-stitched cards and wedding stationary - to order - for your friends and family who are celebrating an anniversary, wedding, birthday or any special occassion. If you have a favourite photo you wish to always treasure then StitchByPost can help with their specialist Hand-Crafted Photo - Chart Kits. Kits that will completely enthrall you, with everything you will need to fully progress to completion of your masterpiece.All the products seen are for sale and if you have a particular request you can always use the mail ordering system. These make excellent gifts and beautiful reminders of your visit to Wales.

Mrs Walker also undertakes commissioned orders of highly specialised and wedding stationary, and general occassions X-stitched works of art cards. These gifts of love and skill by StitchByPost makes it worth revisiting this part of Wales.

🏛 historic building   🏛 museum   🏛 historic site   🏞 scenic attraction   🌿 flora and fauna bog, designated a Site of Special Scientific Interest, are home to a variety of rare plants such as bogbean, round leafed sundew and royal fern. The park's visitor centre has an exhibition that describes both the history and the natural history of the park.

PEMBREY
5 miles W of Llanelli on the A484

🏞 Pembrey Country Park   🏞 Cefn Sidan

This village lies on the flat lands which border Carmarthen Bay to the east of Llanelli, and during World War II a Royal Ordnance Factory produced munitions for the Allied Forces here. At the factory's peak, in 1942, it covered some 500 acres and employed 3,000 people. It ceased production in 1965, and since then the land has been landscaped to produce **Pembrey Country Park**, which offers visitors an unusual mix of pine forests, sand dunes and beaches as well as a dry ski slope, a toboggan run, a miniature railway and an adventure playground. Pembrey Pines Trail is a four-mile walk through dunes and woodland, with splendid views. There's also a visitor centre, and to the east lies Pembrey Saltmarsh, a local nature reserve and a Site of Special Scientific Interest. The park also includes **Cefn Sidan**, a blue flag beach that is one of Europe's best and safest, and from which there are glorious views over the Gower coastline.

KIDWELLY
7½ miles NW of Llanelli on the B4308

🏛 Parish Church of St Mary   🏛 Kidwelly Castle
🏛 Kidwelly Industrial Museum   👻 Gwenllian

This historic town, whose charter was granted by Henry I in the 12th century, boasts a 14th century bridge over the River Gwendreath and the **Parish Church of St Mary**, originally built as the church of a Benedictine priory in 1320.

However, the most interesting and impressive building is undoubtedly the remarkably well preserved Norman **Kidwelly Castle**, which stands on a steep bluff overlooking the river. The castle spans four centuries, but most of what remains today is attributed to Roger, Bishop of Salisbury who died in AD 1139 and also founded the priory. One of Wales' best kept secrets, Kidwelly Castle gives a fascinating insight into the evolution of a medieval castle into a domestic dwelling of more settled times.

For hundreds of years, the ghost of **Gwenllian**, daughter of the King of Gwynedd and the wife of the Prince of South Wales, was said to haunt the countryside around the castle. During an attack on in 1136 which Gwenllian led, she was decapitated and legend has it that her headless ghost was unable to find rest until a man searched the battlefield and returned her skull to her. Princess Gwenllian was certainly a warrior, and she was perhaps also a writer. Some have attributed parts of *The Mabinogion* to her, and if the attribution is correct, she would be Britain's earliest known woman writer.

On the outskirts of the town, marked by its 164ft redbrick chimney, lies the **Kidwelly Industrial Museum** - housed in an original tinplate works dating from 1737 Here visitors have a unique opportunity to see how the plate was made as well as learning something of the county's industrial past. The museum contains Britain's sole surviving pack mill.

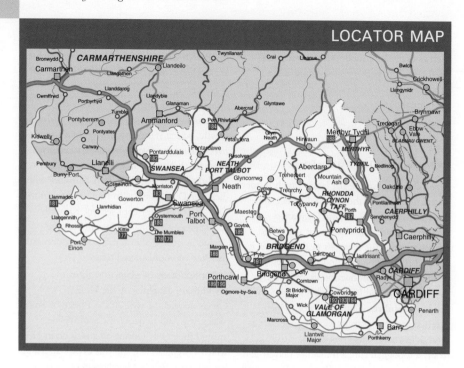

LOCATOR MAP

ADVERTISERS AND PLACES OF INTEREST

🏚 historic building   🏛 museum   🏛 historic site   🍂 scenic attraction   🌿 flora and fauna

9| Gower Peninsula & Heritage Coast

The delightful city of Swansea, with a population of 226,000 (including its hinterland), is the second largest city in Wales, and marks the gateway to the southernmost bulge of Wales, the lovely Gower Peninsula, a region designated an Area of Outstanding Natural Beauty, much of it owned by the National Trust. The Gower's southern coastline is made up of a succession of sandy, sheltered bays and along its whole coastline it is dotted with charming and relaxed seaside resorts.

This is also an area rich in natural beauty, with a long history that can be explored not only at the Gower Heritage Centre but also through its various castles, religious sites and ancient monuments. The area has many small family farms that yield some of the finest produce in south Wales, with the Gower in particular being known for its cockles and its laverbread (edible seaweed).

The Vale of Glamorgan is characterised by gentle rolling hills, genteel towns, a coastline rich in heritage and history, pretty villages and rich farmland. This is where Norman warlords built their castles, and where, at Llantwit Major, one of the country's oldest seats of learning was founded.

Behind the coastal region lie the valleys of southwest Wales which were known the world over for their coal mining and heavy industry. The best known is the Rhondda Valley, where only one mine survives from the numerous collieries that provided coal, not just for this country but many parts of the world. However, though mining has all but gone, the heritage remains. The towns and villages, where life revolved around the colliery, the chapel and the male voice choirs, survive. These famous choirs were formed mainly by coalmining and iron working communities of the south Wales valleys, and in the quarries of north Wales. Most of them welcome visitors dropping in on rehearsals as well as attending concerts.

In many cases, nature has reclaimed the hills and vales once scarred by the mining industry and, while pride in the industry remains, the various new country parks and nature reserves developed on the sites of the old mines are giving the area a new hope, and a new appeal.

Rhossili Bay

Swansea

🏛 Swansea Castle	🏛 Parish Church of St Mary
🏛 Waterfront Museum	🏛 Swansea Museum
🐦 Bonnie Tyler	🏛 Glynn Vivian Art Gallery
🏛 Egypt Centre	🌱 Clyne Gardens
🏛 Dylan Thomas Centre	🏚 Maritime Quarter
🌱 Plantasia Botanic Gardens	🐦 Sir Harry Secombe
🐦 Catherine Zeta Jones	🐦 Michael Heseltine
🐦 Rowan Williams	

Swansea, the second city of Wales, was founded in the late 10th century by Sweyne Forkbeard, King of Denmark. Its English name means 'Sweyne's Ey' - ey being an inlet. **Swansea Castle**, which gained notoriety in the 18th century when the northern block became a debtors' prison, was first built by the Norman Henry de Newburgh in the late 11th century. However, it was all but destroyed by Owain Glyndwr in the early 1400s when he ransacked the town that had grown up around the fortification.

As early as the 14th century, shipbuilding and coalmining were important industries in the area and, by 1700, Swansea was the largest

port in Wales. Smelters from Cornwall arrived here, attracted by the plentiful supply of coal, and copper works also flourished. Nelson's ships were covered in Swansea copper, and at one time 90% of the country's copper was smelted here and, in the heyday of the industry, other metals such as tin, lead, nickel and zinc were imported to the town for smelting and refining. In the 19th century Swansea porcelain was another famous product.

Much of the traditional industry has disappeared now, and the old dock area has been transformed into a marina surrounded by stylish waterfront buildings. This **Maritime Quarter** is arguably the most impressive part of the town and is alive with cafés, pubs and restaurants. The new **Waterfront Museum** on Oystermouth Road has exhibits and displays from the early days of the port right through to the devastating bombing raids of World War II. There is plenty to see and learn at the museum.

The town is also home to the **Swansea Museum**, the oldest in Wales, but up to date, combining bygone Swansea history and culture with new exhibitions and events. Among the displays are Swansea porcelain, the Cabinet of Curiosities, a Welsh kitchen and the Mummy of Tem-Hor. More artefacts from Egypt can be seen at the **Egypt Centre**, where over 1,000 objects, from impressive painted coffins to everyday household items, can be seen which date back as far as 3500 BC. At the **Glynn Vivian Art Gallery** in Alexandra Road a broad spectrum of the visual arts is on display. Based on the bequest of Richard Glynn Vivian, the gallery houses an

Swansea Marina

international collection of Swansea porcelain and various Old Masters as well as numerous paintings and sculptures by 20th century artists including Hepworth, Nicholas, Nash, Ceri Richards and Augustus John.

The **Parish Church of St Mary** was founded in medieval times, though it was probably built on the site of a 6th century monastery. The church was rebuilt in the 1890s when the 14th century chancel and tower and the 18th century nave were pulled down. However, this Victorian church was burnt down in February 1941 when it was bombed. Rebuilding continued until 1959.

At **Plantasia Botanic Gardens**, housed in the walled garden of Singleton Park, visitors can wander around a glass pyramid with three climatic zones - tropical, humid, arid - and 5,000 exotic plants. The hot house is also home to numerous exotic insects, fish and reptiles, such as leaf cutting ants, and there is a butterfly house where the various colourful species fly freely. **Clyne Gardens**, at Blackpill off the A4067 Mumbles road, are known in particular for their marvellous rhododendrons, including National Collections, their imposing magnolias and an extensive bog garden. In 2001 the rhododendrons captured 23 awards from the Royal Horticultural Society. These 19th century landscaped gardens were laid out by the Vivian family, who were also responsible for nearby Sketty Hall, a 19th century version of an Italian parterre garden.

No mention of Swansea would be complete without referring to the town's most famous son, Dylan Thomas, who described the town as viewed from his hillside home:

Ugly, lovely town crawling, sprawling, slummed, unplanned, jerry-villa'd, and smug-suburbed by the side of a long and splendid curving shore......

His former home on steep Cwmdonkin Drive in the Uplands district displays a blue plaque with the simple inscription, "Dylan Thomas, Poet, 1914-53. Born in this house". The house can be viewed by appointment. Cwmdonkin Park, close to his home, was much loved by Thomas, whose poem *The Hunchback in the Park* was set there. The **Dylan Thomas Centre** in Somerset Place is dedicated to the poet's life and works, with the exhibitions featuring some of his original manuscripts, letters to friends and family and a moving American documentary about him. There are Dylan Thomas Trails to follow in the city centre, Uplands, Mumbles and Gower, and the annual Dylan Thomas Celebration attracts visitors from around the world.

The city was also the birthplace of other well know people. **Sir Harry Secombe, Catherine Zeta Jones, Michael Heseltine, Rowan Williams** (Archbishop of Canterbury) and the singer **Bonnie Tyler** were all born here.

If Dylan Thomas was Swansea's most famous son, its most famous dog was Jack (known as 'Swansea Jack'), a black retriever who lived in the city and died in 1937, aged seven. He was reputed to have saved 27 humans and two dogs from drowning and was awarded the canine Victoria Cross. In 2002 he was named 'dog of the century'.

Gower Peninsula

BISHOPSTON
3 mile SW of Swansea off the A4118

🌢 Bishopston Valley

The sheltered **Bishopston Valley** contains an extensive area of ancient woodland that supports a wide variety of plants and birds. A

PRESENCE

22 Pennard Road, Kittle, Swansea SA3 3JS
Tel: 01792 232499
e-mail: presencegifts4you@btinternet.com

People visiting Swansea who are looking for great gift or souvenir ideas always head for **Presence**, on Pennard Road. This entrancing shop, with its bright blue facia and its window stacked with a fascinating array of framed prints, teddy bears, cards and ceramics, has become a firm favourite since John Mizen opened it over two years ago.

The interior is light and spacious, with plenty of room to browse round everything on offer. You will not be hurried, though John is always on hand to advise and help. It is one of the few shops in south Wales that stocks the wonderful 'Gotta Getta Gund' range of teddy bears, described as the 'most huggable bears in the world'. They come from America, and now have a large following in this country as well. They make the ideal present for children of all ages. Also stocked are the Terramundi money pots, in a range of bright colours, shapes and stripes that is sure to please everyone.

But Presence doesn't just end there. It also stocks the famous Lily-Flame candles made by Helen Cawton. They have soft, sensual aromas that add a pleasant, welcoming fragrance to any room. Plus there is a range of cards and other gift items that all represent great value for money. Presence also offers a next-day framing service at competitive prices. John has been offering this service from before he opened his shop, and he has become something of an expert.

---

two-mile footpath leads along the valley from Kittle to Pwll Du.

MUMBLES

4½ miles SW of Swansea on the A4067

🏚 Oystermouth Castle   🏚 Parish Church of All Saints

🏛 Lovespoon Gallery   🌱 Langland Bay

🎞 Mumbles Passenger Railway   🐾 Thomas Bowdler

This charming Victorian resort grew up around the old fishing village of Oystermouth, which has its roots in Roman times and where the Normans built a castle to defend their land. Now in ruins, **Oystermouth Castle** was built by William de Londres, and was later the home of the de Breos family. The gatehouse, chapel and great hall all date from around the 13th and 14th centuries. Surrounded by small but beautiful

grounds overlooking the bay, the ruins are now the scene of re-enactments which chart the history of the castle and, in particular, the siege of the fortress by Owain Glyndwr.

The village is now a popular sailing centre, with numerous pubs, a restored late-Victorian pier and, on the headland, a lighthouse guarding the entrance into Swansea harbour. The **Parish Church of All Saints** is built on ths site of a Roman villa, and originally dates from the 12th century, though it was restored in Victorian times. Inside there is a memorial to the famous Mumbles lifeboat, and in the churchyard is the grave of **Thomas Bowdler** (1754 - 1825), the literary censor, who published an expurgated edition of Shakespeare in 1818 and gave our language the word 'bowdlerise'. His *Family Shakespeare* omitted words and expressions which he

---

🏚 historic building   🏛 museum   🎞 historic site   🌱 scenic attraction   🐾 flora and fauna considered could not be read aloud by a father to his family. Sex was out, but cruelty and violence remained largely unexpurgated. Bowdler died at Rhydding, near Swansea, in 1825, leaving a bowdlerised version of Gibbon's *Decline and Fall of the Roman Empire*.

An unusual attraction in Mumbles is the **Lovespoon Gallery**, where visitors will find an amazing variety of these unique love tokens. Lovespoons were traditionally carved from wood by young men and presented to their sweethearts as a token of their devotion. The custom dates back many centuries, but in these less romantic days the spoons are often bought simply as souvenirs of Wales.

Oystermouth Castle

The **Mumbles Passenger Railway** was the world's first, and ran from Mumbles north into Swansea. From 1807 to its closure in 1960, the five-mile line used horse, sail, steam, battery, petrol, diesel and electricity. On Bank Holidays in the mid-Victorian period it was

COVER TO COVER

58 Newton Road, Mumbles, Swansea SA3 4BQ
Tel: 01792 366363
e-mail: sales@cover-to-cover.co.uk
website: www.cover-to-cover.co.uk

Opened in September 1999, **Cover to Cover** has become one of the most popular shops in the delightful Victorian seaside village of Mumbles, outside Swansea. An inviting bookshop

where you can browse through quality fiction, an eclectic mix of non-fiction titles, plus a range of books on local, Swansea and Welsh interest.

The children's area is very popular with soft seats for little ones to settle and enjoy their books. The range stocked is excellent from Beatrix Potter to Harry Potter.

But Cover to Cover also sells an interesting selection of gifts, including leather wallets, bookmarks, key rings, journals, an award-winning fragrance range, photo frames, soft toys for children, and much more.

In Spring 2007 Cover to Cover launched their online book business with plans to include gifts later. This is a shop not to be missed.

SHAKERSHACK

Castleton Walk Arcade, Newton Road, Mumbles,
Swansea SA3 4AX
Tel: 01792 368378
e-mail: shakershack@tiscali.co.uk
website: www.shakershack.co.uk

Shakershack is a unique country store set in an arcade in
Mumbles. It is a wonderful American/French style shop selling a wide range of gifts ideas for all
the family at very competitive prices, and is one of the few distributors of the famous McCall and
Barn range of candles in the UK. Browse here, among the colourful and intriguing displays, to your
heart's content, then choose a suitable souvenir or gift for a loved one. They will treasure it.

526 Mumbles Road, Oystermouth, Swansea SA3 4DH. (01792)368212
www.joes-icecream.co.uk
For the very best in delicious ice cream you can't beat Joes.
Made in Swansea since 1922, this famous award winning brand boasts
three ice-cream parlours, with its unique taste you are transported to
ice cream heaven. Try the traditional knickerbocker glory or one of the many
sundaes. Also on offer are a selection of sandwiches and homemade cakes. When
you vist this beautiful part of Wales make sure you experience the wonderful taste
of Joes.

known to carry up to 40,000 passengers.

Beyond The Mumbles - the name is derived from the French *mamelles* meaning 'breasts' and is a reference to the two islets of the promontory beyond Oystermouth - lies the lovely Gower Peninsula, designated an Area of Outstanding Natural Beauty. Gower's southern coast is made up of a succession of sandy, sheltered bays and the first of these, **Langland Bay**, is just around the headland from the village.

PARKMILL

8 miles SW of Swansea on the A4118

🏰 Pennard Castle   🏛 Gower Heritage Centre

This village is home to the **Gower Heritage Centre** which is itself centred around a historic water mill built in the 12th century by

the powerful le Breos family, the Norman rulers of Gower. Originally constructed to supply flour for nearby **Pennard Castle**, now in ruins, this water mill is a rare survivor in Wales of a rural complex that would once have been found in most villages and hamlets. The Heritage Centre has displays on the history of this beautiful region along with a farming museum. Visitors can also tour the mill, where the restored machinery grinds flour on most days. Younger visitors to the centre can make friends with the farm animals and everyone will enjoy wandering around the craft units and workshops where a wheelwright, a potter, a blacksmith and a mason can be seen plying their trades

The castle was originally built of wood in the 12th century by Henry de Beaumont, Earl

🏛 historic building   🏛 museum   🏛 historic site   🗺 scenic attraction   🌿 flora and fauna of Warwick, when he became the lord of Gower. Later, it was rebuilt in stone, and the ruins you see today are from that period.

PENMAEN
7 miles SW of Swansea off the A4118

🏠 Parish Church of St John the Baptist

Tradition has it that a village, Stedwarlango, is buried here beneath the sand dunes. The National Trust owns an area that includes High Pennard, topped by a prehistoric hill fort, and Three Cliffs Bay, where there are old lime kilns, an ancient burial chamber and a pillow mound - an artificial warren used to farm rabbits. Cut into the rocks is Minchin Hole, a geological Site of Scientific Interest where evidence has been found of mammals and early man. The **Parish Church of St John the Baptist**, though it was heavily restored in Victorian times, has a wealth of memorial tablets.

OXWICH
11 miles SW of Swansea off the A4118

🏠 Parish Church of St Illtud 🏠 Oxwich Castle

🔾 Oxwich Point 🌱 Oxwich Nature Reserve

One of Gower's prettiest villages, Oxwich lies huddled along a lane at the western end of a superb three-mile-long beach. Once a small port exporting limestone and also a haven for smugglers, Oxwich is today a marvellous holiday area with safe bathing, clean beaches, wind surfing and water skiing. The village has some picturesque cottages of the traditional Gower style which include one that was once occupied by John Wesley. The 13th century **Parish Church of St Illtud**, half hidden by trees, is well worth seeking out as its ancient font is believed to have been brought here by St Illtud himself. There are several interesting carved tombs within the building, and the

chancel ceiling was decorated in 1931 by a scenic artist who worked at Sadler's Wells in London.

Just to the south of the village lies **Oxwich Castle**, a grand Tudor manor house built around a courtyard. Although this was probably the site of an earlier fortification, the splendid house was established by Sir Rice Mansel in the 1520s and added to by his son, Sir Edward Mansel, whose building work includes the Elizabethan long gallery. The Mansel family's time at this lavish mansion was short lived, and after they left in the 1630s the house fell into disrepair, although the southern wing was used as a farmhouse and the southeast tower still survives to its full height of six storeys.

For walkers there are plenty of footpaths to explore and the walk to **Oxwich Point**, in particular, provides some magnificent views of the Gower Peninsula. Close to the beach lies part of the **Oxwich Nature Reserve**, home to many rare species of orchid as well as other plant life and a variety of birds.

KNELSTON
12½ miles SW of Swansea on the A4118

🏠 Parish Church of St David 🪨 Arthur's Stone

To the north of this attractive village lies **Arthur's Stone**, a large burial chamber capstone. Traditionally, this is said to be the pebble which King Arthur removed from his shoe while on his way to the Battle of Camlann in the 6th century. According to legend, Arthur threw the stone over his shoulder and the stone lies exactly where it landed. Up until the 19th century, local girls would take part in a ritual here to discover whether their lovers were true or not. At midnight during the full moon, the girls would place a honey cake soaked in milk on the stone and then crawl under it three times. If their lovers were true, they would appear before them. The **Parish Church of St David** is 14th century, and has some interesting memorials within it. It was built by Henry de Gower, Bishop of St Davids. It has a west tower with a saddleback roof that contains the oldest (and some say loudest) bell on the Gower Peninsula.

RHOSSILI
16 miles SW of Swansea on the B4247

🏛 Parish Church of St Mary   🏛 The Warren

🍃 Worm's Head   🍃 Rhossili Beach

This village, on the westernmost area of the Gower Peninsula, is thought to have been named after St Fili, who is said to have been the son of St Cenydd. The **Parish Church of St Mary**, which dates from the early 13th century, has a superb late Norman carved archway over the door. Inside is a memorial plaque to a Gower man, Edgar Evans, who is perhaps better known as Petty Officer Evans, who died in the ill-fated expedition to the Antarctic led by Captain Scott in 1912.

The original village, and its parish church dedicated to St Sili or Sulien, stood near the beach, and in the 13trh century was engulfed by the shifting sand dunes during a storm. It is said that the site, now called **The Warren**, was once a Celtic monastery founded by St Cynwal.

To the west of Rhossili lies **Worm's Head**, an island which is a National Nature Reserve. Reached by a causeway at low tide, there is public access to the island, but those making the crossing should take great care not to be cut off by the tide. Worm's Head marks the southern edge of Rhossili Bay, where **Rhossili Beach** can be reached by a steep downhill climb. At low tide, the remains of several wrecks can be seen, most notably the

Helvetia, which was wrecked in 1887. The beach is very popular with fishermen, surfers and bathers.

LLANGENNITH
15 miles W of Swansea off the B4271

🏛 Parish Church of St Cenydd   🍃 Burry Holms

This quiet village is home to the largest church on the Gower Peninsula. The **Parish Church of St Cenydd** was built in the 12th century on the site of a monastery founded six centuries earlier by St Cenydd himself, which was later destroyed by Vikings. Inside, now mounted on a wall, is a curious gravestone thought to mark the resting place of the saint. He was born on the Gower Peninsula, and legend tells us he walked with a limp due to a withered leg. He was cast adrift in a basket on the Loughor estuary because of it, but was rescued by gulls and brought up by angels. To the west of the village and marking the northern edge of Rhossili Bay lies **Burry Holms**, another small island which can be reached via a causeway at low tide. On the island are the remains of an Iron Age earthwork and also a monastic chapel dating from the Middle Ages.

LLANRHIDIAN
10½ miles W of Swansea on the B4295

🏛 Weobley Castle   🏛 Llanelen

🏛 Parish Church of St Illtyd

Close to the wild and lonely north coast of the Gower Peninsula, where some of the finest beaches in the country can be found, this village is also close to **Weobley Castle**. Dating from the early 14th century and built by the de Bere family, Weobley is more a fortified manor house than a castle and stands today as one of the few surviving such houses in Wales. On an isolated site overlooking the

THE BRITANNIA INN

Llanmadoc, North Gower, Swansea SA3 1DB
Tel: 01792 386624
e-mail: viv.davies@tiscali.co.uk
website: www.britanniainn.co.uk

The **Britannia Inn** is a picturesque pub and restaurant situated in a quiet corner of the Gower Peninsula, in the village of Llanmadoc.

The Inn dates from the 17th century and many of the original features are preserved; in the bar there is the original bread oven, and in the restaurant the beams are thought to have been taken from ships which were "lanterned" ashore by wreckers.

Martin and Lindsey took over in October 2006, they are both chefs of considerable international experience having travelled and worked in New Zealand, Australia, SE Asia, South Africa and Central America. This experience is reflected in the excellent food that is served in the restaurant which is full of character. The food is prepared from fresh local produce, their signature dish being 'cockle, crab and butternut ravioli'.

The cosy bar serves an excellent selection of cask conditioned ales, lagers and stouts.

Outside the Inn there are extensive beer gardens to the front and to the rear, with excellent views over the Loughor Estuary and the added interest of an aviary and small pet area. There are three guest rooms available.

eerie expanse of Llanrhidian Marsh, this house has been remarkably well preserved and visitors can gain a real insight into the domestic arrangements of those days and, in particular, the owners' desire for comfort. In the late 15th century the house came into the hands of Sir Rhys ap Thomas, an ally of Henry VII, and further improvements were made including the addition of a new porch and an upgrade of the accommodation in the private apartments. As well as seeing the interior of this impressive house, visitors can also view an exhibition on the Gower Peninsula - its history and other ancient monuments.

Weobley Castle

🎭 stories and anecdotes　🐦 famous people　🎨 art and craft　🎵 entertainment and sport　🚶 walks

THE NEST

100 St Teilo Street, Pontarddulais, Nr Swansea SA4 8SS
Tel: 01792 882425
e-mail: samantha@samantha32.wanadoo.co.uk

With cream, wooden walls and exposed wooden floors, **The Nest** is a special shop, stuffed full of goodies that are sure to please and impress everyone.

It is situated in the small town of Pontarddulais, north west of Swansea just off the M4, and is owned and managed by Samantha Johnson. After a time living in London she moved back to her homeland to bring up her children and begin a career with Shelter Cymru. Since opening the shop in 2006 it has gone from strength to strength with Samantha's mum holding the fort 4 days a week and Samantha and her husband working there on their days off from their normal jobs. All the staff are very knowledgeable about everything they stock, and are always on hand to offer friendly help and advice. Browse the shop's colourful interior with no obligation to buy. Take your time, and you will almost certainly find that present you have been looking for or a souvenir of your trip to Wales. The place has a fascinating quality, and you will be impressed by the outstanding value-for-money prices.

It sells a wide range of goods such as retro kitchen storage, heart shape slate coasters, bedding, quilts, cuddly toys, jewellery, games, accessories, pottery and children's crockery. Some items are exclusive to the shop, like the wooden letters which are cut to shape in the States and then sent over to be hand painted by Samantha. Popular with the boys are the used American car number plates mainly in red, white and blue colourways. She especially likes French and American goods, and has an in-depth knowledge that she is willing to share with her customers. Such names as Greengate quilts, Emma Bridgewater crockery, with their bright patterns, St Eval candles from Cornwall, loveable Jellycat toys, high-quality Egmont children's cuddly toys, Surfboard clocks, Rosie Flo colouring books, Grand Illusions pottery and a whole lot more grace her shelves and displays, and the cuddly toys especially, some of which are made in Belgium, are available nowhere else in the country. Samantha also makes her own Christmas fabric decorations, and these delightful objects are also on sale in the shop.

If you bring your children along, and they are well behaved, Samantha will present them with a sweet. If the grown ups are also well-behaved, they might be given a sweet or two as well. There are toys in the shop to keep the children happy while their parents browse. The shop sits in the heart of the town, on the main street, and can't be missed. So if you're travelling along the M4, turn off at Pontarddulais, pay it a visit and have a look round. You will be made more than welcome.

🏛 historic building   🏛 museum   🏚 historic site   🏞 scenic attraction   🌱 flora and fauna

THE MASONS ARMS

Ryh-y-Pandy Road, Morriston, Swansea SA6 6PB
Tel: 01792 842535

For good food, great dink and light snacks you just can't beat **The Masons Arms** in Morriston, near Swansea and just off the M4 motorway. It is a picturesque inn - whitewashed with hanging baskets and a feeling of 'olde worlde' charm about it. The interior is equally as delightful, with open log fires, old wood, framed prints on the wall and a warm, Welsh welcome that is second to none.

It is a family run inn, owned and managed by mine hosts Anne and Kieran, who take great pride in the high standards of service, the keen prices and the overall ambience, which speaks of cosiness, friendliness and a 'country pub' atmosphere. It is a favourite with locals, which is always a god sign!

There is a well-stocked bar serving real ales plus a good range of beers, lagers, cider, wines, spirits, liqueurs, and, should you be driving, soft drinks. Bar lunches and light snacks are served, with the produce used in the kitchen being fresh and sourced locally wherever possible. No frozen stuff here!

One of the joys of the inn is the live entertainment, and you are invited to come along and listen to the live music and take part in the karaoke (but only if you want to!).

Good, honest country pubs with bags of atmosphere are hard to find nowadays, so The Mason's arms are something special. Call in and see for yourself.

GOWER PENINSULA & HERITAGE COAST

The **Parish Church of St Illtyd** is medieval, and has a fortified tower. It has strong links with the Knights of St John of Jerusalem, and in 1880 a curious carved stone was unearthed in the churchyard. Known as the 'Leper Stone', it is Irish in origin, and seems to show St Anthony and St Paul meeting in the desert.

Close to Llanrhidian is the site of the legendary lost village of **Llanelen**. During the reign of Edward VI in the mid 16th century, a ship ran aground in the Burry estuary, and the people of Lhanelen rescued the crew members and made them welcome. However, unknown to everyone, the crew were infected with the plague, and eventually everyone either died or fled, abandoning the village. An archaeological dig between 1973 and 1985 uncovered foundations of simple cottages and

what was thought to be the foundations of a church. Two memorial stones at the entrance to St Illtyd's Church commemorate the village.

LOUGHOR

6½ miles NW of Swansea on the A484

🏰 Loughor Castle

A strategic location on the mouth of the River Loughor gave this village prominence and importance down the centuries. The Romans built their station of Leucarum here in the 1st century and, in the early 12th century, a Norman nobleman, Henry de Newburgh, built **Loughor Castle** on the edge of the Roman site. Unfortunately, all that is left of the stronghold, which protected the confluence of the Burry Inlet and the River Loughor, is the ruined 13th century square tower.

📖 stories and anecdotes   🦜 famous people   🎨 art and craft   🎭 entertainment and sport   🚶 walks

HILARY BRYANSTON ARTIST & ART TUITION

Graig-y-Betting Gwrhyd Road, Pen Rhiwfawr, Swansea SA9 2SA
Tel: 01639 831309
e-mail: info@hilarybryanston.co.uk
website: www.artcymru.co.uk / www.hilarybryanston.co.uk

If you are looking for a relaxing, enjoyable day, why not visit the art classes organised by artist **Hilary Bryanston**? Her studio is situated in a remote, idyllic setting on the Gwrhyd Mountain, six miles north of Pontardawe near Swansea. This gives you the opportunity to spend a day painting or drawing, wood and stone carving, making ceramics or creating mosaics with a professional artist who will give you all the help, advice and encouragement you need to improve your craft and talent. Longer courses are on offer as well, and accommodation at competitive prices is always available. Walking and birdwatching are other ways to enjoy this landscape.

Hilary is a respected artist who has exhibited all over the country, including London, Birmingham, Cardiff and Wolverhampton, and is listed in Frances Spalding's definitive book, *20th Century Painters and Sculptors*. She studied at various art colleges in both Wales and England, and now tutors in painting ceramics where she has gained an enviable reputation at passing on her skills. She calls herself a 'painter of the

imagination', inspired by a diet of the local spectacular landscapes and beach scenes near where she lives.

The classes are aimed at both the beginner and the more advanced, and are not only stimulating but extremely enjoyable and sociable affairs. Why not book a day for yourself and see? Hilary is approachable and friendly, and will personally welcome you to her beautiful cottage high in the Welsh hills.

Port Talbot

🏠 Baglan Bay Energy Park   🐾 Red Dogs of Morfa

Port Talbot grew out of a small community called Aberafan. Well known for its steel industry, it was named after the Talbot family, who were responsible for the development of the town's docks in the 19th century. Now called the Old Docks, this area saw significant expansion again in the 20th century when a new deep water harbour was opened by the Queen in 1970. Today Port Talbot is home to factories and processing plants, and also to the solar centre of **Baglan Bay Energy Park**, which explains the history of the area and its power generating potential.

Coal mining has taken place in the area around Port Talbot for centuries and during this time many superstitions have grown up. In 1890, the miners at Morfa Colliery reported seeing ghostly images in and around the colliery. They were said to be fierce hounds, which became known as the **Red Dogs of Morfa**, and they would run through the streets with their appearance being accompanied by a sweet, rose-like scent which filled the mine shaft. Such were the number of eerie manifestations that on the morning of 10th March 1890, nearly half the morning shift failed to report for work. Later the same day, there was an explosion at the colliery - 87 miners died in the disaster.

🏛 historic building   🏛 museum   🏚 historic site   🏞 scenic attraction   🌿 flora and fauna

Around Port Talbot

NEATH
4 miles N of Port Talbot on the A465

🏛 Neath Abbey   🏛 Parish Church of St Illtyd

🏛 Neath Museum and Art Gallery   🖌 Neath Fair

While Neath's industrial history dates back to the late 16th century, when the first copper smelter in South Wales was built here by Cornishmen, the town has its origins in Roman times. Remains of Roman Nidum can still be seen close to the ruins of **Neath Abbey**, which was founded in the 13th century by Richard de Granville on land seized from the Welsh in around 1130. At first it was a daughter house of Sauvigny in France, but it later became Cistercian. It was a wealthy establishment, always wanting to expand its land holdings, and this led it into many disputes with Margam Abbey, to the south east of Port Talbot (see also Margam). The buildings were converted into a mansion for Sir John Herbert in the 16th century and it was later used to house copper smelters. It was also de Granville who built **Neath Castle**, in the mid 12th century, around which the town grew and whose scant remains can be found near a town centre car park.

The **Parish Church of St Illtyd** was founded in the 6th century by the saint of the same name. Legend has it that this was where he used to come on retreat, and a wooden church was erected on the site. The present church is the result of a restoration of 1850, though there are still some Norman and Early English details - notably the font - to be seen. It was again restored in 2003.

Housed in the Gwyn Hall in the centre of thr town, the **Neath Museum and Art Gallery** has permanent displays on the history of the town, including finds from the time of the Roman occupation, as well as regularly changing art and photographic exhibitions. The Museum has many hands-on activities, including grinding corn, using a Celtic loom and making a wattle fence.

Held each September, **Neath Fair** is the oldest such event in Wales, founded by Gilbert de Clare in 1280.

ABERDULAIS
6 miles NE of Port Talbot off the A4109

🖼 Aberdulais Falls

From as early as 1584 the power generated by the magnificent National Trust-owned **Aberdulais Falls** has been harnessed for a number of industries, including copper smelting and tin plating. Today, the waterwheel, the largest currently in use for the generation of electricity, makes the Falls self-sufficient in environmentally friendly energy. The Turbine House provides access to a unique fish pass.

CRYNANT
9 miles NE of Port Talbot on the A4109

🏛 Cefn Coed Colliery Museum

In the beautiful Dulais Valley, **Cefn Coed Colliery Museum** provides a wonderful opportunity for visitors to discover what life was like for the miners who worked underground in some of the most difficult conditions experienced anywhere in the world. Through photographs, maps and other exhibits, the tradition and legacy of mining are brought to life. The museum also has a well-stocked souvenir and gift shop, with one of the best selections of genuine and reproduction miner's lamps in the region. It is ideal for finding a special present from Wales.

CYNONVILLE
6 miles NE of Port Talbot on the A4107

🏛 South Wales Miners' Museum   🖼 Afan Forest Park

Virtually surrounding the village (to the north,

GOWER PENINSULA & HERITAGE COAST

L & A THE OUTDOOR CENTRE

Goytne, Port Talbot SA13 2YP
Tel: 01639 885509
e-mail: info@landaoutdoorcentre.co.uk
website: www.landaoutdoorcentre.co.uk

L & A, the Outdoor Centre can be found in a uniquely beautiful south Wales valley adjoining the 10,000 acres of forestry at Margham Park. It is the ideal place for people or groups looking for a peaceful holiday or break and yet within easy distance of things to do and see. It is near the Afan Park Mountain Biking Centre and Glyncorrwg Ponds, only 30 minutes west of Cardiff, and a few minutes from Port Talbot, with its shops, bars, clubs, pubs and supermarkets.

It boasts superb self-catering accommodation in 13 two-storey cabins that come complete with three upstairs bedrooms, a fully-equipped kitchen (where crockery, cutlery and cooking utensils are provided), dining table and chairs, a comfortable lounge with colour TV, and a WC plus shower. The décor in each is smart and modern, with extremely comfortable furniture and plenty of space. They are located overlooking a mountain stream, with outdoor furniture and facilities for barbecues. All bed linen is provided.

In addition, for larger groups there are three eight-bedded bunk houses with wc and shower but no cooking facilities and a 38-bedded bunkhouse with four toilets and shower room.

Pets are most welcome at L & A the Outdoor Centre, and it also has a bar and restaurant, the Watering Hole, where you can relax over a drink or eat superb food prepared from fresh local produce wherever possible. The centre also boasts a lecture theatre, function room with bar and catering facilities, wireless internet and business facilities, activity and play areas and an outdoor heated swimming pool.

Within a short radius of the centre there is just so much to do. In addition to what has already been mentioned, there is ample opportunity to take part in horse riding, walking and rambling, golf, fishing, canoeing, rock climbing, surfing, abseiling and a whole lot more. Why not make the 30 minute journey to the Grand Hotel in Swansea, which is owned by the centre, and indulge in some fine dining?

L & A, the Outdoor Centre offers the very best in holiday facilities for families of groups looking for something a bit different, and the prices represent amazing value for money. So pick up the phone and make your booking now.

🏛 historic building   🏛 museum   🏛 historic site   ☘ scenic attraction   🌱 flora and fauna west and south) lies the **Afan Forest Park**, a large area of woodland where there are trails for cycling, walking and pony trekking. At the Park's Countryside Centre an exhibition explains, with the aid of hands-on displays, the landscape and history of the Afan Valley. The **South Wales Miners' Museum**, also at the centre, illustrates the social history of the valleys' mining communities.

PONT-RHYD-Y-FEN
3½ miles NE of Port Talbot on the B4287

🐦 Richard Burton   🐦 Ivor Emmanuel

This mining village in the Afan Valley was the birthplace of the actor **Richard Burton** (1925 - 1984), who was born Richard Walters Jenkins. He was the 12th of 13 children born into a Welsh speaking family. His father was a

coal miner and his mother died in childbirth two years after he was born. Consequently, he was brought up in Port Talbot by his much older sister. He was legally adopted by his schoolmaster at grammar school, Philip H. Burton. It was also the birthplace, in 1927, of singer **Ivor Emmanuel**. Like Burton, he too had a tragic childhood, as his mother, father, sister and grandfather were killed when a German bomb fell on the village. He was a great friend of Richard Burton.

MARGAM
3 miles SE of Port Talbot on the A48

🏛 Margam Abbey   🏛 Parish Chutrch of St Mary

🏛 Margam Stones Museum   🌳 Margam Country Park

To the southeast of the town lies **Margam Country Park** surrounding a mansion built in

---

LOVESPOONS WALES

264a Margam Road, Margam, Port Talbot, West Glamorgan
Tel: 01639 681100
e-mail: paul@lovespoons-wales.co.uk
website: www.lovespoons-wales.co.uk

Looking for the perfect Celtic gift when visiting Wales? Then head for **Lovespoons Wales** in Margam, just outside Port Talbot. These traditional tokens of love used to be carved by young men to give to their intended sweethearts. They also showed to the sweetheart's father that the young man was industrious and good with his hands, always a good sign!

Of course, not all the spoons were accepted, and no doubt the young man would nurse a broken heart until someone else came along. But there's no need for that at Love spoons Wales - there's a huge range of these exquisite spoons, all carefully crafted by Paul Wadge and his team in the time-honoured manner. Many have traditional designs, including a heart and sometimes a keyhole, signifying a young man's desire to share a home with his loved one. Nowadays, other designs can be incorporated, and special commissions are always undertaken.

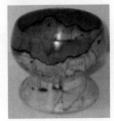

Lovespoons Wales also makes turned objects from wood - everything from bowls to vases, as well as pierced work and goblets. Though they are all individually hand-turned, the prices at Lovespoons Wales are amazingly reasonable, and you are sure to find something that will appeal to you. They make the perfect gift for an anniversary, and smaller versions of the love spoons themselves can be given as favours at weddings. So come along to Lovespoons Wales and admire the many beautifully crafted objects on show.

🎭 stories and anecdotes   🐦 famous people   🎨 art and craft   🎟 entertainment and sport   🚶 walks the 1840s by the Talbot family. The land once belonged to **Margam Abbey**, a Cistercian house which was founded in 1147 by Robert, Earl of Gloucester (see also Neath). Following a violent revolt by the lay brothers, the abbey went on to become one of the wealthiest in Wales but, at the time of the Dissolution of the Monasteries, the estate passed on to Sir Rice Mansel, who built the first mansion on the estate in 1537.

The park today boasts several buildings left by previous owners including the **Parish Church of St Mary**, (the former abbey church, and all that remains of the abbey itself), a classical 18th century orangery, recently restored monastic gardens, a unique fuchsia collection and a restored Japanese garden from the 1920s. This huge recreational area - the park covers some 800 acres - also includes a visitor centre, waymarked trails, a deer park, bird of prey centre and the **Margam Stones Museum**, where visitors can see a collection of Roman, Celtic and Norman carved stones.

Pontypridd

🏠 Pontypridd Museum   🐿 Sir Geraint Evans

🐿 Stewart Burrows   🐿 Tom Jones

This friendly valley town is justly proud of its past, which is revealed in the **Pontypridd Museum** housed in an old Baptist chapel close to Pontypridd's historic stone bridge over the River Taff. As well as its industrial heritage, the town has a long tradition of music and in the main park are two statues commemorating Evan and James, a father and son songwriting team who were responsible for composing the words and music for the Welsh National Anthem, *Land of my Fathers* (*Hen Wlad fy Nhadau*).

Perhaps better known to today's visitors, however, are the two opera stars **Sir Geraint Evans** (1922- 1992) and **Stewart Burrows** (born 1933), who came from the same street in nearby Clifynydd. **Tom Jones** (born 1940), the international star, was born in Trefforest, a mile or so south east of the town. Just outside Pontypridd, at Fforest Uchaf Farm, Penycoedcae, is the **Pit Pony Sanctuary**, where visitors can meet more than 25 horses and ponies, including several retired pit ponies. Also here are pit pony memorabilia and a reconstruction of a typical pony-powered Welsh drift coalmine.

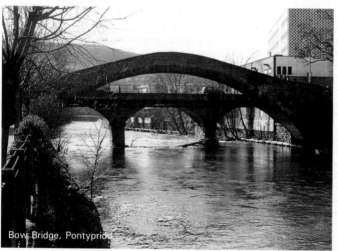
Bow Bridge, Pontypridd

Around Pontypridd

LLANTRISANT
4 miles SW of Pontypridd on the B4595

🏛 Parish Church of Saints Illtyd, Gwyno and Dyfod

🏛 Llantrisant Castle 🏛 Royal Mint Museum

🏛 Royal Mint 🌱 Dr William Price

The **Parish Church of Saits Illtyd, Gwyno and Dyfod** give the town its name - the enclosure, or church, of the three saints. It dates from 1246, with later additions and modifications. The east window, designed by Morris Burne Jones, is one of only three church windows that features a beardless Christ and, behind the altar in the Lady Chapel, is a curious stone known as the 'Ressuection Stone', thought to date from the 7th century. The church also has a baptistery where those being baptised can choose either a traditional baptism or full immersion. All that remains of 13th century **Llantrisant Castle** is part of a round tower known as the Raven Tower. It was built in about 1250 by Richard de Clare, Lord of Glamorgan, to defend this area against the Welsh. It was probably to this castle, in 1326, that Edward II and Hugh Despenser were brought after falling into the hands of Queen Isabella.

Though some of the traditional heavy industry still remains, Llantrisant is best known nowadays for being the home of **The Royal Mint**, within a 38-acre site, which transferred here from Tower Hill, London in 1967. It produces coins, not just for the United Kingdom, but for countries all over the world. At the **Royal Mint Museum** there is a permanent display of coins, medals, dies and drawings, along with a shop, café and a programme of events and exhibitions.

Standing in the town centre is a statue of a figure dressed in a fox skin head-dress. This is the town's memorial to **Dr William Price**, an amazing and eccentric character who lived from 1800 to 1893. Espousing many causes, some of which scandalised straight-laced Victorian Britain, Price was a vegetarian who believed in free love, nudism and radical politics. His most famous deed took place in 1884, when he cremated his illegitimate son Iesu Grist (Jesus Christ), who had died in infancy. As a result of the controversy, and the ensuing court case, cremation became legal in Britain. To commemorate his centenary, the council constructed a heather garden which can be seen as one enters the town.

PORTH
3 miles E of Pontypridd on the A4058

🏛 Bacchetta's Italian Café Museum

The industrialised areas of South Wales

🎭 stories and anecdotes 🐦 famous people 🎨 art and craft 🎭 entertainment and sport 🚶 walks

attracted many Italian immigrants in the 1920s and 1930s. Many of the immigrants opened up cafes, and in Porth is the **Bacchetta's Italian Café Museum**, situated above the station Café. Here you can see exhibits and artefacts connected with the cafés and their families.

TREHAFOD
1½ miles NW of Pontypridd off the A4058

🏛 Tower Colliery Visitor Centre

🏛 Rhondda Heritage Park

In the Rhondda Valley alone there were once 53 working mines in just 16 square miles but, although they have all but gone, the traditions of coal mining live on. When the Lewis Merthyr Colliery closed in 1983, it re-opened as the **Rhondda Heritage Park**, a fascinating place where former miners guide visitors around the restored mining buildings. As well as seeing the conditions in which the miners worked and hearing stories from miners whose families worked in the mines for generations, visitors can also see exhibitions on the role of the women in a mining village, the dramatic history of the 1920s strikes for a minimum wage and the tragedy of mining disasters. Between 1868 and 1919 in Rhondda one miner was killed every six hours and one injured every two minutes. The cultural and social history of a mining community, through brass bands, choirs and the chapel, is explored and visitors also have the opportunity to put on a hard hat and travel down the mine shaft in a cage.

ABERDARE
9 miles NW of Pontypridd on the A4233

🏛 Aberdare Museum   🏛 Tower Coliery Visitor Centre

🞾 Dare Valley Country Park   🐦 Griffith Rhys Jones

Situated at the northern end of the Cynon valley, Aberdare, like other valley towns, is famous for its strong music tradition - particularly male voice choirs. In Victoria Square is a statue of the baton waving choir conductor, **Griffith Rhys Jones** (1834-1897).

Aberdare Museum has many artefacts and photographs about the Cynon Valley, and in particular the 1984-85 miners' strike. Wales' last deep mine, the Tower Colliery, is now owned by the miners who work in it. Situated a few miles west of Aberdare, the **The Tower Colliery Visitor Centre** has photographs and displays about the mine and the life of its miners. The whole of the landscape of Aberdare was once shaped by coal mines and heavy industry, but with the closure of the mines the countryside is, through ambitious land reclamation and environmental improvement schemes, returning to its pre-industrial green and lush natural state. Just a short distance from the busy town centre is **Dare Valley Country Park**, which was opened in 1973 on former colliery land and where trails tell of the natural and industrial history of the area.

Merthyr Tydfil

🏛 Cyfarthfa Castle Museum and Art Gallery

🏛 Joseph Parry's Ironworker's Cottage

The main road in this area of Wales, the A645, acts as a dividing line. To the south are the historic valleys once dominated by coal mining and the iron and steel industries, while, to the north, lie the unspoilt southern uplands of the Brecon Beacons National Park. This rigidly observed divide is explained by geology, as the coal bearing rocks of the valleys end here and give way to the limestone and old red sandstone rocks of the Brecon Beacons. The close proximity of the two different types of rock also explains the nature and growth of

🏛 historic building   🏛 museum   🏚 historic site   🞾 scenic attraction   🐦 flora and fauna industry in this particular area of South Wales as the iron smelting process required not just coal but also limestone. The iron ore was locally available too. These ingredients all came together in the most productive way at Merthyr Tydfil and this former iron and steel capital of the world was once the largest town in Wales. It took its name from the martyr St Tudful, the daughter of the Welsh chieftain Brychan (see also Brecon). She was martyred by the Irish for her Christian beliefs in AD 480.

Described as 'the most impressive monument of the Industrial Iron Age in Southern Wales', **Cyfarthfa Castle** (see panel below) is a grand mansion situated in beautiful and well laid out parkland. The castle was commissioned in the 1820s by the ironmaster William Crawshay, who constructed the grand house to overlook the family's ironworks, which at the time were the largest in the world. Today, this mansion is home to the **Cyfarthfa Castle Museum and Art Gallery**

which not only covers the social and industrial history of Merthyr Tydfil and the surrounding area but also has an extensive collection of fine and decorative art. The parkland, too, is well worth exploring, and at the visitor centre information on the park's amenities and natural history can be found.

Joseph Parry's Ironworker's Cottage, in Chapel Row, provides a contrasting view of life in Merthyr Tydfil during its heyday. A superb example of a skilled ironworker's home, the cottage gives an interesting insight into the living conditions of those days. It was here that Joseph Parry, the 19th century composer famous for writing the haunting hymn *Myfanwy*, was born; on the first floor is an exhibition of his life and work.

Another of the town's claims to fame lies in the political sphere: it was the first constituency in Britain to return a socialist Member of Parliament when, in 1900, Kier Hardie was elected to Westminster.

Cyfarthfa Castle Museum & Art Gallery

Brecon Road, Merthyr Tydfil CF47 8RE
Tel/Fax: 01685 723112

Built in 1824, **Cyfarthfa Castle** is an impressive monument to the industrial revolution. Once a Regency mansion, it now houses a magnificent museum and art gallery. The basement atmospherically recalls over 3,000 years of history in this important Welsh town, whilst the restored upper floors are a grand setting for the srt displays and eclectic collections from the ancient world.

Cyfarthfa Castle is set in 160 acres of parkland containing formal gardens, sweeping lawns, a lake, children's play facilities, a model railway and much more.

The Castle and park are situated on the edge of the Brecon Beacons National Park and make a great day out. Open daily 1st April - 30th September 10am-5.30pm; 1st October - 31st March, Tuesday-Friday 10am-4pm and Weekend 12-4pm. Closed Mondays.

🎭 stories and anecdotes   🐦 famous people   🎨 art and craft   🎵 entertainment and sport   🚶 walks

Around Merthyr Tydfil

PONTSTICILL
3 miles N of Merthyr Tydfil off the A465

🚂 Brecon Mountain Railway

From here the **Brecon Mountain Railway** travels a short, scenic route up to Pontsticill Reservoir in the Brecon Beacons National Park. The charming vintage steam trains follow the tracks of the old Merthyr Tydfil to Brecon line, which has been re-opened by railway enthusiasts.

ABERFAN
4 miles S of Merthyr Tydfil off the A4054

🏛 Memorial Gardens

This former mining village still carries about it a feeling of infinite sadness. On the morning of the 21st October 1966 a great mountain of coal waste slid down onto the village, engulfing Pantglas School and about 20 houses, and killing 144 people, of which 116 were children. It was a disaster of international proportions. The then chairman of the National Coal Board, Alfred Robens, rather than visit the disaster site straight away, decided instead to attend a ceremony where he was installed as Chancellor of Surrey University. This, and his later insistence that the causes of the disaster had been hitherto unknown springs beneath the slag heap (when in fact they had been known about), blackened his name forever in Wales.

People come to the village nowadays, not as tourists, but as people who want to spend time reflecting in the **Memorial Gardens**, built on the site of the school.

Bridgend

🏰 Newcastle Castle   🏰 Coity Castle

🏛 South Wales Police Museum

Known in Welsh as Pen-y-Bont Ar Ogwr (meaning 'the crossing of the River Ogmore'), this bustling market town lies at the confluence of the Rivers Ogmore, Garw and Llynfi and it was once regarded as so vital a route that it had two castles, one on either side of the River Ogmore. The remains of 12th century **Newcastle Castle** lie on the west riverside while the more extensive ruins of 14th century **Coity Castle** stand guard on the other. Originally built by the Norman Payn de Turberville and strengthened over the following three centuries, Coity Castle was finally abandoned in the late 16th century, having withstood a siege by Owain Glyndwr 150 years earlier.

Bridgend's distinction as a market town dates back as far as the early 16th century. and down the ages there have been tanneries, a woollen factory and local potteries in the area. However, for the last 250 years or so, Bridgend has been an agricultural market centre supporting the industrial towns in the valleys. In the South Wales Police HQ is the **South Wales Police Museum**, with displays, artefacts and photographs of policing in the area.

Around Bridgend

EWENNY
1 mile S of Bridgend on the B4265

🏰 Ewenny Priory   🏰 Parish Church of St Michael

🏺 Ewenny Pottery

This charming rural village is home to **Ewenny Priory**, whose church is now the

---

🏰 historic building   🏛 museum   🏛 historic site   🐾 scenic attraction   🌿 flora and fauna

Ewenny Priory

Parish Church of St Michael. It was founded in 1141 by Maurice de Londres, the son of William de Londres of Ogmore Castle. This is one of the finest fortified religious houses in Britain and, while its precinct walls, towers and gateways give the priory a military air, it is believed that they were built for reasons of prestige rather than defence. Close by lies 400-year-old **Ewenny Pottery**, said to be the oldest working pottery in Wales.

TONDU
3½ miles N of Bridgend on the A4063

🏚 Tondu Heritage Park   🌱 Parc Slip Nature Reserve

The nationally important Tondu Ironworks have now been incorporated into the **Tondu Heritage Park**, while the site of an old colliery and open cast coal workings have been developed into the **Parc Slip Nature Reserve**. The reserve's network of paths lead

visitors through the various different wildlife habitats, such as grassland, woodland and wetland, where a wide variety of plants, birds and animals have made their homes.

BETWS
5 miles N of Bridgend off the A4063

🏚 Bryngarw House   🍃 Bryngarw Country Park

Just south of the village lies **Bryngarw Country Park**, which throughout the year presents a variety of enchanting landscapes including woodland, grassland, water features and formal gardens. A visitor centre provides information on the country park and on the many species of plants and birds to be found here. Perhaps the most interesting feature of the park is the exotic Japanese Garden, which was laid out in 1910 and where there are not only a series of interlinked ponds and an oriental tea garden pavilion, but also superb azaleas, rhododendrons, magnolias and cherry trees.

The house at the centre of the estate, **Bryngarw House**, was built in 1834 by Morgan Popkin Treherne as a 'small but elegant dwelling'.

MAESTEG
8 miles N of Bridgend on the A4063

🏚 Tabor Chapel

This ancient market town was the centre of iron making in the 1820s, but the last great furnace was 'blown out' in 1886; one of the ironworks is now a sports centre. Maesteg was once linked to the coast at Porthcawl by a tramway, traces of which can be seen at Porthcawl. The **Tabor Chapel** in Maesteg was where *Land of My Fathers* was first sung in public in 1856. The Welsh words were written by Evan James, the music by his son James James. For 112 years, Talbot Street was the only alcohol-free high street in Britain, so covenanted in the will of the teetotal spinster after whom the street was named. In the summer of 2002, a restaurant challenged the covenant, and the magistrates ruled in his favour.

LLANGEINOR
5 miles N of Bridgend on the A4064

🏛 Parish Church of St Ceiwyr

This pretty village is home to the **Parish Church of St Ceiwyr**, built on the site of a 6th century monastic cell founded by St Ceindaughter of King Brychan, who gave his name to Breconshire. It has a fine 15th century nave, a 16th century tower and a Norman font.

HOEL-Y-CYW
4 miles NE of Bridgend off the B4280

🍃 Mynydd y Gaer

To the northeast of the village lies **Mynydd y Gaer**, a wonderful 1,000-feet high viewpoint which provides spectacular views across the valleys to the north and the Bristol Channel to the south.

LLANTWIT MAJOR
8 miles SE of Bridgend off the B4265

🏛 Town Hall   🏛 Parish Church of St Illtyd
🏛 Llantwit Major Castle

This delightful town is perhaps the Vale of Glamorgan's most historic settlement, Its **Town Hall** is medieval, and still very much in use today. It was here, in AD 500, that St Illtyd founded a church and school. One of the great Celtic saints who travelled in Britain, Ireland and Brittany, St Illtyd was a contemporary of both St David and St Patrick. Although little is known of him, he

does feature in the book *The Life of St Samson of Dol*, which was written around 100 years after his death. The church and school he founded here are believed to be the oldest learning centres in the country. The imposing **Parish Church of St Illtyd** seen today is a combination of two buildings, one an early Norman structure and the other dating from the late 13th century. Inside can be seen a fine collection of Celtic crosses which includes St Illtyd's or St Samson's cross, which was found buried in the church grounds on top of two skeletons. **Llantwit Major Castle** - often referred to as the 'Old Place' - is in fact a ruined manor house at the centre of the town.

ST DONAT'S
7½ miles S of Bridgend off the B4265

🏛 St Donat's Castle   🍃 Nash Point
🏛 Parish Church of St Donat

Close to the village lies **St Donat's Castle**, which was built in the 13th century. It came into the possession of the Stradling family through marriage in 1292, and they stayed in the castle until 1738. A more recent owner was the American newspaper magnate William Randolph Hearst. Hearst, whose life was fictionalised in the classic Orson Welles film *Citizen Kane*, spent huge sums of money restoring and furnishing this historic building, where he entertained film stars and other well known figures. To the west of the village lies **Nash Point** (see walk on page 322) a headland with two lighthouses and the remnants of an Iron Age fort. This area of the coast is overlooked by limestone cliffs which through wind erosion have begun to resemble giant building blocks. The present **Parish Church of St Donat** dates originally from Norman times, but it has been much altered over the years. Within the Lady Chapel are tombs of members of the Stradling family.

SOUTHERNDOWN
4 miles S of Bridgend on the B4265

🏰 Daven Castle   🌿 Glamorgan Heritage Coast Centre

This popular holiday centre, overlooking Dunraven Bay, is home to the **Glamorgan Heritage Coast Centre**, which has displays and information about the 14-mile long stretch of wild and beautiful coastline, which begins in the west at Newton. Overlooking are the scant remains of **Dunraven Castle**, which is actually a 19th century mansion. It was inhabited right up until the 1940s, but was partially demolished in 1963.

OGMORE
2½ miles S of Bridgend on the B4524

Lying at the mouth of the River Ogmore, this pretty village is close to a ford across the River Ewenny where the ruins of **Ogmore Castle** can be seen. It was built originally in timber in the early 12th century by William de Londres, and rebuilt in stone by his son Maurice. This was once the foremost stronghold in the area although all that can be seen today are the remains of a three storey keep and the dry moat. The castle grounds are said to be haunted by a ghost known as Y Ladi Wen (The White Lady) who guards the treasure thought to be buried here. For its part, the River Ogmore is supposed to be haunted by the tormented spirits of misers who died without disclosing where they had hidden their riches. Legend has it that these spirits will be released from their misery only when their hoards are found and thrown into the river, downstream of the castle.

Another story tells of the daughter of Maurice de Londres. It seems that the Norman knights regarded all the game in the area as theirs by right. The local population, however, had no other food but the abundant game, and took to poaching. Being caught poaching usually meant the death sentence, and after one such incident, Maurice's daughter intervened, saying that the Welsh should have an area of land where they could hunt.. As it was her birthday, her father, as a birthday present, told her to walk in a circle until nightfall, when she should return to the same spot she started from. The land within that circle would be common land, and anyone could hunt there. Maurice's daughter duly set out, and by nightfall had marked out a vast expanse of land. Her father kept his word, and it is said that Southerndown Common, still in existence today, is that self same area of land.

A marked walk leads from the castle across meadows lying between the Ewenny and Ogmore rivers to Merthyr Mawr.

MERTHYR MAWR
2 miles SW of Bridgend off the A48

🏰 Candleston Castle   🏰 Dipping Bridge

🌿 Merthyr Mawr Warren

Situated down river from Bridgend, this delightful village of thatched cottages bordered by meadows and woodland lies on the edge of **Merthyr Mawr Warren**, one of the largest areas of sand dunes in Europe.

Bridge at Merthyr Mawr

🎭 stories and anecdotes   👤 famous people   🎨 art and craft   🎡 entertainment and sport   🚶 walks

Nash Point

Distance: *2.8 miles (4.5 kilometres)*

Typical time: *75 mins*

Height gain: *90 metres*

Map: *Explorer 151*

Walk: *www.walkingworld.com ID:1893*

Contributor: *Peter Salenieks*

ACCESS INFORMATION:

Marcross is approached along minor roads from the B4265 to the West of Llantwit Major. A private road leads from Marcross to the Car Park. Cars cost one pound per day in 2003 (50p after 5pm).

ADDITIONAL INFORMATION:

This walk will take about 75 minutes. The foreshore between Waypoints 3 and 4 is not accessible around high water.

DESCRIPTION:

Nash Point is a popular venue for outdoor activities such as walking, sea angling and birdwatching. This walk takes in part of the Glamorgan Heritage Coast, which was the first designated heritage coast in Britain, together with points of archaeological and geological interest.

Start at the entrance to the car park, where light refreshments are available in season. Follow the footpath down into Cwm Marcross, passing an interpretive sign and cross Marcross Brook by a small, wooden footbridge. Walk up the other side to reach the site of an Iron Age promontory fort. This is a Scheduled Ancient Monument. It is one of a series of promontory forts

situated along the coast of the Vale of Glamorgan that were built between about 700 BC and the Roman invasion of Wales in 76 AD. Only a small remnant of the fort has survived centuries of erosion and undercutting of the cliffs.

Follow the footpath along the clifftop, crossing several stiles before dropping down into Cwm Nash. There are fine views of cliffs, bays and coastal scenery. Children should be supervised closely, as the footpath is unfenced in places. The walk proceeds along the rocky foreshore to Nash Point. This offers a fresh perspective on the horizontally bedded rocks of the Lower Lias series that form the coastline. There is some unusual rock scenery, together with opportunities to explore the beach and rock pools.

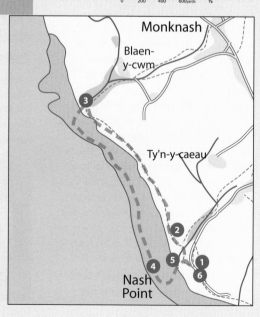

Note that the foreshore between Waypoints 3 and 4 is not accessible around high water. Consult the local press for details of the tide times before you start and plan your day accordingly.

FEATURES:

Sea, Toilets, Birds, Great Views, Cafe, Ancient Monument

WALK DIRECTIONS:

1 | Follow the footpath down into Cwm Marcross, passing an interpretive sign. Cross Marcross Brook by a small, wooden footbridge and walk up the other side to reach the site of Nash Point Promontory Fort.

2 | Cross the dry-stone wall via a stile and continue north-west along the clifftop footpath. This leads over several more stiles before descending into Cwm Nash.

3 | Turn left (south-west) beside Nash Brook and walk along the foreshore to Nash Point (if the tide is high, then return along the clifftop footpath instead).

4 | Walk around Nash Point, crossing a series of rock pavements and a stony beach to reach the outflow of Marcross Brook.

5 | Join a footpath on the right (east) side of Marcross Brook and ascend towards the entrance to the car park.

6 | Walk from the head of the footpath to the café at Nash Point to complete the route.

Now a Site of Special Scientific Interest, the dunes offer the perfect habitat for a wide variety of plants and animals.

Surrounded by the dune system are the remains of **Candleston Castle**, a 15th century fortified manor house that was, until the 19th century, the home of the powerful Cantelupe family. Local children believe the house to be haunted but the biggest mystery of Candleston is the fate of the village of Treganllaw (meaning 'the town of a hundred hands') which is thought to have been engulfed by the dunes. Parts of *Lawrence of Arabia* were filmed here.

On the road approaching the village is the 15th century **Dipping Bridge** which has some interesting holes in its parapet through which in the old days sheep were pushed into the river for their annual dip! An inn used to stand close to the bridge, where, it was claimed by locals, travellers were murdered for their money. People dismissed this as a far fetched story until the inn was pulled down, and skeletons were dug up in the grounds.

NEWTON
4½ miles W of Bridgend off the A4106

Dating back to the 12th century, the village was founded as a 'new town' and by the 17th century was a thriving port from where grain and knitted stockings were exported. The imposing limestone **Parish Church of St John the Baptist** was originally built by Sir Thomas de Sandfford family for the Knights of the Order of St John of Jerusalem in the late 12th or early 13th century, though some of what we see nowadays is 15th century. Thomas had obviously been on the Crusades, as he named his son and heir Jordan.

PORTHCAWL
6 miles W of Bridgend on the A4229

📷 Porthcawl Museum   🏛 Porthcawl Harbour

Porthcawl is one of the region's most popular resorts, with clean sandy beaches at Sandy Bay, Trecco Bay and the quieter Rest Bay, along with an amusement park that provides a wide variety of rides, from white knuckle roller coasters to more gentle carousels. This is also a haven for surfers, sailors and fishing enthusiasts, while the headlands above Rest Bay are the site of the famous Royal Porthcawl Golf Club.

THE ATLANTIC HOTEL

West Drive, Seafront, Porthcawl CF36 3LT
Tel: 01656 785011 Fax: 01656 771877
e-mail: enquiries@atlantichotelporthcawl.co.uk
website: www.atlantichotelporthcawl.co.uk

The Atlantic is a popular, personally run hotel on the seafront at Porthcawl, a short walk from the town centre, the harbour and the Royal Porthcawl Golf Club. The hotel has single, double and twin-bedded rooms, and family rooms for children sharing with their parents. All have en suite bathrooms, satellite TV, telephone and tea/coffee trays, and many enjoy superb sea views of the Glamorgan Heritage Coast across the channel to the hills of Devon and Somerset. With golfing, sailing, fishing, sandy beaches and family entertainment virtually on the doorstep, and easy access to the M4 (J37) and the major centres of Cardiff and Swansea, the Atlantic is an excellent choice for both leisure and business guests.

LA ROCHELLE BRASSERIE

9-10 Well Street, Porthcawl,
Vale of Glamorgan CF36 3BE
Tel: 01656 782330
website: www.la-rochelle-porthcawl.co.uk

A distinctive gabled building on a corner site in Porthcawl is the setting for one of the most inviting and popular eating places in the region. Just 100 yards from the seafront, **La Rochelle Brasserie** has something of the look of a traditional tavern, and spindle-back chairs and glass-topped wooden tables assist the delightful ambience that chef-patron Warren Evans has created.

The main menu is supplemented by a two-course lunch and evening special menus and a pre-theatre menu, and the cooking by Warren and his team shows influences from home, Europe and further afield. Most of the dishes are just that little bit different, showing a winning combination of classic technique and imaginative contemporary touches: duck breast with a honey and raspberry glaze; mussels in creamy chicken broth; king prawns in a sticky garlic and chilli glaze; fresh tuna stuffed with goat's cheese; hickory beef kebab.

Several dishes can be ordered as either starter or main course, and the exceptional food is complemented by an extensive, well-chosen wine list.

The more dignified side of Porthcawl centres around the Edwardian promenade, a legacy of the prosperous days when this was a port exporting coal and iron. The history of the town can be discovered at **Porthcawl Museum** in John Street, where there is a fascinating collection of artefacts, costumes and memorabilia on display, while at **Porthcawl Harbour** there are still several historic buildings which date from the heyday of this busy port. During the summer, two veteran steamships leave the harbour for trips along the Bristol Channel and across to Lundy Island.

KENFIG

6½ miles W of Bridgend off the B4283

🏰 Kenfig Castle 🏚 Kenfig Pool

🌱 Kenfig National Nature Reserve

This village was originally founded in the 12th century by Robert, Earl of Gloucester, who also built **Kenfig Castle** here. However, some 300 years later the sands of Kenfig Burrows had swamped the settlement and the medieval town lies buried in the dunes although the remains of the castle keep are still visible. The settlement was actually a borough of some importance, with its own charter, town walls, a thriving High Street and a Guildhall, The

legend of **Kenfig Pool** has it that on a quiet day when the water is clear, the houses of the buried town can be seen at the bottom of the lake and the bells of the old church can be heard ringing before a storm.

Today, this marvellous area of dunes to the northwest of the present village is the **Kenfig National Nature Reserve**. With over 600 species of flowering plants, including orchids, a freshwater lake and numerous birds, this is a haven for all naturalists as well as ramblers.

Penarth and the Vale of Glamorgan

Penarth

🏛 Washington Gallery 🏚 Comeston Medieval Village

🏚 Lavernock Point 🏚 Flat Holm

🌳 Cosmeston Country Park

Often described as the 'garden by the sea', Penarth (the name means 'cliff's head' or 'bear's head' in English) is a popular and unspoilt seaside resort which developed in Victorian and Edwardian times. Built for the wealthy industrialists of Cardiff's shipyards immediately to the south of the city, this

---

📖 stories and anecdotes   👤 famous people   🎨 art and craft   🎭 entertainment and sport   🚶 walks

once fashionable town has lost none of its
late 19th and early 20th century elegance and
style, typified by the splendidly restored pier,
the promenade and the formal seaview
gardens. If the town seems to have been lost
in a time warp, a visit to the **Washington
Gallery**, housed in an old cinema on Stanwell
Road, will dispel this view through its
exciting collection of modern and
contemporary art.

In the early 1980s a team of archaeologists
uncovered the remains of a medieval village
to the south of the town. It grew up around a
manor house belonging to the Constantin
family (some of the first Norman invaders in
Wales) in the 12th century. However, in the
mid 14th century the Black Death reached
the village, killing around one third of the
population, and following a period of decline
it was left to decay. Today, **Comeston
Medieval Village** is a tourist attraction, and
several of the village's buildings have been
reconstructed, allowing visitors, with the
help of costumed characters, to gain a real
insight into life in a medieval village in AD
1350.

The village is in **Cosmeston Country
Park**, an area of lakes, woodlands and
meadows created from a disused limestone
quarry. A peaceful and tranquil habitat for
many birds and animals, with a wide range of
plant life, the country park has a visitor
centre, picnic areas and a café.

In 1897, **Lavernock Point**, to the
southeast of the country park, was the site of
Marconi's early experiments in radio
transmission and the scene of the historic
reception of the words "Are you ready?",
which were transmitted to **Flat Holm**, an
island some three miles offshore. A tiny
island with a wealth of wildlife, Flat Holm

also has a history that dates back to the Dark
Ages, when it was used by monks as a retreat.
Vikings, Anglo Saxons, smugglers and
cholera victims are known to have sought
refuge on the island, which was also fortified
twice, once by the Victorians and again in
World War II. Today, it is a Site of Special
Scientific Interest, with a local nature reserve
that is home to the largest colony of gulls in
Wales.

AROUND PENARTH

BARRY ISLAND
5 miles SW of Penarth on the A4055

- Barry Island Railway Heritage Centre
- Barry Castle   Cold Knap Roman Buildings
- Welsh Hawking Centre
- Barry Island Pleasure Park

Barry Island is not an island but a peninsula
which faces the much larger town of Barry
itself, whose natural, sheltered harbour has
been used since Roman times; **Cold Knap
Roman Buildings**, to the west of this seaside
resort, are all that remains from those days. A
popular place for holidaymakers for
generations, Barry Island offers its visitors all
the traditional seaside resort trappings, from
sandy beaches to a funfair, as well as views
across the Bristol Channel to the Devon coast.
The latest all-weather attraction is the **Barry
Island Railway Heritage Centre**, which has
opened its extended line from Barry Island
into the neighbouring Waterfront Dock
Development. The **Barry Island Pleasure
Park** has over 50 rides for kids of all ages,
such as a log flume, a haunted mine, roller
coaster and carousel. In the town of Barry
itself are the scant remains of **Barry Castle**,
including a 14th century gatehouse. To the

COWBRIDGE
12½ miles W of Penarth off the A48

🏛 Parish Church of the Holy Cross   🏰 Town Walls

🏛 Cowbridge Museum

This handsome and prosperous town had its origins in a Roman settlement, which by the 4th century had grown into a small town. Recent archaeological digs have uncovered the remains of many Roman buildings, including a bath House. It has been the principal market town of the Vale of Glamorgan since medieval times and is today noted for its quality shops, crafts and restaurants. The original Norman grid layout of the town is visible to this day, particularly in the mile-long main street, and Cowbridge's mid 14th century **Town Walls** and gatehouse still stand.

Barry Island

north of the resort is the **Welsh Hawking Centre**, where 200 birds of prey have their homes and there are regular flying demonstrations.

GLYNDWR VINEYARD AND B&B
Llanblethian, Cowbridge, Vale of Glamorgan
Tel: 01446 774564
e-mail: glyndwrvineyard@hotmail.com

Rewind and recharge your senses in the stunningly beautiful, individual, twin bedded lodge which serenely adjoins orchards, fields and a six acre vineyard. Enjoy fresh Welsh produce for breakfast - to enjoy on your own sunny verandah, overlooking ponds, lawns and woodland whilst watching wildlife pass by undisturbed. Forget the restrictions of time with a kitchenette to enjoy snacks and drinks at any time of day or night.

Secluded but not isolated, you are a stroll away from the village pub with its delicious food and local beer. Twelve miles west of Cardiff, a short drive from the sea and one mile from the charming market town of Cowbridge with its unique shops and choice of quality restaurants and historic inns.

Glyndwr vineyard is the oldest family run vineyard in Wales, producing award-winning red, rose, white and vintage sparkling wines. Enjoy trails, group tours and tastings in their own cellars by appointment.

📖 stories and anecdotes   🐦 famous people   🎨 art and craft   🎭 entertainment and sport   🥾 walks

HAVARD & HAVARD ANTIQUES

59 Eastgate, Cowbridge, Vale of Glamorgan CF71 7EL
Tel: 01446 775021
e-mail: info@havardandhavard.com
website: www.havardandhavard.com

Philip and Christine Havard were brought up with Welsh furniture, learning to appreciate its unique combination of beauty and practicality. Thus they brought a wealth of experience when they opened **Havard & Havard Antiques** here in the heart of Cowbridge on St David's Day 1992.

The main displays on the two floors concentrate on 18th and 19th century Welsh country pieces, including classic dressers, dining tables and chairs and corner cupboards. They also keep a stock of distinctive period objects, along with a new range of textiles and cushions from Cefyn Burgess.

New for 2007 is the garden section with antique and contemporary garden furniture; sculptures and water features. The owners, who are members of LAPADA, are always ready with advice on styling of both period and modern interiors to reflect their owners' lifestyle and personality. Opening hours are 10 to 5 Tuesday, Thursday, Friday and Saturday.

THE LINEN CUPBOARD

2 Penny Lane, Cowbridge, Vale of Glamorgan CF71 7EG
Tel: 01446 771150
e-mail: info@thelinencupboardcowbridge.co.uk   website: www.thelinencupboardcowbridge.co.uk

The Linen Cupboard enjoys a pleasant setting alongside a stream just off the main street of Cowbridge. Owner Melanie James, who took over the premises in October 2005, has filled her delightful shop with a wide selection of lifestyle items, homeware and gifts, the great majority from British manufacturers and suppliers. The range includes bedding and accessories, cushions and throws, door stops, soft toys and smaller items like soaps, candles, Fair Trade crochet work and silk flowers.

The Linen Cupboard is the largest stockist of Cath Kidston in Wales, and among other top names in stock are Wendy Woods quality linen and cottons, cushions and soft furnishings in hand-embroidered linen and silk, unique embroidered bags, purses and cosies from Poppy Treffy,

lovable soft toys from Anne-Claire Petit and the Danish maker Maileg, and bone china mugs by Stubbs of Norfolk. The shop offers a popular, practical wedding list and a gift wrapping service using a choice of Cath Kidston, Nina Campbell and Emma Bridgewater paper.

🏛 historic building   🏛 museum   🏛 historic site   🌀 scenic attraction   🌿 flora and fauna

South Gate, Cowbridge

The large **Parish Church of the Holy Cross**, originally dedicated to St Mary, dates from around 1300. It has a fortified tower in which are a peal of 13 bells. The **Cowbridge Museum**, within the old town hall cells, has artefacts, photographs and displays on the history of the town. The work of local craftspeople can be seen at the **Old Wool Barn Art & Centre**, which has studio workshops set around an attractive courtyard.

ST NICHOLAS
6 miles NW of Penarth on the A48

To the south of the village lie **Dyffryn Gardens** which, as part of the Dyffryn estate, were landscaped in the 19th century. One of

the finest surviving Thomas Mawson gardens in Britain, Dyffryn offers a series of broad sweeping lawns, Italianate terraces, a paved court, a physick garden and a rose garden as well as a vine walk and arboretum. Perhaps the most impressive features are the Pompeian Garden and the Theatre Garden where open air plays and concerts are held.

ST HILARY
10 miles W of Penarth off the A48

▦ Beaupre Castle

To the south of the village lies **Beaupre Castle**, which is in two parts. The earliest part, to the south, was built in about 1300 on one side of a small courtyard. In the 16th century the castle was owned by Sir Rice Mansell, who began building a new Tudor building on the north side, again round a court. The work was finished by William Bassett and his son Richard. The well-preserved outer gatehouse, with its exuberant carving, dates from this time.

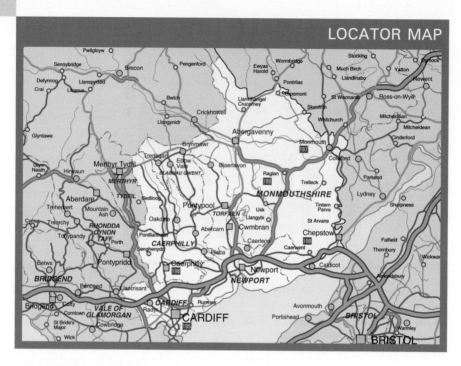

ADVERTISERS AND PLACES OF INTEREST

10 | Cardiff & Monmouthshire

History, ancient and modern, abounds in this region of South Wales, with the distinguished ruins of Norman fortifications and the remains of the industrial past of its valleys. An area of contrasts, like much of Wales, it would be easy to pass straight through this region on a journey to the Gower Peninsula or Pembrokeshire, but that would be to miss out on much of the Welsh heritage.

The valleys of the Wye and Usk offer some truly glorious scenery as well as the equally breathtaking sight of Tintern Abbey. An inspiration for both poets and artists, this abbey was at one time one of the richest in the country and the magnificent ruins beside the River Wye are still a stirring sight. This area, too, is one that saw much contest between the Welsh and the English, so not surprisingly there are numerous fortifications to be seen and explored. The Three Castles - White, Skenfrith and Grosmont - provided a valuable defence from their strong yet isolated positions while most towns of note also had their own fortress.

Monmouthshire itself, for many years, was fought over politically. Was it an English county or a Welsh one? Henry VIII, in 1535, divided Wales into 12 counties and placed Monmouthshire in England. The waters were muddied even further when people began referring to the 'Principality of Wales and Monmouthshire'. And to make matters worse, the Church in Wales was disestablished in 1920. As Monmouthshire at that time was within the Welsh diocese of Llandaff, that meant that what was nominally a English county did not have churches belonging to the Church of England.

In 1974, at local government reorganisation, the matter was settled when Monmouthshire was legally placed in Wales. However, even today there are still groups of people who want to return Monmouthshire to England, and a minor political party called the English Democrats are calling for a referendum on the matter.

The largest city in the area is Cardiff, the capital city of Wales and a place which is successfully blending the ancient with the modern. The Romans occupied various sites in this area, but it was heavy industry and the influence of the Bute family that made Cardiff such a powerful port. The home of Welsh rugby, the superb Millennium Stadium and a recently rejuvenated waterfront, Cardiff is a city that vibrates with life, energy and enthusiasm.

To the north lie the valleys that provided so much wealth until the decline of coal mining and the iron industry. Much of the land that was once an industrial wasteland has been reclaimed by nature, with the help of sensitive human intervention, but there are still some monuments to the great industrial age remaining, chiefly at the Big Pit Mine and Blaenavon Ironworks.

Cardiff

🏯 Cardiff Castle	🏯 Pierhead Building
🏯 Llandaff Cathedral	🏛 National Museum
🏯 Metropolitan Cathedral of St David	
🏛 Welsh Regiment Museum	🏛 Dr Who Exhibition
🏛 Cardiff Bay Visitor Centre	🏛 Techniquest
🏛 Cardiff Bay	🏛 National Assembly	🐾 Cathays Park
🐾 Roath Park	🐦 Shirley Bassey	🐦 Shakin' Stevens
🐦 Roald Dahl	🖉 Wales Millennium Centre
🖉 Norwegian Church Arts Centre	
🔑 Cardiff Bay Church Tour	🔑 Cardiff Centenary Walk
🖉 Millennium Stadium	

The capital city of Wales is a delightful place with an unexpected beauty, a long history, a sporting tradition and an exciting rejuvenated waterfront that is attracting visitors in their thousands. The Cardiff area was first settled by the Romans in the 1st century, but from their departure a few centuries later to the arrival of the Normans in the 11th century, little was recorded of life around what is now Cardiff. In 1091, Robert FitzHamon built a primitive fortress on what remained of the Roman fortification and this was, over the years, upgraded to a stone castle around which the town began to develop. Overrun by Owain Glyndwr in the early 15th century, the town and its castle came into the hands first of the Tudors and then of the Herbert family and their descendants, the Marquisses of Bute.

It was given city status in 1905, but was not declared to be the official capital of Wales (Caernarfon was the other contender) until 50 years later. It now has a population of about 320,000.

However, Cardiff is very much a product of the Industrial Revolution and its story is intertwined with that of John Crichton-Stuart,

2nd Marquess of Bute (1793 - 1848), who began developing the town. The family controlled the docklands and, as the town began to thrive as a coal exporting port, it made a vast fortune. Cardiff became the biggest coal-exporting port in the world, and at its peak in 1913 more than 13 million tons of coal were exported from the docks.

Some of this wealth was poured back into the rebuilding of **Cardiff Castle** (see panel on page 334). A no expense spared project initiated by the 3rd Marquess (who was reputed to be the richest man in the world), the castle is an extravagant and opulent Victorian version of a castle of the Middle Ages, designed by the eccentric architect William Burges. With his flamboyant imagination allowed to run riot, Burges created magnificent rooms rich in murals, stained glass and marble which have to be seen to be believed. However, while the building is very much a flight of wealthy Victorian fancy, outside in the grounds can be seen the well-preserved medieval castle keep and stonework dating from Roman times. Visitors to the castle today also have the opportunity to look around the **Welsh Regiment Museum** within the Black and Barbican Towers and look out over Cardiff from the top of the Norman keep.

As might be expected in a capital city, Cardiff is home to many of the national treasures of Wales and at the superb **National Museum** there is a vast collection of archaeology, natural history (including 55,000 live leaf-cutter ants!) and ceramics as well as permanent exhibitions on the Evolution of Wales and Man and the Environment. The art gallery is home to a fine collection that includes the largest body of Impressionist paintings outside Paris and the best Welsh art.

🏯 historic building	🏛 museum	🏛 historic site	🐾 scenic attraction	🐦 flora and fauna

National Museum, Cardiff

full vision of the complete development which, among other aims, is reuniting the city with its dockland. The **Wales Millennium Centre** is an arts and cultural centre of world importance. Perhaps the single most important part in the revival of the Bay is the massive Cardiff Bay Barrage, a barrier that stretches for a kilometre across the mouth of the Bay. Of particular interest to children at Cardiff Bay is **Techniquest**, the country's leading science discovery centre, where visitors can explore many aspects of science and technology through a range of interactive exhibits. The former church for Norwegian sailors, which is where the author Roald Dahl was baptised, is now the **Norwegian Church Arts Centre** which maintains the links which have grown up over the years between the two nations.

Although Cardiff's famous Arms Park, the home of rugby football for so many years, has gone, its replacement, the **Millennium Stadium**, which was christened by hosting the last great sporting event of the 20th century, the Rugby World Cup Final in November 1999, is set to become an equally revered shrine to the Welsh national game and is already proving a highly successful replacement for Wembley. Visitors to the stadium can see the hallowed turf and learn how the pitch was laid, find out how the 8,000 ton roof opens and closes, and walk from the Welsh players' dressing room, through the tunnel and on to the pitch.

The museum and gallery, along with the City Hall, are located in **Cathays Park**, where there are other civic buildings and also various departments of the University of Wales.

The area once known as Tiger Bay is one of the country's most exciting and imaginative regeneration developments. Now called **Cardiff Bay**, this revived waterfront is home to the new **National Assembly** (known as Y-Senedd in Welsh), the impressive **Pierhead Building** which was built in 1896 for the Bute Docks Company and the **Cardiff Bay Visitor Centre** (known locally as 'The Tube'). At this award-winning tubular building, visitors can see a futuristic exhibition which lays out the

Cardiff has achieved new fame as the place where the BBC television series *Dr Who* is made and filmed, and at the Red Dragon Centre on Hemingway Road is the **Dr Who**

Cardiff Castle

Cardiff Castle Grounds, Cardiff,
South Glamorgan CF10 3RB
Tel: 02920 878100
website: nationaltrust.org.uk

Cardiff Castle is an unusual blend of Roman fort, medieval castle and fanciful Victorian gothic mansion.

The Romans established a fort on the site in the 1 st century AD, but the square 8 acre fort that remains today was built in the 4th century. When the Normans built their castle in the late 11th century what remained of the Roman walls was buried under earth ramparts. The walls were revealed during excavations in 1889, and were rebuilt on the original foundations - clearly visible in places -between 1922 and 1925.

The Norman motte had a stone shell keep added in the 12th century. Further reinforcements were added by the De Clare family in the 13th and early 14th centuries. The keep gained a gatehouse and fore-buildings linked by a massive ward wall to a new tower in the south - the Black Tower. The wall and the keep's fore-buildings were demolished by 'Capability' Brown in the 1770's during re-development of the site. The moat that surrounded the motte was also filled in, but has since been restored and modern stone now marks the position of the old wall and fore-buildings.

In 1423, Richard Beauchamp, Earl of Warwick, built a new tower and hall block on the western wall of the site. This was improved in the late 16th century by the Herbert family who converted it into a luxurious and well appointed house. For most of the 17th and 18th centuries the house was left empty and fell into disrepair. In 1766 the house came into the possession of Lord Mountstuart, the future 1 st Marquess of Bute. He began a programme of demolition and re-building that was continued by his grandson, the 2nd Marquess.

The 2nd Marquess of Bute gained immense wealth through the exploitation of mineral resources on his Glamorgan estates and his development of Cardiff as a centre for industrial trade. When he died suddenly in 1848 he left an infant son, John Patrick Crichton Stuart, as "the richest baby in Britain". The 3rd Marquess was to become one of the richest men in the world, and he lavished money on building projects at many of his properties. In 1869 work began to remodel Cardiff Castle to the designs of the Gothic Revival architect William Burges. The great wealth of Lord Bute provided Burges with the freedom to design and build his most fanciful schemes. A visit to Cardiff Castle without viewing the interiors would mean missing out on some of the most remarkable rooms ever created during the Victorian era. To fully appreciate the work of William Burges it is worth visiting nearby **Castell Cach** which was rebuilt as a summer retreat for Lord Bute and features more of Burges' gothic fantasy creations.

🏛 historic building   🏛 museum   🏛 historic site   🔱 scenic attraction   🌿 flora and fauna

Exhibition. It has props and costumes from the latest series, as well as from previous series. It's the place to hang out with Daleks and Cybermen.

A mile or so from the city centre stands **Llandaff Cathedral**, a beautiful building set in a grassy hollow beside the River Taff. The cathedral suffered severe bomb damage during World War II and part of its restoration programme included a controversial Epstein sculpture, *Christ in Majesty*, which dominates the interior. Inside, visitors will also find some delightful medieval masonry, a marvellous modern timber roof and some works of art by members of the Pre-Raphaelite movement. In Charles Street in the city is Cardiff's 'other cathedral' - the **Metropolitan Cathedral of St David**. It was built as a Roman Catholic church in 1887, and became a cathedral in 1916. Two miles north of the city centre, **Roath Park** is a 19th century urban park with handsome trees, formal flower beds, a wild area and a memorial to Scott of the Antarctic.

A great way to explore the city centre is to follow the **Cardiff Centenary Walk**, which takes in most of the sites and historic landmarks. It's about 2¼ miles long, and has numbered way markers on the pavements. A free guidebook and map are available. The **Cardiff Bay Church Tour** is a guided walk round the many churches around Cardiff Bay. It takes in the Norwegian Church, a Mosque and a Greek Orthodox church.

Many famous people wre born in, or lived in, Cardiff. Perhaps the most famous is **Shirley Bassey** the internationally known singer. She was born in the former Tiger Bay area, which has now been completely redeveloped. Another singer born in the city is **Shakin' Stevens**, the rock star. Born

Michael Barrett in 1948, he was born in the Ely district. The late children's writer **Roald Dahl** (1916 - 1990), was born within the large Norwegian community that flourished in the city, and was baptised in the Norwegian Church. He stayed in the Llandaff area and attended the cathedral school.

Around Cardiff

ST FAGANS
3 miles W of Cardiff off the A48

🏛 Museum of Welsh Life   ⚔ Battle of St Fagans

On the outskirts of Cardiff, this picturesque village is home to the **Museum of Welsh Life** in the large grounds of St Fagans Castle, a splendid mansion. Founded in 1948, this is a museum unlike any other, as it contains an assortment of buildings, collected from all over Wales, which have been re-erected in these glorious surroundings. Ranging from a Celtic village and a 17th century farmhouse to a Victorian schoolroom, a farmyard complete with animals, a pre-war grocery, a terrace of iron-workers cottages, a toll keeper's cottage and a House for the Future, each of the 40 or so buildings has been furnished to reflect a period in its history. As well as this superb collection, the museum holds demonstrations on traditional craft skills, and visitors can enjoy a delightful stroll round the formal gardens, the Italian Garden, the modern knot garden and the terraces that descend to a series of fishponds.

The **Battle of St Fagans** took place in 1648, when a detachment from the New Model army defeated Parliamentary troops who had defected. At the time there was dissention among some of the Parliamentarian troops, as they had not been given food or money for a long time, and they feared that they might eventually be sent home without remuneration. So some of them fought under the Royal Standard under the command of the governor of Pembroke Castle.

TONGWYNLAIS
3 miles NW of Cardiff on the A470

🏛 Castell Coch

Situated in the Taff Valley and hidden by trees, **Castell Coch** appears to be a fairytale castle of the Middle Ages, yet it only dates from the 19th century. Built on the site of a 13th century castle, Castell Coch was designed by the eccentric architect William Burges for the 3rd Marquess of Bute as a companion piece to Cardiff Castle. As the Marquess was reputed to be the wealthiest man in the world - the family owned the thriving Cardiff docks - money was no object and so this elaborate castle was constructed. While the medieval

illusion of the place is maintained by the working portcullis and drawbridge, the interior decoration is perhaps even more astonishing. All perfectly preserved, each room is a masterpiece, with eye-catching details such as paintings of butterflies on the domed ceiling of the drawing room, scenes from *Aesop's Fables* and Greek mythology on the walls, and bird and animal mouldings around the doors. The Marquess planted a vineyard in the castle grounds which, it is said, produced the only commercially made wine in Britain between 1875 and 1914. There are now more than a dozen commercial vineyards in Wales alone.

NEWPORT

🏛 St Woolos Cathedral   🏛 Transporter Bridge

🍃 W.H. Davies   🍃 Johnny Morris

🏛 Newport Museum and Art Gallery

Interior Detail, Castell Coch

With a population of about 120,000, Newport is the third largest city in Wales. It achieved city status in 2002 to mark the Queen's Golden Jubilee. The Romans settled in the area in the 1st century and the town's **St Woolos Cathedral**, splendidly situated on the hilltop, is just the latest building on a site which has been a place of worship since the 6th century. The church was founded by St Gwynllyw (Woolos is the English version of his name), who was, before his conversion, a cruel and wicked man. He is said to have had a dream one night that he would go to a hill and find there a white ox with a black spot. He went the next day and, finding the ox, saw it as a sign from God and became a devout Christian. It is said that he died in AD 500.

The church started off life as a wooden structure not long after the saint died. It was

Scenery Near Newport

VIII's uncle, Jasper Tudor. In the **Newport Museum and Art Gallery** there is a range of displays on the town's origins, including a Roman mosaic floor which was excavated close by. Not to be missed here are the John Wait teapot display and the Fox collection of decorative art. An impressive reminder of Newport's more recent past is the massive **Transporter Bridge** across the River Usk. Specially designed in 1906 by Frenchman Ferdinand Arnodin to allow traffic to cross the river without disrupting the movement of shipping. Basically, a cradle is suspended on wires from a gantry that spans the river, and this carries vehicles back and forth. The bridge is one of very few of its kind, one being in Middlesbrough, while two others are in France.

Among the city's famous sons of Newport was the late **Johnny Morris** the TV star and the poet **W.H. Davies**, who penned the famous lines:

What is this life if, full of care,
We have no time to stand and stare.

To the west of the town lies **Tredegar House and Park**, one of the finest examples of Restoration architecture in Wales and the

then replaced by a Saxon stone building, and some of the stonework in the present Galilee Chapel may be from this church. The rest of the building is Norman and later. It did not become a pro-cathedral until 1929, when the diocese of Monmouth was created. Finally, in 1949, it achieved full cathedral status. In the graveyard of the church are the graves of some of the soldiers of the Welsh Regiment who were killed in the Battle of Rorke's Drift during the Zulu Wars of South Africa.

Newport Castle, the remains of which can still be seen, was built in the 14th century by the d'Audele family, and replaced an earlier timber structure near what is now the cathedral. In the 15th century it was strengthened by Humphrey Stafford, who went on to become the Duke of Buckingham. In the 16th century it was lived in by Henry home of the influential Morgan family for more than 500 years. Visitors can tour the rooms and discover just what life was like here, both above and below stairs, as well as finding out something of this great Welsh family. Its more colourful and famous members include Sir Henry Morgan, the notorious pirate, Godfrey, the 2nd Lord Tredegar, who survived the Charge of the Light Brigade and whose horse is buried in the grounds, and Viscount Evan, whose menagerie included a boxing kangaroo. The park that surrounds the house is equally impressive, with early 18th century walled formal gardens, an orangery with restored parterres, and craft workshops. Visitors can take a carriage drive through the parkland and children have their own adventure playground.

Around Newport

CAERLEON

2½ miles NE of Newport on the B4236

🏛 Caerleon Castle   🏛 Parish Church of St Cadoc

🏛 Legionary Museum   🪶 Arthur Machen

🏛 Caerleon Roman Fortress and Baths

Despite its close proximity to Newport, Caerleon has managed to maintain the air of a rural town, but its chief attraction is the remarkable Roman remains. Caerleon is one of the largest and most significant surviving Roman military sites in Europe, set up in AD 75 by the 2nd Augustinian Legion and originally called Isca. A substantial Roman town grew up around the military base and among the remains to be seen at **Caerleon Roman Fortress and Baths** are a large amphitheatre where thousands watched the gladiators, the only surviving barracks to be seen in Europe and a complex system of Roman baths which

were the equivalent of today's sports and leisure centres. Finds excavated from the remains are on show at the **Legionary Museum** where, along with the weapons, mosaics and models, visitors can see one of the largest collections of engraved gem stones.

Caerleon Castle was originally built of timber in 1085 by Norman invaders, though the ruins you see today date from the 12th century and later. It fell to the Welsh in 1217, but was recaptured by the Enlgish before again being taken by the Welsh in 1231. The **Parish Church of St Cadoc** is largely 15th century, though a church had stood here long before this. The lower parts of the tower are thought to be 12th century. The church contains some impressive stained glass.

However, Caerleon has more to offer than Roman and Norman remains - impressive though they are - and the town has some fine examples of timbered buildings. It also has links with King Arthur, one local legend even suggesting that the Roman amphitheatre was the site of King Arthur's Round Table. Caerleon's most famous son was the writer of dark, brooding ghost and fantasy books, **Arthur Machen**. He wrote this fond tribute to his birthplace:

I shall always esteem it as the greatest piece of fortune that has fallen to me, that I was born in that noble, fallen Caerleon-on-Usk, in the heart of Gwent....

Alfred, Lord Tennyson, visited Caerleon, staying at the riverside Hanbury Arms while seeking inspiration for his *Idylls of the King*.

PENHOW

7 miles E of Newport off the A48

🏛 Parish Church of St John the Baptist

🏛 Penhow Castle

This hamlet is home to Wales' oldest lived-in

🏛 historic building   🖼 museum   🏛 historic site   🪶 scenic attraction   🌱 flora and fauna

Penhow Castle

fortress, the 850 year old **Penhow Castle**, which still has its stout Norman keep and an impressive 15th century Great Hall complete with minstrels' gallery. It is no longer open to the public. Adjacent to the castle is the **Parish Church of St John the Baptist**, which is very picturesque, and well worth a visit. Its tower is 12th century, and it was built by the St Maurs family, who also built the castle.

CAERPHILLY

10 miles W of Newport off the B4623

🏰 Caerphilly Castle　　🏛 Caerphilly Visitor Centre

🎭 Tommy Cooper

The town is famous for its distinctive white crumbly cheese. It was first made in 1831, and

originated in the farms surrounding the town. During World War II and for a few years after, the making of the cheese was prohibited. A few years ago the industry started up again, and it is now possible to get loccaly made cheese once more. The **Caerphilly Visitor Centre**, as well as providing tourist information, has an exhibition on local history and culture, a display of Welsh crafts and a fine Welsh food shop. The town is dominated by the massive **Caerphilly Castle**, which is not only one of Britain's largest castles (only Windsor and Dover are its equal) but is also one of the finest surviving examples of medieval military architecture in Europe. This great fortress was built largely in the late 13th century by the Norman Lord Gilbert de Clare. Along with the 'wall within walls' defence system, he also employed a mighty water defensive arrangement that included lakes and three artificial islands. The castle was restored in the 19th century by the Marquess of Bute, but nothing seems to be able to restore the castle's

📖 stories and anecdotes　　🐦 famous people　　🎨 art and craft　　✐ entertainment and sport　　🚶 walks

Rhyd-y-gwern Woods

Distance: *2.2 miles (3.5 kilometres)*

Typical time: *90 mins*

Height gain: *150 metres*

Map: *Explorer 152*

Walk: *www.walkingworld.com ID:2476*

Contributor: *John Thorn*

The walk starts at the Forestry car par marked 'Llwyn Hir', near Rudry. It is advised to park in clear view of the road to deter car thieves.

Very dog friendly - no traffic, sheep or stiles. Graded as easy but a short steep slope just before point 3 and a few muddy patches after rain. Pub (The Maenllwyd) 400 yards from the start - or the Hollybush at Draethen. The

1:50,000 map does not mark all the paths. Lots of flowers : Violets, Cowslips, Primroses, Wood Anemones and Bluebells through the spring. You may find orchids around points 5 and 6 in the summer. Lots of history: there were silver, lead and coal mines in this area - hence the uneven landscape.

DESCRIPTION:

A lovely walk on woodland paths - beautiful in the spring when covered in bluebells and wood anemones - with traces of an industrial past.

FEATURES:

Pub, Flowers, Butterflies, Industrial Archaeology, Woodland

WALK DIRECTIONS:

1 | Walk up the car park area and pass the barrier. About 50 yards after the barrier turn left uphill on a path. Continue ahead, ignoring junctions on the left and right. Just after the path levels out turn right at a crossing. When you reach a forest road, opposite a gate to a disused quarry turn left and follow this up, bearing round to the right.

2 | At a wide area with access to a lane on the left, take the footpath directly ahead. At the top of the slope turn right with a fence to your left. At the corner of the fence, opposite a gnarled beech tree, turn left following the path with the field boundary on your left. The path climbs steeply past a stile.

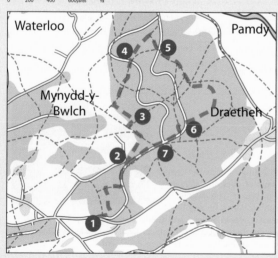

Waterloo

Pamdy

Mynydd-y-Bwlch

Draethen

3 | Just over the top of the ridge, turn right on a wide level path; after 10 yards turn left downhill; after another 50 yards bear left. Cross 2 small streams and follow the well-worn path through the woods. At a stile on the left (view across to the hills above Caerphilly) bear right.

4 | Cross the forest track. After about 300 yards turn right at a 'crossroads' and follow the path round to the right.

5 | Cross another forest track. Go down into the woods, bearing round to the right past some fallen trees. Cross a stream and continue through a small clearing (a good picnic place). Go round the clearing and under the trees on a wide path. At one point you need to veer off to the left to avoid fallen trees: turn right on a wider path then left to resume the route. Continue across a smaller path, bear left at a fork, cross another path and continue uphill as the woods change to deciduous. Near the top of the hill, bear round to the right between two fenced pits. After 200yards, ignore a small path then bear left.

6 | Cross the forest track. Continue straight ahead then left at a junction to pass a large yew tree, join the wide track and turn right

7 | At a wide junction go straight ahead. When you reach point 2, bear round to the left following the forest track down and back to the start.

famous leaning tower, which manages to out-lean even the famous Leaning Tower of Pisa. Today the castle is home to an intriguing display of full size working replica siege engines.

Caerphilly was the birthplace of the much-loved comedian **Tommy Cooper** (1921 - 1984), though he moved to Devon when he was a few months old.

DERI
14 miles NW of Newport off the A469

Parc Cwm Darran

To the north of Deri, in beautiful Darran Valley, lies **Parc Cwm Darran**, a glorious country park which, along with the adventure playground and informative Visitor Centre, also has a six-acre coarse fishery.

PONTLLANFRAITH
11 miles NW of Newport on the A4048

Gelligroes Mill

Close to this town lies **Gelligroes Mill**, a 17th century water mill restored to full working order. In the early 20th century the mill was owned by Arthur Moore, a radio enthusiast, who on the night of 11th April 1912 claimed to have heard distress signals from the sinking *Titanic*. No one believed Arthur until two days later, when the news reached England of the disaster.

CWMFELINFACH
9 miles NW of Newport on the A4048

Ynys Hywel Centre   Sirhowy Valley Country Park

Covering some 1,000 acres of both woodland and farmland, the **Sirhowy Valley Country Park** provides the ideal opportunity to walk, cycle or ride along the park's numerous trails. The Full Moon Visitor Centre has all the details of the park's natural history and of other activities here while, in the heart of the country park, is **Ynys Hywel Centre**, a converted 17th century farmhouse which has conference facilities and a weekend coffee shop.

CWMCARN
7 miles NW of Newport on the B4591

🍃 Cwmcarn Forest Drive

🍃 Mabinogion Sculpture Trail

Just to the west of the town lies **Cwmcarn Forest Drive**, a seven-mile stretch of high forest road that provides some of the most magnificent panoramic views of the South Wales countryside and the Bristol Channel beyond. Another attraction is the **Mabinogion Sculpture Trail**, which depicts characters from the Celtic folklore tales of the *Mabinogion*. The drive's visitor centre has details of the route and what can be seen at various points and also a coffee shop and a gift shop selling local handicrafts. There are also a campsite and a mountain bike trail.

RISCA
5 miles NW of Newport on the B4591

🏛 Fourteen Locks Canal Centre

To the south of Risca, at High Cross on the Monmouthshire Canal, is the **Fourteen Locks Canal Centre**, where this complicated systems of locks was constructed to raise and lower barges some 168 feet in just half a mile with only the minimal wastage of water. There are several walks from the centre, which take in the locks, ponds, channels, tunnels and weirs, as well as the countryside in which the centre is sited. Open from Easter to September, the visitor centre has a display that follows the opening (in 1796), the growth and the heyday of the Monmouthshire Canal and

the decline that started when the railways began to take over from water transport

NELSON
14 miles NW of Newport on the A472

🏛 Llancaiach Fawr Manor   🍃 Nelson Handball Court

As well as boasting the open-air **Nelson Handball Court** dating from the 1860s (and still in use), this village is home to **Llancaiach Fawr Manor**, a handsome Elizabethan manor house which has been lovingly restored to reflect the year 1645 and the time of the Civil War. During this turbulent time, the Pritchard family lived here and visitors can meet members of the family and their servants, all in authentic costumes, as they carry on with their daily lives. As well as preparing meals, gardening and exchanging gossip of the day, a number of activities from that time, such as archery and falconry, are staged.

The building is said to have eight ghosts, and visitors get the chance to meet some of them on the special ghost tours.

Pontypool

🏛 Pontypool Museum   🏛 Junction Cottage

🍃 Pontypool Park   🍃 Llandegfedd Reservoir

Known to have been in existence before the time of the Normans, Pontypool is credited with being the home of the Welsh iron industry. The first forge here is believed to have been in operation as early as 1425, and the first ironworks opened in 1577. It is said that the first iron working forge in America was started by emigrants from Pontypool in the mid 17th century. This valley also prides itself on being the earliest place in Britain to have successfully produced tin plate, which it did in in 1720. Today the town's industrial heritage can be explored at the **Pontypool**

🏛 historic building   📷 museum   🏛 historic site   🍃 scenic attraction   🐦 flora and fauna

Museum, where both the industrial and social history of the town and surrounding Torfaen valley is detailed. The museum is located in the late Georgian stables of Pontypool Park, once the home of the Hanbury family, who were, appropriately, owners of a local ironworks. **Pontypool Park** is a 19th century landscaped park whose main attractions include a shell grotto and a unique double-chambered ice house. The formal Italian gardens have recently been restored with the help of Heritage Lottery funding.

Pontypool Museum

The canals, too, have played an important part in the development of Pontypool and this particular legacy is recalled at **Junction Cottage**, a toll keeper's cottage of 1814 lying at the junction of the Monmouthshire and Brecon Canal and the River Lwyd.

However, industry seems worlds away at **Llandegfedd Reservoir**, to the east of Pontypool, where the lake and surrounding countryside provide numerous opportunities for fishing, sailing, walking and bird watching.

once itself dominated by heavy industry. Today, the mines and large works have gone and major environmental improvement schemes, including planting forests, have taken away many of the old eyesores. Not far from the town are some interesting and historic places including the **Llanyrafon Mill and Farm Museum** and the **Llantarnam Grange Arts Centre. Greenmeadow Community Farm**, set within the town's planned green belt, is home to all manner of farm animals, and farm trails, a children's adventure playground and an unusual dragon sculpture are among the other attractions which go to provide a popular and entertaining day out. If you'd rather go shopping, then the **Cwmbran**

Around Pontypool

CWMBRAN
3 miles SW of Pontypool on the A4051

📷 Llanyrafon Mill and Farm Museum

🖼 Llantarnam Grange Arts Centre

🌱 Greenmeadow Community Farm

🎯 Cwmbran Shopping Centre

This new town in the old industrial valleys of South Wales was founded in 1949 and was

Llanyrafon Mill

Shopping Centre is said to be the largest undercover shopping centre in Wales.

ABERTILLERY
6 miles NW of Pontypool off the A467

The **Arbertillery And Disrrict Museum,** on the ground floor of the Metropole Conference and Cultural Centre, tells the story of this former mining town and the surrounding area from the Bronze Age up until the present time. There is a recreation of a miner's kitchen and many artefacts and displays about the mining industry.

BEDWELLTY
7 miles W of Pontypool on the A4048

🏛 Parish Church of St Sannon

The **Parish Church of St Sannon** is medieval in origin. Inside, on the south wall, is the famous iron gravestone of Mary Rowlands, who died in the 1770s. For over 200 years it lay in the churchyard, yet it shows little sign of rusting, a testimony to the quality of the iron made around here at the time.

BLAENAVON
6 miles NW of Pontypool on the B4246

🏛 Cordell Museum   🏛 Blaenavon Ironworks

🏛 National Mining Museum of Wales

🏛 Pontypool and Blaenavon Railway

Despite once having been associated with the heavy industries of coal mining and iron working, Blaenavon is set in surprisingly pleasant countryside which can be further explored by taking the **Pontypool and Blaenavon Railway**, the highest standard gauge track to have survived in Wales. Half the site lies within the Brecon Beacons National Park.

The oldest colliery in Wales, Big Pit Mine,

closed in 1980, but has been reopened as the **National Mining Museum of Wales**, with former miners and engineers from the site giving guided tours accompanied by plenty of anecdotes. Visitors (children must be at least five years old and a metre tall), armed with helmet, lamp and battery pack, can travel down a 90 metre shaft in a pit cage and walk through the underground roadways, air doors, stables and engine houses which were built by past generations of mineworkers and where thousands of miners, some of them children, laboured in arduous conditions. On the surface at this site, designated Britain's 18th World Heritage Site by UNESCO, there are more buildings to explore, including the winding engine-house, the blacksmith's workshop and the pithead baths.

The other side of the town's industry, iron working, can be discovered at the **Blaenavon Ironworks**, a marvellous site that not only represents an important aspect of the Industrial Revolution but is also one of Europe's best preserved 18th century ironworks. Built against a cliff-face in the 1780s and then at the cutting edge of technology, the ironworks, whose power came from a steam engine, became the second largest in Wales. Visitors to the ironworks and the **Cordell Museum** can see the whole process of production, including the row of blast furnaces and ingenious water balance tower by which the material was transported. Here, too, the human element of the vast ironworks is covered, as a small terrace of workers' cottages, built between 1789 and 1792, has been preserved.

The **Parish Church of St Peter**, built in 1804, is the oldest building in Blaenavon, and has many features made of iron. It was built by the ironmasters of the ironworks, Samuel

Hopkins and Thomas Hill, and given to the parish. The town is Wales' book town, and now has many second-hand bookshops in its main street.

EBBW VALE
10 miles NW of Pontypool on the A4048

🌳 Festival Park

This old steelmaking town, whose member of Parliament was once the formidable orator, social reformer and driving force behind the National Health Service, Aneurin Bevan The town was transformed by the 1992 Garden Festival. Following the event, the garden site was developed into **Festival Park** with houses, shops and a range of leisure activities.

A monument to Aneurin Bevan stands on the outskirts of the town, which still has a number of fine houses which were built by the wealthy steel and coal magnates of the area.

TREDEGAR
12 miles NW of Pontypool on the B4256

🏛 Elliot Colliery Winding House

🌳 Bryn Bach Country Park

🐿 Aneurin Bevan 🐿 AJ Cronin 🐿 Neil Kinnock

This pretty town was the birthplace of **Aneurin Bevan**, founder of the National Health Service and Member of Parliament for Ebbw Vale. The ashes of Bevan, in 1960, and of his wife Jennie Lee, in 1988, were scattered in the hills above Tredegar. It was in the town that the novelist **AJ Cronin** worked as a doctor and where he collected information for his book, *The Citadel*, which was later made into a film starring Robert Donat and a television series with Ben Cross. Brown tourist signs lead to the **Elliot Colliery Winding House**, now a museum of a colliery

that once employed more than 2,000 people.

Close by lies **Bryn Bach Country Park**, a 600-acre area of grass and woodland, with a 16-acre man-made lake, an abundance of wildlife, a visitor centre and opportunities for walking, fishing, canoeing, climbing and abseiling. **Neil Kinnock**, the former Labour leader, was born in Tredegar.

RHYMNEY
12½ miles NW of Pontypool off the A469

Rhymney was once a coal mining town, and is nowadays famous because of the poem written by coal miner and later school teacher Idris Davis called the *Bells of Rhymney*. It was about a coal mining accident, and the poem was later set to music by the folk singer Peter Seeger. The words mention many towns in South East Wales, but the bells of Rhymney are called the 'sad' ones.

ABERGAVENNY
8½ miles N of Pontypool on the A40

🏛 Parish Church of St Mary 🏛 Abergavenny Castle

🏛 Abergavenny Museum 🏛 Museum of Childhood

🌳 Blorenge

Abergavenny has sometimes been called the 'gateway to South Wales', and is a particularly pleasant and thriving market town. It sits within the Usk Valley, with the Brecon Beacons National Park to the north. The town can trace its history back to the Roman fort of Gobbanium established here in either AD 57 or AD 58. In the early 12th century the Norman knight Hameline de Balun built a castle here, and founded a priory. The **Parish Church of St Mary**, once the priory church, dates from the 14th century and later. Inside there is are fine choir stalls and medieval altar tombs. Here, too, is the Norman

Abergavenny Castle, where in 1175 the fearsome Norman lord, William de Braose, invited the Welsh lords to dine and then murdered the lot while they were disarmed at his table. Not very much remains, as King Charles I ordered it to be destroyed. Today, the rebuilt keep and hunting lodge of the castle are home to the **Abergavenny Museum** where exhibits from prehistoric times to the present day detail the history of the town and surrounding area. Displays include recreations of a Victorian kitchen and a saddler's workshop. The castle and its grounds have been open to the public since 1881.

Abergavenny is a popular place during the summer. Surrounded by glorious countryside, it is a place from where all manner of activities, including walking, pony trekking and canal cruising, can be enjoyed. A little way south of town, the 1,834ft **Blorenge** is a popular tourist spot. One of the car parks at its base is called Foxhunter. It was presented by Colonel Sir Harry Llewelyn in memory of his wonderful show jumper, who died in 1959 and is buried nearby.

LLANTHONY
9 miles N of Pontypool off the B4423

🏠 Llanthony Priory

In the beautiful Vale of Ewyas, also known as Llanthony Valley, **Llanthony Priory** was built on a spot which has links with the beginnings of Christianity in Wales, and in the 6th century was chosen by St David for a cell. The priory grew out of a hermitage founded by the Norman William de Lacy in the 11th century.

The beauty and tranquillity of the location have inspired many people. Eric Gill and Walter Savage Landor are among those who

made their homes here. For many years the site was in a state of near decay, but the Welsh Office graded it as an Ancient Monument and so ensured its survival.

Monmouth

🏠 Monnow Bridge   🏠 Monmouth Castle

🏠 Round House   🏠 Great Castle House

🏠 Parish Church of St Mary   🏛 Castle Museum

🏛 Nelson Museum and Local History Centre

🏛 Regimental Museum   🏛 Naval Temple

🌿 The Kymin   🌱 King's Garden

🐚 Geoffrey of Monmouth   🐚 Charles Stuart Rolls

This prosperous and charming old market town grew up at the confluence of three rivers - the Wye, Monnow and Trothy - which are all noted for their fishing. The River Wye

Monnow Bridge, Monmouth

🏠 historic building   🏛 museum   🏛 historic site   🌿 scenic attraction   🌱 flora and fauna

is crossed by a five arched bridge built in 1617, but the Monnow boasts the most impressive of the town's bridges. **Monnow Bridge** is one of Monmouth's real gems, and its sturdy fortified gatehouse, dating from the 13th century, is the only one left of its kind in Britain. When work was undertaken some time ago on the bridge to strengthen it, the foundations of the previous wooden bridge, dating from about 1180, were discovered, directly under the present one. The gatehouse was not part of this new bridge, however. It was added in the early 14th century as part of the towns defences.

The Wye Valley, Monmouth

Long before the bridge was constructed, the Normans built **Monmouth Castle** here in around 1068. Later rebuilt by John of Gaunt in the late 1300s, the castle was the birthplace of his grandson, later Henry V, in 1387. Much later, in the 17th century, **Great Castle House** was built by the 3rd Marquess of Worcester from the ruins of the castle, and he lived here while his other homes, Badminton and Troy House, were being rebuilt. Today, the castle houses both the **Castle Museum** and the **Regimental Museum** where the histories of the castle and the Royal Monmouthshire Royal Engineers are explored. The **King's Garden** is a recreation of a small medieval courtyard garden, planted with herbs that would have been common around the time of Henry V.

Another interesting building in the town is the 14th century **Parish Church of St Mary**, formerly a priory church, whose eight bells are said to have been recast from a peal which

Henry V brought back from France after his victory at Agincourt. The story goes that as Henry was leaving Calais, the ringing of bells was heard and he was told that the French were celebrating his departure. He immediately turned back and took the bells to give as a present to his native town.

One of the graves in the churchyard is that of an obscure house-painter called John Renie, who died in 1832 at the age of 33. His headstone is an acrostic of 285 letters that reads "Here lies John Renie". This epitaph can be read over and over again, upwards, downwards, backwards and forwards, and if doglegs and zigzags are also included, it is apparently possible to read "Here lies John Renie" in 45,760 different ways. The memorial also records the deaths of his two sons, one at the age of one year and nine months, the other at the age of 83. An earlier Monmouth man, **Geoffrey of Monmouth**, was the Prior at St Mary's before becoming Bishop of St Asaph in North Wales. It was probably in Monmouth that Geoffrey wrote his massive work, *A History of the Kings of Britain*, with its legends of King Arthur and Merlin.

Also in the town is the **Nelson Museum and Local History Centre**, where a fascinating collection of material and artefacts about the great Admiral can be seen. This interesting collection of memorabilia was accumulated by Lady Llangattock, the mother of **Charles Stuart Rolls** of Rolls Royce fame, who, while born in London, had his ancestral home nearby. The history of the town is illustrated in displays in the same building. The exploits of the Hon Charles Rolls in cars, balloons and aeroplanes are featured here; one of the most evocative pictures is of Rolls in the basket of his 'Midget' balloon at Monmouth Gasworks in about 1908. Some five miles from the town is the Rolls estate where Charles grew up and developed an early interest in engineering and motoring that led to his forming the Rolls-Royce company. Charles died in an air accident in 1910 and his statue, along with a monument to Henry V, can be seen in the town's main Agincourt Square. He is buried in the churchyard of St Cadoc's, at Llangattock-vibon-Avel, not far from Monmouth.

Just to the west of the town, and practically on the border with England, lies **The Kymin**, a National Trust-owned hill overlooking the River Wye. From here there are spectacular views across the picturesque landscape. The **Round House**, also found here, was erected by the Kymin Club in 1794. The members of this club were local worthies who liked to hold open-air lunch parties on the Kymin. They decided to construct a building so that they could picnic inside in bad weather, and the

ENVEE

92 Monnow Street, Monmouth, Monmouthshire NP25 3EQ
Tel: 01600 711557
e-mail: enquiries@envee.co.uk   website: www.envee.co.uk

For the very best in stylish fashions and accessories, you just can't beat Envee, situated in the High Street, right in the heart of Monmouth. It has been in existence for just over a year, and already it has earned an enviable reputation for chic, well-designed fashion accessories such as shoes and handbags.

It is owned and managed by Yvonne Perry, who is developing a wealth of experience in the retail fashion industry, and she and her staff are always on hand to offer advice and help if needed. The shop is a cornucopia of delights - bright, colourful and full of the kind of accessories that any woman would appreciate. The range of shoes in particular is spectacular, with everything from high fashion to sensible day wear with just a hint of glamour. And the bags have to be seen to be believed. Everything from fun items such as bags featuring American licence plates to feisty shoulder bags and elegant handbags for an evening engagement.

All the big names are here - Roberta Botella, Riva, Claudina, Tamaris, Azurée Cannes, Arcadia, Bourne, Littlearth, Fiorelli, Caprice, Marino Fabiani, Strutt Couture and so many more. There is free car parking nearby, and the shop is open from 8.30 am to 6 pm from Monday to Saturday, as well as Sunday.

A truly enjoyable shopping experience with a relaxed atmosphere, soft music and a babbling water feature in the background. Come along and see for yourself.

🏠 historic building   🏛 museum   🏛 historic site   🌀 scenic attraction   🌿 flora and fauna result is the Round House - round so that the views could be enjoyed from every part of the house. Offa's Dyke footpath (see Prestatyn) runs through the land. Nearby is the **Naval Temple**, opened in the early 19th century to commemorate the Battle of the Nile.

Around Monmouth

TRELLECK
4½ miles S of Monmouth on the B4293

🏛 Parish Church of St Nicholas   🏚 Harold's Stones

🏚 Preaching Cross   🏚 Tump Turret

🐦 Bertrand Russell

Trelleck's name means 'Three Stones' and these large prehistoric monoliths can be found to the southwest of the village. For reasons unknown they are called **Harold's Stones**. They do not represent all the historical interest here, as the **Parish Church of St Nicholas** is also worth visiting. It dates from the 13th and 14th centuries, and stands on the site of a church built in the 7th century and endowed by the ancient kings of Gwent. The **Preaching Cross** in the churchyard probably dates from that period. Close to the church a

mound known as **Tump Turret**, which is all that remains of a Norman motte and bailey.

To the east of the village is the Virtuous Well, also called St Anne's Well. The water is full of iron, and it was once drunk as a curative. In medieval times, Trelleck was one of the most important towns in Wales, and a local field, where stone and masonry have been discovered, is said to mark the location of its main buildings.

The village was the birthplace of the philosopher **Bertrand Russell** (1872 - 1970). He was the grandson of the 1st Earl Russell.

TINTERN PARVA
7½ miles S of Monmouth off the A466

🏛 Tintern Abbey   🏛 Parish Church of St Mary

🏚 Old Station

This riverside village, which nestles among the wooded slopes of the lovely Wye Valley, is a very beautiful place, and the whole of the valley between Monmouth and Chepstow is designated an Area of Outstanding Natural Beauty. Here are found the enchanting ruins of **Tintern Abbey**, which lie beside the river. The abbey was founded by Cistercian monks in 1131 and largely rebuilt in the 13th century by Roger Bigod, the Lord of Chepstow Castle. The monks farmed the rich agricultural land as well as dedicating themselves to their rigorous regime of religious devotions right up until the time of the Dissolution. A rich and powerful abbey in its day, Tintern is now a majestic ruin with much delicate tracery and great soaring archways, in a glorious

Preaching Cross, Trelleck

🎭 stories and anecdotes   🐦 famous people   🎨 art and craft   🏃 entertainment and sport   🚶 walks

Tintern Abbey

Distance: *3.1 miles (5.0 kilometres)*

Typical time: *95 mins*

Height gain: *185 metres*

Map: *Outdoor Leisure 14*

Walk: *www.walkingworld.com ID:213*

Contributor: *Peter Salenieks*

Tintern lies between Monmouth and Chepstow in the Wye Valley. The Abbey is just off the A466, at the southern end of the village. There is a car park just off the main road. If this is full, the car park for Tintern Abbey is at the rear of the Abbey, beside the River Wye.

ADDITIONAL INFORMATION:

This walk will take about 95 minutes. It can be combined with a visit to Tintern Abbey. Contact the Information Centre on 01291 689251 for information about when the Abbey is open.

DESCRIPTION:

Whilst Tintern is best known for its Abbey, there is evidence of earlier settlements dating back to the Bronze Age. The name "Tintern" is derived from Dyn Teryn (or King's Fort). It is where King Tewdrig chose to live as a hermit in the 6th century, before defeating the Saxons in his final battle at nearby Pont y Saeson. The Abbey was built on the ruins of Tewdrig's hermitage in 1131 and became the first Cistercian Abbey in Wales. It was rebuilt between 1270 and 1301 to reflect the growing wealth and power of the Cistercian order and it continued to prosper until 1536, when the Abbey was dissolved by King Henry VIII.

The opening of the Wye Valley Railway in the 1870s hastened the growth of Tintern and the Wye Valley as tourist attractions, prompting some restoration of the Abbey ruins. They were visited by poets and artists, including Wordsworth and Turner. William Wordsworth first visited Tintern in 1793 and returned five years later, when he wrote the poem 'Lines composed a few miles above Tintern Abbey', saying that *"no poem of mine was composed under circumstances more pleasant for me to remember than this."*

This linear walk starts at Tintern Abbey, passing The Anchor public house to reach the River Wye. It follows the western bank of the Wye towards Tintern, where gifts and refreshments are available, before crossing the river via a bridge. After walking a short distance back along the eastern bank, wooded paths lead uphill to Offa's Dyke Path, which is followed to the Devil's Pulpit. This is a small limestone rock that juts out from the cliffs. It looks down over Tintern Abbey from the hills beside Offa's Dyke on the eastern side of the River Wye. Local legend has it that the devil stood upon the Devil's Pulpit to preach to the monks below, tempting them to desert their order. After admiring the view, retrace your route to reach the start.

FEATURES:

River, Pub, Toilets, Church, Wildlife, Birds, Great Views, Cafe, Gift Shop, Tea Shop, Woodland

WALK DIRECTIONS:

1 | Start at the car park opposite Tintern Abbey and walk north along a minor road that leads towards the River Wye. Pass The Anchor public house on your left and stop when you reach a footpath on the left (west), which is

adjacent to a mini-roundabout at the end of the road.

2 | Follow the footpath along the western bank of the river. After the footpath turns inland towards Tintern, pass a whitewashed house on the left and continue along a minor road to reach a T-junction. There is a footpath sign directly ahead.

3 | Turn left (south) and walk a short distance along the minor road to a junction with the A466. Turn right (north-west) and walk along the pavement, passing a hotel on your left and an art gallery and gift shop on your right. Continue until you reach a minor road junction on your right, which is just past the Abbey Mill Cafe.

4 | Walk north-east along the minor road towards the River Wye and cross the footbridge. Continue east along the footpath on the eastern side of the river, passing a footpath on the right (which leads to the riverbank). A footpath on the left leads uphill,

with several metal posts at the start. Follow the footpath uphill. Shortly after it levels off, there is a footpath junction beside a short section of stone wall on the left (north).

5 | Take the right-hand footpath and follow it for a short distance, until you reach another footpath junction marked by a wooden post with a footpath sign. Take the right-hand footpath and continue for a short distance to reach a footpath junction.

6 | Turn left and follow the footpath uphill, as it ascends the northern side of a narrow spur. As the gradient levels off, the footpath bears around to the right (south-east). A short flight of wooden steps can be seen on the left, just past a large uprooted tree on the right. Ascend the wooden steps to reach a track junction marked by a wooden post with a footpath sign. An antenna can be seen on the opposite side of the track. Turn right (south-east) and walk a short distance along the track to reach a footpath junction with a stone marker.

7 | Bear left at the junction and follow the footpath uphill to reach Offa's Dyke Path.

8 | Turn right (south) at the footpath sign and walk along Offa's Dyke Path until you reach a footpath junction and a sign at a right-hand bend.

9 | Continue west along Offa's Dyke Path from the footpath sign to reach the Devil's Pulpit at a left-hand bend. There is a sign to mark the Devil's Pulpit. Tintern and the Wye Valley can be seen below through a clearing in the trees. Retrace your route back to the start.

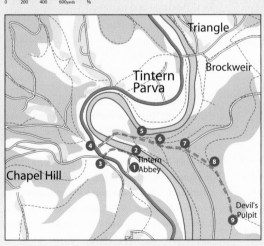

Tintern Parva

setting that has inspired painters and poets such as Turner and Wordsworth.

However, the abbey is not the only ruin in the vicinity. The ruins of the former **Parish Church of St Mary** lie close to the Beaufort Hotel, and originally served the parish of Chapel Hill, to the asouth of Tintern Parva. The church remained in use until 1972, but was burnt down in 1977.

A mile from the abbey, along the A466 Chepstow-Monmouth road, is the Victorian **Old Station** which now acts as a visitor centre for the Wye Valley. Here, too, are a countryside exhibition, a collection of signal boxes, a gift shop and a model railway.

CHEPSTOW
12½ miles S of Monmouth on the A48

🏯 Chepstow Castle   🏯 Parish Church of St Mary

🏯 Town Gate   🏛 Chepstow Museum   🏚 Port Wall

This splendid old market town, which lies on

the border with England, takes its name from the Old English 'chepe stow', meaning 'market place'. It occupies a strategic crossing on the River Wye between England and Wales, and indeed looks across the river into England. Situated on a crag are the well-preserved ruins of **Chepstow Castle**, which William Fitzosbern, Earl of Hereford, began building in 1067 as a base for the Norman conquest of south east Wales. Its importance can be judged from the fact that it was built of stone, when most Norman fortresses of the time were in motte and bailey form and built from earth and timber. The castle began life as a keep, and towers, walls, fortifications and gatehouses were added to prepare it for the Welsh wars, in which, as it happened, it played no part. It is open throughout the year.

A major exhibition within its walls, 'A Castle at War' relates its history, and a group of local people have come together to form the Chepstow Garrison; dressing up and re-enacting scenes from Chepstow's past, they have become a popular attraction for both local residents and tourists.

Built at the same time as the castle keep, and by the same William Fitzosbern, is the **Parish Church of St Mary**. It was the church of a former Benedictine priory which suffered considerable damage after the Dissolution of the Monasteries in 1536. It suffered further damage in 1701 when the massive central tower collapsed. The vast three-storey original nave gives some idea of the grand scale on which it was built. The church contains some imposing and interesting monuments, including the Jacobean tomb of Margaret Cleyton with her two husbands and 12 children. This lady paid for the town's gatehouse to be rebuilt in 1609. Also entombed here is Henry Marten, friend of Oliver Cromwell and signatory to the death warrant of Charles I. Marten spent many years imprisoned in Chepstow Castle, in the tower that now bears his name. William Fitzosbern also founded the Abbey at Cormeilles in Normandy, a town with which Chepstow is now twinned.

Opposite the castle is **Chepstow Museum**, housed in an elegant 18th century merchant's house, and here the rich and varied history of this border town is revealed. The museum has displays on the town's many industries, including shipbuilding, fishing and the wine trade. Chepstow was at one time an important centre for shipbuilding, and one of the many photographs in the exhibition shows the closing stages in the building of *War Genius* in National Shipyard No1 in 1920. Ships were built well into the 1920s, and the tradition was

revived during World War II with the construction of tank landing craft.

Throughout the town itself, the medieval street pattern is still much in evidence, along with surviving sections of the town wall, called the **Port Wall**, and the impressive **Town Gate**. But Chepstow is also a thriving modern town, and its attractions include an excellent racecourse offering both Flat and National Hunt racing; the highlight of the jumping season is the valuable and prestigious Welsh Grand National. The racecourse lies within the grounds of historic Piercefield Park. Piercefield Picturesque Walk was created in the 1750s by Valentine Morris the Younger and follows the Wye river cliff up to the Eagle's Nest. Chepstow is at one end of Offa's Dyke (see Prestatyn), the 8th century

SCANDIA

35 Moor Street, Chepstow, Monmouthshire NP16 5DE
Tel: 01291 627272

For designer shoes and gifts in Chepstow, head for **Scandia**, which has branches on Moor Street, Chepstow and Priory Street, Monmouth. They are owned and managed by Else Grete Skov-Newton, who originally hails from Denmark, and have a great range of fashion shoes and accessories to suit every woman.

The shop in Chepstow is housed in a delightful, listed building dating from the 17th century, still with its original breams and old fireplace. Both shops are open six days a week, and place great emphasis on quality, good design and superb value for money. Else has lived in the area for 28 years, and people come, not just from Monmouthshire, but from all over, to select and buy their footwear and accessories.

Famous names such as Farfalla, Esino, Orlando, Vaneli, Marco Tozzi, Capollini, Cefalu and Riva can be bought here, as well as a wonderful range of gifts, candles and other accessories.

Else and her staff are knowledgeable about the shoes they stock, and are always willing to offer help and advice when you make a purchase. The service is always efficient and friendly, something in which the staff take great pride. They also take a great pride in their knowledge of this beautiful area of Wales, and can point you in the direction of the many attractions, be they historic, cultural, scenic or sporting - that Monmouthshire has to offer. Pay a visit. You'll be amazed at the huge range and the realistic prices.

🎬 stories and anecdotes   🖋 famous people   🎨 art and craft   ✒ entertainment and sport   🚶 walks

defensive ditch and bank built by the King of Mercia. It is also the starting point for the long-distance Wye Valley and Gloucestershire Way walks.

Caldicot Castle

CALDICOT
15 miles S of Monmouth on the B4245

🏛 Caldicot Castle

🏛 Parish Church of St Mary

Caldicot Castle dates from Norman times and was restored for use as a family house in the 1880s. It was originally built by Humphrey de Bohun on a much earlier fortified site in the early 13th century. Of particular note is the sturdy round keep and the gatehouse dating from the 14th century. The castle, which is set within a wooded country park, hosts occasional medieval banquets.

The **Parish Church of St Mary** dates originally from the 12th century, though it is now mainly from the 14th and 15th centuries. It was founded by Milo Fitzwalter on the site of an earlier church dedicated to St Bride.

CAERWENT
14 miles SW of Monmouth off the A48

🏛 Parish Church of St Stephen   🏛 Venta Silurum

Close to the Wentwood Forest, this town - which is now more of a village - was the site of **Venta Silurum**, a walled Roman city built by the invaders for the local Celtic Silures tribe. Sections of the Roman defences still remain and are some of the best preserved in Britain, while inside the walls can be seen the remains of the forum basilica and the Romano-Celtic temple. Venta Silurum is thought to have been the largest centre of civilian population in Roman occupied Wales, and covered over 44 acres. It is yet another suggested site for King Arthur's Camelot.

Much of the present village is built of stone taken from the Roman site, including the **Parish Church of St Stephen**, which was built in medieval times.

RAGLAN
6½ miles SW of Monmouth off the A40

🏛 Raglan Castle   🏛 Clytha Castle

To the north of this village of shops and inns and a mix of old and modern buildings, lies **Raglan Castle**, one of the finest late medieval fortresses in Britain. Built towards the end of the Middle Ages, and thus in relatively peaceful times, the castle was also constructed with comfort in mind and it represents wealth and social

Venta Silurum, Caerwent

🏛 historic building   🏛 museum   🏛 historic site   🗱 scenic attraction   � flora and fauna

aspirations as much as military might. Started in 1435 by Sir William ap Thomas, who fought at Agincourt, the building work was continued in the same lavish manner by the next owner, William Herbert, who was responsible for the addition of the formal state apartments and the magnificent gatehouse. Despite being more a palace than a fortress, Raglan Castle withstood one of the longest sieges of the Civil War. To the west lies **Clytha Castle**, a folly designed by John Nash for an owner of the Clytha Park estate in memory of his wife.

The village indirectly gives its name to the 'Raglan sleeve', which is joined to the main part of a pullover in a diagonal manner, from collarbone to armpit. It was named after Fitzroy James Henry Someset, 1st Baron Raglan (1788 - 1855), who lost his arm at the Battle of Waterloo

USK

11½ miles SW of Monmouth on the A472

🏰 Usk Castle   🏛 Parish Church of St Mary

🏛 Gwent Rural Life Museum

This delightful small town, which takes its name from the river on which it sits, was founded by the Romans in AD 75. Well known for its excellent local fishing - the River Usk is a fine salmon river - the town attracts fishermen from far and wide. Also noted for its floral displays and historic buildings, Usk is home to the **Gwent Rural Life Museum**, housed in several historic buildings, which tells the story of life in this Welsh border region from Victorian times up until the end of World War II. Among the many themes covered here are domestic and agricultural life and exhibits ranging from

THE SHIP INN

8 High Street, Raglan, Monmouthshire NP15 2DY
Tel: 01291 690365

The Ship Inn is a delightful 16th century stone built pub that combines all the best traditions of an 'olde worlde' inn with modern standards of service and great value for money. It has a fine reputation, both with locals and visitors, and its oldest customers must be the 12 ghosts that are said to haunt it! One - called Mr. Bridges - is so pleased with the service that there is even a special chair set aside for his convenience!

The interior has bare stone walls, old beams and an open fireplace where a fire burns during the winter months. It sells a great range of drinks, from real ales to beers, wines, spirits (the alcoholic kind!) and soft drinks. And the food is outstanding. So much so that you are well advised to book in advance for evening meals. All the produce used is sourced locally wherever possible, ensuring maximum freshness and flavour. The menu includes such favourites as steaks with all the trimmings, tasty cottage pie, chicken and mushroom pie, lasagne, curries, sliced ham, egg and chips and faggots served with peppered mash, onion gravy and peas.

Teas and fresh-ground coffees are also available, and within the outdoor courtyard are tables and chairs for eating and drinking al fresco during the warmer months. This is a pub that takes its customers seriously, and always offers a warm welcome.

hand tool crafts to mechanisation.

Usk Castle was built in the early 12th century, and passed to and froe between the English and the Welsh. It was strengthened by Gilbert de Clare in the late 13th and early 14th century when he built the tower keep. De Clare was eventually killed at Bannockburn, and it then passed to Elizabeth de Burgh and eventually the Mortimer family. The Duchy of Lancaster, which owned it next, allowed it to fall into decay.

The **Parish Church of St Mary** was formerly the church of a Benedictine priory for nuns founded in the 12th century, and has a 15th century roodscreen.

LLANVETHERINE
9 miles NW of Monmouth on the B4521

🏛 White Castle

🏛 Parish Church of St James the Elder

To the south of the village lies one of the 'Three Castles', **White Castle**, which is so called because when it was built the masonry was rendered with gleaming white plaster, patches of which can still be seen. Starting life as a simple earthwork not long after the Norman Conquest, White Castle was rebuilt in stone during the late 12th and 13th centuries to provide, along with Skenfrith and Grosmont castles, a triangle of fortresses to control this strategic entry point into Wales. Situated in a beautiful and isolated place, the ruins are still able to conjure up the romance of the Middle Ages. Much later, during World War II, Hitler's deputy, Rudolf Hess, fed the swans on the castle's moat while held at a local mental hospital following his mysterious flight from Nazi Germany. The **Parish Church of St James the Elder** dates from the 14th century, though it was restored in 1872. The Arts and Crafts pulpit dates from 1900.

GROSMONT
9½ miles NW of Monmouth on the B4347

🏛 Grosmont Castle   🏛 Parish Church of St Nicholas

This village takes its name from the French, 'gros mont', meaning 'big hill'; it is the site of **Grosmont Castle**, the most northerly of the 'Three Castles'.

Now in ruins, Grosmont started life as a steep earthen mound but, after having been replaced by a stone fortification, it was unsuccessfully besieged by both Llywelyn the Great and Owain Glyndwr. During exploration of the ruins, an Arabic 'faience jar' was found here - undoubtedly a relic from the Crusades. The 13th century **Parish Church of St Nicholas** has an octagonal tower surmounted by a spire. The nave has an unusual tomb - the stone carving of the recumbent knight above it was never finished.

SKENFRITH
5½ miles NW of Monmouth on the B4521

🏛 Skenfrith Castle   🏛 Parish Church of St Bridget

At this point the Monnow Valley forms something of a gap in the natural defences of the Welsh Marches and its was here that the Normans built **Skenfrith Castle** (NT), the last of the 'Three Castles' - the others being White and Grosmont. Situated beside the river, Skenfrith Castle was built in the 13th century by Hubert de Burgh and is noted for its fine round tower keep and its well-preserved curtain wall. Once the troubled domain of medieval warlords, this border region is today peaceful and undisturbed. The **Parish Church of St Bridget** dates from the 13th century with later additions, and sits close to the River Monnow, where there are still the remains of a medieval quay.

ABERAERON TIC

The Quay, Aberaeron, Ceredigion SA46 0BT
Tel: 01545 570602
Fax: 01545 571534
e-mail: aberaerontic@ceredigion.gov.uk

ABERDULAIS

The National Trust, Aberdulais Falls, Neath SA10 8EU
Tel: 01639 636674
Fax: 01639 645069
e-mail: aberdulais@nationaltrust.org.uk

ABERDYFI TIC

The Wharf Gardens, Aberdyfi, Gwynedd LL35 0ED
Tel: 01654 767321
Fax: 01654 767321
e-mail: tic.aberdyfi@eryri-npa.gov.uk

ABERGAVENNY TIC

Swan Meadow, Monmouth Road, Abergavenny,
Monmouthshire NP7 5HH
Tel: 01873 857588
Fax: 01873 850217
e-mail: abergavenny.tic@monmouthshire.gov.uk

ABERYSTWYTH TIC

Terrace Road, Aberystwyth, Ceredigion SY23 2AG
Tel: 01970 612125
Fax: 01970 612125
e-mail: aberystwythtic@ceredigion.gov.uk

BALA TIC

Penllyn, Pensarn Road, Bala, Gwynedd LL23 7SR
Tel: 01678 521021
Fax: 01678 521021
e-mail: bala.tic@gwynedd.gov.uk

BANGOR TIC

Town Hall, Deiniol Road, Bangor, Gwynedd LL57 2RE
Tel: 01248 352786
Fax: 01248 352786
e-mail: bangor.tic@gwynedd.gov.uk

BARMOUTH TIC

The Station, Station Road, Barmouth,
Ceredigion LL42 1LU
Tel: 01341 280787
Fax: 01341 280787
e-mail: barmouth.tic@gwynedd.gov.ukynedd.gov.uk

BEDDGELERT TIC

Canolfan Hebog, Beddgelert, Gwynedd LL55 4YD
Tel: 01766 890615
Fax: 01766 890615
e-mail: tic.beddgelert@eryri-npa.gov.uk

BETWS-Y-COED TIC

Royal Oak Stables, Betws y Coed, Conwy LL24 0AH
Tel: 01690 710426
Fax: 01690 710665
e-mail: tic.byc@eryri-npa.gov.uk

BLAENAU FFESTINIOG TIC

Unit 3, High Street, Blaenau Ffestiniog,
Gwynedd LL41 3HS
Tel: 01766 830360
Fax: 01766 830360
e-mail: tic.blaenau@eryri-npa.gov.uk

BLAENAVON TIC

Blaenavon Ironworks, Stack Square, Blaenavon,
Torfaen NP4 9RQ
Tel: 01495 792615
Fax: 01495 791388
e-mail: blaenavon.ironworks@btopenworld.com

BORTH TIC

Cambrian Terrace, Borth, Ceredigion SY24 5HU
Tel: 01970 871174
Fax: 01970 871365
e-mail: borthtic@ceredigion.gov.uk

BRECON TIC

Cattle Market Car Park, Brecon, Powys LD3 9DA
Tel: 01874 622485
Fax: 01874 625256
e-mail: brectic@powys.gov.uk

TOURIST INFORMATION CENTRES

BRIDGEND TIC
McArthur Glen Design Outlet (Wales), The Derwen,
Bridgend CF32 9SU
Tel: 01656 654906
Fax: 01656 646523
e-mail: bridgendtic@bridgend.gov.uk

BUILTH WELLS TIC
The Groe Car Park, Builth Wells, Powys LD2 3BL
Tel: 01982 553307
Fax: 01982 553841
e-mail: builtic@powys.gov.uk

CAERLEON TIC
5 High Street, Caerleon, Newport NP18 1AE
Tel: 01633 422656
Fax: 01633 422656
e-mail: caerleon.tic@newport.gov.uk

CAERNARFON TIC
Oriel Pendeitsh, Castle Street, Caernarfon,
Gwynedd LL55 1ES
Tel: 01286 672232
Fax: 01286 678209
e-mail:
caernarfon.tic@gwynedd.gov.ukTIC@gwynedd.gov.uk

CAERPHILLY TIC
Lower Twyn Square, Caerphilly CF83 1JL
Tel: 029 2088 0011
Fax: 029 2086 0811
e-mail: tic@caerphilly.gov.uk

CARDIFF TIC
Cardiff Visitor Centre, The Old Library, The Hayes,
Cardiff CF10 1NE
Tel: 08701 211 258
e-mail: visitor@cardiff.gov.uk

CARDIGAN TIC
Theatr Mwldan, Bath House Road, Cardigan,
Ceredigion SA43 2JY
Tel: 01239 613230
Fax: 01239 614853
e-mail: cardigantic@ceredigion.gov.uk

CARMARTHEN TIC
113 Lammas Street, Carmarthen SA31 3AQ
Tel: 01267 231557
Fax: 01267 221901
e-mail: carmarthentic@carmarthenshire.gov.uk

CHEPSTOW TIC
Castle Car Park, Bridge Street, Chepstow,
Monmouthshire NP16 5EY
Tel: 01291 623772
Fax: 01291 628004
e-mail: chepstow.tic@monmouthshire.gov.uk

CONWY TIC
Castle Buildings, Conwy LL32 8LD
Tel: 01492 592248
Fax: 01492 573545
e-mail: conwytic@conwy.gov.uk

DOLGELLAU TIC
Ty Meirion, Eldon Square, Dolgellau,
Gwynedd LL40 1PU
Fax: 01341 422576
e-mail: tic.dolgellau@eryri-npa.gov.uk

FISHGUARD HARBOUR TIC
Ocean Lab, The Parrog, Goodwick, Fishguard,
Pembrokeshire SA64 0DE
Tel: 01348 872037
Fax: 01348 872528
e-mail: fishguardharbour.tic@pembs.gov.uk

FISHGUARD TOWN TIC
The Library, High Street, Fishguard SA65 9AR
Tel: 01348 873484
Fax: 01384 875246
e-mail: fishguard.tic@pembrokeshire.gov.uk

HARLECH TIC
Llys y Graig, Harlech, Gwynedd LL46 2YE
Tel: 01766 780658
Fax: 01766 780658
e-mail: tic.harlech@eryri-npa.gov.uk

TOURIST INFORMATION CENTRES

HAVERFORDWEST TIC
Old Bridge, Haverfordwest, Pembrokeshire SA61 2EZ
Tel: 01437 763110
Fax: 01437 767738
e-mail: haverfordwest.tic@pembrokeshire.gov.uk

HOLYHEAD TIC
Stenna Line, Terminal 1, Holyhead, Anglesey LL65 1DQ
Tel: 01407 762622
Fax: 01407 761462
e-mail: holyhead@nwtic.com

KILGETTY TIC
Kingsmoor Common, Kilgetty, Pembrokeshire SA68 0YA
Tel: 01834 814161
Fax: 01834 814161
e-mail: info@tourismpembrokeshire.com

KNIGHTON TIC
Offas Dyke Centre, West Street, Knighton,
Powys LD7 1EN
Tel: 01547 529424
e-mail: oda@offasdyke.demon.co.uk

LAKE VYRNWY TIC
Unit 2, Vyrnwy Craft Workshops, Lake Vyrnwy,
Powys SY10 0LY
Tel: 01691 870346
Fax: 01691 870346
e-mail: laktic@powys.gov.uk

LLANBERIS TIC
41b High Street, Llanberis, Gwynedd LL55 4EU
Tel: 01286 870765
Fax: 01286 871924
e-mail: llanberis.tic@gwynedd.gov.uk

LLANDOVERY TIC
Heritage Centre, Kings Road, Llandovery,
Carmarthenshire SA20 0AW
Tel: 01550 720693
Fax: 01550 720693
e-mail: llandovery.ic@breconbeacons.orgeconbeacons.org

LLANDRINDOD WELLS TIC
Auto Palace, Temple Street,
Llandrindod Wells LD1 5HU
Tel: 01597 822600
Fax: 01597 829164
e-mail: llandtic@powys.gov.uk

LLANDUDNO TIC
Library Building, Mostyn Street, Llandudno,
Gwynedd LL30 2RP
Tel: 01492 876413
Fax: 01492 872722
e-mail: llandudnotic@conwy.gov.uk

LLANFAIRPWLLGWYNGYLL TIC
Station Site, Llanfairpwllgwyngyll, Anglesey LL61 5UJ
Tel: 01248 713177
Fax: 01248 715711
e-mail: llanfairpwll@nwtic.com

LLANGOLLEN TIC
Y Chapel, Castle Street, Llangollen LL20 8NU
Tel: 01978 860828
Fax: 01978 861563
e-mail: llangollen@nwtic.com

MACHYNLLETH TIC
Royal House, Penrallt Street, Machynlleth SY20 8AG
Tel: 01654 702401
Fax: 01654 703675
e-mail: mactic@powys.gov.uk

MERTHYR TYDFIL TIC
14a Glebeland Street, Merthyr Tydfil CF47 8AU
Tel: 01685 379884
Fax: 01685 350043
e-mail: merthyr_tic@hotmail.com

MILFORD HAVEN TIC
94 Charles Street, Milford Haven,
Pembrokeshire SA73 2HL
Tel: 01646 690866
Fax: 01646 690655
e-mail: milford.tic@pembrokeshire.gov.uk

TOURIST INFORMATION CENTRES

MOLD TIC
Library Museum & Art Gallery, Earl Road,
Mold CH7 1AP
Tel: 01352 759331
Fax: 01352 759331
e-mail: mold@nwtic.com

MONMOUTH TIC
Shire Hall Agincourt Square, Monmouth,
Monmouthshire NP25 3DY
Tel: 01600 713899
Fax: 01600 772794
e-mail: monmouth.tic@monmouthshire.gov.uk

MUMBLES TIC
The Methodist Church, Mumbles Road,
Swansea SA3 4BU
Tel: 01792 361302
Fax: 01792 363392
e-mail: info@mumblestic.co.uk

NEW QUAY TIC
Church Street, New Quay, Ceredigion SA45 9NZ
Tel: 01545 560865
Fax: 01545 561360
e-mail: newquaytic@ceredigion.gov.uk

NEWPORT TIC
Museum & Art Gallery, John Frost Square,
Newport NP20 1PA
Tel: 01633 842962
Fax: 01633 222615
e-mail:
newport.tic@newport.gov.ukt.TIC@newport.gov.uk

NEWPORT (PEMBS) TIC
2 Bank Cottages, Long Street, Newport,
Pembrokeshire SA42 0TN
Fax: 01239 820912
e-mail: newportTIC@pembrokeshirecoast.org.uk

NEWTOWN TIC
The Park, Back Lane, Newtown, Powys SY16 2PW
Tel: 01686 625580
Fax: 01686 610065
e-mail: newtic@powys.gov.uk

OSWESTRY MILE END TIC
Mile End Services, Oswestry, Shropshire SY11 4JA
Tel: 01691 662488
Fax: 01691 662883
e-mail: tic@oswestry-bc.gov.uk

OSWESTRY TOWN TIC
The Heritage Centre, 2 Church Terrace, Oswestry,
Shropshire SY11 2TE
Tel: 01691 662753
Fax: 01691 657811
e-mail: ot@oswestry-welshborders.org.uk

PEMBROKE TIC
Visitor Centre, Commons Road, Pembroke,
Pembrokeshire SA71 4EA
Tel: 01646 622388
Fax: 01646 621396
e-mail: pembroke.tic@pembrokeshire.gov.uk

PEMBROKE DOCK TIC
Irish Ferries, Ferry Terminal, Pembroke Dock,
Pembrokeshire SA72 6JZ
Tel: 01646 622753
Fax: 01646 622753
e-mail: pembrokedock.tic@pembrokeshire.gov.uk

PENARTH TIC
Penarth Pier, The Esplanade, Penarth,
Vale of Glamorgan CF64 3AU
Tel: 029 2070 8849
e-mail: penarthtic@valeofglamorgan.gov.uk

PORTHCAWL TIC
Old Police Station, John Street, Porthcawl,
Bridgend CF36 3DT
Tel: 01656 786639
Fax: 01656 782387
e-mail: porthcawltic@bridgend.gov.uk

PORTHMADOG TIC
High Street, Porthmadog, Gwynedd LL49 9LD
Tel: 01766 512981
Fax: 01766 515312
e-mail: porthmadog.tic@gwynedd.gov.uk

TOURIST INFORMATION CENTRES

PRESTEIGNE TIC
The Judges' Lodging, Broad Street, Presteigne,
Powys LD8 2AD
Tel: 01544 260650
Fax: 01544 260652
e-mail: presteignetic@powys.gov.uk

PWLLHELI TIC
Min y Don, Station Square, Pwllheli,
Gwynedd LL53 5HG
Tel: 01758 613000
Fax: 01758 613000
e-mail: pwllheli.tic@gwynedd.gov.uk

RHAYADER TIC
The Leisure Centre, North Street, Rhayader LD6 5BU
Tel: 01597 810591
e-mail: rhayader.tic@powys.gov.uk

RHYL TIC
Rhyl Childrens Village, West Parade, Rhyl,
Denbighshire LL18 1HZ
Tel: 01745 355068
Fax: 01745 342255
e-mail: rhyl.tic@denbighshire.gov.uk

SAUNDERSFOOT TIC
The Barbecue, Harbour Car Park, Saundersfoot,
Pembrokeshire SA69 9HE
Tel: 01834 813672
Fax: 01834 813673
e-mail: saundersfoot.tic@pembrokeshire.gov.uk

ST DAVIDS TIC
National Park Visitor Centre, The Grove, St Davids,
Pembrokeshire SA62 6NW
Tel: 01437 720392
Fax: 01437 720099
e-mail: enquiries@stdavids.pembrokeshirecoast.org.uk.

SWANSEA TIC
Plymouth Street, Swansea SA1 3QG
Tel: 01792 468321
Fax: 01792 464602
e-mail: tourism@swansea.gov.uk

TENBY TIC
The Croft, Tenby, Pembrokeshire SA70 8AP
Tel: 01834 842402
Fax: 01834 845439
e-mail: tenby.tic@pembrokeshire.gov.uk

TYWYN TIC
High Street, Tywyn, Gwynedd LL36 9AD
Tel: 01654 710070
Fax: 01654 710070
e-mail: tywyn.tic@gwynedd.gov.ukC@gwynedd.gov.uk

WELSHPOOL TIC
Vicarage Garden, Church Street, Welshpool,
Powys SY21 7DD
Tel: 01938 552043
Fax: 01938 554038
e-mail: weltic@powys.gov.uk

WREXHAM TIC
Lambpit Street, Wrexham LL11 1WN
Tel: 01978 292015
Fax: 01978 292467
e-mail: tic@wrexham.gov.uk

INDEX OF ADVERTISERS

INDEX OF ADVERTISERS

INDEX OF ADVERTISERS

Looking for more walks?

The walks in this book have been gleaned from Britain's largest online walking guide, to be found at *www.walkingworld.com*.

The site contains 300 walks across eastern England, so there is plenty more choice in this region alone. If you are heading further afield there are walks of every length and type across England, Scotland and Wales – ideal if you are taking a short break as you can plan your walks in advance.

Want more detail for the walks in this book? Next to every walk in this book you will see a Walk ID. You can enter this ID number on Walkingworld's 'Find a Walk' page and you will be taken straight to the details of that walk.

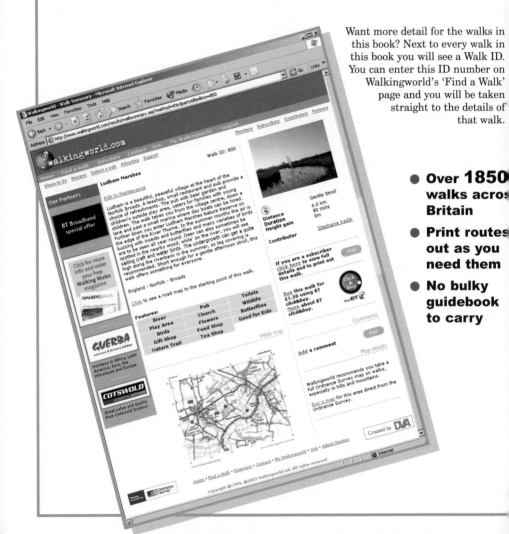

- **Over 1850 walks across Britain**

- **Print routes out as you need them**

- **No bulky guidebook to carry**

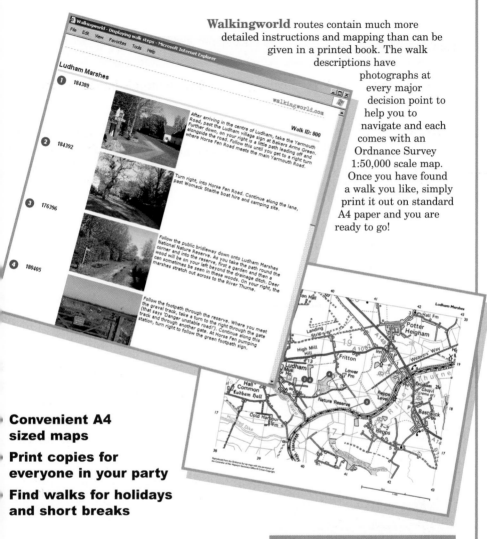

Walkingworld routes contain much more detailed instructions and mapping than can be given in a printed book. The walk descriptions have photographs at every major decision point to help you to navigate and each comes with an Ordnance Survey 1:50,000 scale map. Once you have found a walk you like, simply print it out on standard A4 paper and you are ready to go!

- **Convenient A4 sized maps**
- **Print copies for everyone in your party**
- **Find walks for holidays and short breaks**

A modest annual subscription gives you access to over 1850 walks, all in Walkingworld's easy to follow format. The database of walks is growing all the time and as a subscriber you gain access to new routes as soon as they are published.

sit the **Walkingworld** website at *www.walkingworld.com*

INDEX OF WALKS

ORDER FORM

To order any of our publications just fill in the payment details below and complete the order form. For orders of less than 4 copies please add £1 per book for postage and packing. Orders over 4 copies are P & P free.

Please Complete Either:

I enclose a cheque for £ [　　　　　] *made payable to Travel Publishing Ltd*

Or:

CARD NO: [　　　　　]　　　　EXPIRY DATE: [　　　　　]

SIGNATURE: [　　　　　]

NAME: [　　　　　]

ADDRESS: [　　　　　]

TEL NO: [　　　　　]

Please either send, telephone, fax or e-mail your order to:

Travel Publishing Ltd, 7a Apollo House, Calleva Park, Aldermaston, Berkshire RG7 8TN
Tel: 0118 981 7777   Fax: 0118 940 8428 e-mail: info@travelpublishing.co.uk

	PRICE	QUANTITY		PRICE	QUANTITY
HIDDEN PLACES REGIONAL TITLES			**COUNTRY PUBS AND INNS TITLES**		
Cornwall	£8.99	....	Cornwall	£5.99	....
Devon	£8.99	....	Devon	£7.99	....
Dorset, Hants & Isle of Wight	£8.99	....	Sussex	£5.99	....
East Anglia	£8.99	....	Wales	£8.99	....
Lake District & Cumbria	£8.99	....	Yorkshire	£7.99	....
Northumberland & Durham	£8.99	....	**COUNTRY LIVING RURAL GUIDES**		
Peak District and Derbyshire	£8.99	....	East Anglia	£10.99	....
Yorkshire	£8.99	....	Heart of England	£10.99	....
HIDDEN PLACES NATIONAL TITLES			Ireland	£11.99	....
England	£11.99	....	North East of England	£10.99	....
Ireland	£11.99	....	North West of England	£10.99	....
Scotland	£11.99	....	Scotland	£11.99	....
Wales	£11.99	....	South of England	£10.99	....
HIDDEN INNS TITLES			South East of England	£10.99	....
East Anglia	£7.99	....	Wales	£11.99	....
Heart of England	£7.99	....	West Country	£10.99	....
South	£7.99	....	**OTHER TITLES**		
South East	£7.99	....	Off The Motorway	£11.99	....
West Country	£7.99	....			

TOTAL QUANTITY [　　　　　]

TOTAL VALUE [　　　　　]

HIDDEN PLACES GUIDES

Explore Britain and Ireland with
Hidden Places guides - a fascinating series of national and local travel guides.

Packed with easy to read information on hundreds of places of interest as well as places to stay, eat and drink.

Available from both high street and internet booksellers

For more information on the full range of *Hidden Places* guides and other titles published by Travel Publishing visit our website on

www.travelpublishing.co.uk
or ask for our leaflet by phoning **0118-981-7777** or
emailing **info@travelpublishing.co.uk**

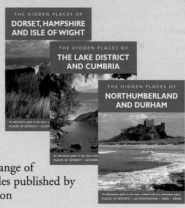

VISIT THE TRAVEL PUBLISHING WEBSITE

Looking for:

• *Places to Visit?*

• *Places to Stay?*

• *Places to Eat & Drink?*

• *Places to Shop?*

Then why not visit the Travel Publishing website...

• Informative pages on places to visit, stay, eat, drink and shop throughout the British Isles.

• Detailed information on Travel Publishing's wide range of national and regional travel guides.

www.travelpublishing.co.uk

READER REACTION FORM

The **Travel Publishing** *research team would like to receive readers' comments on any visitor attractions or places reviewed in the book and also recommendations for suitable entries to be included in the next edition. This will help ensure that the* **Country Living** *series of* **Rural Guides** *continues to provide its readers with useful information on the more interesting, unusual or unique features of each attraction or place ensuring that their visit to the local area is an enjoyable and stimulating experience. To provide your comments or recommendations would you please complete the forms below and overleaf as indicated and send to:*

The Research Department, Travel Publishing Ltd, 7a Apollo House, Calleva Park, Aldermaston, Reading, RG7 8TN

YOUR NAME:

YOUR ADDRESS:

YOUR TEL NO:

Please tick as appropriate: COMMENTS ☐   RECOMMENDATION ☐

ESTABLISHMENT:

ADDRESS:

TEL NO:

CONTACT NAME:

PLEASE COMPLETE FORM OVERLEAF

READER REACTION FORM

COMMENT OR REASON FOR RECOMMENDATION:

READER REACTION FORM

The **Travel Publishing** *research team would like to receive readers' comments on any visitor attractions or places reviewed in the book and also recommendations for suitable entries to be included in the next edition. This will help ensure that the* **Country Living series of Rural Guides** *continues to provide its readers with useful information on the more interesting, unusual or unique features of each attraction or place ensuring that their visit to the local area is an enjoyable and stimulating experience. To provide your comments or recommendations would you please complete the forms below and overleaf as indicated and send to:*

The Research Department, Travel Publishing Ltd, 7a Apollo House, Calleva Park, Aldermaston, Reading, RG7 8TN

YOUR NAME:

YOUR ADDRESS:

YOUR TEL NO:

Please tick as appropriate: COMMENTS   RECOMMENDATION

ESTABLISHMENT:

ADDRESS:

TEL NO:

CONTACT NAME:

PLEASE COMPLETE FORM OVERLEAF

READER REACTION FORM

COMMENT OR REASON FOR RECOMMENDATION:

....

....

....

....

....

....

....

....

....

....

....

....

READER REACTION FORM

The **Travel Publishing** *research team would like to receive readers' comments on any visitor attractions or places reviewed in the book and also recommendations for suitable entries to be included in the next edition. This will help ensure that the* **Country Living series of Rural Guides** *continues to provide its readers with useful information on the more interesting, unusual or unique features of each attraction or place ensuring that their visit to the local area is an enjoyable and stimulating experience. To provide your comments or recommendations would you please complete the forms below and overleaf as indicated and send to:*

The Research Department, Travel Publishing Ltd, 7a Apollo House, Calleva Park, Aldermaston, Reading, RG7 8TN

YOUR NAME:

YOUR ADDRESS:

YOUR TEL NO:

Please tick as appropriate: COMMENTS ☐   RECOMMENDATION ☐

ESTABLISHMENT:

ADDRESS:

TEL NO:

CONTACT NAME:

PLEASE COMPLETE FORM OVERLEAF

READER REACTION FORM

COMMENT OR REASON FOR RECOMMENDATION:

....

....

....

....

....

....

....

....

....

....

....

....

READER REACTION FORM

The **Travel Publishing** *research team would like to receive readers' comments on any visitor attractions or places reviewed in the book and also recommendations for suitable entries to be included in the next edition. This will help ensure that the* **Country Living series of Rural Guides** *continues to provide its readers with useful information on the more interesting, unusual or unique features of each attraction or place ensuring that their visit to the local area is an enjoyable and stimulating experience. To provide your comments or recommendations would you please complete the forms below and overleaf as indicated and send to:*

The Research Department, Travel Publishing Ltd, 7a Apollo House, Calleva Park, Aldermaston, Reading, RG7 8TN

YOUR NAME:

YOUR ADDRESS:

YOUR TEL NO:

Please tick as appropriate: COMMENTS ☐   RECOMMENDATION ☐

ESTABLISHMENT:

ADDRESS:

TEL NO:

CONTACT NAME:

PLEASE COMPLETE FORM OVERLEAF

READER REACTION FORM

COMMENT OR REASON FOR RECOMMENDATION:

....

....

....

....

....

....

....

....

....

....

....

....

READER REACTION FORM

The **Travel Publishing** *research team would like to receive readers' comments on any visitor attractions or places reviewed in the book and also recommendations for suitable entries to be included in the next edition. This will help ensure that the* **Country Living series of Rural Guides** *continues to provide its readers with useful information on the more interesting, unusual or unique features of each attraction or place ensuring that their visit to the local area is an enjoyable and stimulating experience. To provide your comments or recommendations would you please complete the forms below and overleaf as indicated and send to:*

The Research Department, Travel Publishing Ltd, 7a Apollo House, Calleva Park, Aldermaston, Reading, RG7 8TN

YOUR NAME:

YOUR ADDRESS:

YOUR TEL NO:

Please tick as appropriate: COMMENTS ☐   RECOMMENDATION ☐

ESTABLISHMENT:

ADDRESS:

TEL NO:

CONTACT NAME:

PLEASE COMPLETE FORM OVERLEAF

READER REACTION FORM

COMMENT OR REASON FOR RECOMMENDATION:

....

....

....

....

....

....

....

....

....

....

....

....

READER REACTION FORM

The **Travel Publishing** *research team would like to receive readers' comments on any visitor attractions or places reviewed in the book and also recommendations for suitable entries to be included in the next edition. This will help ensure that the* **Country Living series of Rural Guides** *continues to provide its readers with useful information on the more interesting, unusual or unique features of each attraction or place ensuring that their visit to the local area is an enjoyable and stimulating experience. To provide your comments or recommendations would you please complete the forms below and overleaf as indicated and send to:*

The Research Department, Travel Publishing Ltd, 7a Apollo House, Calleva Park, Aldermaston, Reading, RG7 8TN

YOUR NAME:

YOUR ADDRESS:

YOUR TEL NO:

Please tick as appropriate: COMMENTS ☐   RECOMMENDATION ☐

ESTABLISHMENT:

ADDRESS:

TEL NO:

CONTACT NAME:

PLEASE COMPLETE FORM OVERLEAF

READER REACTION FORM

COMMENT OR REASON FOR RECOMMENDATION:

....

....

....

....

....

....

....

....

....

....

....

....

TOWNS, VILLAGES AND PLACES OF INTEREST

TOWNS, VILLAGES AND PLACES OF INTEREST

TOWNS, VILLAGES AND PLACES OF INTEREST

TOWNS, VILLAGES AND PLACES OF INTEREST

TOWNS, VILLAGES AND PLACES OF INTEREST

TOWNS, VILLAGES AND PLACES OF INTEREST

TOWNS, VILLAGES AND PLACES OF INTEREST

TOWNS, VILLAGES AND PLACES OF INTEREST

TOWNS, VILLAGES AND PLACES OF INTEREST

TOWNS, VILLAGES AND PLACES OF INTEREST

TOWNS, VILLAGES AND PLACES OF INTEREST